15⁰⁰

15⁰⁰

FROM THIS LAND

"Minnesota's Enterprises" by George Dixon

Pictorial Research by Virginia M. Westbrook

Introduction by Linda Kelsey

Produced in Cooperation with the
Minnesota Chamber of Commerce and Industry

Windsor Publications, Inc.
Northridge, California

FROM THIS LAND

A History of Minnesota's Empires, Enterprises, and Entrepreneurs

Deborah L. Gelbach

Frontispiece: *Each of the 10,000 lakes has as many moods, few lovelier than those of twilight. Photo by Matt Bradley*

Page six: *On a sunny July afternoon, Minneapolis reflects the energy of a vigorous American city boldly approaching the twenty-first century. Photo by Greg L. Ryan/Sally A. Beyer*

Windsor Publications, Inc.—History Books Division
Vice-President/Publishing: Hal Silverman
Editorial Director: Teri Davis Greenberg
Design Director: Alexander D'Anca
Director, Corporate Biographies: Karen Story

Staff for *From This Land*:
Senior Editor: Pamela Schroeder
Production Editor: Susan L. Wells
Photo Editor: Teri Greenberg
Developmental Editor: Karl Stull
Copy Editor: Maryanne L. Kibodeaux
Assistant Director, Corporate Biographies: Phyllis Gray
Editor, Corporate Biographies: Brenda Berryhill
Production Editor, Corporate Biographies: Una FitzSimons
Layout Artists, Corporate Biographies: Barbara Moore, Mari Catherine Preimesberger
Sales Representatives, Corporate Biographies: Henry Hintermeister, Joseph Belshan,
    Merl Gratton
Senior Proofreader: Susan J. Muhler
Editorial Assistants: Didier Beauvoir, Thelma Fleischer, Alyson Gould, Kim Kievman,
    Michael Nugwynne, Kathy B. Peyser, Pat Pittman, Theresa Solis
Art Director: Christina Rosepapa
Designer: Tanya Maiboroda

Library of Congress Cataloging-in-Publication Data
Gelbach, Deborah L., 1947-
    From this land.
    "Produced in cooperation with the Minnesota Chamber of
Commerce and Industry."
    Bibliography: p. 374
    Includes index.
    1. Minnesota—Economic conditions. 2. Minnesota—Economic
conditions—Pictorial works. I. Title.
HC107.M6G45   1988   330.9776'053   88-199
ISBN 0-89781-231-X

CONTENTS

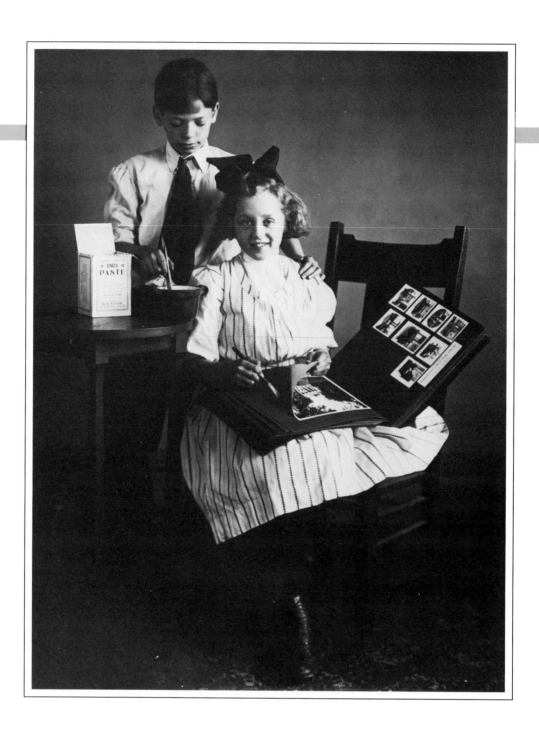

Public interest in photography boosted small St. Paul industry. The H.B. Fuller Co. found a market for its dry paste among people who wanted to preserve evidence of their lives in photograph albums. Courtesy, Minnesota Historical Society

INTRODUCTION

Not unexpectedly, the first white men to walk the Indian's earth that became America's Midwest brought with them the values and expectations of seventeenth-century Europe, the old order. Bold in their belief in mercantilism and the certainty of their faith, Nicolet, Hennepin, Radisson, Duluth, and their countrymen sought the riches of Cathay and the salvation of souls. In their wake followed more Europeans, then citizens of a young United States, then new immigrants—the men and women who would call Minnesota "home" and whose lives and work would shape a new order.

That new order, or rather the drama of its emergence in Minnesota, the significance of its achievements, and the relevance of its values, is the foundation of this compelling book.

In creating her moving account of some of America's most vital history, Deborah Gelbach has focused on people, ideas, and action, and ultimately on values. Beneath the human drama and authenticating detail of her narrative lie the great issues and patterns which shape our nation and our society, articulated with insight and compassion.

Ms. Gelbach offers us a Minnesota of startling contrasts and immense energy, at once a vast arena of capricious nature, a laboratory of social change, and a proving ground of technology. Here is a storied realm of magnificent forests for lumbering, great lakes and mighty rivers for waterpower and navigation, the ores of the Mesabi for iron and steelmaking, and rich soil for agriculture in volatile truce with ravenous locusts, ferocious winters, floods, and drought. Technology has forged its ceaseless change with railroads, river steamboats and whaleback ore boats, mills and elevators, and supercomputers. Nor have the world's tides of depression and war neglected Minnesota's fortunes.

Nearly every significant issue faced by Americans in modern times has had a lively test in Minnesota, often with lasting impact across the nation. The complementary and competing interests of agriculture and industry, of farm and city, of grower and distributor, capital and labor, government and private citizen have clashed and cooperated.

In Minnesota, those issues have generated fascinating variations in its social and economic institutions—cities grand and modest, tiny farms and mighty agribusinesses, corporations, cooperatives, unions, trade associations, private colleges and public universities, political parties of every hue and stripe.

And always there are the real, ungeneralized, men and women whose humanity drives Ms. Gelbach's narrative. Under her evocative spell we share with Josiah Snelling, Henry Sibley, and Alexander Ramsey the challenge of bringing order to a frontier land. We exult with Cadwallader Washburn and Edmund La Croix as their middlings purifier assures market domination for Minnesota millers. Grim fascination grips us as James J. Hill, Jay Cooke, John D. Rockefeller, and J.P. Morgan broker Minnesota's and the nation's wealth. We wake on chilly Depression mornings and dial WCCO to hear the report from "Market Lady" Mildred Simons or the reassuring voice of Marjorie Husted as Betty Crocker. We nod in admiration at Sister Elizabeth Kenny's crusade against polio's crippling effects. And we delight one more time in the optimistic rhetoric of Hubert Horatio Humphrey.

Then we join Deborah Gelbach in examining the Minnesota of today and assessing our capacity to shape for this magnificent land a future worthy of its trust and the trust of our heirs. And finally we treasure our heritage as burnished by this estimable work.

Linda Kelsey

Linda Kelsey

*No tree is more reminiscent
of the North Woods than the
elegant, supple white birch, delight
of painters, canoe makers, and
boys. Spring light graces these examples along the Big Fork River.
Photo by Matt Bradley*

CLAIMING AN ABUNDANT LAND

Fourteen years after the Pilgrims reached the coast of America, a Frenchman named Jean Nicolet stepped out of a birch-bark canoe near the site of modern-day Green Bay, Wisconsin. Wearing a silk damask robe embroidered with oriental bird-and-flower patterns, Nicolet believed he was correctly dressed to officially open the trade route from New France, on the St. Lawrence River, to China. With an eye toward the meaning of the moment, he raised his pistol and fired two shots into the air.

On the shore a delegation of Winnebago chieftains observed Nicolet and quietly agreed that they were being visited by a white god. As it turned out, the Winnebago lands were not in China, and Nicolet's ceremonial dress was premature. On the other hand, the country was thick with fur-bearing beaver and muskrat, which the Winnebagos were happy to share with the god from the sea.

It was 1634. The British crown had already imposed the first in a long series of taxes on the New England colonists, and the trouble that would lead to the American Revolution almost 150 years later had begun to brew. But to the north, in the colonies of New France near present-day Montreal, a tiny band of French explorers and missionaries itched to find trade routes to China in the name of their country and their king. They longed for furs to send home and people to convert to Christianity. Since the early 1600s when adventurers first began to explore the lands along the St. Lawrence and Ottawa rivers, there were rumors that just beyond the horizon lay an enormous body of salt water. On the other side, so it was believed, were all the luxuries of the land of Cathay.

Nicolet (pronounced Nic-o-lay) had been selected by New France's founder, the visionary Samuel de Champlain, to find the passage to Cathay. Nicolet believed that France was on the verge of a lucrative trade breakthrough and he wanted to be the man to make it happen. With Huron Indians as guides and emissaries, and canoes filled with trinkets to trade, he followed the rumor west.

Despite years of service to New France, Daniel Greysolon, Sieur Duluth, never realized his lifelong dream of finding a passage through the wilderness to the Pacific. Courtesy, Northeast Minnesota Historical Center

Although Nicolet was not successful in finding the Orient, he was one of the first French explorers to map the Straits of Mackinac and the northern coast of Lake Michigan. More important to Minnesota history, however, were the enthusiastic stories he carried back to Quebec. His tales enticed other explorers to search for the passageway to China and, along the way, establish working relations with Indians who could supply them with beaver and muskrat pelts.

But in the discovery business, time and patience are key ingredients to success. The headwaters of the Mississippi River were still undiscovered in 1655, and the largest Great Lake—Lake Superior—was, for the most part, uncharted. The land that would become Minnesota was just beyond the horizon for the French explorers.

In 1655 a pair of brash young explorers—Pierre Esprit Radisson and his brother-in-law Médard Chouart, Sieur de Groseilliers—set out to push farther than any previous French explorer had gone. Some historians think the two men reached the south shore of Lake Superior and pushed inland, possibly even reaching Prairie Island on the Mississippi River where Hastings is today.

Leaving his brother-in-law to raise corn for their return trip, Radisson spent another four months traveling and establishing trading relations with the Sioux, or the "nation of the beefe" (buffalo hunters) as he called them. Greatly impressed with the fertility and beauty of the country and astonished by the herds of buffalo and antelope, flocks of pelicans, and the abundance of sturgeon and other fish, Radisson believed that the land west and south of Lake Superior was a land of great opportunity for New France, even if it didn't lead to the mythical Cathay.

When Radisson and Groseilliers returned to Quebec, their canoes overflowed with beaver skins (called "castors" by the early French voyageurs). They carried reports of newly discovered Indian tribes and rich western lands for the French to claim as their own. But politics cut short their heady excitement. The two men had not been properly licensed as French explorers, and their furs were taken away from them. Feeling betrayed by their own country, Radisson and Groseilliers worked their way to England, where they eventually chartered the Hudson's Bay Company—the fur-trading company that would eventually become so powerful that it would leave its mark on two centuries of economic growth in the Americas.

By 1660 New France's trade tentacles reached out in an enormous triangle from Hudson Bay to the watershed between the Mississippi River and Lake Superior, and east to Quebec. As French voyageurs fanned out across the country, their canoes loaded with trade goods, the French Royal government's interest in the new continent was rekindled. Money and management talent were pumped into fur trading, map charting, and exploration. Hardy Jesuit priests accompanied the explorers, sometimes in search of Indians to convert to Christianity and sometimes as explorers in their own right.

So intoxicating were the potential riches along the shores of the Great Lakes and their tributaries that the French government decided to claim the region all for itself. On June 14, 1671, in the same year that John Milton published *Paradise Regained* in England, agents representing the French Royal government held an elaborate ceremony at Sault Ste. Marie to proclaim to all the world that this new paradise belonged to France. A wooden cross was placed high on a hill, and the French coat of arms was nailed just above it. While their Indian guests looked on, a handful of Frenchmen sang a hymn and then listened as an agent of King Louis XIV read a proclamation announcing that the French Sun King was also king of Lake Huron and Lake Superior "and all other countries, rivers, lakes and tributaries, both discovered and undiscovered, bounded on the one side by the Northern and Western Seas and on the other by the South Sea . . ."

It is doubtful that the Indians understood the implications of the elaborate French pageant which ended with a great bonfire in the darkness of the early summer evening.

Before the decade was over, Daniel Greysolon, Sieur Duluth (Dulhut), led another group of French explorers into Lake Superior country. Like so many before him, Duluth

Father Louis Hennepin named the mighty waterfall on the Mississippi River for his patron saint, Saint Anthony. Courtesy, Minnesota Historical Society

was looking for something more than beaver pelts; he too had his heart set on finding the Northwest Passage to the Orient. Duluth left Montreal in the autumn of 1678, and the following summer reached the shore of Lake Superior where the city that bears his name stands today. That year he made a trip to a large Sioux village on Mille Lacs Lake, where he heard another rumor about a great salt sea to the west. Duluth had no way of knowing that the salt sea was probably Great Salt Lake in Utah.

Nevertheless, the rumor encouraged Duluth. In subsequent months he followed the Bois Brule River (in Douglas County, Wisconsin) and portaged to the St. Croix River. On the St. Croix he traveled to its confluence with the Mississippi.

In the meantime Father Louis Hennepin, a Belgian friar, had joined Robert Cavelier, Sieur de La Salle, in a 1679 expedition of Lakes Ontario, Erie, Huron, and Michigan and the Illinois and Mississippi rivers. After traveling for more than a year the party split up; La Salle returned to Montreal and the rest of the party canoed into the arms of a band of Sioux, who captured them and moved them up the Mississippi River, then northward to the Sioux villages around Mille Lacs Lake.

Rumor of the white men's capture traveled slowly overland, and when Duluth eventually heard it he set out to investigate. Five months after they were captured, Duluth freed Father Hennepin and the rest of the party, and, as the story goes, sharply criticized the Indians for their behavior. The Sioux apparently felt apologetic for betraying the white men's trust, for later that autumn when Duluth, Hennepin, and the other Frenchmen decided to travel south again by way of the Rum River, the chief of the Sioux traced the route on a piece of paper and marked its portages. For history's sake, the rough drawing was probably the first map of Minnesota to be seen by Europeans.

The next year, 1682, La Salle led an expedition down the Mississippi and claimed the whole Mississippi River Valley for France.

As the seventeenth century rolled into the eighteenth, the French weren't the only people who were laying claim to the land we call Minnesota. The Sioux (Dakota) and Chippewa (Ojibway) Indian nations had been pushing and pulling their way across the face of northern Minnesota for decades, sometimes boiling over into battle as the Sioux were gradually driven out of the forests by the Chippewa, who were in turn being forced west, out of the northern Great Lakes area, by the powerful Iroquois.

Ownership of the land and its riches were the spoils of the conquerors. The land was bountiful, and possible to traverse. Under a bright blue, early-summer sky it appeared to be paradise.

The Three Maidens rock formations testify to the power of the glaciers that reshaped Minnesota's topography. These three "erratics" transported many miles by moving ice came to rest near Pipestone when the glacier melted. Courtesy, Minnesota Historical Society

MOTHER OF THREE SEAS

Long before any human beings arrived, about 2,700 million years ago, Minnesota was mountainous, with spectacular volcanoes a common occurrence. Rock formations around Lake Superior are evidence of the volcanic action that shook the land. But time, erosion, changing temperatures, and massive ice sheets altered the landscape. About two million years ago temperatures across the northeastern part of North America and northeastern Europe dropped, and tremendous glaciers spread out over the land. Everything touched by the glaciers was absorbed, including boulders as large as buildings and entire forests, adding weight to the icy masses as they lumbered along.

The glaciers reshaped the face of Minnesota, leaving behind great glacial deposits, and building the network of rivers, streams, and lakes that would make exploration possible for the voyageurs and shipping so inexpensive for the millers, farmers, and lumber barons who would eventually inhabit the land.

From glacial deposits and scratches on rocks geologists have calculated that there were probably four major glacial advances across Minnesota, beginning about two million years ago and ending a mere 11,000 years ago.

About 11,000 to 13,000 years ago the climate began to warm up and the glacial ice melted. Although streams and rivers cut through the silt and other deposits to carry some of the meltwater away, more than 15,000 lakes of all sizes and shapes remained to dot the Minnesota landscape. Minnesotans can thank the Laurentide Ice Sheet for the fact that there is one square mile of water for every twenty square miles of land today.

There were giants among the lakes in those first thousand or so years following the retreat of the glaciers. Prehistoric Lake Aggasiz is estimated to have been about 700 miles long and 250 miles wide; it covered much of present northwestern Minnesota, northeastern North Dakota, southern Manitoba, and southwestern Ontario. Lake Aggasiz' outlet was what is now the Minnesota River Valley, and the fertile agricultural land of the Red River Valley was carved from the ancient lakebed. Of particular importance to the French voyageurs were the border lakes which formed in the wake of the glaciers; these lakes became the pathways to the rich bounty of the interior north.

The Great Lakes were created from the old preglacial basins which had been deeply scoured into the earth by the ice and then dammed up by moraines as the glaciers retreated. Because of the glaciers, the Duluth-Superior harbor is the largest inland port in today's United States.

Glaciation was largely responsible for the fertility and diversity of Minnesota's soils. As the glaciers cut down ancient mountains they left behind gentler slopes that could be farmed by the waves of pioneers who were to come.

By the time the first human discovered the great river network that made long-distance travel possible, the land of Minnesota had become a major source of water for the rest of the continent. Centrally located in North America, Minnesota is a crest from which water drains north to Hudson Bay, south to the Gulf of Mexico, and east to the St. Lawrence River, emptying into the Atlantic. By the end of the Ice Age, Minnesota had become the Mother of Three Seas—north, south, and east.

THE FLEUR-DE-LIS AND THE UNION JACK

The brand of regionalism that would color Minnesota's political history and industrial growth in the eighteenth, nineteenth, and twentieth centuries can arguably be traced back to the glaciers. Because glaciation had created such a variety of soils and land forms, the wilderness became the repository of a rich variety of resources. In the north, vast expanses of coniferous forests attracted a lumber industry that pumped money and labor into the state between 1850 and the turn of the century. In the southern and

The beaver lured trappers and traders in search of fortune into the American wilderness. The fur trade not only helped to satisfy the European taste for beaver hats, but also brought European goods into Indian lodges and formed the foundation for the interaction of two very different cultures. Courtesy, Minnesota Historical Society

western parts of the state, grasslands covering rich black soils lured pioneer farmers, giving birth to agriculture, one of the largest industries in the state. And, like a partial boundary between the two topographic regions, a zone of hardwood forests—elm, oak, and maple—eventually provided wood for shelter and light industry.

Another Minnesota resource was iron ore. Beneath the surface of the earth, changes in temperature, pressure, chemical mix, and oxygen content had been enriching taconite rock deposits with iron for millions of years.

But before iron ore changed the industrial picture in Minnesota, metal—in the form of household items and weapons—played a large part in ending the traditional Indian way of life. First, the Indians learned to depend on the kettles and knives the traders exchanged for their furs. Then, in about 1700, the Chippewa, who lived on the southern shore of Lake Superior, learned to use guns. This gave them the advantage over the Sioux tribes who stood in their way as they continued to push south. For the next six decades the Sioux and Chippewa battled fiercely, the Sioux desperately trying to hold onto the lands their ancestors had lived upon possibly as far back as 600 B.C.

The French had a similar problem. So large were their landholdings in North America that they were nearly powerless to prevent incursion from another major power—such as the British. But the rival British were marching out from the East Coast to establish their own trade relations with the Indians, and there was little that France could do to stop them. And unlike the French, the British had plans to domesticate the wilderness. Under the expansionist monarchy of King George III, the British sent a steady stream of settlers to North America, and intended to add it to their empire.

By 1756 the territorial conflicts between France and Britain had precipitated a world war. Called the Seven Years' War, it spilled over into Europe, India, and North

America—wherever the British and French had influence. The North American phase of the Seven Years' War, called the French and Indian War, was precipitated by the British claim to the Ohio River Valley. The French wanted the British to stay east of the Appalachians.

In the North American wilderness the French and their Indian allies were defeated. Across the Atlantic, the Treaty of Paris, signed in 1763, ended the Seven Years' War and France's claim to any military or political power in North America. All land east of the Mississippi fell under British rule.

After the war the British jumped onto the Orient Express. Offering $100,000 to anyone who discovered the legendary waterway from Hudson Bay to the Pacific, Britain's government made the western exploration a top priority. Robert Rogers, then commander of the British Fort at Mackinac, was appointed to lead an exploration overland to the Pacific coast. Rogers sent a young fellow by the name of Jonathan Carver ahead to take a proper British look at the wilderness and to build a working relationship with the Indians.

In early September, 1766, Carver set out from Mackinac for the Mississippi River, arriving about October. Leaving his canoes at the junction of the St. Croix and Mississippi rivers, he walked overland through the gathering winter cold toward the Falls of St. Anthony. Although still loyal to the French, the Indians were friendly enough, and Carver spent the winter with them. In the spring he was invited to join an Indian council that was held in a magnificent cave overlooking the Mississippi River—today called Carver's Cave. There Carver made a long speech to the Indians, telling them of the great power of the King of England and declaring his country's intention for friendship.

With Indian relations established—at least for the moment—Carver happily wrote in his journal that some day mighty kingdoms would rise in the wilderness and "stately and solemn temples, with gilded spires reaching to the skies" would take the place of Indian tepees.

By late spring Carver had hooked up with the exploration party that Rogers had sent. Their first stop was to pick up supplies and trading goods at Grand Portage, a nine-mile stretch of land linking Lake Superior and the Pigeon River. (For more than a century French traders and trappers had used Grand Portage as a gathering spot at the end of the hunting season; under British rule, Grand Portage had become the center of a widening area of trade.) But Carver and his men were disappointed to discover that besides failing to send their supplies, Rogers was in prison—accused of treason. For Carver it was the end of an expedition but the beginning of his career as a travel writer. His book, *The Travels of Jonathan Carver through the Interior Parts of North America in the Years 1766, 1767 and 1768,* became popular among the ladies and gentlemen of British society back in Mother England.

Carver was the first of many earnest young British pathfinders. As the American Revolution heated up on the East Coast, British and Scottish fur traders poured into the new country in a frenzy for furs. But even in the wilderness the law of supply and demand governed economic reality. As competition forced prices down, margins became tight for the traders and their backers. Already a century old, the Hudson's Bay Company of Montreal was virtually a monopoly, and it dictated terms that made the blood of many traders boil.

To protect themselves and to stabilize mounting competition in the fur trade, a group of vigorous Scots and British pulled together as a cooperative in 1783, forming the North West Company—a loose confederation of partnerships backed by Scottish interests in Montreal. It was the North West Company that made border-lake canoe routes famous throughout the world, giving the well-established Hudson's Bay Company a run for its money. With an active inland base at Grand Portage and a number of other posts across the face of Minnesota, the North West Company thrived for thirty years. Then the competition between the two companies became so fierce that they

Jonathan Carver, sent by the British in 1766 to explore the area around the St. Croix and Mississippi rivers and to establish a relationship with the Indians, predicted that their "stately and solemn temples with gilded spires reaching to the skies" would eventually take the place of Indian tepees.

St. Anthony Falls' wilderness state lasted until Fort Snelling soldiers erected a sawmill. This lithograph of the falls by Henry Lewis dates from circa 1854. Courtesy, Minnesota Historical Society

actually attacked people and property, and the North West Company started to unravel. First Congress passed an act forbidding it to trade south of the Canadian border. Then, under pressure from the British, it was forced to merge with the Hudson's Bay Company.

At Grand Portage it was not uncommon for more than a thousand British "Norwesters" to gather during the summer months. They spent their time exchanging stories of wintering on Leech Lake or Sandy Lake in central Minnesota, or along the Red River Valley deep in the heart of Sioux territory.

Fur trade was conducted on a credit system. In exchange for kettles, cloth, beads, guns, tobacco, and spirits, Indians promised to supply traders with beaver and other skins and furs. In the fall Indian delegations would arrive at a trading post to select supplies and equipment. The trader would keep a careful account of the Indians' charges and would expect payment in the spring—frequently at inflated prices. For a tin kettle worth about $2.50, an Indian might be expected to haul in about sixty muskrats, valued in those days at $12.00. The more the Indians grew accustomed to European products, the more dependent they became on the traders. In one year the North West Company supplied more than 16,000 gallons of liquor for trade. It was a system that brought traditional tribal values to the brink of extinction.

ONWARD AMERICA . . .

In the wilderness—far away from the commercial thrusts of the Eastern Seaboard—the effect of the American Revolution was little more than a laborious management shift in the fur-trading business. Like the French before them, the British reluctantly gave up their holdings. Unlike the French, however, the British took their time about their departure.

Before the Treaty of Paris was signed between the British and the Americans in 1783, Benjamin Franklin negotiated border terms with British diplomats who wanted to draw a line west from Montreal along the 45th parallel, straight to the Mississippi River—approximately where the Twin Cities are located today. In the British plan everything south of the 45th parallel was to belong to the United States; everything north was to belong to England.

Fortunately for the lumbermen and miners yet to come, Franklin drove a hard bargain with the British. The boundary that was finally adopted was drawn west from Lake Superior through something called "Long Lake," then up to the northwest point of Lake of the Woods and west from there. But Franklin and his diplomatic team had no accurate maps of the area for a number of years, and the treaty boundaries raised more questions than they answered. Conflicting British and American claims finally resulted in a compromise in 1818 which named the Pigeon River as the Canada/United States boundary west from Lake Superior, and drew the remainder of the boundary line where it is today.

It wasn't until nearly twenty-five years after the Revolution that the American government turned its attention to the vast country beyond the Eastern Seaboard cities. President Thomas Jefferson's interest in his country's wartime acquisitions was piqued by Napoleon, who, in 1803, sold what was left of his colonial empire in North America to the United States for about $15 million—roughly three cents an acre. The Louisiana Purchase received hearty approval from the public and the press. Now open to exploration were the lands extending north and west of the Mississippi River. To find out more about this vast area, Jefferson sent the Lewis and Clark expedition west toward the Pacific in 1804. The next year Lieutenant Zebulon Pike was commanded to explore the upper Mississippi to its source.

When Pike left St. Louis, Missouri, in August 1805, he had a number of missions to accomplish. First, he hoped to win the confidence of the Indian tribes who lived along the Mississippi River Valley and, eventually, to win some of their lands to establish American military posts. Also, he wanted to be certain that the British were no longer occupying American lands. Driving him forward through the snow and the cold winter, however, was his personal hope of finding the headwaters of the Mississippi River.

In a 70-foot keelboat with an entourage of one sergeant, two corporals, and seventeen privates, Pike reached the mouth of the Minnesota River in about four weeks. On what is now called Pike's Island, Pike and his men built a camp and raised the American flag. The next day a group of Sioux came over to find out who they were and what they were doing. An earnest soldier and an able talker, Pike established cordial relations with them, and in a few weeks a formal council was held at which Pike asked the Sioux to make peace with their Chippewa enemies, give up trade with the British, and sell the United States two (carefully chosen) pieces of land for military forts—one at the mouth of the St. Croix River and the other at the mouth of the Minnesota. The price he negotiated with the Indians came to 1.28 cents per acre.

Though he had accomplished his mission for the Jefferson administration, Pike couldn't leave the country without trying to discover the source of the Mississippi River. Reason should have told him to wait until spring. But Pike was a man in a hurry, and he pushed himself and his men upriver in the teeth of a bitter Minnesota winter. As bad as the cold and the howling snow were, however, nothing caused Pike as much concern as the continual signs of an active British trade. At Sandy Lake, about fifteen

In 1805 Zebulon Pike was sent by President Jefferson to the upper Mississippi region to make the American presence known. Though, officially, Pike was to try to gain the confidence of the Indians of the area and thereby obtain some of their lands for American military posts, his personal dream was to find the headwaters of the Mississippi. He was successful in his mission for the Jefferson administration, but not in finding the source of the Mississippi. From Cirker, Dictionary of American Portraits, *Dover, 1967*

The American Fur Company took over the trading post at Fond du Lac, near Duluth, fifteen years after its establishment. Missionary work, a school, and an experimental fishing industry supplemented fur trading at the post. Courtesy, Northeast Minnesota Historical Center

miles north of present-day McGregor, Pike's cold, hungry, and weary party groped its way through the gates of a North West Company fur-trading post. They rested there for twelve days, well-treated and fed by the British traders, before pushing on to another British post at Leech Lake, some fifty miles to the northwest. In his haste, Pike declared Leech Lake to be the source of the Mississippi River.

History would prove Pike wrong about two things: he missed the actual source of the Mississippi by more than twenty miles, and he misjudged the position of the British traders.

In fact, the days of British authority over Minnesota's resources were running out. American entrepreneurs were beginning to see the potential for wealth that was waiting to be plucked. In New York, John Jacob Astor, a German immigrant, was one of those American entrepreneurs. In 1808 he founded the American Fur Company, which would soon become one of the major forces behind the economic growth of the Upper Mississippi River Valley, the Great Lakes, and as far west as the Oregon Territory.

The American Fur Company would also set the tone for big business in America. Through the first thirty-five years of the nineteenth century, the company amassed money, prestige, and power until it monopolized the fur trade. By diversifying its interests, the company proved to be as nimble as it was lusty. At the same time that Astor was establishing a trade loop that included Leipzig, London, and Canton, his fur company was building up its land holdings in America, developing food-producing farms for its employees, creating commercial fisheries on Lake Superior, and managing lead and copper mines.

Astor's fingers reached into Minnesota's interior after the War of 1812, when the United States government declared that no foreign country would be allowed to operate a fur trade within its borders. As usual, Astor's timing was right. In 1815 the Sioux nation pledged loyalty to the United States, leaving the military free to build outposts in the wilderness. Besides preserving the peace, they would protect American trade.

THE SELKIRK COLONISTS

They called him the Prairie Chicken because he had a shock of fiery red hair that swept back from his forehead like a crest. His name was Josiah Snelling, and in 1820 he was sent by the U.S. Army to the Minnesota wilderness to build the fort that would bear his name. Colonel Snelling had a temper that matched the color of his hair, but under his leadership in the 1820s, Fort Snelling—the northernmost military post in the United

Nicknamed the "Prairie Chicken" because a shock of red hair swept back from his forehead like a crest, Josiah Snelling was anything but a coward. In the 1820s, under his leadership, Fort Snelling became a vanguard of settlement in the West. From Cirker, Dictionary of American Portraits, *Dover, 1967*

The Métis drove caravans of up to 800 carts along the Red River trails, bringing supplies to the Selkirk settlement near Winnipeg and returning to St. Paul with furs. Each cart carried 800 pounds of goods and traveled from Pembina to St. Paul in thirty to forty days. Courtesy, Minneapolis Public Library

States—became a vanguard of Western settlement. Built high on the bluffs above the confluence of the Minnesota and Mississippi rivers, the fort looked down on a valley where two major cities would be built before the end of the century.

Snelling was a man who explored possibilities. Logs for his fort were cut along the Rum River and rafted down to a sawmill built by his men at the Falls of St. Anthony. Limestone for the outer walls was quarried nearby. In the fertile clearings near the fort, the soldiers grew wheat, oats, corn, and garden vegetables, including 4,500 bushels of potatoes in 1824. Inside the fort, Snelling and his wife, Abigail, promoted cultural events for the officers, their families, and their visitors. Just outside, Indian leaders, Indian agents, and fur traders picked their way through two centuries of hostilities between the Chippewa and the Sioux tribes, trying to maintain a semblance of peace.

Three years after Snelling assumed command, the fort saluted the first steamboat to reach the area. The *Virginia*'s trek marked the beginning of an important communications link between St. Louis and the Minnesota hinterland. It was only a matter of time before settlers, household goods, and investment dollars, as well as mail and news, would flow north.

Within a few years of its founding the great fort offered protection and human companionship for settlers who had fallen on hard times. One such group who needed help was from the Selkirk Colony, a band of Scottish and Swiss immigrants who had settled along the Canadian Red River Valley. The Selkirk Colony had been plagued by disasters from its founding in 1811 to its finale in the 1830s, including floods, droughts, failed crops, and bloody rivalries between the North West Company and Hudson's Bay Company traders.

In 1827 a number of Swiss and French Canadian families broke away from the colony to resettle in the United States. Having heard about Fort Snelling from American Fur Company traders, the families packed their belongings into oxcarts and walked from the settlement near present-day Winnipeg to the fort. Poverty-stricken, hungry, and desolate, the Selkirk refugees sought the protection of the fort while trying to decide what to do next. Many headed down the Mississippi and settled at Galena and other points south, while others quietly started to farm on military reservation land north of the fort and west of the Mississippi River. Within the next decade, 500 more people arrived at Fort Snelling from the Selkirk Colony. Since settlement of the territory was not officially permitted by law—all the land surrounding the military reservation was Indian land—the Selkirkers who stayed on lived at the favor of the military government.

What was wanted was land on which to build permanent homes and businesses. Pressured by land speculators, lumbermen, and settlers, the government negotiated treaties with the Sioux to obtain the large triangle of land between the St. Croix and Mississippi rivers. When the treaties were ratified in 1838, settlers from the Red River Valley were ordered away from the military reservation land. Pushed from the fort, the settlers from the Selkirk Colony moved down the Mississippi and established a new settlement, which would eventually become St. Paul, today the state capital.

Through the decades, a primitive but workable financial system, based on credit, had been built on the fur trade. But in the 1830s silk became the fashion rage in Europe,

Martin McLeod of Montreal, pictured here about 1850, sought shelter at Fort Snelling in the mid-1830s. He stayed on as a trader for the American Fur Company throughout the 1840s and later exerted his literary influence on the first Territorial Legislature by authoring the bill to establish common schools in Minnesota. Courtesy, Minnesota Historical Society

Henry Sibley was asked by a delegation of pioneers in 1846 to lobby in the halls of Congress for the formation of a new territory. At first he was unsuccessful, but three years later, with Senator Stephen A. Douglas' help, he was able to convince Congress to pass a bill creating the Territory of Minnesota. From Cirker, Dictionary of American Portraits, *Dover, 1967*

and the demand for fur dropped nearly overnight. Like toppling dominoes, the effect was quickly felt in the pockets of American fur traders, who were threatened not only by the sudden collapse of their European market but also by the advance of farming, lumbering, and settlements on their trapping territory.

The undoing of the fur industry was a jolt to the struggling frontier economy. Money grew scarce. For the American Fur Company, the Panic of 1837, as the financial crisis was called, was not a total surprise, though management was shocked that it came as quickly as it did. After 1838 the fur trade in the Minnesota wilderness was gradually replaced by logging, milling, and farming.

Once the 1837 treaties with the Sioux Indians were sanctioned by Congress, wavelets of hardy white settlers washed over the ancient hunting and fishing grounds. Many were attracted to the newly opened country by the thick stands of white pine that grew along the St. Croix River, and by the dollars that expanding American lumber markets could offer. By the early 1840s lumbering had become a booming business in and around the ceded Indian lands of the St. Croix River Valley. A few small sawmills cropped up, followed by families of subsistence farmers.

Because early farming was such difficult work—even on Minnesota's rich river-valley soils—agriculture got off to a slow start. Families who were able to cut through the tough prairie topsoil could only provide for themselves. Life was primitive and lonely, with limited rewards for the few who stuck it out.

As families continued to push west, however, the trickle of settlement soon became a steady flow. In Washington, D.C., Congress tried to make sense—and states—out of the territories that were being populated. Between 1834 and 1849 the lands around Fort Snelling west of the Mississippi belonged to four different territorial governments—Michigan, Wisconsin, Iowa, and finally, after lengthy debate, Minnesota.

The people who had made their homes in the delta between the St. Croix and Mississippi rivers felt that they deserved some representation in Congress and a government to provide structure during the westward expansion. Becoming a territory would mean federal assistance for road building and schools. It would also mean mail delivery and courts for trying people who broke the law. In 1846 a delegation of pioneers from the delta area asked Henry Sibley, a deft negotiator formerly with the American Fur Company, to promote their cause in the halls of Congress. For his efforts, and at his own expense, he was able to get a bill passed in the House that would allow the creation of a new territory. But the Senate was less inclined to put its stamp of approval on the idea. Of overriding concern to members of Congress was the simmering slavery issue, and Sibley understood that he would have to bide his time before trying again.

In his memoirs Sibley wrote that a number of names had been suggested by various House members for the proposed territory, including "Itasca," "Algonquin," "Chippewa," "Jackson," and "Washington." By compromise, the House chose "Minnesota," derived from a Sioux word meaning "water with clouds on it."

By 1848 the push for status as a territory had become a hot political issue. On the Fourth of July the citizens of Stillwater organized a parade and celebration to demonstrate their serious intentions of becoming a full-fledged territory of the United States. Six weeks later, a convention of sixty-two representatives was held at Stillwater to add an official delegation to the voice of its citizens. Once again Sibley was asked to go to Washington on behalf of the Minnesota territory. This time, with considerable help from Illinois Senator Stephen A. Douglas—a friend and long-time colleague—Sibley was successful. The bill passed on April 3, 1849. Bordered by the St. Croix and Mississippi rivers on the east, the new territory extended to the Missouri River on the west. Within the boundaries of the new territory were about 25,000 Sioux and Chippewa, and a mere 5,000 settlers.

Six days later the whistle of a steamboat rounding the bend of the Mississippi called out the news to the townspeople of St. Paul, the newly named capital. A major battle had been won.

For Yankees the music of St. Anthony Falls reverberated with the rhythm of waterwheels driving sawmills, flour mills, and woodworking machinery. Courtesy, Minnesota Historical Society

INDUSTRIALIZING THE FRONTIER

T hrough the 1850s America was in a mood to celebrate. To show the world it was made of the right stuff, America held a world's fair at New York City's Crystal Palace in 1853. Only four years old, the Minnesota territorial government grabbed the opportunity to promote settlement and business growth along its riverbanks, appointing William G. Le Duc, a pioneer Minnesotan, as the director of Minnesota territorial marketing. Le Duc was given an expense budget ($300), a mission (to captivate the New York City press), and a directive (to attract potential settlers). With an Indian canoe, a few photographs of the landscape, wild rice from the northern lakes, furs from the timberlands, and grains from an infant farming belt, Le Duc put together a rustic exhibition that, for many Easterners, put the Minnesota Territory on the map. Legend tells that Le Duc also transported a live buffalo with him to New York City. For all his trouble, however, the buffalo was declined entrance at the door.

Minnesota was not lacking for boosters like Le Duc, and their words echo the thriving sense of optimism abroad in the territory. In 1849 the *Minnesota Pioneer* lauded Minnesota as the "new" New England. "Minnesota, we foresee, will be the destination of the largest current of emigration from the Eastern States . . . ," the newspaper proclaimed.

> Here they will find an unqualified healthy climate, fertile and well drained lands, and upon the Mississippi, the best market for mechanical products in the Union. With such a population will come not only arts but science and morals. Our Falls of St. Anthony with hundreds of water powers upon other streams will be turned to manufacturing purposes. Thrifty towns will arise upon them. Our undulating prairies will rejoice under the hand of husbandry; these hills and vallies [sic] will be jocund with voices of school children, and churches shall mark the moral progress of the land.

To advertise "the undulating" prairies and "thrifty towns" along Minnesota's waterways, the Territorial Legislature appropriated money in 1855 to pay a full-time immigration commissioner whose job was to meet every incoming ship of immigrants in New York City's harbor and describe to them the bounty of the land. Between ship arrivals the commissioner wrote pamphlets for those Europeans who hadn't yet made the journey to America.

Thousands of settlers disembarked from steamboats at the St. Paul levees on their way to claim land on the prairies. The influx of people in the 1850s broke all migration records in spite of the fact that boat traffic was limited to fewer than nine months of the year. Courtesy, Minnesota Historical Society

Between 1849 and 1860 Minnesota's population soared—from 5,000 to 172,000. Throngs of immigrants bound for Minnesota helped propel the Mississippi steamboat industry to new levels of success. By 1858 sixty-two steamboats were regularly plying their way to St. Paul, carrying potential settlers—many from Germany and Norway—looking for good farming soil. Steamboat traffic flourished on the Minnesota River as well. After the building of Fort Ridgely, near present-day New Ulm, steamboats carried pork, flour, and other goods upriver to the soldiers, and gold for the Indians in payment for the lands they had ceded. By 1858 Fort Ridgely counted 394 steamboat landings within the year.

The Red River of the North was the third major river system in Minnesota to carry steamboat traffic. This traffic was necessary to open up the northern regions of the territory, and the St. Paul Chamber of Commerce in 1858 offered a cash prize to anyone who successfully navigated the river. Businessman and hotel builder Anson Northrop sailed a steamboat to Crow Wing on the Mississippi River, then took the boat apart—board by board, gear by gear. With thirty-four teams of oxen, he hauled his steamboat across more than eighty miles to the Red River, where he launched his craft and claimed his prize. It was a number of years, however, before steamboats regularly appeared in Breckenridge and Ortonville and the other Minnesota communities that were springing up along the river.

Each spring when the ice finally broke up, usually in late April, dozens of hardy steamboats chugged their way through a countryside that was becoming increasingly dotted with towns. On the lower Mississippi, citizens in the villages of Winona, Wabasha, Read's Landing, Red Wing, Frontenac, and Hastings stood on the banks, waving the steamboat crews on to St. Paul.

Beyond the rapidly growing towns of St. Cloud and Sauk Rapids, St. Anthony and its sister city, Minneapolis, snapped with importance as the logging industry stretched its enterprising fingers into the white pine forests of the north country. Along the Minnesota River, villages such as Shakopee, St. Peter, Mankato, and New Ulm attracted families of immigrants who transplanted their traditions and ethics of hard work into the Minnesota prairie.

The Minnesota Territory was fast becoming a land of business opportunities. Minnesota could offer water power for milling and manufacturing, pine for lumbering, waterways for inexpensive transportation, and rich soil for farming.

In the 1850s, breweries, tanneries, and foundries grew up alongside shops, hotels, physicians' offices, and lawyers' firms. Underpinning the growth was capital, brought upriver by the financiers whose banks soon marked the main street of every town and village. Building towns became a favorite occupation of land speculators who were willing to gamble that they had the formula that would attract enough people to make their town a successful venture. Between 1855 and 1857, 700 towns were laid out, with platted lots for many thousands more people than were actually living in the territory at the time.

SEALED FATE

While young farming families unloaded their baggage from the steamboats, policy-makers in St. Paul were busy authorizing and designing a seal that would signify the territory's potential. In 1849 Territorial Governor Alexander Ramsey and congressional delegate Henry Sibley supervised the selection of the design. After considerable thought they agreed that the best drawing was offered by Seth Eastman, an Army cap-

Steamboats linked Minnesota and the rest of the country until after the Civil War. The winter freeze, however, halted the flow of goods and people for several months, and by March supplies ran low. So, a bonus was offered to the first boat that would brave the thawing river in the spring. Courtesy, Minnesota Historical Society

tain stationed at Fort Snelling whose illustrations of contemporary Indian life were well regarded.

What Eastman's penwork communicated was that the white man's civilization was pressing the Indian into obscurity. Against a distant background of Minnehaha Falls, an Indian brave on a horse is seen turning away from a settler who has cut into the soil with his plow and into a tree with his ax. Eastman's drawing, later incorporated into the state's seal, forecast the heavy price the Sioux and Chippewa nations would pay throughout the nineteenth century. Mary Henderson Eastman, the artist's wife, wrote a poem reflecting her husband's work. Her words are poignant, not because she crafted her thoughts well but because they represent the zealousness of the new arrivals that doomed the two proud Indian nations.

> Give way! Give way young warrior!
> Thou and thy steed give way!
> Rest not, though lingers on the hills,
> The red sun's parting ray.

The spread of civilization across the face of Minnesota was sure and steady. Lured by promotional pieces such as the small book called *Minnesota and Its Resources*, families from Maine to Ohio joined the steady flow of immigrants from western Europe. What they wanted was land—land on which they could build farms and homes for themselves and as a heritage for their children. What they brought with them were energy and determination, qualities that fostered Minnesota's entrepreneurial spirit.

Having conquered the hardships of their westward adventures, the new arrivals felt increasingly hemmed in by the Indian lands that surrounded them. They complained ruefully to their territorial leaders that more land should be tamed for farming. The public and the press argued that too many dollars were leaving with the steamboats in payment for foodstuffs which could be better and less expensively grown by Minne-

The pastoral image of St. Anthony Falls attracted Southern gentry seeking summer vacations in the north, and their patronage supported riverfront hotels. Courtesy, Minnesota Historical Society

Against a distant background of Minnehaha Falls, an Indian brave on a horse is seen turning away from a settler who has cut into the soil with his plow and into a tree with his ax. Seth Eastman, an Army captain stationed at Fort Snelling, submitted this watercolor in 1849 as the basis for the Minnesota State Seal. Courtesy, Minnesota Historical Society

sota farmers. In the 1850s, almost everyone believed that farmlands were the key to Minnesota's long-term economic solvency.

Two treaties were signed with the Sioux in 1851, expanding the agricultural potential of the territory west from the Mississippi River. For a little more than $1.6 million, the federal government bought 24 million acres of land, reaching across the lower half of Minnesota from the Mississippi on the east to the Bois des Sioux and Big Sioux rivers on the west.

With such a wide expanse of rich agricultural land available, many farmers began planting more than their own families or animals could eat, and selling the rest. As transportation to markets grew better, agriculture fostered new spinoff industries. Within the decade twenty-two meat-packing plants were opened to handle a growing livestock business down on the farms. In 1854 a mill opened at St. Anthony to commercially process local wheat. The mill's owners had a difficult time when it first opened, but only four years later eighty-five flour mills were thriving across the state in such places as Marine, Northfield, Winona, and Hastings, as well as St. Anthony, Minneapolis, and St. Paul.

In 1855 the first agricultural fair was held in Minneapolis to celebrate a diverse and strong agricultural base. Families from the surrounding countryside hauled their best crops and livestock to town. Shanghai and Chittagong chickens, Leicester sheep, yellow dent corn, butter and cheese, squash, pumpkins, and potatoes were admired as if they were the crown jewels of England.

Indian land holdings were also hemming in another infant industry. Ancient white pines—so big, legend says, that it took sixteen grown men standing fingertip to fingertip to reach around one of them at the base—crashed to the earth as teams of loggers moved north on the St. Croix and Rum rivers. Demand for Minnesota pine was on the upswing. Wood was needed for houses, shops, schools, and churches in the brand-new towns, but more titillating to the businessmen paying the loggers' wages was the profit to be made downriver from their white gold.

No one doubted that the lumber industry needed elbowroom. The industry itched for the pine in Lake Superior country. The federal government accommodated by tempting the Chippewa with offers of payments and trading credits in exchange for

The Falls of St. Anthony gave Minnesota great industrial potential, and by 1863 mills flanked these Mississippi River falls. Courtesy, Minnesota Historical Society

the land east of the St. Louis River. In 1854 the first of a number of treaties was signed in the north country to secure land for Minnesota settlers and speculators. By the end of 1855 the Indians had signed away their rights to most of the land in Minnesota Territory.

Traveling up nearly any river in the 1850s, it was common to see smoke rising from the chimneys of settlements. Too impatient to wait for the federal land surveys that followed treaty signings, homesteaders marked their property lines by blazing trees or building small fences. Under the 1841 Preemption Act, families could choose 160 acres of land, build a home and begin farming, and not pay for the land until the government got around to putting it up for sale. Then the family living on the land had first claim to it and could buy it at the lowest price.

MINNESOTA
AND
ITS RESOURCES
BY
J.W. BOND

FALLS OF ST. ANTHONY

REDFIELD
110 & 112 NASSAU STREET
NEW YORK.
1853.

Though this book contained only two illustrations, its powerful words created pictures in people's minds that made them pack their belongings and move to Minnesota. Courtesy, Minnesota Historical Society

GROWING TOGETHER—GROWING APART

There was a great celebration in 1854 when the first railroad tracks reached the Mississippi River at Rock Island, Illinois. The East Coast was finally linked to the heart of the continent, and settlers could board the train in a major Eastern city, travel overland to Rock Island, and then hop a steamboat going north. Getting to Minnesota had become relatively easy.

Twelve hundred people—including Millard Fillmore, the thirteenth president of the United States—rode the first train from Chicago to Rock Island. There, seven steamboats waited to transport the partying crowd to St. Paul. As the steamboats rounded the last bend outside the city, the mood of the citizens of St. Paul was electric. For them, statehood was as close at hand as the steamboats.

With federal help, the territory built roads to connect the growing centers of trade such as Stillwater, St. Paul, Minneapolis, and St. Anthony with the farming communities at Monticello and Crow Wing. From the north, hundreds of Red River oxcarts hauled furs from the outposts and settlements around the old Selkirk Colonies to St. Paul. By 1858, trade between the Red River villages and southern Minnesota had become so lucrative that a caravan of 600 oxcarts arrived in St. Paul, filled with furs that would soon be bound for the Eastern markets.

With better roads Minnesotans enjoyed better communication, not only with each other but with the outside world as well. Instead of one mail delivery to St. Paul every week or so, the mail regularly rode the rails from the East, and was then transported by steamboat and stagecoach to the end of the line. But the letters were frequently filled with disquieting news about the growing bitterness between the North and South over slavery.

In 1858, 600 oxcarts laden with furs (such as those shown here) arrived in St. Paul from the Red River villages. The carts were constructed of wood without any type of metal. Courtesy, Stearns County Historical Society

While nearly every citizen of the territory favored statehood, there the harmony ended. In 1855 the Republican party was founded in the wake of the disintegrated national Whig party. Opposing slavery and supporting a transcontinental railroad and free land for settlers, the Republican party dominated the farming centers in southeastern Minnesota.

On the opposite side of the political fence were the Democrats, who, in Minnesota, were generally lukewarm on the issue of slavery. The Democratic platform of the day insisted that the citizens of every new state and territory in the Union vote to decide whether to become a slave state or a free state. As the party of popular sovereignty, the Democrats counted their heaviest support within the larger cities of St. Paul, St. Anthony, and Stillwater.

While the parties squabbled back and forth over the size and shape of the potential state, and the location of the capital, the territory entered a new era. In 1856 Democrat Henry Rice took the cause of Minnesota's statehood to Congress. Introduced as a bill by Senator Stephen Douglas, the request came at a time when pro- and anti-slavery interests were delicately balanced in Congress. If Minnesota became a state, how would it lean? Southerners generally assumed that Minnesota citizens would reject slavery, so they voted against the measure.

Nevertheless, the Minnesota Enabling Act was passed on February 26, 1857, giving the territory the power to draft a state constitution. The struggle to statehood had been so bitter, however, that Republicans and Democrats held their own conventions and drafted separate constitutions. When Henry Sibley was finally elected governor in a very close and bitter race with his Republican opponent Alexander Ramsey, voting fraud and deception charges were tossed from one end of the political spectrum to the other. In the end, the Democrats added a few Republican changes and sent their constitution to Congress for consideration. During the following months Congress again debated the ramifications for the slave states should Minnesota's request for statehood be allowed. Finally, in May 1858, Minnesota was officially admitted to the Union.

END OF THE ROAD

By the time the steamboat *Milwaukee* carried the news about statehood up the Mississippi in the spring of 1858, the territorial settlers' confident expectations of prosperity had disappeared. Paralleling the Panic of 1837, which signaled the end of the frontier fur trade, the Panic of 1857 ended land speculation fever and immersed the country—including its newest state—in a choking depression.

The financial troubles of the late 1850s exploded when the Ohio Life Insurance and Trust Company of New York failed. For years the credit system had been ballooning, inflated by land speculation. Using credit, Minnesota families had ordered household goods, kept up on the latest Eastern styles, and snapped up pieces of land. When Eastern creditors nervously called in their loans, the citizens of Minnesota couldn't pay their debts.

Suddenly there weren't two nickels to rub together in the entire territory, and the doors of burgeoning businesses slammed shut. Up and down the dusty streets of such towns as Hastings, Alexandria, and Anoka, banks, hotels, and stores closed down. Word quickly came that credit rates from the East had jumped from 3 percent to an unheard-of 10 percent. No one could afford to pay off their loans or refinance past speculation. Packing their bags, professional land-buyers hurried down to the wharves to catch the earliest steamboat out of town. Oil lamps and newfangled gas lights (in St. Paul) burned late in the offices of lawyers and civil authorities as land foreclosures seemed to outnumber the late-summer crop of mosquitoes. Within weeks after the panic swept up the rivers, another nail was driven into the coffin of economic prosperity. Earlier in the year, the Territorial Legislature had passed an act that provided significant land grants and tax breaks to four railroad companies empowered to build lines across the countryside. The goal was to quickly connect towns with points East. Under the act, as soon as a railroad company completed a twenty-mile stretch of road, it was to receive title to another 120 sections of land, until every village in Minnesota Territory could call itself a whistle stop.

When the panic hit, however, the chartered railroad companies—the Minnesota and Pacific Railroad Company, the Transit Railroad Company, the Root River Valley and Southern Minnesota Railroad Company, and the Minneapolis and Cedar Valley Railroad Company—suddenly found themselves in a tight spot. To take advantage of the land grants, the four companies would have to raise money for the construction of the first twenty miles of track. Their dilemma, of course, was that there was no money in the territory to raise. The Transit Railroad Company—a corporation that was empowered by the legislature to build a road from Winona through St. Peter to the Big Sioux River—even tried to sell 500,000 acres of its land grant at one dollar an acre. Finding no buyers, the owners fled back to the state capital and pleaded for help.

The public was more than sympathetic to the plight of the railroads. Wanting a national rail system was patriotic, and everyone dreamed of a system that would pull the territory together—politically and geographically. By February 1858, a little over six months after the panic had begun, a bill appeared in the Territorial Legislature to provide $5 million in bonds, backed by territorial credit, to help the railroads begin work.

With the introduction of the $5 million loan bill, legislators demonstrated their belief that supporting big business also supported the little guy who needed to work, and that pumping some money into the economy would help to get things moving again. The bill declared that upon the completion of grading any ten miles of railroad, a railroad company would receive secured bonds in $100,000 increments, for which it would pay interest and the principal when due. The bill passed easily, and a popular election held in May 1858 confirmed the public's overwhelming support of the $5 million loan. Winona town officials reported that out of 1,182 votes, only one person voted against the measure.

But financial disaster still prevailed in the late summer and fall of 1858, when the railroads began construction and were expecting to use the new state's support to invigorate their cash flow. Money was still tight, and the value of the state's bonds sank owing to the depression. Railroad company executives soon realized that they were trapped in a quicksand from which there was no escape. By 1859 the public's confidence in the railroads' ability to keep their end of the financial bargain had been lost, so much so that critics proclaimed that the companies had never intended to lay tracks at all, that they had tricked the good citizens of Minnesota from the first. And where grading had been done, the quality was inadequate. Furious, citizens pointed to a public outlay of $2.25 million in special bonds that had provided 240 miles of poorly executed, discontinuous gradings.

Translating the so-called railroad scheme into cartoon form, an illustrator named R.O. Sweeny circulated to the papers in the state a broadside drawing showing a team of gophers in top hats pulling a cartload of legislators down a railroad track. From beneath, the track and the gopher train were supported by the backs of Minnesota citizens. So widely known was Sweeny's cartoon at the time that the new state quickly became known as the "Gopher State."

THE "BANNER WHEAT STATE"

Elected the second governor of the state of Minnesota in 1860, Alexander Ramsey defeated his personal friend and political rival Henry Sibley, launching a tradition of Republican political domination that would last nearly forty years. As he took his oath of office, Ramsey spoke of two missions he wanted to accomplish within the first months of his administration. With his term coming on the heels of the depression, he first intended to tackle cost-cutting policies in state government; within a year he cut expenditures by 36 percent. His second goal was to turn his state's support to the Union cause, marching whenever possible against the onslaught of secessionist and pro-slavery foes.

In the spring of 1861 he was in Washington, D.C., appealing for federal financial aid for the state, when he heard that Fort Sumter (at Charleston, South Carolina) had fallen and that Union troops had been forced to evacuate it. Ramsey hastened to the office of the Secretary of War and pledged 1,000 men to help defend the Union. Thus

In 1860 Alexander Ramsey became the state of Minnesota's second governor. He was the first governor, however, to volunteer his state's men for the Union army. Courtesy, Minnesota Historical Society

Chief of the Sandy Lake tribe of Ojibway, Po-go-Nay-ke-Shick carried on the perpetual struggle between his people and the Dakotas. The fighting ended with the banishment of the Dakotas after the uprising of 1862. Courtesy, Minnesota Historical Society

Little Crow's participation in the 1862 uprising has obscured his role as a negotiator. As chief of the Mdewakanton Sioux, he sought peaceful ways for Indians and whites to live together until he saw no alternative but the use of force. Courtesy, Minnesota Historical Society

Minnesota became the first state to answer President Abraham Lincoln's call for troops.

The Civil War revived the sense of national loyalty that had been flagging for a few years in Minnesota. Setting their own financial worries aside, Minnesotans pitched in with their support to help settle the slavery issue once and for all. Accompanied by furled flags and blaring trumpets, more than 25,000 men left for the battlefields of Bull Run and Chickamauga.

In the early days of the war, no one could imagine the devastation that lay ahead for those men, their families, and the country. At Gettysburg, 215 of the First Minnesota regiment's 262 men lay dead or severely wounded on the battlefield.

On the homefront, the Sioux Indians, who had ceded most of their hunting and fishing grounds in the treaties of 1851, were now confined to reservations in the Minnesota River Valley. They deeply regretted the loss of their ancestral lands, and their disillusion was intensified when their crops failed during the summer of 1861. Bureaucratic holdups in Washington had delayed land payments to the Sioux, making it impossible for the Indian tribes to buy the supplies they needed, thus compounding their resentment toward the white society. Finally, one late-summer day in 1862, four wandering Sioux hunters killed five settlers at Acton, in Meeker County. The Indian nation, led by Chiefs Little Crow and Shakopee, rallied in an all-out commitment to war. Before Minnesota's political leaders received word about the murders the next morning,

Delays in government land payments to the Sioux made it impossible for the tribes to buy necessary supplies. These bureaucratic hold-ups, coupled with the Sioux's resentment over the loss of their ancestral lands, precipitated a bloody Indian war. In retaliation, President Lincoln ordered the hanging of thirty-eight Sioux warriors. The mass execution, pictured here, took place in Mankato. Courtesy, Minnesota Historical Society

a large war party had already attacked the Lower Sioux Agency, looting and burning the buildings and killing traders. Like a prairie fire, the Indians' bitterness burned across the countryside, quickly turning into one of the nation's bloodiest Indian wars. Governor Ramsey called out extra troops and put Henry Sibley in charge of the entire force.

Within five weeks, the white man had once again achieved the upper hand. As many Indian families attempted to flee to Dakota Territory for safety, more than 1,700 Sioux and mixed-blood sympathizers were captured. Three hundred of the more serious offenders were tried immediately, sentenced to death, and held for the final word of condemnation from President Lincoln. Lincoln's decision, however, reflected leniency. On the day after Christmas in 1862, thirty-eight Sioux, instead of 300, were hanged at Mankato in a mass execution. Ironically, Chiefs Little Crow and Shakopee were not among them; they had escaped capture. The remaining prisoners were banished to a reservation in what is now South Dakota.

With demand for Minnesota wheat at an all-time high to feed the boys in blue, the farmlands deserted during the Indian war were again put under the plow. New threshing machines, combination reaping and mowing machines, and improved plows—manufactured in Minnesota plow factories—helped ease the farmers' job. Between 1860 and 1865 the state's wheat harvest more than doubled, from a little over 5 million to 9.5 million bushels.

During the Civil War, Minnesota was an official "banner wheat state" for the country, and ambitious entrepreneurs capitalized on the need to grind wheat into flour so that it could be shaped into loaves. In 1860 there were only eighty-one flour mills in the state. Over the next decade more than 400 more were built, primarily in the heart of the wheat-growing region in the southern half of the state. By 1869 there were thirteen mills in Minneapolis alone, producing 250,000 barrels of flour in one year. Minnesota had the winning combination of rich soil for raising wheat and water power for grinding it into flour. Along the Root, Mississippi, and Minnesota rivers, mills symbolized the domestication of the land.

The need for food in the Union camps also helped stimulate the growth of a healthy beef and pork market. And Minnesota wool was used for army uniforms. By the time the war-weary survivors straggled home to their farms late in 1865, Minnesota's econ-

Indian people such as this Ojibway woman adopted white dress even as they continued to build traditional dwellings and confine their children in cradle boards. Courtesy, Northeast Minnesota Historical Center

omy had blossomed. Farmers saw wheat prices triple between 1861 and 1866, and a sense of confidence was slowly working its way across the state.

Encouraged by the Homestead Act, which Lincoln had signed into law in 1862, a wave of young families arrived. The act enabled them to settle on 160-acre plots, improve the land over a period of five years, and eventually buy their farms from the federal government for small administrative fees. Towns like Winona and New Ulm flowered as the state's population blossomed. From 172,000 citizens in 1860, the state grew to 440,000 within the decade—a population increase matched only by Kansas and Nebraska.

Still smarting as a nation from the severe depression following the Panic of 1857, the Lincoln administration took steps to reduce the possibility of future bank failures and wildcat lending. The National Bank Act, passed in 1863, established a system of federally run banks and the eventual national control of banking transactions. For the hundreds of new businesses starting up in Minnesota after the Civil War, the act helped restore confidence in bank notes. Still to come, however, was relief from the exorbitantly high interest rates that could be demanded because of a general lack of available money.

Farmers and small businessmen were not the only ones looking for more opportunities following the war. The lumber business was growing into a sizable industry as millions of board feet of Minnesota white pine were floated down the Mississippi to

Six years after the Panic of 1857, the National Bank Act was passed, establishing a nationwide system of federally run banks. The First National Bank in Minneapolis, pictured here in 1866, provided office space for other businesses. Courtesy, Hennepin County Historical Society

markets in Chicago, Rock Island, and St. Louis. For the returning Civil War veterans the industry's prosperity was good news. Lumber companies were as hungry for manpower as they were for stands of pine. Commercial mills grew in the wake of the lumbermen's advance around the Falls of St. Anthony, at Stillwater and Marine on the St. Croix River, and at Winona where John Laird, his brothers, and his cousins, James and Matthew Norton, processed the logs that floated down the streams of Wisconsin and Minnesota. The Laird, Norton Company eventually became one of the largest lumbering operations in the upper Midwest.

Minnesota lumber played a large role in the Midwest's growth. Cities such as Kansas City, Des Moines, and Omaha were built from the rafts of lumber that arrived steadily throughout the last half of the nineteenth century. But lumbering was a highly competitive business and through its heyday in Minnesota, nefarious land deals—taking advantage of the bargain prices offered to settlers by the Homestead Act—were negotiated among lumber barons in smoke-filled rooms. The newspapers of the day hinted loudly that great fortunes were being made behind the backs of Minnesota's citizens. As in all economic growth, there is a trade-off; and here a loss of wilderness resources was the price that was paid for development. From the St. Croix north, the land was ruthlessly stripped, leaving behind a wasteland of stumps and slashings. For places such as Duluth and Cloquet, lumbering greatly contributed to the growth of the community and the prosperity of the citizens who lived there. But in the years following the Civil War, it was hard to keep the trade-offs in balance.

TRACKING PROGRESS

Minnesota shared the economic prosperity that permeated the new Midwest after the Civil War. Like its sister states of Kansas, Iowa, and Wisconsin, Minnesota was transforming itself from a frontier territory to an industrial center. Progress was marked by immigrants coming in and foodstuffs going out at the wharves.

By the end of the 1860s, progress was also marked by the type of transportation that carried eager settlers, produce, and grain in and out of the river towns. Prompted by President Lincoln's signature on the Pacific Railroad Act in 1862, the railroads were swiftly working their way across the country, linking landlocked Midwestern towns with the ports of Europe and the Orient.

At first, railroad trafficking and agricultural development were considered equal partners in success. As they moved away from subsistence-level farming, Minnesota farmers realized that they needed a system of transportation that would move their produce and grains to the user swiftly. Besides wanting to keep their crops from spoiling, the farmers wanted to be sure they were able to move their wheat when it was advantageous to sell. The railroad companies did more than their share in stimulating settlement along the tracks. For them, long-term gain was directly related to their ability to establish the dependence of both shippers and receivers on the railroad. Railroad corporations also needed to sell the lands the government gave them in order to finance construction.

Once again the Minnesota Legislature rolled up its sleeves to try its hand at railroading. Soon the Minnesota and Pacific Railroad Company rose from the ashes of the recent depression, renamed the St. Paul and Pacific Railroad. Construction began as soon as plans and state statutes were formulated. Money was found to link St. Paul and St. Anthony in 1862, to extend to Anoka the following year, and to stretch to Sauk Rapids, fifty miles to the north, by 1866. Little Duluth, poised at the edge of Lake Superior, waited patiently for the chance to build a major shipping business, but it wasn't until 1871 that a railroad linked the port with southern farms.

Trade between the Middle West and the East Coast was humming as railroad lines laced their way across the countryside. But along with the whistle of the train

Oliver H. Kelley, who arrived in St. Paul in 1849 from Boston, settled in Itasca in 1850. Though city-bred, Kelley became a "book farmer" and advocated experimentation and information exchange among farmers. In 1864 Kelley became a clerk under the U.S. commissioner of agriculture, and two years later he came up with the idea of a national farmers' organization. The following year Kelley and six friends founded the Order of the Patrons of Husbandry, also known as the Grange. From Cirker, Dictionary of American Portraits, *Dover, 1967*

came new problems for farmers. Minnesota farmers in the 1860s and early 1870s took their crops to the nearest collecting point, where they were paid the regional price minus a dealer's commission for handling the grain and the price of shipping it to market. Prices fluctuated along with the speculative spirit of the East Coast commodities market. Farmers had no control over the payment they would receive for their work.

On the other hand, the railroad companies had considerable control over the amount they could charge for hauling. They used their increased clout to command higher and higher shipping rates, squeezing dealer margins and eventually the farmers' profits.

In the first decade of growth, the railroads held most of the cards. Frequently, there was not enough competition to force railroad companies to hold the line on rate increases. They considered the level of competition (the transportation options in the area), the nearness to a regional market, and the personal goodwill they felt toward each shipper, and then charged what the traffic would bear. It became common practice for the railroads to set preferential rates for larger shippers or to underweigh and underclassify grain shipments. For Minnesota farmers the rate fluctuations were a bitter pill to swallow, as prices for wheat dropped after the Civil War. What was needed— and needed immediately—was a uniform and fair system of grain inspection and grading, and a rate structure that would be the same for everyone.

Hoping to fight fire with fire, the St. Paul Board of Trade tried to form a cooperative in 1865 that would pull together all the upper Mississippi River grain collection points. Although it was a weak attempt, and failed because of local rivalries, it was the springboard for an agrarian crusade that lasted a number of decades.

In 1867 Oliver H. Kelley, a Minnesota farmer and a clerk at the Bureau of Agriculture in Washington, D.C., recognized that farmers would not be able to strengthen their position unless they joined forces against the railroads and elevator operators. To help them, Kelley founded the National Grange. In 1868 he returned home, and Minnesota farmers were ripe for his ideas. Grange meetings were organized in tiny halls across the state, and by the following year forty Granges had been established in Minnesota. Five years later Kelley's idea had exploded into 20,000 chapters located throughout the country.

Through the last half of the 1860s and most of the 1870s, Grangers collaborated to influence public opinion and legislative action. Along with Congressman Ignatius Donnelly, Minnesota's renowned orator and social reformer, Grangers helped pave the way for regulation of railroad rates. Laws passed in Minnesota during 1871 and 1874 established railroads as public highways, set maximum levels for shipping rates, and created the position of Commissioner of Railroads as overseer of all railroad business within the state.

The Grange movement also laid the foundation for other important movements in Minnesota that would eventually attempt to unite the interests of farmers and laborers against exploitation by big business. It was a standoff that would root itself in the politics of Minnesota and feed sectional conflicts in the state throughout the last quarter of the nineteenth century and well into the twentieth.

While the rhetoric heated in town halls and meeting rooms, the railroad companies were laying tracks across the state. And with the growth of the network came the growth of competition. The Southern Minnesota, the Winona and St. Peter Railroad, and the Hastings and Dakota Railroad ran parallel lines west. To the north, the Lake Superior and Mississippi Railroad was cutting pathways through the pineries toward the port city of Duluth, while the St. Paul and Pacific Railroad was heading toward the fertile Red River Valley. In 1869 a golden spike was driven into a railroad tie at Promontory, Utah, where the Union Pacific and the Central Pacific met to finally link West and East. On hand to watch that moment in history were 500 Minnesota citizens.

Minnesota had its own brand of railroad heroes. In 1873 James J. Hill, a young immigrant from Canada, began reorganizing the failed St. Paul and Pacific Railroad,

Ignatius Donnelly won a place in the hearts of ordinary folk by his outspoken defense of their interests in his publications and in the Minnesota Legislature. He is also remembered as first resident and promoter of the "paper" town of Ninninger, Minnesota, and as a science-fiction author. Courtesy, Minnesota Historical Society

James J. Hill earned the nickname "Empire Builder" by constructing a network of railroads that linked St. Paul with Canada and Duluth with the Pacific. His business succeeded because he matched a keen head for juggling materials and men with his own persistent hard work. Courtesy, Minnesota Historical Society

and thus began a long upward battle to build his own railroad line across the northern plains of the Dakotas, over the mountains of Montana, and west to Puget Sound. Hill's Great Northern Railroad, when completed in 1893, opened new stands of pine to the lumber barons as well as trade opportunities with the Orient. Within months Hill was shipping southern cotton to Seattle for shipment to Japan, as well as flour from Minneapolis, textiles from New England mills, and ores from Colorado mines.

As a power broker and empire builder, Hill was unmatched throughout the last half of the century. His ability to wheel-and-deal his way through the fine print on railroad-regulating legislation dazzled his opponents. His drive and ambition juxtaposed with his paternalistic care of those he favored has become as legendary as his vision.

NO GOING BACK

By the early 1870s the landscape of Minnesota was dotted with new centers of settlement, which were linked together by the telegraph and more than 800 miles of railroad track, fed by a booming agricultural industry, and enriched with the products Minnesota manufacturers could provide—boots and shoes, agricultural implements, and clothing. Clustered around the confluence of the Minnesota and Mississippi rivers, the cities of St. Paul, St. Anthony, and Minneapolis prospered as logs rolled through the rapids around the millraces, grain filled local storage elevators, and tourists seeking a healthful climate paraded along the boardwalks.

Lumbering, flour milling, and transportation powered Minnesota's growth, bringing dollars from the rest of the country with every blast of a steamboat or locomotive whistle. By 1872, when St. Anthony and Minneapolis became one city, the area was known as a center for railroads, manufacturing, milling, and finance. As the head of navigation on the Mississippi River—and the jumping-off place for many new arrivals—St. Paul was a transportation hub as well as a center for the banking, insurance, and printing industries.

Above the Falls of St. Anthony, Minneapolis cradled the lumber that roared downriver from the north and built mills and furniture manufacturing plants. An animal feed industry grew fat with the grain that arrived daily on trains that were reaching farther north and west. Bakeries thrived. So did a clothing manufacturing industry that put bread on the table for an increasing number of laborers.

The seeds of civilization were swelling in other towns as well. From surrounding farms, produce and dairy products arrived regularly in villages such as Crookston, St. Cloud, Winona, and Albert Lea, where elevators, cheese factories, and creameries soon sprang up. In Duluth, businessmen looked eastward toward the Great Lakes and speculated that grain could be brought by train to the inland port, then shipped through the lakes, down the St. Lawrence River, and eventually to the waiting tables of Europe. In fact, Duluth's potential as a great shipping center was so well known among the great financiers and builders of the day that Jay Cooke, promoter for the Northern Pacific Railroad, made Duluth the eastern terminal for his railroad line. By the 1880s the city was becoming a port known throughout the world.

The success of hundreds of farm families hung on the decisions of these members of the Northern Pacific Expedition, who plotted the route of the Northern Pacific Railroad in the summer of 1869. The men are pictured in their camp at Glenwood, Minnesota. Courtesy, Minnesota Historical Society

Only two decades after Minnesota had become a territory, a subtle shift began in its economic foundations. Instead of living off the land, some families looked for steady wages in the factories and mills. Instead of living on isolated farms, they wanted neighbors, the convenience of grocery stores, and regular mail delivery. Instead of living from one growing season to the next, these Minnesota families hoped to put some money away for a rainy day, order a new stove from Montgomery Ward, or even visit the Boardwalk in Atlantic City.

While Minnesota's pine swirled in the eddies around the lumber mills and industrial chimneys belched smoke, a new class system slowly worked its way into urban life. Frustrated by poor working conditions, low wages, and long hours, working men and women pulled themselves together against those they believed profited from their toil. By 1883 the first labor union—the Knights of Labor—had an active organization in the state, touching off a political rivalry between business and labor interests that

Soft sandstone underlying the hard limestone ledge around the Falls of St. Anthony gave way to the persistent scouring action of moving water, and on October 5, 1869, a tunnel built there collapsed. Courtesy, Minnesota Historical Society

would last decades, paralleling the efforts of the Grangers who represented the small Minnesota farmer.

Between the end of the Civil War and the country's centennial, the citizens of Minnesota learned to accept the accelerated pace of change that accompanies industrialization. It was a time when interests were divided between labor and business, city and village, north timber country and southern farmland—even between those who were concerned about the preservation of Minnesota's natural resources and those who favored exploitation.

It was also a time of learning just how far civilization can push before it starts to destroy its own foundation. On Tuesday, October 5, 1869, a tunnel that had been built between Hennepin and Nicollet islands collapsed. The river formed an enormous maelstrom, whirling its way through the tunnel, ripping the roof as though it were made of sand. People from Minneapolis and St. Anthony hurried to the riverbank where they watched three mills on Hennepin Island tumble into the Mississippi River.

A wave of fear choked many of those who watched as word spread that the Falls of St. Anthony would be destroyed. The general assumption that the waterpower of the falls was inexhaustible was gone forever. On October 6, 1869, the *Minneapolis Tribune* acknowledged that the Falls of St. Anthony were vital to the economic security of the state's industries. "Every moment of time, is how precious no man knows, so long as that mighty rush of water, irresistible in its power of demolition, is free to undermine and subvert the prosperity of these two cities," it declared.

As hundreds of men worked day and night to save the falls in the days following the tunnel's break-up, Minnesotans learned that a strong economic future could not be taken for granted.

The 1869 collapse of the tunnel between Hennepin and Nicollet islands proved only a temporary setback in the taming of the mighty Mississippi. The following year engineers persisted in their efforts to harness the waterpower. Courtesy, Minnesota Historical Society

Mueller and Company Grocers of Rochester decorated a young lady in dried fruit to lure people to their shop in the 1880s. Courtesy, Olmsted County Historical Society

GILDING "THE LILY OF THE WEST"

CHANGES IN THE WIND

E arly in the summer of 1873 the homesteading farmer in southern Minnesota had good land beneath his feet, credit when he needed it, and a market for all the grain his family could produce. Before him—as far as the eye could see—was the wheat that would guarantee his future.

But riding the early-June wind were hordes of Rocky Mountain locusts, swirling and gnawing their way east through the tender grasses, stripping the countryside. The farmer and his family could do little but watch as the grasshoppers dropped into their fields and demolished the waving stalks of wheat. When the swarm moved on, the family was left with only the hope that they could survive the winter to plant again in the spring.

They weren't alone in their troubles. Throughout the state, newspapers reported swarms of locusts so large that they eclipsed the sun. The roar of their frenzied feeding sounded like a prairie fire. From Rock, Pipestone, Lincoln, Redwood, Renville, Brown, Watonwan, Blue Earth, and Faribault counties, farmers reported losses totaling millions of dollars that summer.

What had been a bad dream for the farmers in 1873 became a nightmare in 1874. The grasshoppers had done more than ruin crops—they had laid eggs. The following spring, black clouds of young hoppers erupted in field after field in search of food, and within days Minnesota was again under siege. The locusts consumed crops as far north as Becker and Aitkin counties and as far east as the Mississippi River.

Pluck, determination, and charity carried many Minnesota farming families through the next three winters. With each spring thaw came hope, and with each planting came disaster. As grasshopper swarms crossed and recrossed the state in search of new feeding grounds, the crisis made inroads into the mainstream economy. Local businesses extended credit to farmers until the money ran out, while food prices soared.

In 1876 newly elected Governor John S. Pillsbury encouraged Minnesotans to do everything they could think of to fight the pests, and listened patiently while one person after another offered solutions. A teacher from New Ulm, Gustav Heydrich,

John S. Pillsbury went into milling when he came to Minnesota in 1855, but his nephew started the company that still flourishes today. In the 1890s, as governor, he encouraged Minnesotans to invent ways to rid the state of the grasshopper plague. Courtesy, Minnesota Historical Society

In this library, Ignatius Donnelly produced both political tirades in support of common people and science-fiction dramas of the past and the future. Courtesy, Minnesota Historical Society

proposed a horse-driven machine that would sweep grasshoppers into a bin and then crush them under the machine's heavy wheels. A Willmar citizen, Andrew Robbins, invented a tar-filled metal pan that would scoop up and trap grasshoppers as the pan was dragged across a field; several hundred of the inexpensive "hopperdozers" were put into operation. In 1877 the town of Le Sueur advertised a bounty of 20 cents a quart for dead grasshoppers, but the number caught so far exceeded the town's coffers that the bounty was reduced to one dollar a bushel. Still the grasshoppers came.

A legislative relief committee, chaired by prominent St. Paul politician Henry M. Rice, distributed many thousands of dollars across the state, feeding and clothing 6,000 people during the winter of 1876 and appropriating $75,000 in 1877 for buying seed grain. Help also came from the National Grange, which collected $11,000 to spread among the stricken families in Minnesota and in other states.

In the spring of 1877 the next crop of locusts hatched and Minnesotans prepared for another year of disaster. But instead of eating their way through the state, the grasshoppers lifted their wings and rode the wind across the border. The ordeal was over.

The grasshopper plague was only one of a series of misfortunes that hit Minnesota farmers in the years after the Civil War. Farm families felt increasingly cut off from the prosperity that the rest of the country enjoyed. Droughts, floods, hailstorms, crop disease, and insects plagued the wheat fields during the 1870s. In addition, farmers felt manipulated by the railroads and by grain-buyers, whom they accused of unfairly grading their wheat.

The De Laval Cream Separator booth at the Morrison County Fair relied on user testimony and a free telephone to boost sales. The separator made possible the production of dairy products on a large scale. Courtesy, Morrison County Historical Society

At the heart of the farmers' troubles was the fact that wheat prices had dropped from an all-time high of $1.50 a bushel during the Civil War to 80 cents a bushel by 1870. Farm families complained that to make ends meet they had to produce two bushels of wheat for every one they had grown in better days. But to grow more crops, they needed more equipment, and that was costly. Life down on the farm had become a struggle.

Through the Grange movement the farmers turned their fears into action. The Grange movement was instrumental in helping to establish a state commissioner of railroads in 1871, and a board of railroad commissioners in 1874, which had the power to develop a rate schedule. The Grange also introduced farmers to the concept of cost savings through cooperative purchasing. The Werner harvester was manufactured and sold through local Granges at half the cost other manufacturers were charging.

In 1875, at the height of its political strength and with a national membership of more than 1.5 million, the Grange movement began to crumble under its own weight. With so many members, it could no longer effectively secure every farmer's needs. Internal dissension eroded its membership base, and within five years the movement lost 85 percent of its membership. By the early 1880s, farmers across the country would regroup into the national Farmers' Alliance. First described as a lobbying organization on behalf of farmers, within a decade the alliance would transform itself into a third party with an agenda all its own.

When wheat became the state's primary cash crop during the Civil War, it breathed life into Minneapolis. Flour mills quickly banked St. Anthony Falls, and dollars for flour pumped up the Mill City's finances. In the Red River Valley, mammoth farms—many thousands of acres in size—supplied wheat for the whole country.

But growing wheat year after year in the same fields depleted the soil, and farmers were left with weakened crops vulnerable to disease and pests. They dismally accepted the fact that an acre of Minnesota soil that grew twenty-two bushels of wheat in the 1860s could only produce eleven bushels in the 1870s. At the same time, rising property

54

taxes and ballooning operating costs made it imperative that a family get the most out of the soil. Advances in machinery—steel plows, binders, threshing machines—made agricultural mass production a possibility, even a necessity.

Properly done, diversified farming could help replace soil nutrients, and at the same time spread the risk of crop failure. By the middle 1870s many farmers in the southeastern counties of Minnesota had augmented their wheat crops with small dairy operations, growing feed crops such as corn and oats for their own use.

By 1878 enough cows were being raised in Minnesota to invigorate the growth of the dairy industry. That year the Minnesota Dairymen's Association was organized to help develop local markets, and the De Laval cream separator opened up the possibility of building large-scale production facilities for dairy products. By the middle of the next decade, sixty creameries and forty cheese businesses had laid the foundation for a cooperative marketing movement that would eventually make Minnesota the nation's largest producer of butter and a leading dairy state.

Thanks to three pioneers in agricultural diversification, Minnesota farmers learned new ways to vary their crops and thus build better lives. Wendelin Grimm, an immigrant from Germany, experimented with an alfalfa seed that could survive Minnesota's winter. Grimm alfalfa quickly became a staple for the state's cattle-raising industry. Another settler, Peter M. Gedio, moved to the shores of Lake Minnetonka where he experimented with fruit trees. His "Wealthy" is today one of the state's most

The importance of a creamery to local farmers is clear in this view of wagons full of milk arriving at the Lake Elizabeth creamery about 1891. Courtesy, Minnesota Historical Society

popular apples. Oren C. Gregg was one of the first Minnesota farmers to try dairying. Having tried and had trouble raising wheat, in the mid-1860s he decided to build a dairy business in the rich grasslands of Minnesota. Gregg's success with winter dairying eventually attracted the interest of officials from the University of Minnesota who wanted to find a way to educate farmers. In 1886, Gregg was hired to carry his message out to the fields and the small towns. One year later he was made chairman of the newly organized Farmers' Institute at the University of Minnesota.

For many years Gregg and his staff provided farmers with much-needed information on crop production, also offering rural women information about the domestic side of running a farm. Through the institute he helped farm families change from single crop farming to diversified agriculture, thus stimulating the growth of the dairy and livestock industries. Under his guidance the day's scientific discoveries in the laboratories were taken out into the farmers' fields.

THE MIDDLINGS PURIFIER AND WASHBURN'S FOLLY

In the post-Civil War Midwest, inventors were making discoveries that were to have far-reaching consequences. In the early 1870s the invention of the middlings purifier, a sifting mechanism used in grinding wheat, bolstered the growth of the milling industry. Despite their troubles with disease, weather, and pests, many Minnesota farmers continued their love affair with wheat through the last quarter of the nineteenth century. But the flour ground from their wheat was poor in quality and appearance. Since the early days of the territory, farmers had been harvesting a hard red wheat that could be planted in the early spring. The more typical winter wheat grown in other parts of the country, which had to be planted in the fall, could not survive Minnesota's severe winters.

Although the early-spring wheat solved the farmers' problems, it caused headaches for the millers. The kernel of the spring wheat, containing the gluten and wheat germ, was too hard to be crushed properly and so was sifted out with the bran. The loss of the "middlings" meant the loss of the wheat's leavening agent as well as important nutrients.

A few small mills in Hastings, Dundas, and Winona discovered ways to make a better-quality flour from spring wheat, but none that could be used in large-scale production. So when Cadwallader Washburn, one of the founders of General Mills,

Right: *Though Minneapolis gained international fame as a milling center, smaller millers also established local reputations of their own. This miller's shop in Waseca offered its own brand, "Waseca White Rose." Courtesy, Waseca County Historical Society*

Facing page: *Cadwallader Washburn, one of the founders of General Mills, was instrumental in revolutionizing the milling industry by helping to perfect the middlings purifier. Courtesy, Minneapolis Public Library*

Minneapolis made history when the Washburn A Mill exploded in 1878. Courtesy, Minneapolis Public Library

Inc., heard that Edmund La Croix had built a crude but workable middlings purifier for a mill in Faribault, he sent his right-hand man, George Christian, to snap him up.

Together, La Croix and Christian worked secretly on La Croix's original invention, and by the time they were finished, middlings could be separated from the bran by a blast of air that lifted the lighter bran particles while the heavier middlings were sifted down. Washburn's head miller, George T. Smith, assisted with the fine tuning of the new equipment and invented an automatic traveling brush that would keep the all-important sifting cloth clean.

Inside the six-story stone mill—called "Washburn's Folly" when it was first built at a cost of $100,000 in 1866—the four men knew that they were on the front line of a major revolution in the milling industry. No doubt Washburn expected his employees to be close-mouthed about their discovery. But the men couldn't completely check their enthusiasm, and the milling community buzzed with the news. It wasn't long before Smith succumbed to a job offer from Washburn's major rival, Charles Pillsbury, and a carefully guarded trade secret became public property.

The effects of the middlings purifier reached every corner of the state. Between 1870 and 1880 Minnesota's wheat crop rocketed from 18 million to 34 million bushels, as increasing numbers of farmers willingly risked the rigors of nature and the pricing quagmires of the railroads to feed the appetites of the Minneapolis mills. The number of mills grew from 210 in the early part of the decade to 436 ten years later. Mills such as the City Mill, the Galaxy Mill, the Zenith and Palisade Flour Mill, and the Northwestern Consolidated Milling Company flanked the banks of rivers across the state.

But the industry's growth was not without setbacks. The millers learned the hard way that flour dust and machinery sparks are incompatible. On May 2, 1878, the Washburn A Mill exploded, killing eighteen workers and completely destroying six surrounding mills. Property losses in the milling district at the Falls of St. Anthony ran more than $1 million, and could have been devastating. Nevertheless, within months bigger and better mills replaced the rubble. New ventilation equipment and iron rollers that reduced the amount of dust emitted by the middlings purifier were installed as a hedge against future disasters. So modern were the new operations, in fact, that the rebuilt Washburn A Mill was said to have been able to produce 4,000 barrels of flour a day, several times what any Eastern mill could produce.

By 1890 the quality of Minnesota's flour was unmatched elsewhere. In that year the Washburn-Crosby Company, of Minneapolis, received the gold, silver, and bronze medals for excellence at the Millers' International Exhibition in Cincinnati, Ohio. From that day on, Washburn-Crosby flour has been called Gold Medal flour.

This high-grade Minnesota flour commanded prices that were triple the dollar-a-barrel which other mills received. Within the decade railroad lines, capitalized with mill money, shuttled Minnesota flour to the East Coast and to the tables of people around the globe. By 1890 Minneapolis was considered the largest mill city in the world.

Rail lines ran through the milling district in Minneapolis. Wheat from the Dakotas and Minnesota went through the milling process and back on the trains for distribution throughout the country. Courtesy, Minneapolis Public Library

THE SPADE, THE SWEATSHOP, AND THE CIGAR

In the years following the Civil War, the country's rich resources were quickly turned into profitable empires by power brokers who talked about net worth in terms of millions of dollars. Along with these new empires came corruption, greed, and, sometimes, failure on a colossal scale. In 1873 the collapse of Jay Cooke and Company (the corporation that had financed the Northern Pacific Railroad) set off a financial panic that swept the country, closing down the New York Stock Exchange for ten days and causing a severe nationwide depression.

As the flour milling industry grew, Minnesota farmers came up against big-business empires as they battled for fair prices with the railroads and with elevator operators. In 1876 the millers formed a buying cooperative, the Minneapolis Millers Association, so that they could have some control over the prices paid for wheat at local elevators, prohibit competitive wheat purchasing by Milwaukee or Chicago buyers, and distribute the wheat as each mill warranted. Since there were no state regulations on grain pricing or grading, growers protested that the close cooperation between the millers and the elevator operators, who often were in the employ of railroads, undercut the value of their wheat.

Tempers flared, and in 1878 the bitter resentment of the state's wheat growers was focused on the congressional campaign between W.D. Washburn, outspoken brother of the builder of the mill known as "Washburn's Folly," and Ignatius Donnelly, champion of the common people. Although Washburn went to Congress and Donnelly went back to the task of commanding his agrarian troops, their campaign did result in a favorable long-term benefit for farmers. Due in part to Donnelly's campaign, in 1885 the state legislature finally established a system of inspecting and grading wheat.

Another important change in the milling industry occurred in 1881. By then, many of the wheat fields in Minnesota had deteriorated so badly that millers were forced to bring in wheat from out of state, where they did not have the control over the wheat

*William D. Washburn, who, in the late 1870s, ran for Congress against Ignatius Donnelly and won, was the original owner of this steamer—*City of St. Louis. *Excursion steamers such as this one were launched on Minnesota's larger lakes. Photo by F.L. Mortimer. From the Dewars Collection, Minneapolis Public Library*

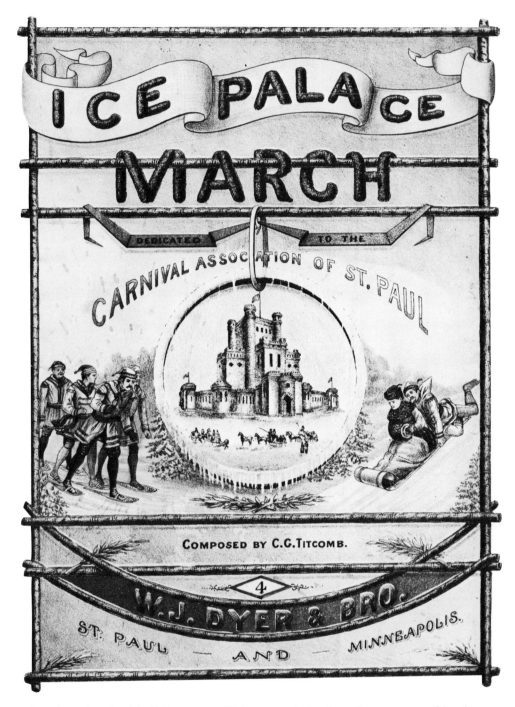

St. Paul proved to the world that its winter climate was an asset rather than a liability by holding a Winter Carnival starting in 1886. Parades and festivities were complemented by the "Ice Palace March" written for the occasion. Courtesy, Minnesota Historical Society

market that they had in Minnesota. This opened the door for a group of businessmen, some representing large wheat purchasers in Chicago and other Eastern cities, to get together in Minneapolis in 1881 and organize a grain market. Called the Minneapolis Chamber of Commerce, the cooperative eventually became one of the largest grain exchanges in the country. The Minneapolis Millers Association dissolved shortly after the chamber was formed.

With the Minneapolis Chamber of Commerce, Minnesota could export both flour milled locally and wheat brought in by train from points west. Before the chamber was formed, the state's annual wheat export was about 215,000 bushels—the rest was ground into flour. But in 1882, 2 million bushels were shipped beyond the state's boundaries, and the amount doubled every year for a decade.

Wheat was gold in the international marketplace as well. In 1878, 107,000 barrels were exported to foreign tables, and in 1900 the wheat shipped from Minnesota totaled one-fourth of all United States flour exports.

Germans outrank all other immigrant nationalities in Minnesota. They brought with them a love of beer and a devotion to the land. Pictured is the Kiewel Brewery Company wagon. Courtesy, Morrison County Historical Society

The expansion of the railroad as well as the flour- and saw-milling industries attracted thousands of settlers, many from overseas, causing the state's population to increase 700 percent from 1865 to 1900. Census figures for 1880 showed 780,773 citizens in Minnesota, 30 percent of whom were born in such places as Germany, the Scandinavian countries, Ireland, the British Isles, Bohemia, Switzerland, Poland, Russia, and France.

Settlers were attracted to a land of plenty, blue skies, friendly people, and prosperity. Their spirit is exhibited in a folk song of the day, called "The Beauty of the West" or "The Lily of the West."

When first I left old Buck Eye,
Location for to find,
I heard of a distant country,
In language most divine.
A land of milk and honey,
And waters of the best,
They called it Minnesota,
The Beauty of the West . . .

I jumped on board a steamer,
The Northern Belle by name,
She soon let loose her anchor,
And we were off again.
She rang her bell at Winona,
And landed me and chest
In this said Minnesota,
The Beauty of the West.

And when we got recruited
A-rambling I did go
I wandered the state all over
I trailed it through and through
It's when I came to a cabin
It's I a welcome guest
In this said Minnesota
The Beauty of the West.

New settlers brought with them a willingness to work and a perennial hunger to improve their lives, but most didn't have the money or understanding of the culture to make wise decisions. Tired from long journeys, poor food, and the anxieties of being away from home, they set up housekeeping where it was cheapest and took the first jobs they could find. The major towns and cities of Minnesota soon supported two very different worlds. One—sedate, tree-lined, and freshly scrubbed—housed the Victorian wealthy. The other—dirty, dilapidated, and overflowing with people—was found in the neighborhoods of the working class.

After the Civil War, Minnesota's primary enterprises—flour milling, lumber, agriculture, and transportation—spawned secondary industries that supplied products and services for the work force as well as for the major industries.

These Swedish tailors in Fergus Falls worked close to windows so they could see their work. Courtesy, Ottertail County Historical Society

Growth in the new manufacturing sector paralleled the fortunes of the major players in Minneapolis and St. Paul, and statistics show an impressive spurt in production between Minnesota's territorial days and the end of the century. In 1850 the gross value of manufactured products was calculated to be about $58,000. By 1880, however, it had increased to $76 million, and ten years later had more than doubled again. Industrial progress in those five decades was so intense that Minnesota rose from thirty-fifth to fifteenth in the nation in number of industrial employees.

But urban working families recognized early on that a healthy business did not necessarily translate into better living conditions for its workers. In fact, quite the opposite was true. Every day more people stepped off the trains or steamboats looking for the key to their fortunes or, at the very least, for steady jobs in the bustling cities of Minneapolis, St. Paul, and Duluth. But as the labor supply grew, wages dropped, as did the workers' influence with their bosses.

Organized protest was not altogether new in Minnesota. In 1854, the journeymen tailors of St. Paul had struck for higher wages, and two years later, St. Paul printers gathered together to discuss their situation. In 1867, difficulty with a subcontractor caused the construction workers who were building the Faribault School for the Deaf, Dumb and Blind to walk off the job, while fifty-two Germans in Minneapolis founded a workingman's society that supported member families without income and helped members find work.

Railroad transportation gave places like Fergus Falls the role of market town, supporting shops and services like barbershops. In this shop patrons could keep their own personal shaving mugs. Courtesy, Ottertail County Historical Society

Conley Camera in Rochester, Minnesota, supplied the Sears, Roebuck Company with cameras. Conley capitalized on Kodak's reputation by using "Rochester Camera Factory" as its name. Courtesy, Minnesota Historical Society

In subsequent years, newspaper accounts show that the journeymen cigar makers, coopers, and mechanics also pulled together to gain strength in bargaining for their respective trades. Unions were formed in small towns such as Lake City and Farmington. Marine engineers united in Duluth.

As the railroads cut across the land, brotherhoods evolved for the workers who were cutting the forests, hammering through the rocks, and laying down the steel bars. In 1870 a Brotherhood of Locomotive Engineers was founded in Austin, followed two years later by a division in St. Paul. Over the next few years railroad brotherhoods spread from one corner of the state to the next. In their infant stage these groups were a fairly congenial reminder to the bosses that labor could organize. But by 1876, when railroads and industry felt the effects of a rising economy, railroad brotherhoods came out swinging, demanding better working conditions and a bigger share of the profit. In 1877 a national strike led by the Knights of Labor against the Union Pacific Railroad made headlines in Minnesota, when the union forced the giant corporation to rescind a number of wage cuts. The following year 6,500 laborers belonged to Minnesota chapters of the Knights of Labor, and with an increasing membership and the sympathy of the newspaper-reading middle class, labor's demands grew into hot political issues. The more than seventy strikes called between 1881 and 1884 cut deeply into the heart of the state's economy.

On the national scene, President Grover Cleveland formed the U.S. Department of Labor, partly in response to the violent Haymarket Square Riot in Chicago. That same riot stepped up the political pace in Minnesota, as farmers and laborers began recognizing common bonds and joining together to influence legislation. In 1886 the Minnesota Farmers' Alliance called a joint meeting with the Knights of Labor, and the result was a list of demands taken to the leaders of both the Republicans and the Democrats.

John H. Stevens characterized the first generation of Minnesota settlers. He earned the title "Father of Minneapolis" by helping to organize the first school, church, library, and agricultural fair in what became Hennepin County. Courtesy, Minnesota Historical Society

Energized and aggressive, the coalition of farmers and laborers pushed for major reforms, instigating a number of legislative bills. But the legislators' interest quickly cooled, and many of the coalition's demands—such as reduced railroad and interest rates, employers' liability laws, and prohibition of child labor—were shelved.

Feeling that they were not being served well by either the Democrats or the Republicans, farmers and laborers across the country soon came to the conclusion that they would have to create a party of their own. In May 1891, 1,400 delegates with a wide range of affiliations gathered in a Cincinnati, Ohio, music hall for the National Union Conference. Proclaiming, "United we stand, divided we fall" and "Opposition to all monopolies," the delegates were rallied by the passionate oratory of Ignatius Donnelly to join the People's Party and nominate a presidential ticket for the 1892 election. After lengthy debate and numerous squabbles, the delegates created a platform that contained the litany of demands the farmer and labor groups had been calling for through the previous three decades.

Members of the People's Party were called "Populists" or "Pops," and what they wanted more than anything was more government regulation of the banking and railroad magnates. Mortgaged to the hilt, many Populists called for a free and unlimited

A surprising array of small industries employed people in large towns and small cities. Little Falls had its own cigar factory in the late nineteenth century. Farmers in Stearns County, just down the Mississippi River, still grow the shade tobacco used for cigar wrappers. Courtesy, Morrison County Historical Society

coinage of silver—a move, they claimed, that would help them pay their debts. Further, the Populists wanted the government to put an end to speculation in stocks, options, and futures, and they wanted the president of the United States to be elected by a direct vote of the people.

Although the Populist party faded on the national level within a few years, it wove new ideas into the texture of society and enabled workers to be heard as loudly as their bosses. In Minnesota, the roots of populism ran deep. And populism would have its say in the state's political future. The balance between the needs of business and those of its workers would become the focus of much political debate in the twentieth century.

TALL TALES AND TALL TIMBER

They say that every time she took a step, another Minnesota lake emerged. And when she bellowed the whole continent shook. She was Babe, the Blue Ox, and she measured forty-two axe handles from eye to eye. As Paul Bunyan's sidekick, the Blue Ox was one of the many legends that grew out of logging camps and followed the logs downriver.

The pine forests of Minnesota were as legendary as the giant lumberjack. Growing to more than 180 feet tall and a typical diameter of three to five feet, the white pines helped finance a diversified industrial base for Minnesota. Lumbering was an essential

Minneapolis needed more coopers than most cities in order to supply barrels for her flour mills and breweries. Schon and Schnitzius enjoyed a convenient location just a few blocks from the Falls. Courtesy, Minnesota Historical Society

ingredient in Minnesota's growth for a hundred years—from the 1830s to the 1930s—but the boom years were the two decades between 1880 and 1900.

Sawmills at Little Falls, Elk River, St. Anthony, Marine-on-the-St. Croix, Anoka, St. Francis, Clearwater, and Princeton were among Minnesota's first businesses, some dating back to the earliest days of the territory. By the late 1860s, Stillwater was considered the state's leading lumber town, drawing logs from the St. Croix River and its tributary, the Snake. But the lands around the St. Croix Valley, which had been vigorously logged since the 1830s, soon became an example for the rest of the state. Accessible pine was disappearing and woods cruisers—men hired to stake out new territories for logging—moved north on the Rum and Mississippi rivers, looking for thicker and better stands of virgin timber.

By 1870, 4,000 men with 2,000 horses and oxen were following the Mississippi River north to log the winter away in Beltrami, Itasca, and St. Louis counties. Duluth was becoming a shipping center for northern-cut pine, and Minnesota lumber was finding its way to construction sites in such cities as New York, Boston, Cleveland, and Chicago. In Minneapolis, fifteen sawmills sliced through logs brought from the lands along the Rum and Mississippi rivers, while Winona flourished as a gateway to the budding southern and western markets, fed by logs from the Mississippi and the Chippewa.

Over the next three decades the lumber industry grew in size and importance as lumber companies found quicker and cheaper ways to get the pine out of the woods and into the mills. The 1880 census shows that Minneapolis had 234 mills which turned $4.5 million worth of logs into lumber worth nearly $7.5 million. By 1890 a number of new businesses—such as planing mills and factories for making sashes, doors, laths, blinds, shingles, furniture, wagons, and boxcars—had grown out of the Minneapolis lumber industry, employing nearly 4,000 people and pumping $1.8 million in wages into the city's development.

Between 1857 and 1889 the number of board feet cut from Minnesota timber jumped from about 100 million to 1 billion. The state boasted that it rose from fourteenth to fourth place nationally in terms of the size of its lumbering industry.

Sawmilling records of all kinds were set in the 1890s. The H.C. Akeley Lumber Company in Minneapolis reported cutting more than 50.5 million board feet in 1890. Two years later a mill in Little Falls—owned by Frederick Weyerhaeuser, a major player in Minnesota's lumber industry—cut 32 million feet; and in Winona, the Laird, Norton Company and the Winona Lumber Company each produced 40 million feet.

With the exception of two or three years following the Panic of 1893 (caused by inflated land prices and a railroad industry that had built its power on credit), the last years of the nineteenth century were the glory days of the lumber industry. Unfettered by concerns about the future of Minnesota's forests, businessmen exploited what they could as cost-efficiently as possible.

This broom factory in Fergus Falls used local raw materials to manufacture a basic necessity for rural as well as village residents. Courtesy, Ottertail County Historical Society

Northern Minnesota's iron ore resources were more than matched by her timber resources. The Virginia Rainy Lake sawmill manufactured lumber to build Range cities and to ship from Duluth harbor. Courtesy, Iron Range Research Center, Pederson Collection

Originally, nearly two-thirds of the state's land had been covered by forests of commercially valuable woods, including white and red pine, spruce, balsam fir, jack pine, white cedar, and tamarack. With the introduction of new machinery and methods, such as steam traction engines for hauling logs out of the woods and narrow-gauge railroads for carrying them to a local mill, loggers were able to move away from the rivers and into the interior of the state.

It took grit to successfully buy and sell Minnesota stumpage. It also took foresight, capital investment, and a good measure of luck. The typical lumberman's philosophy was to buy land cheap, cut timber fast, get out, and move on before bad luck caught up with him. Fortunes teetered while loggers fought logjams on sluggish rivers and diseases such as smallpox in the camps. Major forest fires, ignited as easily by the sparks from a train engine as by lightning, exploded fireballs of pine across uncut timber stands. In 1894 more than 418 people, 248 from the town of Hinkley, died in a forest fire that burned over five counties.

But as the stakes grew and the price for stumpage increased, a small number of businessmen emerged with control of large tracts of forested land. By the end of the nineteenth century, the lumber industry, like the flour-milling industry, had become big business, concentrated in the hands of a few who had the formula to make it pay.

Frederick Weyerhaeuser was one of those men. Socially reclusive, he knew how to build an organization and how to time the acquisition of new land, often skirting the edges of the land laws. As his holdings grew northward from Rock Island, Illinois, in the 1870s and the 1880s, and westward in the 1890s, he made lumbering history. As early as 1872, Weyerhaeuser laid the foundation for a lumbering syndicate called the Mississippi River Logging Company. Though only one of 100 partners, he was the one who knew the size of the others' holdings, and he dictated the terms of the syndicate through its climb to power over the next forty years. The objective of the syndicate

As logging moved further north, timber had to be hauled further to the sawmills. Some logging companies laid tracks into the woods to get the trees out, but few of these lines survived the decline of the industry. Photo by William Roleff, Two Harbors, Minnesota. Courtesy, Minnesota Historical Society

was to gain enough control of the rivers to monopolize the logging traffic from Minnesota and Wisconsin. The syndicate acquired rich lands, logged them, and then divided the revenue according to the amount of stock each syndicate partner held.

The key to the company's success was capital, organization, and political clout. By the 1890s, Weyerhaeuser and his associates had also learned the value of working in close harmony with the railroads. In 1890, Weyerhaeuser purchased the Minnesota land grant of the Northern Pacific Railroad. The next year, he moved his offices next

Right: *Life in a lumber camp was rugged and routine. The men spent most of their time in the woods, so their quarters were strictly utilitarian. They spent their free time washing clothes, playing cards, and making music. Photo by William Roleff, Two Harbors, Minnesota. Courtesy, Minnesota Historical Society*

Above: *Frederick Weyerhaeuser appears in this turn-of-the-century oil painting. At about the time this portrait was painted, Weyerhaeuser's Pine Tree Lumber Company formed the economic backbone of Little Falls, Minnesota. Today the family fortune helps support the Morrison County Historical Society, which is housed in the F.A. Weyerhaeuser Museum. Courtesy, Minnesota Historical Society*

Thomas B. Walker is pictured about 1880. Nineteenth-century big business left a cultural legacy in Minnesota. T.B. Walker's fortune endowed one of the nation's premier modern art museums, the Walker Art Center. Photo by J.A. Brush, Minneapolis, Minnesota. Courtesy, Minnesota Historical Society

door to James J. Hill, who had just consolidated his vast railroad interests into the Great Northern Railroad. The two men grew to be friends as well as business allies. In 1892 Weyerhaeuser's organization bought 50 million feet of stumpage from the St. Paul and Duluth Railroad. Two years later, Hill sold Weyerhaeuser 990,000 acres of timberland from the old St. Paul and Pacific land grant.

In 1900 the Weyerhaeuser Timber Company was formed to purchase the vast tracts of land in the West held by the ailing Northern Pacific Railroad, which had been left gasping for breath by the severe Panic of 1893. During the first decade of the new century, the Weyerhaeuser Timber Company had bought considerable land in Washington, Oregon, Idaho, and California, causing land prices to skyrocket. Having bought timberland in Washington for $6 an acre, Weyerhaeuser sold it a few years later for $120 an acre. When he died in 1914, his empire included 10 million acres of timber extending from Canada to Mexico, from Maine to Puget Sound.

Thomas B. Walker was another businessman who understood how to use the railroads to build a lumber empire. Walker came to Minnesota in 1862 to sell grindstones. Finding the market poor, he took a job as a surveyor for the St. Paul and Duluth Railroad. While working on the crew, Walker learned how to read the commercial value of a forest—a skill that would earn him a place in history as one of Minnesota's leading lumber barons.

Over several years, Walker learned that it was much less expensive to ship dried lumber than to haul green logs. He also discovered the value of building small mills close to the logging site, eliminating the costs and uncertainties of river drives.

Walker was attracted to the rich pine along the upper Red River. Through the 1880s he operated the Red River Lumber Company on the Clearwater River, a tributary of the Red River. Once the logs were cut into lumber, they were hauled by rail from Walker's mill at Crookston to Winnipeg. A new northern market was tapped for the first time.

In 1887 Walker began doing business with H.C. Akeley, a businessman from Michigan who intended to build a sawmill at St. Cloud. Walker offered to sell Akeley half interest in his northern timber tracts, which were potentially valuable but remote from the main river systems. Walker had a plan. By crisscrossing their timberlands

Railroad construction continued throughout the nineteenth century as more lines linked every county in the state to the national network. As the prairies filled up with farmers, there was plenty of freight to support dozens of different companies. Photo by Manderfeld and Goede. Courtesy, Minnesota Historical Society

The Minneapolis and St. Louis Railroad provided an essential link between farmers in southern Minnesota and the flour mills in Minneapolis. Like the Soo Line, the M & St.L.R.R. was a miller's road, built to gain independence from competition in Chicago and Milwaukee. Courtesy, Minnesota Historical Society

with rail lines, the two men would be able to haul the pine to their mills easily. The method proved to be much more cost-efficient than the river drives, especially since few logs were lost or damaged. The Walker-Akeley mill at St. Cloud grew quickly, and during its heyday was one of the largest sawmills in the world.

Minnesota's industrial triumvirate—lumber, flour milling, and the railroads—established the state's position in international trade. The industries drew strength and capital resources from each other, and the respective barons frequently dabbled in each other's affairs. Minneapolis politician and lumberman William D. Washburn, a member of the flour-milling family, financed the building of the Minneapolis, St. Paul and

Sault Ste. Marie Railroad to provide a more direct route for shipping Minneapolis flour through the Great Lakes to the East Coast. The Soo Line, as it was soon to be called, also gave the Washburn interests access to fine forestland in the north. By 1890, 31.93 percent of the Soo Line's tonnage was in lumber, while 24.77 percent was in grain.

The railroads of Minnesota were powered by major decision makers such as James J. Hill, the Washburns, and Walker, but they were built by teams of laborers who scraped up topsoil, laid tracks, and built bridges through summers that were too hot and autumn rains that chilled them to the bone. Side by side, workers of many nationalities inched their way across the state—a mile a day—for a solid daily wage of two dollars.

In 1872, fifteen railroad companies had laid about 2,000 miles of track in Minnesota. Rail connected the Twin Cities and Lake Michigan, as well as Duluth and the Red River Valley. But railroad construction was only in its infancy. Capitalized by an industrial base that was growing stronger every day and vitalized by an exploding population, by 1890 the railroads had woven a network of more than 5,000 miles.

For Minnesota, the railroads were the key to every dimension of its growth. Its industrial base, agricultural prominence, population expansion, and financial strengths were directly linked to the tracks that had helped industrialize every corner of the state. A Pullman car made travel to Minnesota comfortable and it helped encourage a fledgling tourism industry. Refrigerated railroad cars boosted southwestern Minnesota's cattle business by ensuring that Midwestern meat would be fresh when it was delivered to U.S. tables. Wheat, flour, and lumber—representative of Minnesotan ingenuity and hard work—were mingled into the global economy. The railroads had brought the world to Minnesota.

Spawned by the railroad, one Minnesota business dramatically improved the material comfort of millions of Americans. A young station agent, Richard W. Sears, began his business in 1886 in this depot in N. Redwood, Minnesota. He quickly relocated to Minneapolis, and then to Chicago to take advantage of better rail connections. Courtesy, Minnesota Historical Society

*The Merchant's National Bank
opened this new building in
St. Paul in 1915. Urban banks
celebrated their success with monu-
mental flamboyance. Courtesy,
Minnesota Historical Society*

MANAGING BIG BUSINESS

A GIANT BURIED IN THE HILLS

For turn-of-the-century Minnesotans reports of international war may have seemed as commonplace as changes in the weather. In 1898 the United States waged a naval war against Spain, then two years later joined an alliance with Britain, France, Germany, Russia, and Japan to quell a Chinese nationalist uprising called the Boxer Rebellion. In the White House, President Theodore Roosevelt was awarded the Nobel Peace Prize for the part he played in ending the Russo-Japanese War, and there was hopeful talk around the country that another Hague Peace Conference would end worldwide hostilities once and for all.

But in July of 1907, disturbing news closer to home caught the public's attention. On the Mesabi Range, in northern Minnesota, a bitter feud between the miners and the Oliver Iron Mining Company (a subsidiary of the United States Steel Corporation) ended in a labor walkout. It was the first time miners had organized a strike in Minnesota. Backed by a spirited and vocal national union, the Western Federation of Miners (WFM), 16,000 Mesabi miners demanded payment of wages by the day rather than by the amount of ore they mined. They also called for a pay increase and an eight-hour work day.

Many Minnesotans worried that a long strike would hobble the state's accelerating economy. As it turned out, the miners' strike wasn't violent or long-lived. Through August, a few minor scuffles between the strikers and deputies ended in injuries on both sides. But the Oliver Iron Mining Company broke the labor action by calling in immigrant strike-breakers, who understood neither the language nor the meaning of collective bargaining. Trainloads of imported laborers arrived daily in the mining towns. By October most of the miners had returned to work, their demands once again only dreams.

Although the Mesabi Range had at that time been producing iron ore for only fifteen years, the great open-pit mines were massive testimonials to the fact that the range was producing half of the nation's iron ore. Mesabi iron ore was not only plentiful, stretching southward to within fifty miles of Duluth and southwest to the thriving lumber town of Grand Rapids, it was also relatively inexpensive to mine. The loose red ore lay under just a few feet of topsoil. It was easily scooped up in steam shovels and dumped into train cars for shipment to Eastern mills.

The Mesabi Range was the second of three mining areas discovered in Minnesota between 1875 and 1911. The Vermilion Range, near Vermilion Lake, was the first. The Cuyuna Range, which runs southwest from Aitkin for about sixty miles, began shipping its iron ore in 1911. Particularly high in manganese (an important ingredient in producing steel), Cuyuna Range iron ore was critical to American industry during World War I when manganese imports were curtailed.

But the leader in iron ore production was clearly the Mesabi Range. By the turn of the century there were more than thirty working mines on the Mesabi Range. Ironically, the Mesabi Range—which single-handedly turned Minnesota into the largest iron ore-producing state in the union—had been bypassed a number of times by explorers and scientists looking for the mother lode.

For twenty-five years, Leonidas Merritt, one of seven brothers, had been ridiculed by his peers as he searched for iron ore in the upper Mississippi wilderness. Merritt

By the 1920s, improved mining techniques and machinery enabled underground miners to work in much safer conditions. Courtesy, Iron Range Research Center, U.S. Steel Collection

Head frames marked the sites of underground mines on the Range. These were worked by experienced Cornish miners brought by the mining companies from Michigan's upper peninsula. Softer ore in horizontal formations in the Mesabi Range lent itself to strip-mining, which required less specialized skills. Courtesy, Iron Range Research Center, Opie Collection

worked as a timber cruiser, and he used a dip compass and a woodsman's persistence to map the areas he believed held ore. In 1890, he took out 141 mining leases and put together exploring parties which he hoped would find enough iron ore samplings to prove his claim. In November, one of the parties struck ore four miles west of present-day Virginia. The discovery rapidly led to the opening of the Mountain Iron Mine, currently one of the largest mines on the Mesabi Range. The following summer, another Merritt explorer noticed how red the soil was around the roots of a fallen tree. His sharp observation led to the opening of the Biwabik Mine.

"Mesabi" is a Chippewa word meaning "a giant buried in the hills." For Minnesota the name was particularly appropriate. When the word about the rich ore reserves leaked out, the north country exploded. Towns such as Ironton, Hibbing, Eveleth, Chisholm, Virginia, and Babbitt sprang up overnight, and the population of St. Louis County more than quadrupled between 1880 and 1910. Many of the newcomers to northern Minnesota, often penniless and lacking in skills, were new to America as well, arriving from Scandinavia, Yugoslavia, Italy, Poland, and Greece. They offered strong backs and, at first, gratitude for the work that would give them a fresh start.

For the miners and their families, life centered around the mines. Daily blasts of dynamite in the pits shook buildings, frightened children, and broke crockery. Their lives were scheduled by whistles that announced the end of shifts and the arrival of the ore trains. The mines were like living organisms, nibbling away at the land around them. The towns of Hibbing and Eveleth had to be moved from their original sites to accommodate the needs of the mines.

Embarrass, Minnesota, was an interim stop on the Duluth and Iron Range Railroad. The railroad was built to carry ore from the Vermilion Range to the ore docks on Lake Superior. The first sixty-eight miles from the Tower-Soudan mines to Two Harbors were completed in 1884. Courtesy, Iron Range Research Center, Tower Soudan Historical Society Collection

Although the Mesabi ore lay in Minnesota soil, the profits soon padded the Eastern industrial coffers of John D. Rockefeller, J. Pierpont Morgan, and Andrew Carnegie. Understanding how critical iron ore was to the new industrial age, John D. Rockefeller was the first major businessman to invest in the Mesabi Range. In 1890, Leonidas Merritt and his brothers were trying to figure out how to transport their iron ore from the range to the shipping docks at Duluth. Neither the Northern Pacific nor the St. Paul and Duluth railroads would have anything to do with their mining venture. Forced to build their own railroad, they created the Duluth, Missabe and Northern Railway, going in debt to do so. By the end of 1892 their debts totaled approximately $2 million.

But the brothers had only begun to spend money; they still needed to buy mining equipment and to build ore docks at Duluth. Early in 1893 they took out a bond for $1.6 million and found an eager buyer in Rockefeller, who took one-quarter of the offering. Astute financial giant that he was, Rockefeller knew that he would move in for a bigger piece of the action when the time was right. As it turned out, the time was right sooner than he expected.

The Panic of 1893 strangled investment markets, and the Merritts quickly realized that they would not be able to sell any more bonds. Once again they placed their future in Rockefeller's hands. He formed a parent company called the Lake Superior Consolidated Iron Mines Company. The Merritts traded their holdings for stock in the company and were left in control of the mining operation. Rockefeller then placed his own mining holdings in the company, invested another $500,000 in the Merritts' railroad, and took first mortgage bonds in the new company.

Over the next two years the brothers—now overwhelmed by the amount of cash they needed to keep their mining operations going—continued to issue stock. But it did not move in the depressed investment market. For the third time, the Merritts

Cities blossomed along Minnesota's Iron Range as merchants flocked to fill the daily needs of mining families. These substantial population centers in the north woods needed a full range of public services. The Chisholm Fire Department fought winter fires with this ski-mounted rig. Courtesy, Chisholm Free Press

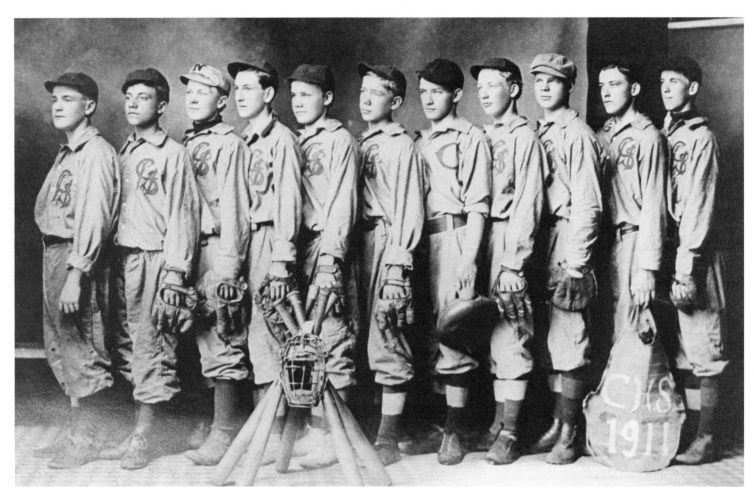

Last names of boys on Chisholm High's 1911 baseball team speak eloquently of the ethnic diversity of Minnesota's Iron Range cities: Nealy, Talus, Rahja, Hirstio, Hudy, Reilly, Kneebone, Anderson, Crellin, and Portugue. Courtesy, Chisholm Free Press

turned to Rockefeller. Obligingly, Rockefeller bought 90,000 shares of their Mesabi stock at $10 a share, granting them an option to recover 55,000 shares within a year at the same price. Only one of the brothers took him up on his offer. By 1895 Rockefeller's name was synonymous with iron ore on the Mesabi Range.

As the Merritts learned, it was not possible to build a mining business on a budget. But there was room on the range for others who had the wit and capital to withstand the lean years. One of those men was Henry W. Oliver, who heard about the Mesabi Range in his hometown of Pittsburgh. In 1892 Oliver paid the Merritts $75,000 to lease the Missabe Mountain Mine, forming his parent company, the Oliver Iron Mining Company. Under the terms of the agreement, Oliver Iron Mining would pay a royalty to the Merritts for each ton of ore shipped.

Almost immediately Oliver recognized the need to infuse more cash into his company so that he could lease more Rockefeller mines and build his operations. He introduced giant steam shovels to make it more cost-efficient to get the ore out of the ground, and also helped form the Pittsburgh Steamboat Company for carrying the iron ore to the steel cities of the East. Correspondingly, he tapped Henry Frick, a manager of Andrew Carnegie's steel companies, and suggested that they make a deal. For $500,000 up front, Carnegie would receive half the control of the growing Oliver company. Over the years Carnegie's power increased along with his interest in Oliver's company.

Far away from the propriety and pleasantries of the Eastern Seaboard, an agreement was made on the Range that helped build the Rockefeller and Carnegie fortunes, and eventually transformed the Mesabi Range into the industrial colossus that it was in the first half of the twentieth century. Rockefeller and Carnegie came to an amiable working agreement: Rockefeller would stay out of the mining operations business, and the Oliver-Carnegie interests would use Rockefeller transportation to get their raw material to the mills. By 1901 Rockefeller owned sixty ships which regularly left the Duluth harbor bound for the East. Oliver and Carnegie agreed to pay Rockefeller a royalty of 25 cents on every ton of ore mined and another 65 cents for every ton of ore carried on one of his ships. In return, Rockefeller stayed out of the Oliver Iron Mining Company's operations.

At the turn of the century four major corporations pulled most of the strings on the Mesabi Range. Carnegie and Oliver operated the Oliver Mining Company; Rockefeller oversaw the expansion of the Lake Superior Consolidated Corporation; J. Pierpont Morgan backed the Federal Steel Company, a holding company that bought and operated mining railroads and ore ships; and James J. Hill formed the Lake Superior Mining Company. Hill originally formed his company to buy Mesabi lands, and eventually placed his properties in a holding company called Great Northern Iron Ore Properties.

These hunters near Hibbing were proud enough of their prize of small game to set up an elaborate photograph to record it. Courtesy, Iron Range Research Center, Opie Collection

The desolate stretches of Minnesota's mining regions had become the playing field for big business. The seats of power were held by men who knew when to move and when not to blink. J. Pierpont Morgan was a master of the game. Envisioning an empire that would lock up iron-ore mining and shipping profits, Morgan sent his negotiators to deal with Andrew Carnegie. In 1901 Carnegie sold him his Mesabi holdings for $500 million. Carnegie next tapped Rockefeller, who by that time was building a petroleum industry, and suggested that Rockefeller sell his mine properties and ore ships. For a little less than $90 million, Morgan took over Rockefeller's interests. Morgan then formed the United States Steel Corporation—the first billion-dollar corporation in the country. United States Steel was a conglomerate of horizontal and vertical holdings that included iron ore and coal mines, steel plants, railroads, and ore ships. The Oliver

In 1893 John D. Rockefeller became the first major businessman to invest in the Mesabi Range, and by 1895 his name was synonymous with iron ore in the area. Oil on canvas by Adrian Lamb. Courtesy, National Portrait Gallery, Smithsonian Institution, Washington, D.C.

Mining Company became a subsidiary of United States Steel, running the conglomerate's mining operations.

Nevertheless, United States Steel was missing one critical component up on the Range. The corporation did not own James J. Hill. Hill, who had vast landholdings on the Mesabi Range, knew that the huge company was already concerned about the day its mines would run out of iron ore. In 1907 Hill made U.S. Steel an offer. In return for allowing the corporation to explore his lands for new iron ore deposits, Hill asked them to pay him a royalty of 85 cents per ton—an unusually high royalty. He also wanted an agreement that their ore would be shipped to Superior on his Great Northern Railroad, at 80 cents per ton. United States Steel sourly accepted his offer. Before the contract was terminated in 1914, the corporation had paid Hill more than $45 million in royalties.

While the newspapers from coast to coast were filled with stories about what the Morgans, Hills, Carnegies, and Rockefellers were doing with their money, there were many who believed that something was fundamentally wrong with the country. When the miners went on strike against the Oliver Iron Mining Company in 1907, nearly seven-eighths of the wealth in America was owned by one percent of the population. It would be six more years before the state would adopt a compensation system to protect workers against industrial accidents and before the unsafe conditions in the mines would draw attention to the plight of the Range worker. The first two decades of the new century were a time when socialism and collectivism seemed like a plausible solution for the worker—and the split between business and labor an insurmountable chasm.

When the Minneapolis Club opened its doors in 1908, its members numbered among the select few who owned motor cars. By the time these prominent businessmen started driving themselves, finding parking space in downtown Minneapolis had become a challenge. Courtesy, Minneapolis Public Library

A boy from Ely posed with some of his toys about 1900. Courtesy, Iron Range Research Center, Opie Collection

HOOKERS AND WHALEBACKS

It was late November 1905 and the steel-gray sky above Lake Superior gave notice of the winter ahead. As Duluth citizens went about their morning business, four freighters, loaded with the last ore shipment of the year, left the protecting arms of Minnesota Point and turned their bows toward the blast furnaces of the East. Looking to the sky, the crews gambled that they could outrun one of Superior's infamous early-winter storms.

But one hour out of Duluth, all bets were off. With tremendous force, a storm blasted the four freighters, dancing the multi-ton ships on the mammoth waves. Every crewman knew that the only hope for survival was a retreat back to the Duluth-Superior Harbor. As townspeople watched, two of the four freighters managed to make it back to the relatively calm waters behind Minnesota Point. The third, although damaged as it rounded the point, limped to safety.

The fourth freighter, the *Mataafa*, was not so fortunate. Churning, frigid water ran fierce and high out of the narrow channel of Minnesota Point, spinning the 4,840-ton *Mataafa* like a top. In the same moment, the freighter was struck from behind by a blast of wind and thrown against the pier. Pelted by sleet and icy water, the crew saw the rudder ripped from their ship and felt the shudder as it was split in two by the waves and rocks.

Miraculously, Captain R.F. Humble and fifteen of his crewmen lived to tell about the storm. The men had made it through the night huddling around a bonfire built of the captain's furniture in the windlass room of the ship. The tragedy, however, lay in the stern of the freighter, where nine men had either frozen to death or were drowned. In the heyday of the iron ore industry—between 1890 and 1920—such drama at sea was a way of life. Without radar, electronic communications, or even the equipment to accurately forecast weather, freighter crews were at the mercy of their shipping schedules and the moody Great Lakes. More than fifty ships were lost on Lake Superior in the 1890s. Between 1900 and 1910, 350 ships had major accidents, at least 84 ships were destroyed, and 250 sailors lost their lives.

Traditions of Victorian elegance, like elaborate picnics in the yard, remained well into the twentieth century. This St. Paul family marked their special occasion with a photograph as well as a feast. Photo by Albert Munson. Courtesy, Minnesota Historical Society

The frequency of shipping disasters paralleled the explosion in the shipping industry at the turn of the century. Standing as sentries to one of the world's best harbors, Duluth and its neighbor, Superior, Wisconsin, grew from sleepy logging towns into thriving cities. The two cities reigned over the vast inland resources of lumber, iron ore, and grain. Transcontinental railroads and local mining railroads made beelines for the Duluth-Superior docks.

Not long after the discovery of Minnesota's abundant iron ore, it became obvious that shipping ore through the Great Lakes was the cheapest and most efficient means of getting the raw material to Eastern mills. A Great Lakes freighter could cover 800 miles with a shipment of ore for about 70 cents a ton, while shipping ore the same distance by railroad could cost up to $5 a ton. It wasn't difficult to calculate the advantage of using Duluth's harbor.

While Mesabi Range ore was being gobbled up by the New York, Pennsylvania, Ohio, and Illinois steel mills, the Eastern states—particularly Pennsylvania—were flush with coal. Coal was needed in Minnesota and points west to fire the turn-of-the-century industrial boom. Lake Superior became a two-way shipping street, and by the mid-1880s five coal docks were built in Duluth. In the next decade, more than 2 million tons of coal were hauled to Duluth, and much of it was used to power the steam shovels that dug the ore on the Mesabi Range. Hand in hand, the coal and iron ore industries grew together. By 1913, Duluth had twenty-four coal docks.

For many years following the discovery of iron ore on the Mesabi Range, the call was out for bigger ships with more holding capacity, greater speed, and more efficient loading and unloading capability. In 1889 a Scottish-born Great Lakes captain,

Built in 1911 as a navigation aid for ore carriers, Split Rock Lighthouse soon attracted tourists admiring the spectacular view of the north shore of Lake Superior. The lighthouse was decommissioned in 1969, but still enjoys great popularity as one of the Minnesota Historical Society's historic sites. Courtesy, Northeast Minnesota Historical Center

Alexander McDougall, designed a steel ship with a flat bottom that could carry great amounts of cargo. His dream was to replace the unreliable wooden vessels that he had known from his youth. From his Duluth home, McDougall sought financing for his ships, which he called "whalebacks" because of their shape. Investors laughed at his design, calling it a "pig boat" because of the flat hoglike bow, so McDougall decided to build the ship himself. His first whaleback barges—No. 101 and No. 102—were built on the Duluth waterfront. As homely as they were, they did what McDougall said they would do—carry the greatest volume of ore at the lowest price. No. 102 hauled nine railroad cars of ore to Cleveland in 1892.

Feeling as if he were on to something big, McDougall wanted to develop a shipbuilding company in Duluth. Again he met with resistance—this time from a coalition of citizens who objected to the potential noise and filth of the operation. McDougall packed up his plans and some investment dollars from Colgate Hoyt (a Rockefeller associate) and moved to West Superior, where he built the successful American Steel Barge Company. During the next three decades his company built nearly three dozen whaleback-shaped barges and steamers, and even a 362-foot luxury whaleback for the 1893 World Columbian Exposition in Chicago. Called the *Christopher Columbus*, McDougall's passenger ship had five decks and all the accoutrements of the finest luxury liners of its time. In subsequent years the ship carried more than 2 million passengers around Lake Michigan.

The whalebacks were the workhorses of the iron ore shipping industry. But their design limited their size, and soon longer and sleeker ships were crowding the waterways. When the Bessemer Steamship Company was formed in 1896, its first fleet of twenty-one ships included the *Queen City*, 400 feet long with a carrying capacity of 3,785 tons. Still, draftsmen of the day tinkered on prototypes of longer ships. By 1904 a 540-foot ship, the *Augustus B. Wolvin*, surpassed all Great Lakes records by loading

McDougall's shipyard built whalebacks to carry Minnesota iron ore from Duluth across the Great Lakes to the steel mills of Ohio and Indiana. Courtesy, Northeast Minnesota Historical Center

People of means could enjoy the freedom of resort living and the amenities of the city thanks to steamers such as the Plymouth, *which carried them from summer residences at Lake Minnetonka to connections with the city transit system. Courtesy, Minneapolis Public Library*

nearly 11,000 tons in ninety minutes. Carrying a cargo of nearly 13,000 tons, the *D.G. Kerr*, at 580 feet, set a new record in 1916.

By 1907 Duluth-Superior was one of the leading ports in the United States; it even outranked New York City for a short time. Iron ore shipments, for example, increased from a total of 12 million tons for the 1890s to more than 135 million tons from 1900 to 1910. In 1900, ships leaving the Duluth-Superior Harbor carried more than 1 million barrels of flour to the East Coast, where it was exported to such countries as Great Britain, the West Indies, Brazil, and Germany. In 1892, the Duluth-Superior port was shipping nearly as much flour as Minneapolis was.

Special freighters, called lumber hookers, carried Minnesota pine to lumberyards in the far corners of the Eastern Seaboard. When the North Shore lumber industry was at its peak, the Duluth and Iron Range Railroad arrived daily at Duluth docks with more than 150 carloads of lumber. The area's sawmilling industry reflected the health of the logging industry—in 1902, Duluth mills sawed a record one billion board feet of lumber. But the pine would soon disappear. By 1925 only one sawmill remained in Duluth, and it handled only the local need for lumber. Minnesota's logging empire had come to an end.

A similar boom-and-bust story can be told of Duluth's commercial fishing industry. In the 1880s Duluth was a collection point for Lake Superior fishing fleets. In the early part of that decade, nearly half a million pounds of whitefish were salted and shipped in barrels. Over the next decade refrigeration made it possible to send fresh frozen fish by rail to the West and South, and by ship to the East. After Lake Superior's whitefish were played out, fishermen turned to lake trout and then to herring. It eventually became evident that the fishermen were taking fish out of the lake faster than nature could replace them. Although a fish hatchery was built by the federal government in 1910 to replenish the waters, it was too little too late. Today the commercial fishing industry in the Duluth area doesn't even meet local demand.

But at the turn of the century, Minnesota's resources looked as if they would last forever. The docks at Duluth-Superior bustled with people and freight, filled with the noise of that optimistic era; the little northern city met the world at Minnesota's back door.

Lumberjacks' appetites were as legendary as Paul Bunyan himself. Camp cooks relied on simple fare in vast quantities to keep the lumbermen fed. The cook at N.B. Shank company's camp #2 obviously took great pride in his calling. Photo by William Roleff, Two Harbors, Minnesota. Courtesy, Minnesota Historical Society

HIT THE ROAD, JACK

Huffing and puffing along the dirt road, a line of Model T Fords rolled through the countryside outside of Clarkfield in Yellow Medicine County, American flags and campaign signs for Charles A. Lindbergh, Sr., fluttering from their open windows. Leading the Ford parade that fine May morning in 1918 was Lindbergh himself, bouncing along the rural backroads of Minnesota to deliver his message.

Banned in Duluth, hanged in effigy in Red Wing and Stanton, Lindbergh had often been dragged from the platform when making speeches against the war. But the small-town voters of the Sixth Congressional District had returned Lindbergh to Congress five times, from 1907 to 1917. Now they wanted to make him their governor. With his Progressive Republican philosophy he was an able and dedicated enemy of big business and big-city political muscle—one who clearly articulated what they so strongly felt. A staunch opponent of America's entry into World War I, Lindbergh believed that the United States should mend its own fences before tampering with its neighbors'. The people of his hometown, Little Falls, agreed with him.

In March 1918, the Farmers' Nonpartisan League—an organization (founded in 1915) that advocated state control of agricultural marketing businesses (elevators, stockyards, flour mills, etc.)—nominated Lindbergh to run against the Republican incumbent, Governor Joseph A.A. Burnquist, in the June gubernatorial primary. Lindbergh and the league were an excellent match. Lindbergh had savvy, Washington

Lake Superior whitefish once graced tables all over the country, but over-fishing caused the industry to collapse. Today smoked fish enjoys a limited statewide market, while the spring smelt run draws fishermen from throughout the region to the mouths of Lake Superior's tributary streams. Courtesy, Northeast Minnesota Historical Center

connections, and a plain talking, kind style of speaking. The league was fresh, energetic, and swelling with new members. Together, they reckoned, they could burst upon the Minnesota political scene and put things right for the farmer.

Although the Nonpartisan League was not a political party, it had an agenda which it wanted a political party to adopt. Its founder, Arthur C. Townley, had recruited enough farmers in North Dakota to gain control of that state's Republican party in 1915 and of the governorship and legislature the following year. He and his followers

turned their attention to Minnesota in 1917. Buying 260 Model T Fords, they fanned out across the state in an all-out effort to influence the 1918 elections.

Townley and the Minnesota farmers felt that they had suffered at the hands of big-business interests, and they wanted economic relief. Buoyed by the belief that they could organize themselves into an active political voice that could change their lives, Minnesotans eagerly paid their $16 membership fee and flocked to meetings. By 1917, 150,000 members in thirteen states were receiving the league's official news magazine, *The Nonpartisan Leader.*

But at 8:30 p.m. on April 2, 1917, when President Woodrow Wilson faced a joint session of Congress and requested that war be declared on Germany and its allies, the country was hurtled into war. In Minnesota the issues that had been heating up the campaign of 1918 were suddenly chilled by the realities of World War I. Economic issues took a backseat to political issues.

While he was a congressman, Lindbergh vehemently opposed any American involvement in the war. But once war was declared, he supported the country's actions. Despite this, he was suspected of being pro-German, and was villified as a man who opposed everything that his county stood for. And because the Nonpartisan League supported his candidacy for governor, that organization was tarred with the same brush.

In June 1918 Burnquist won the gubernatorial primary. But the election was also a show of support for the league, as Lindbergh received three times the number of votes

The Duluth Boat Club made a name for itself long before summer recreation became a statewide industry. With two clubhouses bracketing a two-and-one-half-mile watercourse, the club trained championship rowing teams. Courtesy, Northeast Minnesota Historical Center

Charles A. Lindbergh, Sr., carried his Nonpartisan League message from farm to farm. The League, however, suffered from accusations of pro-German sympathies, so Lindbergh lost to the war governor, Burnquist. Courtesy, Minnesota Historical Society

as there were league members in the state. Still the lesson was clear—the voice of the farmers in Minnesota still couldn't be heard over the roar of big business. To increase the size of their voting bloc, they needed support from another embattled group—labor.

By August 1918, the Nonpartisan League had a plan. On August 25, a joint committee of the Minnesota State Federation of Labor and the Nonpartisan League endorsed a candidate to represent their combined views in the gubernatorial campaign. To make certain that their candidate's name appeared properly on the ballot, they organized the Farmer-Labor Party. It was a coalition that would remain firm—in spite of their loss the following November to Burnquist—and it would gather enough momentum through the next decade to significantly change conditions for working people and farmers.

In 1922 the Nonpartisan League and its sister group, the Working People's Nonpartisan Political League, selected Henrik Shipstead, a dentist from Glenwood, as their senatorial candidate to oppose popular statesman Frank B. Kellogg, a traditional Republican and the incumbent. The Farmer-Labor platform included recommendations for conservation programs, payment of a soldier's bonus from an excess-profits tax, use of the unemployed on state-sponsored public works programs, and an enforced economy in public expenditures. It also recommended a tonnage tax on all iron ore mined in Minnesota, an issue that had been held at bay by the clout of United States Steel since the turn of the century. Shipstead handily defeated Kellogg. For the Farmer-Labor Party, it was a moment to savor.

BUSTING UP THE BUSINESS BOOM

In 1922 the tax on iron ore tonnage passed as an amendment to the Minnesota Constitution. This was an important development for every voter in Minnesota. On one side, businessmen worried that the tonnage tax would doubly tax mining companies, setting a poor precedent for future business legislation. They pointed out that, for a number of years, an *ad valorem* property tax had been imposed on the mining companies by the Iron Range communities. Companies operating mines within a town's corporate limits paid property taxes based on the mine's value from the time the iron ore was discovered to the time the mine was played out. Until 1921, there was no limit on the percentage of ore value that a town could force a mining company to pay. A state tonnage tax would place an additional burden on the mining companies, business argued, by increasing operating costs, which could eventually mean layoffs for the miners.

On the opposite side of the issue were the many taxpayers who believed the tonnage tax would fairly check what they believed were excess profits made by businessmen such as Carnegie and Oliver. They believed it was only right to make the out-of-state investors pay for destroying their wilderness and consuming a nonrenewable resource.

And there was another compelling reason for voters to support the tonnage tax. Public hostility toward big business was growing throughout the United States. Until

Many people saw the progressive spirit of the turn of the century as a threat to morality. They suspected that urban living undermined traditional values. The city missions sought to rectify the trend by preaching to the populous on the streets of Minneapolis. Courtesy, Minneapolis Public Library

Top: *A substantial town like Little Falls had several fire stations by 1900 as well as a younger generation eager to grow up to be firemen. Courtesy, Morrison County Historical Society*

Bottom: *The* Nonpartisan Leader *carried the agenda of the Nonpartisan League to its members with hard-hitting editorials and cartoons as well as articles that provided examples of effective action. Courtesy, Minnesota Historical Society*

IN THE NAME OF PATRIOTISM!

The Liberty Loan department of the First National Bank of Minneapolis really got into the spirit of the war effort in 1916. World War I stimulated a great deal of business in urban as well as rural banks. Courtesy, Hennepin County Historical Society

Joseph A.A. Burnquist (pictured here) won the 1918 gubernatorial primary over Charles A. Lindbergh, Sr. Burnquist, who served in the Minnesota legislature from 1908 to 1912, as lieutenant governor from 1912 to 1915, and as governor from 1915 to 1921, gained both respect and hatred for his suppression of dissenters during World War I. Photo by Paul Thompson. Courtesy, Minneapolis Public Library

the Sherman Anti-Trust Act was passed by Congress in 1890, business did pretty much what it wanted to do. The Sherman Act prohibited corporations from monopolizing interstate or foreign trade to inhibit normal competition. In the wake of the Sherman Anti-Trust Act, politicians across the country took up the cause of the "common people," and it looked as though big business had finally met its match.

The Sherman Act gave Minnesota Governor Samuel R. VanSant a legal foothold to stop a massive railroad merger in 1901-1902 that would have consolidated the Great Northern, Northern Pacific, and Burlington railroads into a single railroad network called the Northern Securities Company. The giant trust had the potential to manipulate the price of both travel and shipping in the United States. One of the company's helmsmen was James J. Hill, president of the Great Northern Railroad; others involved were Edward H. Harriman, head of the Union Pacific, and J. Pierpont Morgan, of United States Steel fame. Led by VanSant's administration, the Northern Securities Company merger was stopped by a decision of the United States Supreme Court in 1904 on the basis of the Sherman Anti-Trust Act.

In 1914 the Sherman Act was bolstered by another anti-trust law, the Clayton Act, which established the Federal Trade Commission, banned price discrimination, barred interlocking directorates, and prohibited certain types of contractual agreements among businesses.

It was in this climate of business reform, led by Minnesota's Progressive Republicans, that legislation for a Minnesota tonnage tax was introduced again and again after the turn of the century. First passed by the legislature in 1908, a tonnage tax calling

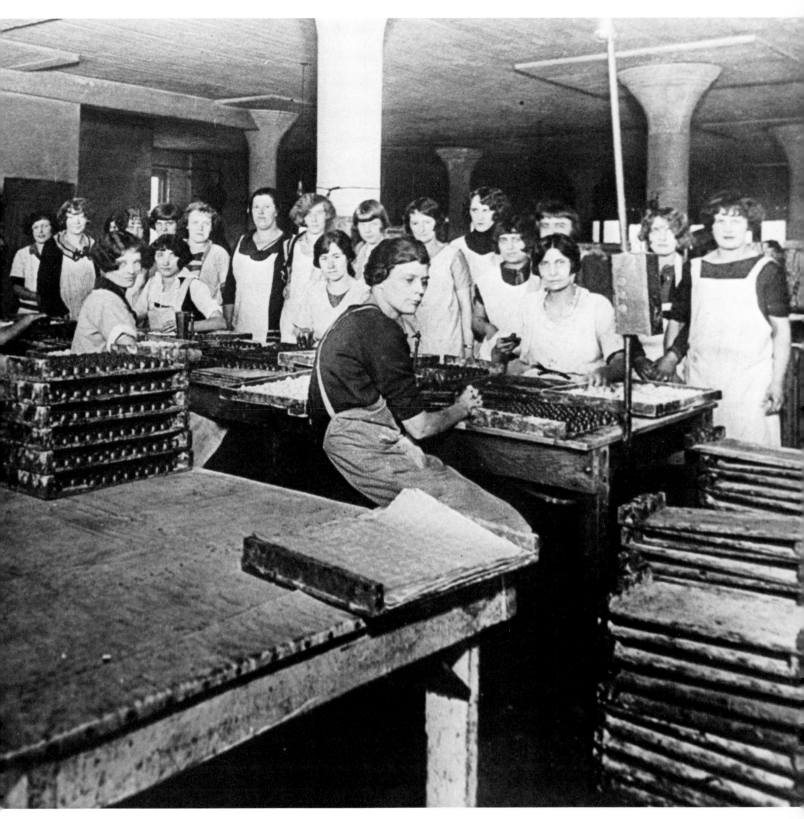

Small factories like the Wahl Candy Company in Duluth depended on women to staff their labor force. These newly enfranchised workers helped spur the Farmer-Labor Party on to victory in the 1922 gubernatorial election. Courtesy, Northeastern Minnesota Historical Center

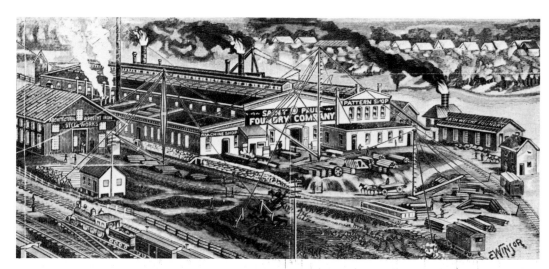

Right: *St. Paul Foundry Company enjoyed a strategic location on the rail line in a city that supplied building materials to the entire upper Midwest. As engineers learned to use more steel in place of masonry construction, this company prospered. Courtesy, Minneapolis Public Library*

Right: *Ford's first manufacturing operation in the Twin Cities began in 1912 with the assembly of the Model T. These workers assemble magnetos in an early version of a moving assembly line where each man pushed the part to the next station. Courtesy, Hennepin County Historical Society*

for a tax of two to five cents on every ton of iron ore was vetoed by Governor John Johnson, a Progressive Republican. For the next fourteen years the tonnage tax was raised during every legislative session, but it wasn't until 1922 that the tax was passed as an amendment to the constitution. Under the new tonnage tax—or occupation tax, as it was called—mining companies were forced to pay 6 percent of the market value of all ores mined or produced. It would be a sore point between business and government leaders for years to come.

While the public was battling big business, the banks in Minnesota were learning that there was a limit to their growth as well. Throughout the state's early history it typically was not all that expensive to found a bank. In fact, so little capital was required

that, according to some cynics, it was probably less costly to build a bank than to take up farming.

In the early 1900s the rise of the manufacturing sector, stimulated in part by the automobile industry and the construction boom in the cities, provided a foundation of capital that invigorated the expansion of the banking system nationwide. With World War I and the accompanying agricultural boom, more banks cropped up across the country than ever before. In Minnesota, small towns from Winona to Alexandria had at least one bank per community; by 1920 there was one bank for every 1,590 people in the state, compared with a national average of one bank for every 3,520 people.

There was little doubt that the states of the Upper Midwest—including Minnesota, North Dakota, South Dakota, and Wisconsin—had more banks than their capital reserves could support during economic bad times. Most of the new banks that had appeared in rural communities thrived during World War I, as agricultural prices increased and a land boom pushed up the price of arable acres. Farmers paid their debts and borrowed more money, pushing land prices to new heights. Heady with optimism, rural bankers put a steady stream of loan dollars into the hands of land speculators and farmers.

But after the armistice was signed and the war was over, in November 1918, the demand for food sharply declined and prices fell. To make matters worse, the newly created Federal Reserve Board tightened up the money supply in an attempt to choke off the nationwide wildcat lending spree.

The National Guard capitalized on national sentiment by using a World War I cannon to draw attention to their recruiting office in Minneapolis in 1921. Courtesy, Minneapolis Public Library

Above: *Minnesota families enjoyed the return to normal life after World War I. Rural people, such as the Abrahamsons of Lanesboro, enjoyed a brief prosperity before the agricultural depression of the early 1920s settled in. Courtesy, Minnesota Historical Society*

Facing page: *St. Paul's lowertown boasted several shoe factories whose skilled workers supported middle-class families living in the comfortable "streetcar" neighborhoods surrounding the city center. Many of these firms, like the Foot, Schultz Company pictured here, constructed modern work space in the first decade of this century. Courtesy, Minnesota Historical Society*

Rural bankers, who had become pillars of their communities, were the first to feel the effects of the new policy. Suddenly a bank's daily business was hardly enough to cover its operating expenses. Many banks closed, and depositors lost their savings and their belief in the banking system. Between 1921 and 1929, 320 state banks and 59 national banks locked their doors. The decrease in the value of Minnesota crops was just as disheartening. In 1919 farming brought about $500 million into the state; ten years later, harvest values had sunk by nearly $20 million.

In the exuberant years of the Charleston, the Model A Ford, and the first sound newsreel, farming families had a difficult time believing that America was the land of plenty. Trying to meet their extensive debts, they were choked by escalating production costs and taxes that tripled during the decade. But their troubles were only the beginning of a depression that would spread nationwide. It was a time to watch, wait, and worry.

Pulling Together

In spite of their problems, farmers and small-business people across Minnesota were encouraged by the lawmaking successes of the Nonpartisan League and the farmer-labor coalition during the 1920s. In 1922 the legislature opened commodity exchanges and livestock markets to cooperative selling agencies and expanded the range of activities open to dairy and other co-ops so that they could better compete in the marketplace.

For Minnesota's farmers the legislature's support of cooperatives was terrific news. In fact, the whole concept of marketing and buying products and services through cooperative clout was probably the best thing they had heard of since the nickelodeon. By 1922 there were approximately 4,500 cooperative associations in the state. The majority were marketing cooperatives, but their number also included buying, producing, insurance, and telephone organizations. In 1921, state cooperative revenues added up to $144 million. Six years later, they had grown to $200 million, a 38 percent increase.

Founded in the same anti-big-business spirit as the Nonpartisan League, dairy cooperatives helped to give farmers control over the market. Led by the spirited Theophilus L. Haecker—a former newspaperman, dairy farmer, assistant to the governor of Wisconsin, and dairy instructor—the co-op movement had begun before the end of the century. By the early 1900s, chapters of the American Society of Equity appeared across Minnesota, fighting an all-out battle with the middleman, who, association members believed, was gaining profits at the expense of the farming family.

After 1907, cooperative marketing efforts for grain farmers were extended from the local market to the terminals in the larger cities. In the spring of 1908 an Equity Cooperative Exchange was organized in Minneapolis to compete with the Minneapolis Chamber of Commerce (the original name of the Minneapolis Grain Exchange). The plan was to create a terminal grain marketing organization that would buy grain from friendly local cooperative elevators. The battle between the two exchanges played across the headlines over the next several years.

Nevertheless, cooperatives had become as much a part of Minnesota as its lakes. In 1921 the Minnesota Cooperative Creameries' Association was organized and immediately attracted 335 members. By shipping their butter in carloads, association members discovered they could save half a cent per pound in shipping costs—a substantial savings. Between 1917 and 1922 the number of shipping cooperatives for potato growers

Above: *Local canning companies provided a tax base for rural towns while ensuring farmers a good price for produce. Contracts between the canning companies and growers took some of the risk out of both enterprises. Courtesy, Le-Sueur Museum*

Facing page: *P.G. Jacobson's ditch and tile machine eased the backbreaking job of draining the prairies of southwestern Minnesota. Minnesota's rich, black soil inspired the name "Blue Earth" for both a county and a city, but the heavy clay needed drainage before it could realize its agricultural potential. Courtesy, Minnesota Historical Society*

increased by 113 percent, and the number of wool growers' co-ops increased by 40 percent.

In the ten years before the bottom fell out of the Wall Street stock market, agricultural cooperatives grew until they gained equal purchasing power with the large private manufacturers and food processors. Many cooperatives joined forces and set up federations. By 1929 Land O'Lakes Creameries, Inc., was a major federation representing 460 creameries and more than 100,000 farmers. While Land O'Lakes fattened the size of its operation, Minnesota became the leading butter-producing state in the country.

During the 1920s an increasing number of other businesses drew sustenance from Minnesota's rich agricultural base. Food processing companies such as the Faribault Canning Company, the M.A. Gedney Company, the Minnesota Sugar Company, and the Minnesota Valley Canning Company built plants in or near the heart of the Minnesota farming country. Trucks carried vegetables from the fields to the canneries, ensuring Minnesota-brand freshness on tables across the nation.

By 1925 the Minnesota Valley Canning Company had created its first "Green Giant" product and was marketing cream-style corn and peas around the country. Six years earlier the state's first sugar beet crop was grown by a Crookston farmer who was financed by a small coalition of businessmen from East Grand Forks. Called the Red River Sugar Company, the coalition (in association with the Minnesota Sugar Company in Chaska) built the state's first sugar beet plant (in 1926 at East Grand Forks). Turning the beets into sugar became an important Midwestern industry over the next two decades.

Facing page: A scientist from Redwing, Minnesota, Alexander Anderson opened the door to the cold cereal industry in 1901 when he discovered a process for puffing wheat and rice. Courtesy, Minnesota Historical Society

Below: Iron workers offered many services in rural towns. Riebold's Blacksmith and Foundry in Waseca made wagons, bobsleds, and harrows, while the foundry cast sash weights, columns for buildings, and other cast-iron products. Courtesy, Waseca County Historical Society

Right: *Automobiles changed the way Americans did business. Rural people could get to town more often, and they often drove further to get "big-city" prices. As a result, many rural shops went out of business in the wake of the automobile era. Courtesy, Minnesota Historical Society*

Below: *Cars brought changes to many small-town businesses. Former livery stables became service stations. The Norr blacksmith shop in Little Falls became a machine shop when they shifted their business from wagon repair to automotive work. Courtesy, Morrison County Historical Society*

W.A. Cady poses next to his electrically driven cream separator in 1924. Electric service in small towns created a gap between rural and village living standards, and farmers wanted modern conveniences. In 1923 Northern States Power teamed up with the University of Minnesota to build a rural line. The Red Wing Experimental Line proved the usefulness of rural electrification. Courtesy, General Electric Company

In the 1920s the meat-packing industry flourished, drawing livestock from the southwestern cornbelt section of the state. Companies such as Geo. A. Hormel and Company in Austin, Armour and Company, Swift and Company, and the South St. Paul Union Stockyards Company in South St. Paul, the Elliot Packing Company of Duluth, the National Tea Packing Company in Fergus Falls, and the Landy Packing Company in St. Cloud employed an increasingly large percentage of Minnesota's workers. By 1929, 7 percent of the Minnesota work force was employed by the meat-packing industry. For many farmers, growing livestock had become more lucrative than growing wheat.

And while businesses that processed farm products cropped up across the state, another change was occurring down on the farm. With electricity and trucking, farming families were discovering convenience. When times were good they were eager to buy the products and services that would break their isolation and ease their labor.

As early as the 1880s Minnesota towns included telephone exchanges in their list of amenities. Unlike many cities, Rochester had only one telephone company, which saved its business people the cost of subscribing to several exchanges. Courtesy, Olmsted County Historical Society

Left: *After a general store, a hotel, and a livery stable and blacksmith shop, a newspaper office was the next most essential business in a small town. Like many others throughout the state, the* Pierz Journal *gave a voice to local people and their problems even as it carried news of the outside world into each of their homes. Courtesy, C.A. Weyerhaeuser Museum*

Below: *Minnesota had one of the first hydroelectric generating stations at the Falls of St. Anthony in 1882. Distribution costs, however, delayed the growth of electrical utilities in sparsely populated areas. Ottertail Power Company took advantage of many waterpower sites among the glacial moraines of western Minnesota to develop one of the most far-reaching utilities in the state. Pictured is one of Ottertail's dams. Courtesy, Minnesota Historical Society*

Right: *Hibbing boasted municipally owned water and light systems within four years of its founding. Relocation of the town in 1919 made modernization of street lighting easy. The resulting "White Way," pictured, gave the town one more claim to fame. Courtesy, Iron Range Research Center, William Opie Collection*

Below: *When this photograph of Bridge Square was taken in 1885, gas lighting was already giving way to electricity. Minneapolis had seen its first electric street lamp in 1883, soon after the St. Anthony Falls hydroelectric station began operation. Courtesy, Minnesota Historical Society*

The Otter Tail Power Company in Fergus Falls is an example of the type of company that rapidly turned a luxury into a necessity for rural people. Having built a small hydroelectric power station in 1909, four Fergus Falls businessmen created one of the area's first full-fledged electric utilities which could run home appliances, turn on lights, and pump water. The only problem for the new utility was how to string the lines from the plant to a growing number of consumers. By 1919, forty-four small towns around Fergus Falls were linked to the generating plant. Three years later eighty-eight towns had been connected to the electric plant. By 1926 the number of towns with electricity had doubled once again, stretching as far as North Dakota. Before the decade was out, electricity was running many farms in the Red River Valley.

Electricity in the backyard corners of Minnesota meant social changes that would sweep out the last traces of isolation for most Minnesotans. By the late 1920s radios were bringing news of people in such faraway places as Rome and Oslo, and up-to-the-hour information that broadened every citizen's horizons.

Horace Mann School in St. Paul offered students access to radio technology in 1922. Minnesota had demonstrated its commitment to education by establishing state-supported schools in the first territorial legislature in 1849. Courtesy, Minnesota Historical Society

Children picketing in front of
Mayor Gehan's office in St. Paul
in 1937 gained publicity but
brought little change in the city
welfare system. Courtesy, Minnesota Historical Society

WEATHERING THE STORM

AGAINST ALL ODDS

I t was an adventure to make a prosperous country proud—a daring young man bound for Paris in a plane he had helped design. Alone, on a late May day in 1927, Charles A. Lindbergh, Jr., set out from New York. This would be only the second transatlantic flight in history—and he would be the first to go it alone.

The people in the United States sat by their radios as Lindbergh's *Spirit of St. Louis* clipped its way across 3,600 miles of sea. A little more than thirty-three hours later, Lindbergh shyly climbed down from the plane at Le Bourget Field in Paris, cheered by 100,000 Europeans.

The warm welcome Europe gave Lindbergh paled next to the frenzy with which the Americans greeted their newfound hero. When Lindbergh and the *Spirit of St. Louis* returned to the United States on the USS *Memphis,* he was met by 200 boats and seventy-five airplanes. On a platform adorned with garlands and American flags, President Coolidge presented the young aviator with the Distinguished Flying Cross. In New York City he was showered with 1,800 tons of ticker tape and blinded by flashing camera bulbs in a parade along Fifth Avenue.

In the following months Lindbergh toured the forty-eight states, telling crowds what aviation could mean for the future of America, and leaving a trail of enthusiastic believers. The "Lindy Hop" was an overnight dance craze and the song "Lucky Lindy" celebrated his "peerless, fearless" success.

Back in Lindbergh's hometown—Little Falls, Minnesota—the aviator's success was every citizen's triumph. On his victorious return flight to Little Falls, Lindbergh circled his hometown, thrilling the crowd of 50,000 with his favorite stunts. He was carried through town in an open Pierce Arrow automobile in one of the largest parades ever seen in Little Falls. Marching bands from Brainerd, Royalton, Pierz, Silver Lake, Red Wing, Chisholm, and Faribault took part, as did the Hibbing Ladies Drum Corps. In a speech at the fairgrounds following the parade, Senator C. Rosenmeier declared, as reported on page one of the August 26, 1927, *Little Falls Herald,* "while Lindbergh's trip across the Atlantic all alone was a great accomplishment and a real service, his greatest service was the setting up of the ideals of fitness and purpose."

Charles Lindbergh, Jr., made history in Minnesota by flying the first airmail routes in 1926. Worldwide fame from his trans-Atlantic flight a year later never diverted him from his devotion to aviation. Courtesy, Minnesota Historical Society

However, the Lindy Hop and the hero worship were soon to become memories from a happier past. On October 29, 1929, the inflated stock market, which had camouflaged an unsound economy, plummeted. Between late October and mid-November stocks lost more than 40 percent of their value, resulting in an economic depression that shook up American business from coast to coast.

In Minnesota, the effects of the crashing economy arrived unforeseen and with unique force. People who had believed President Coolidge's 1925 declaration that "the business of America is business," and who had tied their future to the business boom, were overwhelmed with the catastrophe.

Between 1920 and 1929, Minnesotans—like the rest of the nation—had quintupled their purchasing power through credit. They had over-consumed, buying pianos, washing machines, vacuum cleaners, radios, refrigerators, and automobiles on the installment plan. Now jobs were lost as corporations went bankrupt. Banks foreclosed loans. Credit dried up. Banks failed.

By 1934 one-third of the working people in Hennepin County were unemployed. Men and women who had lost their jobs and exhausted their savings, and in many cases forfeited their homes, had no choice but to "go on relief." Those who were employed were paid so little that they were barely able to pay for their necessities.

The Great Depression that followed spared no part of the state. By 1932, 70 percent of the miners on Minnesota's Iron Range had lost their jobs. By 1933 most of the Iron Range was shut down as industrial activity failed.

Commodity prices went into a slide that would not abate for years. Between 1929 and 1932 wheat prices fell from $1.20 to a little less than 50 cents per bushel. In 1931 the income of Minnesota's dairy farmers was one-fourth what it had been before the crash.

Minnesota citizens faced additional problems over which they, now, had no control. The timber resources of the state were almost depleted. Minneapolis was losing its leadership position as a flour milling center to Kansas, Missouri, and New York. Drought and clouds of grasshoppers ravaged the fields. Transportation lines between the East and the West were being rerouted, and goods were being shipped through the Panama Canal instead of through the Twin Cities and Chicago.

The Panama Canal quickly undermined the transcontinental freight business, so the Fairbanks-Morse Company, a St. Paul scale manufacturer, set up this display of its wares to travel around the upper Midwest in search of better sales. Courtesy, Minnesota Historical Society

All businesses received rough treatment from the Depression, but in Minnesota well-managed, conservatively run businesses survived in many cases. Some, such as General Mills, showed a steady increase in net income between 1930 and 1933. Others went into a frightening decline in the first two years, then recovered through skill and new products.

Minneapolis Honeywell is a case in point. In 1931 and 1932 Honeywell cut its number of employees in half. It added flour sifters, needed by the Pillsbury company, to its product line, and the number of employees returned to normal. Honeywell then bought the Brown Instrument Company of Philadelphia, and, by the end of 1936, its sales and the number of employees tripled. Dayton's department store in downtown Minneapolis kept itself afloat and made a profit each year of the Depression by promotional advertising and innovative sales events.

Others failed. Only a few days after the crash, Wilbur A. Foshay, a prominent Minneapolis businessman and the builder of the tallest—and one of the most up-to-date—office buildings in Minneapolis, declared bankruptcy. He had built a shaky commercial empire in Canada, the U.S., Mexico, and Central America. His huge enterprise included utility companies, hotels, mills, manufacturing companies, retail stores, and some banks. He also was heavily invested in the stock market. Wilbur A. Foshay was one of the many businessmen who could not hold out. (Subsequently he was indicted for using the mails in various types of stock fraud.)

Many of the businesses tried hard to help those who had lost jobs or businesses or hope. The Association of Commerce in St. Paul ran a "Give Double to the Community Chest" campaign; 3M offered an employee benefit plan; the Citizens Alliance in Minneapolis operated an employment bureau. Churches and community groups did what they could and local welfare offices worked long hours. Newspapers, in their editorials, tried to persuade firms to keep people employed, but it was not long before it was evident that these valiant local efforts alone would not be sufficient. Confidence in the buoyancy of private enterprise crumbled, and citizens turned to government—at all levels—for solutions to their economic problems.

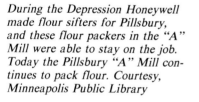

During the Depression Honeywell made flour sifters for Pillsbury, and these flour packers in the "A" Mill were able to stay on the job. Today the Pillsbury "A" Mill continues to pack flour. Courtesy, Minneapolis Public Library

On May 27, 1930, all of Wilbur Foshay's assets were sold at public auction. The prominent Minneapolis businessman who had built one of the tallest office buildings in Minneapolis was forced to declare bankruptcy due to heavy losses in the stock market. Foshay's tower included a penthouse suite designed for his personal use. Courtesy, Minnesota Historical Society

These men gathered in front of the Minnesota State Capitol building about 1935 to demand effective unemployment insurance. Courtesy, Minnesota Historical Society

It was in this climate of gathering desperation that Floyd B. Olson became the first Farmer-Labor governor in 1930, winning the election by a comfortable majority. Olson's talents combined political idealism with backroom negotiating savvy. Through his three terms as governor, he called for reform after reform, with only moderate success, having insufficient legislative or judicial backing to build a comprehensive state program. However, some noteworthy laws were passed in his administration. A state income tax to support the public schools in Minnesota became law in 1933. In February 1933 this governor ordered that there be a two-year period between delinquency and mortgage foreclosure, which the legislature reluctantly made into law. Injunctions in labor disputes were banned.

In his second term (1932-1934) Olson and the new President of the nation, Franklin D. Roosevelt, were philosophically in tune. Roosevelt's New Deal called for two R's—recovery and reform. People needed work today and security for tomorrow. The New Deal quickly put into place programs designed to put money into the hands of the people, thus relieving immediate distress. At the same time, Roosevelt believed his New Deal offered an economic foundation upon which a system of permanent employment could be created, including public works projects and compulsory unemployment insurance.

Olson's objectives for Minnesota were right in step with Roosevelt's plans for the New Deal. When Roosevelt spoke at a Jefferson Day banquet in the Twin Cities (April 18, 1932), he referred to Olson as "my friend and colleague." In his speech Roosevelt repeated his call for a fairer distribution of the national income, and focused his remarks on recommendations for helping farmers, factory workers, small-business people, and professionals to get on their feet again.

Roosevelt's speech received rave reviews across the state. Newspaper accounts noted the close alliance that was building between Roosevelt and Olson. Through the next several years President Roosevelt and Governor Olson kept in close communication. Rumors circulated that Olson would be asked to take a cabinet position. No offer was publicly extended, but the governor's policies were flavored with New Deal purpose.

During his administration Olson directed much of his attention at two bank-holding corporations: Northwest Bancorporation (or Banco) and First Bank Stock Corporation (which later changed its name to the First Bank System). These holding corporations were formed in 1929 by Midwestern bankers to strengthen the Ninth Federal Reserve District's weakened bank system and to prevent their banks from being consumed by Eastern interests. Minnesota bankers knew there was strength in numbers. Under the new system member banks continued to operate fairly autonomously while the parent holding company provided specialized services and capitalization against economic adversities.

The holding company concept worked well, even in the worst years of the Depression. Within a year Northwest Bancorporation had acquired ninety banks in several states. By 1931 this holding company had a controlling interest in 127, many of them from small Midwestern towns. While banks failed across the country, no member of either corporation was forced to close its doors.

In spite of the fact that the two banking systems provided financial stability during a chaotic period, Olson was convinced they were growing too big and too powerful, too fast. He launched a legislative inquiry, followed by an investigation by the State Banking Department. A suit was brought against the officers of Northwest Bancorpo-

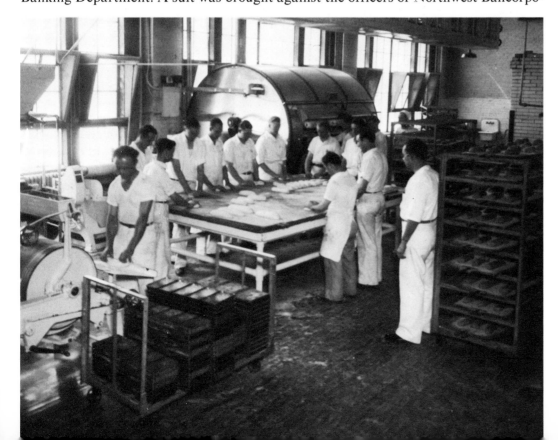

Dunwoodie Industrial Institute retrained people who had lost their jobs. In this 1937 bread-baking class, men learned new skills in the hope of entering a different line of work. Courtesy, Minnesota Historical Society

ration for fraudulent stock sales and manipulation. Though these measures did not turn up enough evidence to indict Banco's officers, the holding company suffered from the negative publicity. By February 1936, all charges had been dropped against the company. Nevertheless, Olson remained convinced that the bank system in Minnesota should be reformed, a belief he held until his death later that year.

Of all the problems Olson faced during his years as governor, he is probably most remembered for the actions he took during the truckers' strike of 1934. In 1934 Minneapolis truckers earned between $12 and $18 for working fifty-four to ninety hours a week. Trapped in a seemingly endless national depression, the truckers, along with other Minnesota workers, were becoming desperate. At the same time the Citizens' Alliance, a group of 800 Minneapolis business leaders, was as vehement about management's rights as the truckers were about theirs. Through the 1920s and into the 1930s the alliance had held the line against the formation of unions in Minneapolis. But its grip was weakening.

In 1933 Congress passed the National Recovery Act to help the country begin its long convalescence. Section 7a of the Recovery Act was the ray of hope that truckers and their compatriots had long been waiting for. Section 7a gave labor the right to bargain collectively, and it prevented employers from firing employees who joined unions.

In Minnesota some of the first to organize were the truckers. Their first big success was a coal driver's strike in February 1934, which completely tied up all coal deliveries in Minneapolis. Next on the agenda for Local 574 of the Teamsters Union was an all-out battle for all truckers. And at the end of April 1934, Local 574 announced its demands for shorter hours, an average wage of $27.50 per week, and overtime pay. The situation was serious, for Minneapolis was a major distribution center in the Upper Midwest, and a truckers' strike could bring the city to a standstill. The *Minneapolis Journal* advised housewives to stock up on groceries and noted that a milk shortage might occur.

Members of the Citizens' Alliance, refusing to bargain with the truckers, waited. On May 16, a strike vote was taken; and within a day, truck traffic was reduced to

Truck farmers in Hennepin County, who had long enjoyed a booming business at the Minneapolis central market, suffered mightily when the truck drivers' strike cut them off from consumers. A temporary market outside the city gave some of them an outlet for produce. Courtesy, Minneapolis Public Library

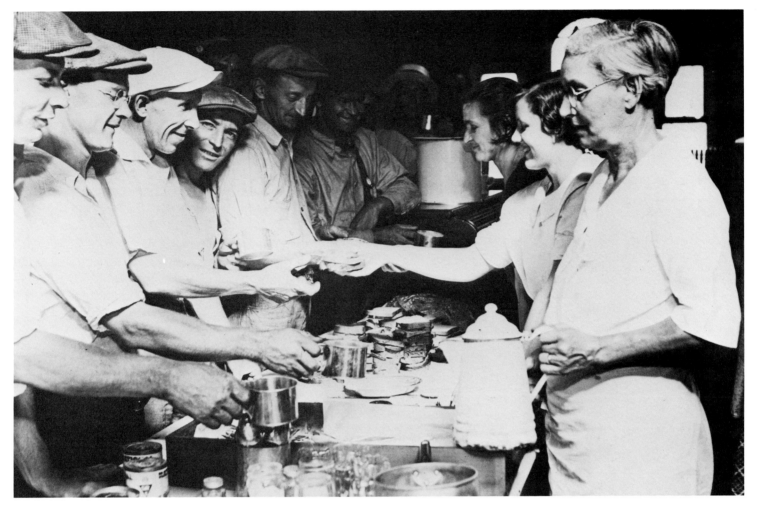

a trickle. The business leaders, who heartily disliked the governor, hoped he would be forced to choose sides between the strikers and the public good. Caught in the middle, Governor Olson threatened to call out the National Guard to distribute food and other necessities if negotiations did not prove fruitful.

Soup kitchens helped feed truckers during the four-month strike. Camaraderie over meals helped strikers keep up their morale. Courtesy, Minnesota Historical Society

In response to the governor's threat, a prominent businessman, Totten Heffelfinger, called for the mustering of citizens—a citizen's army—to help get trucks through the picket lines and distribute food. On May 22, 1934, more than 20,000 people gathered at Minneapolis' central market. Special deputies from the citizens' army squared off against the truckers. Local radio stations covered the event, play-by-play. When a striker tossed a crate of tomatoes through a plate glass window, the fight began in earnest. Two leaders of the citizen's army were shot and killed and scores of people were injured.

The following day Governor Olson ordered in the National Guard, and a temporary truce was called while negotiations between the opposing groups proceeded. The trucks were moving, but the tension remained, and both sides were preparing for the round. Then the employers broke off the talks again, and on July 16, 1934, union members voted to strike once again.

This time violence was a certainty. Four days later, when a truck was sent out on the Minneapolis streets with an armed convoy of police, a striker's truck attempted to block it. The police, armed with shotguns, opened fire at the truck. Within ten minutes sixty-seven people had been wounded; two were dead.

A friend of the working class down to his socks, Governor Olson agonized over his next decision. When the federal mediator, Father Francis J. Haas, declared that a plan for settlement had been drawn up, Olson called for agreement from both sides. When he didn't get it, Olson brought in 3,400 troopers from the National Guard to impose martial law on the city of Minneapolis. Special permits were given to certain categories of trucks so that commerce could begin. When the union proclaimed it would call another strike, the governor ordered a dawn raid on strike headquarters and the arrest of the strike leaders. Two days later he ordered a similar raid on the offices of the Citizens' Alliance.

By August a few employers had accepted the federal mediator's plan, and pressured other members of the Citizens' Alliance to accept it as well. On August 21, 1934, the alliance agreed to the plan. The four-month strike had resulted in a loss of more than $5 million in wages, and had cost the state more than $450,000. Bitterness between labor and business would divide the state politically for years to come.

EASING HARD TIMES

A fruit company truck was overturned when it tried to cross picket lines during the truckers' strike. Courtesy, Minnesota Historical Society

While the truckers' strike is a dramatic example of the general desperation of the working people of the time, the unemployed were organizing themselves for action, too. On April 6, 1934, 3,000 men and women who were out of work stormed into the Minneapolis City Hall-Courthouse, armed with rocks, bottles, and sticks, determined to bring

their plight to somebody's attention. In the skirmish three policemen and a woman by-stander were seriously injured. The courthouse halls became filled with so much tear gas that the building had to be closed for the rest of the day.

In spite of people's financial woes, there was a bright spot. The unpopular Eighteenth Amendment, which prohibited the sale or transportation of liquor in the United States, had been repealed. In December 1933, citizens in thirty-six states, including Minnesota, had voted in favor of the Twenty-first Amendment, and drinking alcohol once again became a matter of personal choice.

In Minnesota, Prohibition ended quietly. The *Minneapolis Journal* reported that the "repeal of the prohibition law had the effect of a lullaby on Minneapolis." According to police records, December 6, 1933—the evening after the repeal was made official—was one of the quietest nights in police history.

While there may not have been shouting in the streets, there was plenty going on behind the storefronts. By January 1934, Governor Olson had signed a state liquor-control law which established rules for the retailing of liquor. This included his insistence that localities have the option to decide whether or not liquor was to be sold within their borders. Sunday closing was mandated. Restaurants, if licensed, could serve liquor

The physical violence between police and striking truckers made such an impression on the public that the Minneapolis truckers' strike became one of the most memorable events in the city's modern history. Courtesy, Minnesota Historical Society

Right: *In May 1934 sixty-seven people were injured and two were killed when an armed convoy of police fired into a crowd of striking truck drivers gathered at the Minneapolis City Market. Courtesy, Minnesota Historical Society*

Facing page: *Millions of smiles such as that on the face of this bartender at Schiek's restaurant in Minneapolis greeted the repeal of Prohibition. Courtesy, Minnesota Historical Society*

with meals. The old kinds of saloons were prohibited, but "cocktail lounges" or "cocktail bars" were allowed. The sale of liquor by the bottle or by the drink by licensed retailers was legal except in communities which had voted to remain dry.

In deference to the dry side of the political aisle, only one bottle-store license could be issued per 5,000 citizens in the large cities, and one license per small town of 1,000 people or more. On-sale licenses could be issued to hotels and clubs as well as to restaurants in cities with over 10,000 people.

The repeal of Prohibition quickly translated into jobs. Breweries that had been closed since 1920 now offered jobs and a hopeful future to job-seekers. In Minneapolis, for example, the Minneapolis Brewing Company renovated its plant and hired 100 new employees. In St. Paul, the Yoerg Brewing Company started up again and the Peerless-LaCrosse Beer Company opened a distribution company to handle the local sales of beer made by the LaCrosse Breweries, Inc. By 1939 there were twenty breweries in business throughout the state, employing 1,700 people.

Abstinence quickly became a forgotten issue for mainstream Minnesotans. The Gluek Brewing Company in St. Paul even targeted sales of their pilsner pale beer to women. An ad in a 1934 issue of the *Minneapolis Journal* read:

Women who like to serve and eat good cheese, cold meats, smoked salmon, kippers, potato chips spread with roquefort, etc. have learned that the mellow, full-bodied flavor of Gluek's beer is the perfect accompaniment. And the chances are that for six months their husbands have also been Gluek enthusiasts. Here's a chance for real family harmony—order a case today.

The woods drew people looking for peace and quiet like members of this camp meeting in Morrison County. Courtesy, Morrison County Historical Society

People from all walks of life were seeking some relief from their trouble, and while social drinking appealed to some, others looked for heroes and excitement on the playing field. Sports became a national obsession during the 1930s. In Minnesota, winning a baseball game became a matter of civic honor.

In the 1880s two professional baseball teams had been formed to represent Minnesota in the American Association. Over the years, the Minor League Minneapolis Millers and the Saint Paul Saints fought hefty battles on the baseball diamonds while their fans simulated those contests before, during, and after the games with plain old civic rivalry. In an article written on August 31, 1934, a veteran sportswriter for the *Minneapolis Journal* captured the spirit of the contest: "Minneapolis has a gaudy lead in this American Association race, a lead of seven games over Milwaukee but, in case you are lighting the old pipe and seeing pennants in the smoke, remember this—the Millers have 19 games left and 15 of them are with St. Paul and Milwaukee." So popular was the civic rivalry during the years of the Depression that hockey teams sporting the same names as the baseball teams carried the contest between Minneapolis and St. Paul into the winter months.

But nowhere were sports quite so popular a draw as they were in the small towns, where dads and moms could watch their sons and daughters compete on a Friday night. In Sauk Centre—home of Sinclair Lewis' fictional *Main Street,* which had been published a decade earlier—1935 newspaper headlines celebrated basketball upsets over Upsala and Osakis. The February 7, 1935, edition of the Sauk Center *Herald* cheered even the girls' drill team, which entertained the "rooters" at the Sauk Centre-Melrose game, proclaiming that "by their yells and gestures and by their contribution Sauk Center can really show visiting towns that they have a team of which they can be proud."

In the 1930s most people believed that women would not need to develop competitive skills to help them in the business world, but women did have opportunities to participate in small-town sports. In Hibbing a coed sports program offered at the Hibbing Junior College taught badminton, basketball, deck tennis, shuffleboard, volleyball, field hockey, archery, swimming, tennis, golf, and Danish gymnastics. Women's competitive sports were so popular that by 1935 the Hibbing Women's Athletic Association had grown into one of the largest organizations at the college.

Enthusiasm for Minnesota-born brawn fanned out across the state as the Depression tightened its hold. Radio sportscasters broadcast the latest successes of the University of Minnesota's Golden Gophers. Native son and former Golden Gopher, Bronko

Eisel's Cafe in Little Falls always served as a meeting place for farmers to discuss economics or politics over platters of bacon and eggs or "beef commercial" (hot beef and mashed potatoes swimming in gravy). Courtesy, C.A. Weyerhaeuser Museum

Nagurski, was making national news on the Chicago Bears professional football team. He was still a home-state favorite.

University of Minnesota Head Coach Bernie Bierman became a legend in those years, as he took his teams into the Big Ten conference championships in 1934, 1935, 1937, 1938, 1940, and 1941. Known for brute power and indefatigable rushing strength, Bierman's teams put their foes to the test and showed Minnesotans a spirit that helped people cope. No matter what else happened during the week, it seemed that everybody wanted to go to the game.

Minnesotans also escaped the Depression at the movies. Business at theaters throughout the state was booming. For two bits an out-of-work miner could watch Clark Gable romance Jean Harlow in *China Seas* or vicariously take on the bad guys with Randolph Scott in Zane Grey's *Thundering Herd.* Laughter helped heal heavy hearts.

You could go to forget, and come home with some dishes if you held a lucky ticket stub. Grand Rapids was the childhood home of Judy Garland, who delighted the whole nation with her rich voice and wholesome appeal, and Minnesotans claimed her as their own.

Horseshoe tournaments fetched considerable local competitive talent as well. Each week players from the Windom, Mountain Lake, Jeffers, Storden, and Westbrook horseshoe clubs went up against each other in fierce rivalry. In fishing country, the city of Brainerd sponsored one of the first Paul Bunyan Expositions.

Federally funded programs of the Depression era did much to build Minnesota's image as a vacation wonderland. Through the Works Progress Administration (WPA) and the Civilian Conservation Corps (CCC), highways, bridges, parks, and playgrounds were built for the traveler's convenience and pleasure. Not only could people get around Minnesota more easily, but there were now places for them to go and things for them to do. In the 1930s, fishing resorts grew like waterlilies in a quiet bay. By 1938, approximately 1,200 lakeside resorts attracted more than 2 million tourists from all over the Midwest.

To the tune of ringing cash registers, the sky-blue waters and the call of the loon across a moonlit lake quickly became the refrain of Minnesota's northern charms. With equal speed, Minnesota towns in the lake country, hard hit by falling farm prices and layoffs in the mines, set themselves up as vacation spots.

The city of Minneapolis began, in 1940, a tradition of holding an Aquatennial in the heat of the summer. Led by an honorary Commodore and a Queen of the Lakes, parades displayed elegant floats representing various businesses and activities; and there were summer sports events and invitational regattas for sailboats on its lakes.

A Virginia Hockey Team posed for a group portrait about 1935. No sport could top the popularity of hockey on the Iron Range. Youngsters grew up on skates, hoping to play on the professional Eveleth Rangers. Although the Rangers have moved away, hockey still reigns supreme in northern Minnesota. Courtesy, Iron Range Research Center, Carl Pederson Collection

Lakes and rivers lured anglers with crappie, walleye, sunfish, northern pike, muskie, and smallmouth bass, while the woods crackled with game and the sun baked out whatever ailed a person. In 1937, 37,000 fishing licenses were issued. Six years later the number of issued licenses had more than doubled.

While some people tested their patience with a line over the side of a rowboat, other vacationers preferred to test their personal best on the golf links. By the end of the Depression, approximately 260 golf courses of varying size, shape, and difficulty had appeared throughout the state, from Alexandria to Winona. Birdieing their way across the greens, Minnesotans celebrated the fact that the work week had been shortened to five days. Weekends had become one of the best things about having a job. Leisure time also meant dollars in the pockets of Minnesotans who waited on tables, cleaned cabins, and drove trains and buses.

For many years Otis Lodge, southwest of Grand Rapids on lovely Sugar Lake, was one of the most glamorous of the lake country resorts. Arthur Otis was way ahead of his time during the Depression years. He built airstrips around the resort and lured planeloads of vacationers with free chicken dinners. Otis even set up an exhibit at the

The Virginia High School baseball team posed about 1925. Schools in Minnesota's Iron Range cities boasted extensive modern facilities where they trained championship teams in many competitive sports. Courtesy, Iron Range Research Center, Carl Pederson Collection

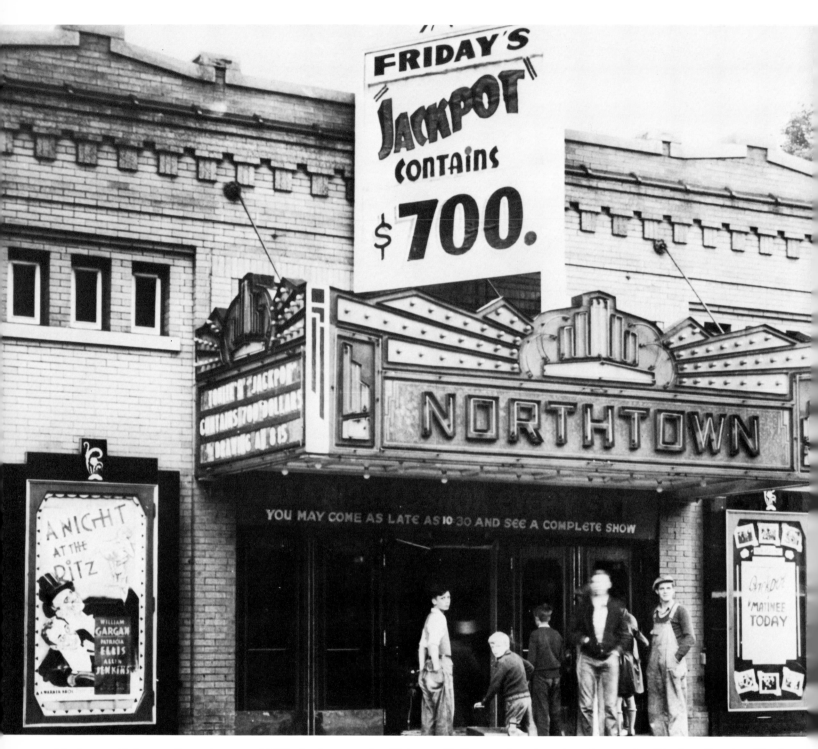

Movies provided some distraction from the grim realities of the Depression. This north Minneapolis theater organized a jackpot drawing to attract customers with the prospect of financial relief as well. Courtesy, Minneapolis Public Library

1937 air show at the Chicago Coliseum, betting that those who liked to fly also liked to fish. By 1940 an expanded airfield received forty-seven planes, including a Northwest Airlines plane filled with twenty-four people.

Minnesota's enterprising tourist industry even warmed the state's pockets during the winter months. Southwest of Minneapolis (near present-day Eden Prairie), a mammoth ski slide was built in 1935. The Minneapolis, Northfield and Southern Railway packed in spectators who would travel to watch ski-jump tournaments in which competitors might make jumps of 200 feet. During the 1930s Minnesota was considered one of the ski capitals of the world.

In the spirit of celebration, the city of St. Paul also revived its citywide Winter Carnival in 1937, after a lapse of nearly twenty years. Here began the tradition of King Boreas of the North, the Winter Carnival parade, fireworks, and outdoor sports events.

134

Across the river in Minneapolis, Winter Sports Week offered competitions in ice hockey, skiing, skating, ice boating, log rolling, tobogganing, and sleighing.

By the end of the decade, vacationers had brought nearly $140 million into the state's flagging economy. Tourism—the latest industry based on the rich resources left behind by the glaciers—showed promise.

VOICES IN THE DARKNESS

Journalist James Madison Goodhue had stepped off the steamboat onto the docks of St. Paul in 1849, when Minnesota was still nine years away from being a state. Determined that the little territory should have a newspaper, within ten days of his arrival Goodhue had the first issue of Minnesota's first newspaper available for distribution.

In Waseca, Herter's Style Show helped to boost the local economy. People who turned out for the entertainment spent money in town, strengthening the local retail businesses. Courtesy, Waseca County Historical Society

Goodhue had intended to name his paper *The Epistle of St. Paul.* Friends, however, cajoled him into changing his mind about that. The *Minnesota Pioneer* soon became the voice and conscience of the emerging state.

In the eighty-five years between the appearance of the first issue of the *Minnesota Pioneer* and the middle of the Depression, getting the word out to the citizens had become big business in Minnesota. By 1937 there were 500 newspapers in the state. Eight of these were metropolitan dailies, including a direct descendant of Goodhue's paper, the *St. Paul Pioneer Press.* In addition to the *St. Paul Dispatch,* the *Minneapolis Tribune,* the *Minneapolis Star* (an offspring of the paper founded by the Nonpartisan League in 1920), the popular *Minneapolis Journal,* and the *Duluth Herald* and *News-Tribune,* there were twenty-six smaller daily papers and a growing number of weekly and monthly papers around the state.

Trolley transportation enabled middle-class workers who lived on the outskirts of the city to get to work with ease. Thus, cities like Minneapolis were able to expand commercial activities long after residential areas filled up. Photo by Norton and Peel, Minneapolis. Courtesy, Minneapolis Public Library

The search for timely news stimulated another Minnesota industry—paper milling. The logging industry had packed its equipment and moved to the Western states after the turn of the century, but the need for paper in the Midwest was growing. In 1916, C.K. Blandin, then publisher of the *St. Paul Pioneer Press,* became aware that this newspaper faced a critical paper shortage, and bought a small mill in Grand Rapids from the Itasca Paper Company. It was a fortunate decision. Within ten years the price of newsprint doubled and annual production at the mill nearly tripled. By 1929 Blandin was more interested in the production of paper than in the production of news. He sold his interests in the newspaper and invested heavily to make his mill—The Blandin Paper Company—one of the most modern paper mills of its time. Despite a depressed market the mill produced 43,000 tons of paper in 1935, and operated at a profit throughout the Depression.

Minnesota's north woods provided great opportunities for the Civilian Conservation Corps. The Cutfoot Sioux CCC Camp (shown here) provided healthy outdoor work with the social aspects of camp life while making a substantial contribution to reforestation. Courtesy, Iron Range Research Center, Nick Radovich Collection

Duluth's incline railway carried residents and tourists up the steep hill to Skyline Drive from 1891 to 1939. Courtesy, Northeast Minnesota Historical Center

Farther north, where the water going over Koochiching Falls drops twenty-four feet, the Minnesota and Ontario Paper Company mill had become a major source of income for Minnesotans living at International Falls. With the mill operating day and night, workers could produce 1,100 feet of paper every minute. Next door, a mill turned waste from the paper plant into wallboard, roofing, and insulating materials for centrally heated homes. Paper manufacturing jobs brought relief to a region that was feeling the pinch of layoffs in the mining industry.

All across the state an increasing number of radio stations brought news, weather, sports, comedy, and a break in the isolation that many people felt. Three major stations served the Twin Cities area: WCCO, WDGY, and KSTP. In the middle of the decade the *Minneapolis Tribune* and the *St. Paul Pioneer Press,* together, invested in a new radio station they called WTCN.

WCCO Radio, founded in 1924, understood the power of the personal message, and its programming reflected this. For farming families, WCCO provided daily market information broadcast from the stockyards in South St. Paul and from the commodity trading floor of the Minneapolis Chamber of Commerce. Through the grim decade of falling prices, market announcer Mildred Simons was a note of stability. Farmers believed she understood what it was they needed to know. Calling her the "Market

Ice boaters on Lake Superior had enough room to work up more speed than they could in their cars on winter roads. Courtesy, Northeast Minnesota Historical Center

Lady," they made her one of the state's first radio personalities in the new era of rapid communications.

In 1930 an experimental radio station was established in Elk River to monitor the progress of the Byrd Expedition to Antarctica. This station communicated with WFAT, the call letters of the radio transmitter on the expedition's supply ship, the SS *Eleanor Bolling,* and allowed residents of Elk River to follow the expedition as closely as if it were a serialized adventure series.

During the Depression, newspapers and local radio stations reported business growth across the state as though it were a beacon in a black sky. When a company expanded and offered the community jobs, it was news. New products were news, too, because every promising step businesses took signaled an opportunity ahead for the unemployed.

Business optimism was expressed in Minnesota during the Depression with enough frequency to keep hope alive. The Minnesota-based 3M Company, for example, was

WCCO Radio quickly earned its place in farmers' hearts. Its clear-channel frequency carried current market prices directly into the kitchen, so a farmer could listen for the latest livestock prices directly from the stockyards in South St. Paul before deciding to set out with his stock. Courtesy, Minnesota Historical Society

having a difficult time keeping up with orders for its new line of colored coating materials for asphalt shingles. On the day the federal government closed down the banks across the country to prevent a nationwide run (March 6, 1933), the 3M Company opened a new roofing manufacturing plant in Wausau, Wisconsin. When questioned by the press, William McKnight, the aggressive young president of the growing company, told reporters that business growth could help to loosen the stranglehold of unemployment. "If every business concern which can afford to do so would undertake now to do work required in the reasonably near future, it would stimulate employment and hasten the return of prosperity. Such companies would find that surprisingly low building costs prevail."

The Minnesota news media were quick with their praise of risk-taking businesses. When demand for products from the Despatch Oven Company of Minneapolis had fallen off so sharply that most of the plant's employees were idle, its visionary president, A.E. Grapp, invented a device that would help miners extract gold from glacial deposits without the use of water. According to news reports in March 1934, Grapp's invention would be snapped up by the mining industry, and could be easily produced by the oven plant's machinery with little additional capital outlay. Whether or not it happened, such attitudes kept people employed a little longer and kept hope alive.

Through the 1930s the news media and regional businesses worked hand in hand in an attempt to stimulate consumer buying. From 1926 to 1936, Betty Crocker's voice over WCCO radio guided homemakers through the problems of feeding their families frugally while providing good nutrition. Through the voice and personality of Marjorie Husted, General Mills could reach directly into each homemaker's kitchen. As the Depression worsened, Betty Crocker was right at the listener's side, providing her with low-cost menus, recipes, and recipe books. Beginning in 1932, coupons in flour products were redeemable for pieces of silverware. The idea was close to marketing genius. Homemakers would get something tangible for consistently using one manufacturer's product. Betty Crocker received the undying loyalty of thousands.

Media and business leaders in Windom also learned that they could help each other. With the town suffering from the poor agricultural market, the *Windom*

3M's first profitable product was sandpaper. Here, St. Paul workers cut rolls of sandpaper into smaller sheets appropriate for industrial or retail uses. Attentive to the needs of their clients who painted cars, 3M soon diversified into the masking tape business. Courtesy, 3M

Established as educational organizations, Junior Homemakers clubs helped young people learn the scientific principles of home economics. In the wake of the Depression, these organizations played an essential role in helping families cope with their severely limited means. Courtesy, Minnesota Historical Society

Reporter gladly filled its pages with news about special celebrations sponsored by the business community. In the fall of 1935, business people sponsored the second annual Halloween party and treasure hunt, with free costume hats and whistles for the children and a dance for grownups in the evening. Clues to the citywide treasure hunt were available with each purchase in a sponsoring merchant's store. Active businesses such as Foss Mercantile Company, Van Nest Motor Company, and Thompson Lands Seed Company also provided their customers with tickets for "Free Silver Day" that same fall. Silver dollars were awarded to those whose tickets were drawn. The grand prize of $25 drew thousands of hopeful players. News reports show that the day was highly successful for everybody.

THE FORGOTTEN ONES

Will Rogers, the cowboy philosopher and social critic, once said the federal government's farm relief policy seemed to mean that the Feds had a responsibility to relieve farmers of everything they owned. His words stuck in the throats of many Minnesota farming families who were battered by falling market prices and periodic droughts.

Roosevelt's New Deal package of help for farming families came in the form of the Agricultural Adjustment Act (AAA). This program, passed in 1933, was based on the theory that restoring farm purchasing power was essential to national economic recovery. The AAA had two primary purposes: to reduce farm production to a level where it would supply the country's staple needs but would not result in surplus for storage or foreign trade, and to push prices up enough so that farmers could get back on their feet. To help finance the crop curtailment programs that were the backbone of the AAA, the new law also imposed a processing tax to be paid by companies that turned farm products such as wheat, corn, rice, hogs, and milk into food products.

The AAA was quickly followed by a supplementary spoonful of federal medicine. Called the Farm Credit Act of 1933, it was designed to help relieve the heavy mortgages farmers carried. Within a year and a half following its enactment, the Farm Credit Act had refinanced more than one-fifth of all farm mortgages.

The AAA's processing tax immediately caused problems by forcing major food-processing corporations to pay sizable sums just to conduct their business. In Minnesota, the processing tax levied against the General Mills Corporation forced it to pay the equivalent of $2.12 on every share of common stock. General Mills joined others in the industry to take action against the processing tax in 1935. They obtained federal injunctions to restrain the government from collecting this tax until the Supreme Court heard the case. In 1936, the Supreme Court halted all farm production control activities.

There was another serious flaw in the construction of the AAA: it did not offer immediate solutions, which the farmers so badly needed. In the fall of 1933, the governors from Minnesota, North Dakota, South Dakota, Iowa, and Wisconsin met to draft a price-fixing proposal to boost prices on staple commodities, such as corn and wheat, high enough to see farmers through the next growing season. They believed that driving prices up through production control would take time they did not have.

But Washington was not in the mood to talk about price fixing. Governor Floyd B. Olson, who presented the governors' proposal to Roosevelt, was stunned by the president's resistance to his pleas. Governor William Langer, of North Dakota, was resentful. He was quoted in the *Minneapolis Journal* on November 5, 1933, as saying that "everybody else, the banker, the insurance man and the railroad man was ahead of the farmer and got their money. There is nothing left for the farmer. The farmer is the forgotten man."

As the motion picture news cameras began to turn, Olson's words had a serious sound:

> Whereas industry has known this Depression for only three years, the farmers have known it for twelve years. In those twelve years, the farmer has seen the prices for his goods go down and down, and the prices of the things he must buy go up and up. All we are asking is parity price for him, a return to him of his purchasing power so that he can buy all the paint you make, all the leather goods you produce, and many other products, and then the Depression will end.

The headlines reporting the president's rejection of a price-fixing program stimulated a fury that swept across the state. Anger turned to threats of striking and blocking highways so that food commodity shipping would be stopped. John Bosch, president of the Minnesota Farmers Holiday Association—a descendant of the defunct Nonpartisan League—urged farmers to fight for their rights and to do whatever they must to hit the economy where it would hurt the most: at the consumer's dinner table.

In Meeker County 400 farmers voted to support a national strike and, despite the fact that the end of the harvest season was only days away, called for immediate action. Activist farmer Evald Nelson wired the state headquarters of the Minnesota Farmers Holiday Association that his county would be off-limits to any farm shipping from that November day forward. In Pipestone County picketing began immediately, and all farm product distributors were coerced into closing their operations. In Chippewa County, Holiday leaders requested that milk distributors pay two cents—to support the costs of the pending strike—for every quart of milk sold. They also demanded that distributors send a supporting appeal to President Roosevelt on the farmers' behalf.

Dairy cooperatives kept the rural economy alive in the 1930s. The Fergus Falls Farmers Cooperative Creamery provided a market for farmers and produced butter at reasonable prices. This woman was photographed cutting butter at the creamery in 1937. From the St. Paul Dispatch-Pioneer Press. *Courtesy, Minnesota Historical Society*

Reconstruction of historic sites made excellent public works projects. Men in Duluth were put to work rebuilding the Fond Du Lac Trading Post near the mouth of the St. Louis River. Courtesy, Northeast Minnesota Historical Center

But the anger demonstrated by farmers who poured their milk into the fields and allowed their crops to rot on the land did not stop the policies that would forever change agriculture in Minnesota. As people lost their farms and moved to the cities in search of work, the population of the state began to shift away from rural areas. At the turn of the century, two-thirds of Minnesota's citizens lived on farms or in small towns of fewer than 2,500 people. But the farm crisis of the Great Depression changed that. By 1940 there were nearly as many people living in the cities as there were in rural communities, and fewer of those people were working on the farms.

Many towns in rural Minnesota actually prospered from the employment programs and money the federal government pumped into the state during the Depression. In the town of Roseau near the northern border, WPA labor built an auditorium and school and repaired the highways. When the federal government established the Rural Electrification Administration (REA) in 1935, it began a massive effort to ensure that every farming family could be plugged into modern life. Battling a lack of interest and resistance to change among the rural families—and sometimes a lack of money—the REA slowly brought electricity to every corner of the state.

Slowly the programs of the New Deal changed the way the larger population centers of Minnesota looked. In Moorhead the Central Junior High School and the first Moorhead Country Club were built with WPA labor and materials, and hundreds of people were employed in the construction. As in so many other places across the state, when the buildings were built, community pride was built as well, even when news reports were dismal.

The Great Depression forced Americans to look closely at their lives. When old ways fail, new methods must be tried. Minnesotans resolutely took part in this reconstruction of their society, which they hoped would be better for everyone.

This busload of Mankato men represented the largest group of volunteers from any one recruiting station. Courtesy, Minneapolis Public Library

MOBILIZING ON MANY FRONTS

ERUPTION OF POWER

On a hot summer night in 1939, an enormous meteor blazed northward over Lake Erie before erupting into a ball of fire. Across New York, Pennsylvania, Ohio, and Canada, thousands of people watched the disintegrating meteor and felt the power of the universe.

At the same time, across the Atlantic millions of Europeans struggled in a world as frightening as blazing meteors. By then Austria, Bohemia, Moravia, Albania, and Poland had fallen in the wake of Hitler's advance.

But on July 12, 1939, the flash of a meteor and the possibility of world war were not foremost on the minds of Minnesotans who were employed by the Works Progress Administration (WPA). As they picketed their work sites through the night, they were more concerned about how to pay their bills. The WPA had given Americans the means to survive economic hardship during the worst of the Depression, but then, after people had grown dependent upon it, the government wanted to dissolve the program.

Billed as a temporary work relief program when it was created as part of President Franklin D. Roosevelt's New Deal in 1935, the WPA meant meaningful work for more than 8 million men and women. Workers built schools, community centers, churches, bridges, and highways; they managed city art projects and sewed clothes for the homeless. For the most part they were paid the prevailing hourly wage of the area, even when that wage was union scale. From 1935 to 1939, WPA projects nationwide cost the federal government more than $11 billion. The well-being of many communities came to depend on the WPA, and in time people forgot that it was meant to be only a temporary measure.

By 1939 the nation's economic gears had shifted, and the country was moving toward recovery. Congress decided it was time to tighten the reins on the WPA, and scaled down costs by limiting the number of worker hours and by standardizing wages. That spring the Emergency Relief Appropriations Act (the Woodrum Act) altered WPA benefits, prescribing layoffs and lowering wages. Hardest hit were skilled laborers, who would be working for far less than union pay.

When WPA workers in Minnesota reported to their jobs on July 5, 1939, after a long Fourth of July weekend, they were met with the grim news that their paychecks would be trimmed to meet new federal guidelines. Building tradespeople in Minneapolis and St. Paul immediately called for a strike. By the next morning work on construction and highway grading projects in the Twin Cities had virtually stopped. When the sun set that evening, an estimated 18,000 people, from the Iron Range to the Twin Cities, were picketing their workplaces.

Organized labor pressured all WPA workers to strike. On July 8 a meeting was held at the WPA warehouse in Brainerd to decide whether to stop work on the twenty-six WPA projects in progress in Crow Wing County. The workers agreed that all work on the Crow Wing sewage disposal plant, the storm sewer, and projects at Boom Lake and Camp Ripley would stop by the following Monday. Of the 1,050 workers employed in construction projects in Crow Wing, at least 900 were expected to picket.

By Monday the strike had turned ugly. In Minneapolis a policeman died after being beaten while trying to escort a WPA worker through a picket line. Claiming the work stoppage was 100 percent effective, workers in Brainerd drove automobiles bearing picket signs up and down the business district. The *Brainerd Daily Dispatch* reported that members of the city council were worried that the storm sewer and sewage disposal plant would not be completed by winter.

Two days later another violent incident erupted in Minneapolis. When 200 non-strikers tried to leave the Second Street WPA project building after their shift, they were confronted by a mob of angry strikers. Police fired on the crowd with both tear gas and bullets. An elderly man was killed and seventeen people were injured, including two children.

Even the most dedicated strikers soon realized they were fighting a losing battle. WPA Commissioner F.C. Harrington warned that the government would not tolerate work slowdowns or stoppages. He announced that WPA workers absent from their jobs for more than five days would be cut from the payroll and replaced.

On Friday, July 15, approximately seventy-two workers on the storm sewer project were fired for failing to show up for work; the next Monday, full crews reported back to work on both the sewage disposal and sewer projects. The *Brainerd Daily Dispatch* summed things up by reporting: "The Brainerd strike, although one of the few outside of the large industrial areas, was carried out in an orderly manner. Both parties agreed that both sides conducted themselves in a manner reflecting to their credit."

Workers in Minneapolis, St. Paul, and Duluth returned to work on Friday, July 21, under a compromise plan devised by Governor Harold Stassen. But over the subsequent months grand jury investigations into the strike resulted in the indictments of 107 men and 55 women from the Twin Cities. Most of those indicted were charged with use of physical force, which under the Woodrum Act was considered a felony. The defendants were grouped, and three separate trials were held. Although the unions protested that the workers were being framed and that Minneapolis had become "the Moscow of America," the juries returned guilty verdicts for many of the defendants. Fear of prosecution severed the chain of labor solidarity among WPA workers. The end of the WPA strike signaled the end of the Depression in Minnesota.

Facing page: Eric Sevareid first put his University of Minnesota journalism degree to use as a field reporter in Europe during World War II. Courtesy, Minneapolis Public Library

SHIFTING TO HIGH GEAR

Geographically, landlocked Minnesota appeared to be sheltered from the winds of war blowing in from Europe by 1939. The people of Minnesota, however, felt anything but isolated from the tempest. Many had families still living in Poland, the Low Countries, or Scandinavia, and the letters from home held frightening news. On September 1, 1939, Great Britain and France declared war on Germany, and radio brought the news into the living rooms of America.

On May 10, 1940, Hitler attacked Belgium and Holland, and the National Red Cross put out a call for contributions to a war relief fund. The St. Paul Chapter of the Red Cross was assigned the task of raising $52,000; within months, it exceeded its goal by more than $14,000. Men and women offered their time as well, sewing

Honeywell produced a radio control box that guided Flying Fortress drones during atom bomb testing. Courtesy, Minneapolis Public Library

clothes, blankets, and surgical dressings, and knitting sweaters and socks for shipment to Europe. Like their neighbors around the state, the women of Crosby and Ironton met each Thursday for a potluck lunch and an all-day knitting and sewing session on behalf of the Red Cross war relief drive.

The effect of Hitler's European war stealthily crept into the Minnesota economy. Many Minnesotans remembered the shortages and inflation that had plagued them during World War I, and so were not surprised when retail prices began to increase. During September 1939 prices for basic commodities rose by 25 percent, foreshadowing the long days of rationing to come.

Several Minnesota companies had established international operations after the Depression. Honeywell, for example, had viewed the world as the marketplace for its central-heating controls. Having opened its first European subsidiary in Amsterdam and set up a headquarters in England, Honeywell became greatly concerned about its employees' safety.

Minnesota companies also recognized that the war effort might be a much-needed shot in the arm economically, particularly for companies that could provide systems and subsystems for defense. As the United States defense program shifted into high gear—in 1941 the federal government appropriated approximately 41 percent of its total budget for defense—manufacturing companies across the country added employees and tooled up for new levels of production. Jobs in factories, ordnance plants, and iron mines were suddenly easier to find, and the multiplier effect worked swiftly. Companies that supplied materials for manufacturing plants grew healthier, and consumers, who for the first time in many years believed their jobs were steady, felt easier about spending the money they had. Among the fastest growing companies were those that manufactured machine tools, electrical machinery, and communications equipment.

After Pearl Harbor, Minnesota's business and labor factions formed a temporary alliance. Newspapers of the time reflected the "let's get down to business" attitude that washed over the state and the nation. In June 1942 the *Shakopee Argus-Tribune* printed an editorial mirroring the nation's commitment: "Secretary Hull joins President Roosevelt in predicting that the war will be long and hard. It's a fight for victory, and we must win the fight . . . For all of us the moral is that, whatever our hopes, we must plan for the worst; we must plan for as long a war as may be necessary to do what we mean to get done."

A major problem facing the War Production Board was how to allocate the nation's resources—how to get workers, raw materials, and manufacturing equipment in the right places at the right time to meet military demands. The most agile minds boggled at the massive organization that was required. In the end, one-third of all federal contracts for ammunition and equipment went to ten of the nation's largest manufacturing plants. General Motors' production contracts, for example, amounted to more than $14 billion.

Minnesota manufacturers grew increasingly concerned that they would not be able to lasso a portion of the defense business. In 1941 the legislature appropriated enough money to establish an office in Washington that would keep an eye out for new war contracts. Minnesota policymakers also devised a system for centralizing the names of all manufacturing plants in the state able to provide subcontracting production work for the prime defense contractors.

Backed by new government defense production contracts, many Minnesota businesses hired every available worker as their plants expanded to meet weaponry demands. Theodore C. Blegen, author of *Minnesota—A History of the State*, notes that it would be impossible to list all the Minnesota companies that contributed to the war effort. Nevertheless, Blegen's abridged list shows the wide range of capabilities in the state. The Minneapolis Honeywell Company, according to Blegen, made sophisticated advances in airplane controls and also created a proximity fuse that would detonate a projectile or bomb at a predetermined distance from a target. Minneapolis Moline produced artillery shells, and Crown Iron Works in Minneapolis developed steel parts for portable bridges, barbed wire entanglement posts, and pontoons. Crown also produced 20,000 tons of fabricated steel used in building military ships at shipyards in Superior, Wisconsin, and Savage, Minnesota.

Like many other small companies that manufactured and sold consumer products, the Owatonna Tool Company (OTC), in Owatonna, had made a good business out of selling tools door-to-door to farmers and mechanics. With the start-up of the war, OTC was one of many to stop its production lines and make some radical changes. OTC's gear pullers were sent to the front by the thousands, and mammoth wrenches for use on America's ships were sent to shipyards by the boxcarload. OTC—bought in 1985 by the Sealed Power Corporation of Muskegon, Michigan—was one of only a few plants in the Upper Midwest to receive five Army-Navy "E" (for excellence) awards during the war.

Larger companies also put the bulk of their production into the war effort. Minnesota Mining and Manufacturing (now called 3M) produced large quantities of adhesive-backed tape which was used for window protection during bombing raids as well as on ships, jeeps, and airplanes. The company also manufactured sheeting used for airplane wings. American Hoist and Derrick, in St. Paul, became a major supplier of marine deck equipment for combat ships and built the cranes, hoists, and derricks that were used in military shipyards.

By the summer of 1942 a second United States army was marching off to work every day—an army of women and men who never saw an enemy's gun but who knew the intimate details of the Allies' weaponry. An employee newspaper for the Federal Cartridge Corporation, the *Twin Cities Ordnance News*, noted that this new production army had its own war cry:

'Keep 'Em Shooting!' That's the new war cry you'll hear on every worker's lips these days! . . . That means that heavy responsibilities rest upon all of us engaged in Ordnance Production: . . . the responsibility to make every minute count; the responsibility to do our work with thoroughness and care . . . to work together as a team.

Northern Ordnance Incorporated, a subsidiary of Minneapolis-based Northern Pump Company, built twin gun mounts and other hydraulic equipment for naval destroyers. Employees of the company were ecstatic when they received a telegram in May 1943 from Rear Admiral W.H.P. Blandy, chief of the Bureau of Ordnance in Washington. "You will be pleased to know that ordnance of your manufacture played a prominent part in the successful action of a United States naval task force which recently fought a Japanese fleet twice its size in a four-hour surface duel off the Komandorski Islands," Rear Admiral Blandy reported, noting that the company's gun mounts, powder, and projectile hoists had helped the Navy outmaneuver and outshoot the enemy. The admiral went on to say that the task force had "executed their almost suicidal mission in magnificent style."

In northern Minnesota the three Iron Ranges hungrily gobbled up new workers as the country's steel mills called for more iron ore. In fact, iron ore shipments to steel plants in the United States nearly doubled between 1939 and 1942, and 66 percent of those iron shipments originated from the Mesabi Range. When the mines needed electrical power, the utilities announced that they would be able to provide sufficient power for all customers, particularly the mines. The Minnesota Power and Light Company informed the public that no federal funds would be required to build additional power facilities during the war effort.

"We recognize our responsibility in the defense program," M.L. Hibbard, president of Minnesota Power and Light, declared in a statement to the *Crosby Courier* in 1941, "and you may be assured that our Company has prepared itself to meet every emergency which may arise in this program of preparedness." Of particular concern

Facing page: Honeywell Regulator company's Moduflow control panels continued to roll off assembly lines throughout the war years. Courtesy, Minneapolis Public Library

Above: *Although the production work that E.F. Johnson did for the military was top secret, the company received public praise for its contribution to the war effort with the presentation of the Army-Navy "E" award in 1944. Courtesy, Waseca County Historical Society*

Facing page: *Honeywell's experience with women workers during World War II taught the company that women's dexterity and attention to detail made them excellent assemblers. Courtesy, Minneapolis Public Library*

to Hibbard was the Cuyuna Range, which he explained was one of the vital spots in the nation's program. A year and a half later the Cuyuna Range reported record shipments of iron ore.

Electricity was also essential for farmers who were suddenly feeding a nation at war. Of 726 Minnesota farms without electricity surveyed in 1942, most had the capability of greatly increasing their yields if electricity were provided. Outside of Warren, in northwestern Minnesota, farmers were able to double the number of laying hens, turkeys, and geese. When electricity was installed, Warren farmers added 415 milk cows, 241 beef cattle, 224 brood sows, and nearly 1,000 feeder pigs.

But private industry wasn't the only source for the war effort. The federal government built a number of munitions plants around the country. Two such plants were located in Minnesota—one in Rosemount, a few miles south of the Twin Cities in Dakota County, and another in New Brighton, then a tiny suburb of St. Paul.

Some of the unsung heroes of the war were the farming families who sold their land to the government and the parents who raised their children in homes close to munitions plants. In Rosemount, the federally run Gopher Ordinance Works spread across thousands of acres of farmland. Although most of the homes were destroyed or moved, a few were kept for use as small satellite offices away from the main plant. An editor for the *Dakota County Tribune* wrote of the stark contrast between the county before and after the war began. "Grotesquely, these farm homes stand out," he noted in December 1942, "the only peaceful reminder of the rolling farmland which soon will be devoted to the outpouring of explosives to blast our way back to a victorious peace."

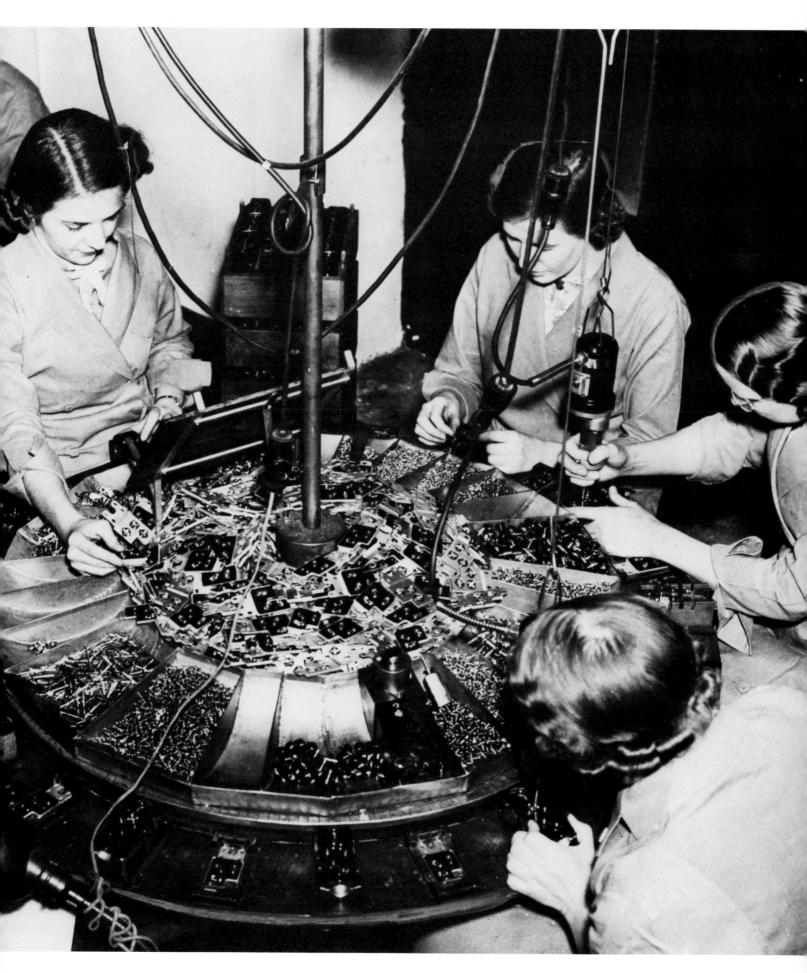

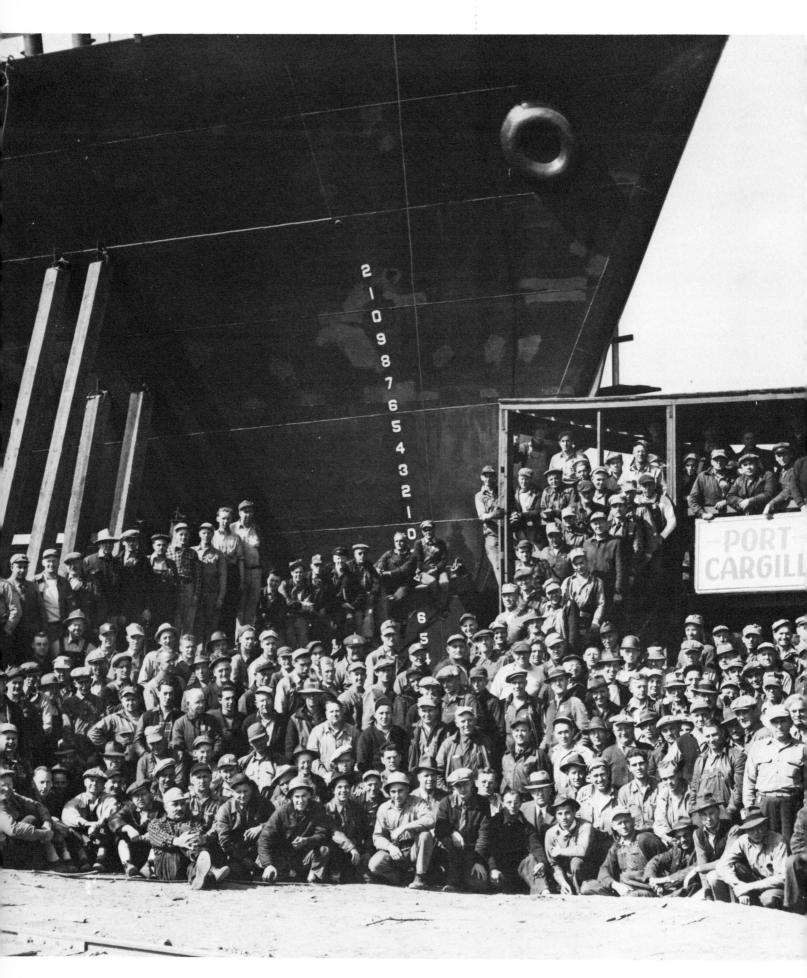

Minnesota also managed to gain a tiny portion of the nation's shipbuilding business. Duluth's shipbuilders manufactured every type of oceangoing vessel, from oil tankers to submarine chasers. But shipbuilding also flourished for a time in Savage, a little town on the Minnesota River in Scott County. In April 1942 the United States Navy announced that it had awarded a $10 million contract to Cargill, Inc., a grain shipping, marketing and elevator company, to build the hulls for oceangoing gasoline tankers at Savage. Once the hulls were completed they were towed down the Mississippi River to New Orleans, where they were rigged for battle duty. County news reports both lauded and regretted the new business: although 1,000 laborers found employment at the shipyards, 800 acres of farmland in Scott and Dakota counties were lost from the tax rolls.

Before the end of the war, the shipyard on the Minnesota River, called the Port Cargill Shipyard, had completed eighteen tankers for the United States Navy, each 310 feet long with a 48-foot beam, capable of carrying 600,000 gallons of gasoline. The corporate history of Cargill, Inc., notes that the vessels built in Minnesota were heavily armed to plow toward the enemy over heavy seas, without the backup of a convoy of ships. The radar system built into the new, modern ships was a breakthrough for a force long vulnerable to sudden air attack. Cargill also built four towboats for the United States Army, which were said to be among the most powerful tugs operating on the inland waterways.

Private industry partnerships with the federal government grew as the war shifted from land to air. The airline industry especially was drastically changed with the advance of the war. Domestic airline services were cut by more than half as the Air Force called pilots into active duty. In 1942, Northwest Airlines, one of the oldest airlines in the United States, operated a bomber modification center for the War Department at Holman Field in St. Paul. More than 5,000 employees designed and equipped—often these were top-secret projects—3,000 aircraft bound for overseas assignments. Northwest Airlines also provided personnel to the Minneapolis Honeywell Regulator Company, which developed and manufactured electronic control systems for aircraft.

Of tremendous importance to the war effort, as well as to the future of the aviation industry, was the ice research conducted at Wold-Chamberlain Airport from 1942 to the end of the war. Under the jurisdiction of the Air Transport Command, and later the Wright Field Army experimental station, researchers made considerable advances in wing de-icing and snow removal techniques. Similarly, the United States Navy's static precipitation research program at Wold-Chamberlain used Northwest flight crews to test radio communications and navigation signal blockouts.

At the Mayo Clinic in Rochester, then half a century old and already one of the leading medical centers in the United States, mechanical and medical research took another critical step forward, this time providing Allied pilots with the G-suit. The G-suit prevented a pilot from being knocked unconscious (due to blood being forced into the extremities) while flying at high speeds and performing intricate maneuvers such as turns and pull-outs.

Facing page: Port Cargill ship-builders gather for a group portrait about 1942. Courtesy, Minnesota Historical Society

"Cold or Hot, Spam Hits The Spot"

SPAM, the spiced ham product made by Geo. A. Hormel & Company in Austin, found its way into American kitchens in 1937 with the help of radio. The makers of SPAM brought WCCO listeners the popular "Jacob Heidrich and His Violin" show three times a week for two years. In 1940 Hormel bought coast-to-coast air time on the "George Burns and Gracie Allen Show." Not long afterward, Burns and Allen introduced "Spammy," their pet pig, to radio audiences, and SPAMwiches became the rave in middle-class households. In just three years 70 percent of the families in urban America were opening the familiar blue cans to serve SPAM—between slices of bread, as an appetizer, and in casseroles.

In 1941 under the provisions of the Lend-Lease Act, SPAM and several other Hormel products went abroad. In his 1942 Christmas Eve broadcast, Edward R. Murrow explained that the British people would have a nice Christmas because, even though "the table would not be lavish, there would be SPAM for everyone."

Minnesota SPAM also attracted the attention of military procurement officers. The day after the attack on Pearl Harbor, the Hormel plant received word that SPAM was to become part of the government's war effort. Just like the ordnance plants that were springing up around the Twin Cities, Hormel's factory was immediately surrounded with steel fences and floodlights. Employees either wore badges to work or were denied entry. Once inside, they turned out thousands of cans of SPAM and combat rations like pork and apples, beef and pork, and ham and eggs. Parachute packs were filled with Hormel luncheon meat. Thousands of tins of Hormel whole chickens were sent to men who would spend the war years far from home.

Hormel's meat-packing business was designated an "essential" industry by the federal government during the war. When the company ran out of nails—one of the many products rationed between 1942 and 1945—the government moved quickly to find a source so that Hormel could close up its shipping crates.

To meet the increased military demand for its products, Hormel expanded its production facilities to four double-shift lines. Even as many employees exchanged their aprons for Army uniforms, Hormel steadily increased its labor force to satisfy Uncle Sam's needs. By the end of 1943 Hormel had hired 1,000 women; the number had increased by approximately one third by 1944, when Hormel's labor pool showed more than 5,000 men and women on its rolls and 1,150 more on military leave.

Companies such as Hormel recognized their obligation to returning service people and assured them they would have jobs waiting for them when the war ended. Hormel went so far as to forward copies of *The Squeal*, its employee publication, overseas. In December 1944, Jay Hormel, president of the company and son of founder George A. Hormel, wrote a letter to his employees serving in the military, telling them, "we still are hoping to be able to offer a full-time annual wage job to everyone who is now on our payroll. That includes those who have come on with us since the beginning of the war as well as those who are on military leave. Your old job will be here for you—the fellow who has taken your place will have to find the next best thing for himself."

As any military strategist would point out, one of the advantages the Allied countries had was access to nutritious food for their armies. But getting food to the "men over there" was frequently as much of a feat as producing the food in the first place. When tin shortages resulted in severe problems for Hormel and other Minnesota-based food supply corporations, packaging became a science.

The Pillsbury Flour Mills Company took the packaging issue seriously, investing in bags that could withstand the stresses of overseas shipping. Reporting on his company's success, Philip Pillsbury noted that they had passed an important milestone in the war effort when the company developed "sacks that could be dropped into the ocean out of Japanese artillery range." The tide would then float the sacks to servicemen on the beachheads.

The ability to adapt to the country's needs was a top issue with corporate management in most major Minnesota companies during the early war years. General Mills turned some of its corporate attention to the production of "roll correctors" for the British Admiralty and eight-inch gun sights for the United States Navy. By 1942, when United States Marines invaded the Japanese-held island of Guadalcanal, the Navy was using torpedo directors developed and manufactured by General Mills. In later months employees of the growing company's Mechanical Division created the "jitterbug" torpedo, which baffled Japanese trackers with its ability to twist and turn through the water.

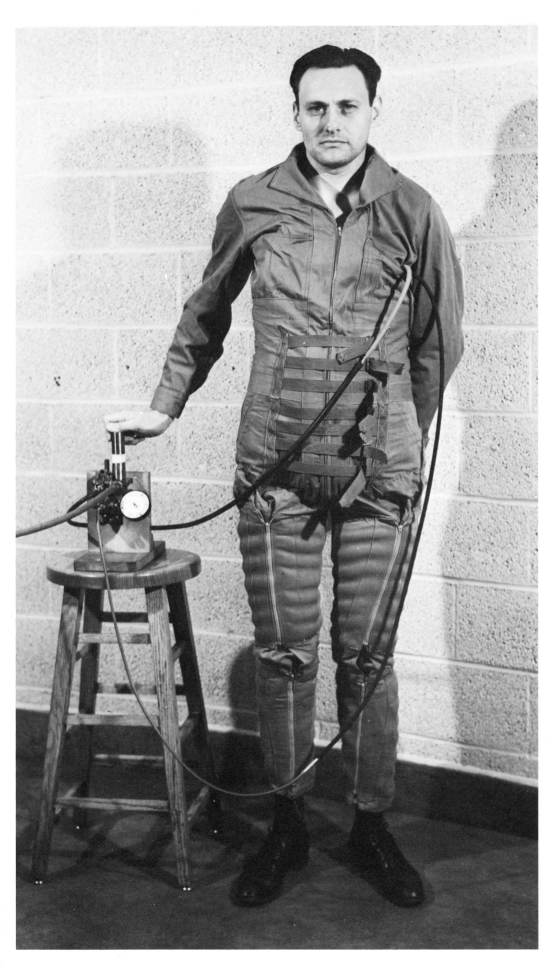

Physicists and physicians at the Mayo Clinic collaborated to design a G-suit that would enable pilots to maintain consciousness under acceleration conditions. Ralph Sturm and others volunteered as human guinea pigs on a centrifuge in the laboratory until the suit design was perfected in 1946. Courtesy, Mayo Clinic

Urged on by the military's pressing needs, General Mills quickly learned the value of diversification. From its shipping docks went boxes filled with gun sights, breakfast foods, vitamins, dehydrated eggs and soups, and sandbags—all carrying the General Mills label. The company also established research facilities to turn soybeans into animal feeds, oils, breads, and other foods. Soybeans came to assume a critical role in Minnesota's postwar food production industries.

World War II was a catalyst for change in many Minnesota industries. Synthetic fibers began to attract the public's attention even before the war, but the need to reserve the bulk of the country's wool for military use prompted the appearance of synthetic-and-wool-blended blankets on the home front. The Faribo Woolen Mills, since 1865 the manufacturer of the Faribo woolen blanket, produced 250,000 olive-drab woolen blankets between 1942 and 1945.

Like many other industries, Faribo Mills took a long look at the changes spurred by the war. And like many other industries, the woolen mill decided to push on with the changes. By 1954 the word "synthetic" had become part of the American vocabu-

Facing page: Efficient transportation played a key role in fuel conservation. An improved channel on the Mississippi River made it possible to ship bulk commodities in fleets of barges. Courtesy, Minnesota Historical Society

lary, and Faribo Mills was producing a line of blankets made entirely of an acrylic called Acrilan. Orlon was later added to make Faribo blankets meet the changing needs of postwar consumers.

"Conservation" was another word that took on added importance for industry during World War II. Most Minnesota manufacturers took seriously their responsibility to conserve the state's resources. Construction materials, industrial metals, rubber, fuel oils, and many foodstuffs were rationed for private use so that they would be readily available for those in combat. Northern States Power Company (NSP), for example, enthusiastically supported the conservation efforts of its employees. At the Black Dog generating plant, workers built a warehouse from wood scraps and railroad ties, and when the company ran out of transformers, it purchased them from secondhand dealers.

NSP's advertising frequently contained messages about the company's conservation efforts. Glowing with pride, the electric utility company reported that it had salvaged 2,519,000 pounds of copper, brass, steel, lead, zinc, rubber, and paper through the war years. "Enough tonnage to build approximately 75 medium-size war tanks to fight the enemy," said one ad.

Above: The rising fame of the Mayo Clinic created a demand for public transportation between Rochester and the Twin Cities. The Jefferson Bus Line, which got its start transporting patients to the clinic, later commissioned an extraordinary series of landscape sculptures for the enjoyment of its passengers. Courtesy, Minneapolis Public Library

ARSENAL OF HEALTH CARE

During World War II, per capita spending on medically related expenses increased an average of 8.5 percent a year. (Between 1945 and 1948, per capita increases were about 3.6 percent annually.) Hospitals were crowded, and physicians, nurses, and laboratory technicians were in short supply. Minnesota's medical workers were saving lives overseas.

The loss of medical talent to the war zones made daily news in Minnesota. Dr. Charles W. Mayo, along with doctors and nurses from the Mayo Clinic in Rochester and the Mayo Foundation (a research affiliate of the University of Minnesota), became part of the U.S. Army 71st General Hospital in 1943. Assembled and trained at Stark General Hospital in Charleston, South Carolina, part of the unit would eventually head overseas for duty in New Guinea. Twelve of the fifty physicians sent to New Guinea on behalf of the 71st General Hospital were from the Mayo Clinic's permanent staff.

From St. Luke's Hospital in Duluth, fifteen staff physicians were called into active duty, including the hospital's only radiologist. Spread thin, those left behind complained bitterly that they could not offer the quality service they felt obligated to provide.

By the end of the war, the days of general practitioners were giving way to increased specialization, cooperation among hospitals, and hospital expansions. But these things cost money, and health care consumers began looking for help to pay for them. Minnesota Blue Cross, the second hospital benefit plan of its kind in the nation, was a timely addition to the health care solution when founded in St. Paul in 1932. In 1940, 75 hospitals in Minnesota were caring for 380,937 Blue Cross subscribers, 23 percent of whom lived outside the Twin Cities, and subscriber numbers nationwide were spiraling upward. By 1952, Blue Cross reported a nationwide enrollment of 40 million.

In 1945 a group of Minnesota doctors, seeing how effective group hospital payment plans had been, thought that a similar plan for prepaying medical expenses might

The Michael Dowling School in Minneapolis responded to the polio epidemic by offering special programs for polio patients. These children were photographed about 1940. Courtesy, Minneapolis Public Library

162

The expanding metropolitan population did not miss the comic section during the newspaper strike of 1949. Minneapolis mayor Hubert Humphrey read the funnies aloud over WCCO Radio to keep readers up-to-date. Courtesy, Minnesota Historical Society

work just as well. Blue Shield was organized in 1946, and by 1947 a combined Blue Cross-Blue Shield benefit package was being offered to families for $60 per year.

When the war ended, hospitals faced crowded conditions. By 1946 the first round of baby boomers nestled in the arms of their parents, and postsurgical wards were as packed as the obstetric units. Many people who had postponed minor surgery during the war could see no reason to delay any longer.

There was also a tragic reason for the crowding in hospitals across the country. In 1946 more than 10,000 cases of polio were treated in Minneapolis alone as a polio epidemic swept the nation. Stricken children arrived by train from out-of-state hospitals, while Mayor Hubert Humphrey pleaded with the federal government to convert the Fort Snelling army barracks into temporary hospital shelters. None of the newly discovered drugs could prevent or cure polio. (Salk's polio vaccine was not developed until 1952; it was released for use in 1955.)

A key figure in the fight against polio was Sister Elizabeth Kenny, an Australian-born nurse who came to Minnesota in 1940. Sister Kenny treated polio victims by applying hot packs and retraining their limbs through physical therapy, rather than im-

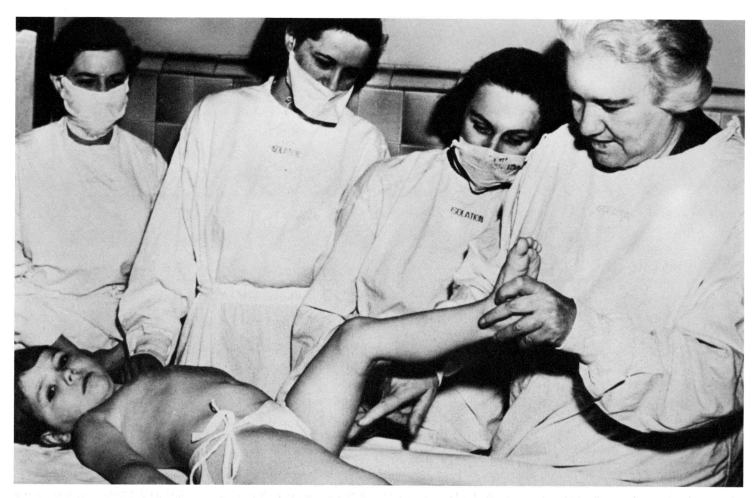

Sister Elizabeth Kenny developed a revolutionary treatment for polio in her native Australia. Her exercise treatment, the basis for modern physical therapy, received cool reception in the United States until she reached Minnesota. There, in 1940, she established the Sister Kenny Institute just in time to train nurses who could respond to the massive polio epidemic. Courtesy, Sister Kenny Institute Archive

mobilizing them in splints or braces, which was the common practice of the day. The Sister Kenny Institute at 1800 Chicago Avenue in Minneapolis was dedicated on December 17, 1942.

The national medical community pointed with great pride to its successes during the 1940s. Because of advances in diagnosis and treatment of disease, and in keeping newborns alive, twelve years had been added to the life expectancy of the average American. Minnesota medical researchers and health care institutions played an important role in the national successes in medicine. Minnesota was building a tradition of excellence in health care that would form the background for the biomedical industry to come.

"YOU SEE WE ARE TIRED . . ."

The United States had been in the war for more than three years when a young soldier stationed in Italy wrote a letter to his family in Montevideo, a town deep in the heart of Minnesota's rich agricultural belt. The young soldier thought longingly of home and hoped that people in the States had not forgotten the men and women who daily engaged in battle.

"You see we are tired," he wrote in his letter. "We are tired of being overseas for 18 months . . . of sleeping on the ground for better than a year . . . of mud and rain and dust and cold . . . We do not know the meaning of furlough or USO, or ice cream and cake, of milk and oranges, of girlfriends and families . . . Of course, if it is necessary or if the risks of war must rest primarily with those who have already toyed with injury and death, we will keep on going with the maximum effort. For we are more than ever for the USA."

The *Montevideo News* published parts of the letter, going on to say that the war touched the neighbors and family members of every soldier and that townspeople must continue to show their loyalty to the cause by buying war bonds. As the editorial pointed out, the farmlands around Montevideo supplied the military with food, and in return Montevideo's farmers had prospered. Farming families bought war bonds to demonstrate their deep-felt patriotism and to support the war effort until victory was won.

Sold nationwide for the first time in May 1941, war bonds not only helped finance the war (costs peaked at 48 percent of the gross national product between 1941 and 1946), but linked the folks at home directly with the action overseas. Every citizen was asked to contribute up to 10 percent of his or her weekly paycheck toward the purchase of bonds.

Minnesotans contributed heavily, even when news reports in 1942 and 1943 were disheartening and victory seemed far away. In 1945 the Minnesota War Finance Committee reported that Minnesota had consistently exceeded all national bond sales quotas. Between July 1, 1941, and December 31, 1945, Minnesotans had purchased more than $824 million in Series E War Savings Bonds, or 109 percent of the national quota.

These troops, photographed in 1943 and stationed in the South Pacific, made new friends by sharing stories of Minnesota. Many Minnesotans saw the world for the first time when they served in World War II. Courtesy, Minneapolis Public Library

Minnesota's commercial banks played an essential role in the financing of World War II. Besides lending to other bond buyers, the banks both handled the large volume of war bond sales and invested heavily in bonds themselves.

The sale of war bonds had a lasting effect on the way Minnesotans conducted their banking business: customers began to demand convenience. The Farmers and Mechanics Savings Bank in Minneapolis was one of the first institutions in the Twin Cities to offer a payroll deduction plan for employees who wanted to purchase bonds. In addition, the bank was open on Monday nights. The payroll deduction plan was so popular that Farmers and Mechanics had more business than it could handle and even stopped taking applications from companies that wished to take part in the plan. In its corporate

Below: This food preparation class display helped Minnesotans get reacquainted with Armour products. Photo by Norton and Peel. Courtesy, Minnesota Historical Society

Facing page: The postwar boom brought prosperity to farmers and businesses alike. These happy farmers won cash prizes for their malting barley. Buyers from Fitger's Brewery in Duluth served on the panel of judges. Courtesy, Fitger's on the Lake

history, Farmers and Mechanics notes that more than half a million bonds were purchased through the payroll deduction department during the war. The bank received a special citation for writing 20 percent of all E bonds sold in Minneapolis.

By buying bonds Minnesotans learned that saving money can pay off in the long run. Saving regularly was a new experience for many workers—during the Depression they did not have much money to save—but peer pressure to sign up for defense bonds helped the idea take hold. Twin Cities Ordnance Plant employees were told by a jubilant management in 1942 that it was the largest plant in the country with 100 percent of its employees signed up for some type of regular contribution to war bonds.

But there was another reason why many people put their money into the 3-percent savings accounts offered by local savings and loan associations—there just was not that

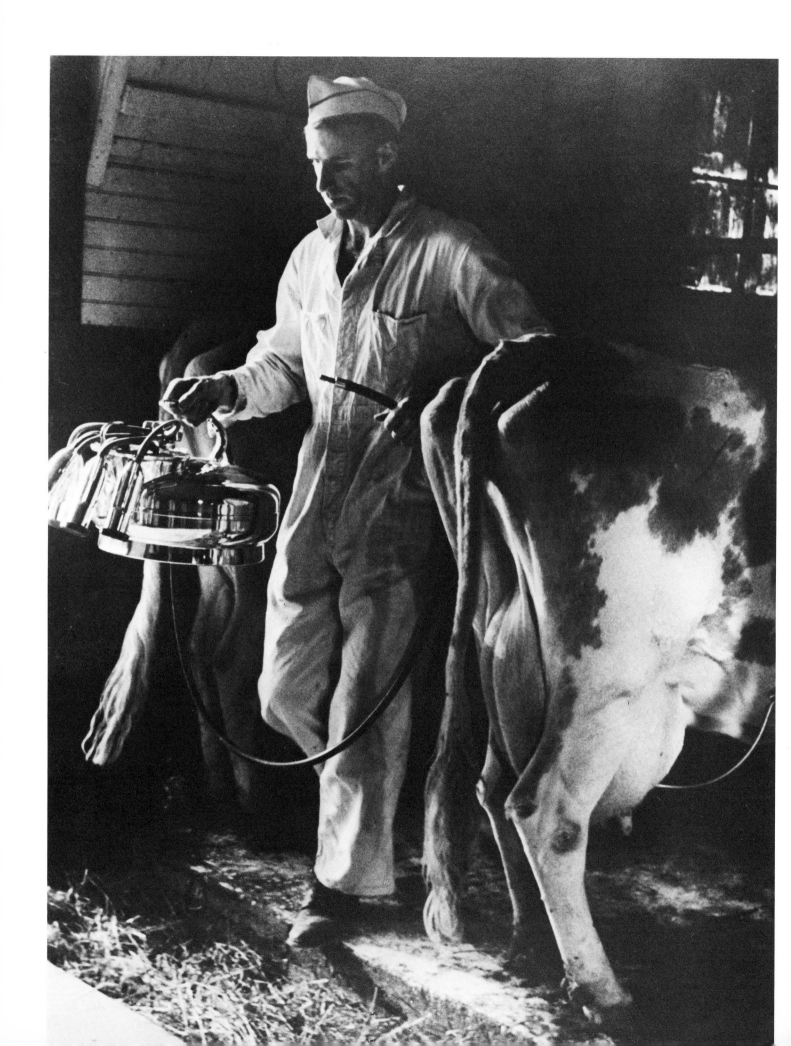

much to buy. New cars were rare, new furniture was often poor in quality, and gasoline rationing limited the traveling that people could do. One Minnesota institution, Twin City Federal Savings and Loan, showed an amazing record of growth during the war years—it more than tripled its savings deposits and doubled its mortgage loans.

Consumer buying habits changed considerably after World War II. When new products came on the market, the public snapped them up. With their checking and savings accounts larger than they had been in years, returning veterans and their families bought cars and appliances, even if it meant putting their names on the dotted lines of credit-package offers.

The major bank corporations in Minnesota felt flush at the end of the war. Banco and its 70-plus affiliated banks across the Upper Midwest (now Norwest Banks) reported that their consolidated deposits had risen from $527 million at the end of 1941 to $1.345 billion at year's end in 1945.

Twin City Federal (TCF) officers were as elated as their counterparts at Norwest. During the 1940s, TCF became, temporarily, the largest federal savings and loan in the United States, growing from a respectable portfolio of $10 million in 1940 to a whopping $200 million in 1950.

Facing page: Dairy farmers praised the advent of electric milking machines, which enabled them to expand their herds. Before rural electrification, few farmers milked more than thirty cows. Courtesy, Minnesota Historical Society

Despite some grumbling from economists who predicted a depression similar to the one that followed World War I, the optimism shown by Norwest Bancorporation, First Banks, and TCF was indicative of the banking industry's overall belief in the growth potential of the Upper Midwest. And the great bank shakeout of the Depression meant that fewer banks were competing for business.

By the end of the decade Minnesota's future looked as happy as a Norman Rockwell illustration. Manufacturing and agriculture were competing for first position in the value of goods produced, and the electronics and plastics industries were coming around the corner. Oil exploration in the Williston Basin in North Dakota had begun, and there was talk on the Iron Range about reclaiming a low-grade iron ore called taconite. Tourism and its attendant business, the recreation industry, sparkled once again after the dark days of gas rationing.

HOMECOMING

Optimism at the end of the war brought weddings, baby announcements, and housewarmings. Along with the burst of technological innovation during and after World War II came shifts in Minnesota's population. In 1940, 30 percent of the state's total population worked on farms; by 1950 only 22 percent of the population farmed. For the first time in Minnesota history, more people lived in urban areas (incorporated towns or cities with populations over 2,500) than in farms and rural villages.

One of the factors in the change was farm mechanization. Farm machinery became more specialized and powerful. Now there were beet lifters, beet loaders, combines, corn pickers, disc harrows, feed grinders, fertilizer spreaders, hay balers, milking machines, and potato diggers. Much of the new equipment was built by Minnesota companies in Minneapolis, St. Paul, Winnebago, Mountain Lake, Glenwood, and Green Isle. With all the diesel-powered muscle available, farmers could do most of the work themselves and had little need for hired hands.

Migrating Minnesotans usually had no trouble finding employment in the cities. Jobs of all kinds were so plentiful that there were often too few applicants for the work available. An article in the *Fairmont Sentinel* on November 14, 1947, announced that jobs were open for individuals with almost any kind of skill: "In fact, there are so many jobs now available for so many varieties of occupations that the employment service has given up trying to keep a full up-to-date list posted on its bulletin board."

Minnesota's urban population was becoming heavily concentrated in three regions: the Twin Cities metropolitan area; the southeast, including Rochester, Austin,

United States Steel's Duluth works enjoyed the two-fold convenience of a nearby supply of iron ore and inexpensive water transportation. Coal came by boat to the Zenith Coal Dock (pictured here) to fire blast furnaces that began production on the eve of World War I. Courtesy, Northeast Minnesota Historical Center

and Winona; and the northeast, including Duluth and the Iron Range cities in St. Louis County. Counties in and around the Twin Cities, such as Anoka, Hennepin, Ramsey, and Washington, experienced the greatest growth.

In Duluth, Minneapolis, and St. Paul—and to a lesser extent, in a few of the smaller towns—new housing communities began to circle the urban cores, frequently in advance of adequate highways, sewers, and good water supplies. Social commentators watched suburban growth with a rueful eye, predicting that America was building pockets of homogeneity that would have a negative effect on the country's spirit.

By the early 1950s the shortage of housing for new postwar families in Minneapolis was forcing them to move to the suburbs south and west of the city, and pressure was put on policymakers to find funds to develop a grid of highways that would make commuting more convenient for those people who lived in the "burbs" and worked downtown. L.P. Pederson, a Hennepin County engineer from 1953 to 1966, remembers trying to convince a busload of legislators that the state should build a highway that would cross the southern section of the Twin Cities, linking the airport with the core of Minneapolis.

As Pederson tells the story, the legislators stepped out of their bus onto a field and tried to imagine a highway that would cross the county from east to west. "Doesn't make much sense to me," one of the legislators noted. "Why would anyone want to spend the taxpayers' money on a highway this far out?"

But in spite of the legislator's attitude, the cities grew and suburbs added suburbs of their own. The first piece of the Crosstown Highway was added to the expanding and increasingly complex highway system in 1967. Today more than 114,000 cars

The Bridgeman-Russell Company established a dairy business in Duluth in 1935 that grew to statewide proportions. Today a person wanting lunch or an ice cream treat in any substantial town looks for the Bridgeman's soda fountain and restaurant. Courtesy, Northeast Minnesota Historical Center

Above: *Two Naval veterans put their technical skill to work in civilian life as they search for a drowned boy in Minneapolis in 1947. Courtesy, Minneapolis Public Library*

Facing page: *After World War II, suburban growth quickly filled the farm fields surrounding Minneapolis and St. Paul. The John Tierney Farm in Richfield was photographed in 1954. From the* Minneapolis Star. *Courtesy, Minnesota Historical Society*

squeeze onto the busy highway every day, a testimony to the fact that city growth frequently takes on a life of its own.

As the 1950s dawned like a sunrise on a summer's day, Minnesotans forgot the troubles they had weathered through the Depression and the war years and began to taste the good life. According to the corporate history of Northern States Power, electrical and gas consumption set all-time records in 1950. That same year NSP added 20,000 new customers—all those new homes and families!—who eagerly plugged in television sets, electric ranges, and phonographs as the costs of electricity continued to decrease.

In the first year of the new decade, living-room stars Ed Sullivan and Arthur Godfrey teamed up to tell the country that color television was right around the corner. People moved out of their kitchens and dining rooms and ate on TV trays. The mood was up—America was strong. In the heart of the country, Minnesotans looked ahead, not behind, and took the job of building progress seriously.

Minnesota celebrated its statehood centennial in 1958 in appropriate form by fitting out a train to carry the celebration throughout the state. Courtesy, Minneapolis Public Library

MINNESOTA MEETS THE WORLD

He had been vice president of the United States for seven months when he returned to Minnesota to speak at the 1965 commencement ceremony at St. Olaf College. Under a brilliant early-summer sky, Hubert Horatio Humphrey leaned into the microphone and reminded the graduates that technology wasn't the only answer to the world's problems. "We must recognize technology's effect on society and insure that it continues to serve us, and not itself," he noted. "There is only one certain way we can achieve this," he said soberly. "It is through education . . ."

The vice president's speech was reported faithfully, without editorial comment, on the front page of the *Northfield News.* But few people paid much attention to his words. For nearly two decades, technological advances had put spirit back into a country that was worn out from war. For a young country on the move, technology was exciting.

Technology brought color television, contact lenses, Sputnik 1, copy machines, aerosol cans, stereo record systems, lasers, and satellite communications. Technology was a computer built at the University of Pennsylvania that could complete 5,000 additions every second; when it was operating, it dimmed the lights of the surrounding city. Clearly, technology was the power of the future. Even as the vice president convinced those St. Olaf graduates of the validity of his message, he was too late. Technology was already in charge of America's destiny.

A new era of space exploration was created when, in 1961, Russian cosmonaut Yuri Gagarin was launched into space aboard a tiny capsule only seven and a half feet wide. When he lived to talk about how it felt to leave earth's gravity, the new era was christened the Space Age.

Far away from the nation's major space centers, Minnesota technology played an essential role in early space experiments. In cooperation with the National Aeronautics and Space Administration (NASA), the G.T. Schjeldahl Company, of Northfield, built a massive communications balloon, 135 feet in diameter and approximately thirteen stories high, that would inflate in space. Launched just a year and a half before Humphrey gave his talk on technology, only blocks from the Schjeldahl plant, the "Satelloon" was called ECHO II, and it would circle the earth—from pole to pole— in a little over two hours, deflecting communications signals as it moved. Four years earlier, ECHO I, also made of Schjeldahl "superpressure" fabrics and Schjeldahl know-how, had captured the imagination of millions as it circled the earth, transmitting radio signals from one part of the globe to the other. By the time the highly sophisticated ECHO II inflated in space in 1964, its older and more primitive sister had traveled nearly 500 million miles and was reportedly beginning to show wear and tear.

Founded in 1955, the Schjeldahl Company would be involved in twenty satellite programs through the decade. But Gilmore Schjeldahl ("Shelly"), founder of the company, used the materials and processes he invented for the space program to build more profitable products as well. Schjeldahl technology made the dome popular—especially as the public got wind of a "Schel-Dome" at Lutsen Resort on Lake Superior, where winter guests could bask by a covered pool as if it were the middle of summer. Schjeldahl technology also created less glamorous products such as packaging machinery.

At the annual meeting of the Packaging Machinery Manufacturers Institute in Gaylord, Michigan, soon after ECHO's launch in 1960, Shelly was asked to talk about his firm's role in building ECHO I. "The ECHO I Satelloon is a good example of packaging," he quipped. "We are the first country in the world to package gas in space."

Whether in preparation for the exploration of outer space or in readiness for an information age that was right around the corner, Minnesota's industrial base swelled with growth possibilities in the first two decades after the end of World War II. Minnesota's adaptable labor pool was heady with new job opportunities as technically oriented companies popped up all over the state. Between 1956 and 1961, the number of new-tech companies increased from 86 to 140, employing more than 40,000 people and commanding $720 million in annual sales. Prompted by an entrepreneurial spirit and available venture capital, companies in Minnesota began manufacturing data processing and mass memory systems, tape recorders, hearing aids, heat-regulation equipment, electronic circuits, sound and video recording tapes, military components, and the prototypes of implantable medical devices.

Surrounded by young upstart companies at home, the father of Minnesota's electronic industry, Minneapolis Honeywell—now, simply, Honeywell, Inc.—ranked 129th among Fortune magazine's listing of the 500 largest industrial companies in the United States. In 1958, Honeywell reported sales of $329.5 million—a long way from the $6.6 billion it reported in revenues in 1985—having increased its sales by almost 2,000 percent between 1939 and 1959. In 1958, with 14,000 employees and an annual payroll of approximately $70 million, Honeywell was the state's largest private employer.

The key to Honeywell's growth was diversification and sophisticated responsiveness to the changing demands of the world. Founded in 1885 to manufacture heat regulator controls, Honeywell created missile guidance systems, instruments, controls, and other components for the military after World War II. By 1959, 25 percent of the company's sales were to the military. At the same time, however, Honeywell was able to maintain its dominant position in electrical controls for residential and industrial heating and cooling systems.

Another company that clearly understood the need for diversification in those years was General Mills. By the end of the 1950s, General Mills was the country's largest flour miller and the 75th largest corporation in the United States. Fifteen percent of General Mills' employees worked for the Mechanical Division, producing navigation and guidance systems, instrument and testing equipment, digital computers, and nuclear equipment engineering. Further, General Mills supported considerable research in optics and meteorology, including high-altitude balloon research. In 1947, General Mills launched one of the first unmanned balloon systems to collect informa-

tion about the earth's atmosphere. Called Project Skyhook, it was launched at St. Cloud carrying a payload of sixty-three pounds; it soared more than 100,000 feet before it landed at Eau Claire, Wisconsin.

St. Paul's claim to corporate fame, 3M (formerly called Minnesota Mining and Manufacturing) ranked 106th in the *Fortune* magazine list of the 500 largest companies in the U.S. In 1959 its electrical products division reported $65 million in revenues. But the company was also gaining international attention for its Thermo-Fax-brand copiers—the world's first dry copiers—and its Scotch-brand tapes. 3M variations of its original "Scotchlite" tapes of the 1940s were used by the electronics industry in the memory units of giant data-processing systems, and by the music industry in recording equipment.

In 1959 the nation's agricultural machinery industry was producing equipment that could harvest grain and can crops quickly and efficiently. Courtesy, LeSueur Museum

In Minnesota, the young computer industry was energized by the appearance of new and tiny companies that would focus on one solution to one problem, and learn how to do it better than anyone else. Frequently these little companies had inexperienced management, unable to withstand the pressures of growth. Often they failed when their product was placed on the market; or they were eaten up by larger, better-managed corporations. Such was the case of Engineering Research Associates, which produced the country's first feasible memory storage system; it was soon acquired by Sperry-Rand (now known as Unisys).

In the late 1950s, Control Data Corporation was considered one of the more promising faces on the computer industry block. Having begun in 1957 with twelve employees, Control Data rapidly strengthened its computer and digital systems operations until, in 1961, it proudly reported having more than 1,250 employees. But as rapid as Control Data's growth was in the first few years of its life, its management was able to nimbly guide it through its entrepreneurial stages without stumbling. One of the reasons for the company's success was its ability to keep one step ahead of its markets, and it concentrated on producing products for the industries its management understood best.

By the late 1950s more than 25,000 Twin Citians were working in technology-related fields, receiving an annual payroll of $120 million and helping to attract sales of more than $400 million. Lured by the profitability of the industry and the optimistic mood of the state's economists, high-spirited entrepreneurs formed and fostered new ventures by the dozens. In March 1959, *The Minneapolis Star* surveyed the metropolitan area to find out just how many new electronics companies were doing business in the area. The newspaper discovered forty-seven new firms employing nearly 4,000 people—many of whom were engineers. Annual gross sales figures for the forty-seven little companies was $50,500,000. Small electronics firms in the Twin Cities at the time included the American Electronics Company in Minneapolis, which manufactured relays, transformers, and switches; Audio Development, which built miniaturized transformers; and Research, Incorporated, which engaged in specialized research in aerodynamics, heat transfer, instrument development, and electronic component production.

Outside of the metropolitan area, even deep in the heart of Minnesota's hunting and fishing centers, other Minnesota electronics firms flourished. A notable example is the E.F. Johnson Company in Waseca, which in the early 1960s was one of the world's largest manufacturers of amateur radio transmitters as well as electronic components and ultra-miniature capacitors for printed circuit equipment. Founded with $1,500 in capital as a mail-order house for ham radio operators in 1923, E.F. Johnson realized its first great surge of growth in 1950, when amateur radio transmitters became popular. In 1961, E.F. Johnson consolidated its operations from several plant locations to a facility costing well over $1 million to build.

Red Wing was the home of Central Research Laboratories, a small company that built laboratory research apparatus and instruments, to be shipped throughout the world. In Mankato, another company that exported many of its products was AEMCO, Inc., which built time switches and controls. Dow-Key Co., Inc., producer of electronic and mechanical coaxial connectors, was located in Thief River Falls. In the middle of Minnesota beer country was the John Oster Manufacturing Company, near New Ulm, which built small motors for use in aircraft. In Rochester, the Waters Corporation built electro-medical instruments.

In the late 1950s rural Minnesota also attracted out-of-state corporations looking for new places to build their production facilities. IBM (then called International Business Machines Corporation) was one such corporation. IBM selected Rochester as the site for its $25 million data-processing plant, and hired close to 2,500 employees. In 1961, T.J. Watson, Jr., then president of IBM, responded to a survey of the quality of business conditions in Minnesota (the survey was conducted by Northern States

Facing page: *A Green Giant research lab and greenhouse were photographed about 1960. The Minnesota Valley Canning Company took its Green Giant brand name from a hybrid pea developed in its own laboratory. The company's commitment to research and development generated the "Heat Unit Theory," which enabled it to pinpoint a "fleeting moment of perfect flavor" and harvest three-quarters of the crop as "fancy" grade. Courtesy, LeSueur Museum*

Power Company, First National Bank of Minneapolis, and Northwestern National Bank of Minneapolis):

> From the time our survey team first arrived in Rochester, we have been given the very finest kind of cooperation and assistance in establishing ourselves there. Local and state governmental officials, as well as business leaders and civic groups, have gone out of their way to make us feel welcome and have helped us in many different ways.
>
> We have been impressed with the progressive attitude and the interest and belief in American business which are characteristic of the people of Minnesota, and are delighted to have so many Minnesotans joining our organization.

JUDGED BY THE COMPANIES WE KEEP

By the middle 1950s more than 3 million people made Minnesota home, and a third of those Minnesotans lived in the three major metropolitan centers of Minneapolis, St. Paul, and Duluth. In 1956 Governor Orville Freeman publicly announced that the labor pool of the state had become one of Minnesota's greatest resources. What Minnesota needed to bolster the economy was enough new industry to keep taxpayers from leaving the state in search of better jobs. In an open marketing letter to the industrial captains of the country, Freeman noted that "Minnesota firmly believes we are judged by the companies we keep. We are proud of those we have, and we are doing our best to increase their number." Freeman added that state policymakers were planning to create legislation to make it more profitable to build a business in Minnesota. But what did he have right away that was better than any other state? People, the governor reminded his readers—a labor pool that was "skilled of hand, steady of mind, and intensely ambitious," displaying the "rugged individualism, the high productivity, and the stability of their forebears."

Additionally, Minnesota had 44 percent fewer labor stoppages than the national average. Minnesotans were well trained for industrial jobs, said the governor. Nearly one-third of the government dollars that were spent for vocational education were applied to trade and industrial skills. And the entrepreneurial spirit was alive and well in Minnesota. People liked to tackle new ideas—in their garages during the long, cold winter months, and in their basements while they escaped August's heat and humidity. Out of those garages and basements in the early 1960s came prototypes of new products that would begin to change the way people lived their lives.

The early 1960s was a creative time for business development, and venture capitalist noses twitched with new business expectations. It was also an optimistic time for new businesses. For the first time in the state's history, manufacturing revenues exceeded the state's agricultural receipts by more than $400 million.

In no Minnesota industry was creative genius quite so busy as in biomedical research. A cousin to industrial electronics, the biomedical business thrived on the unlikely combination of medicine and engineering. Creative sparks flew when physicians and engineers sat across the table from each other. And some of those sparks lit fires that energized a number of Minnesota's major industries.

Earl Bakken, founder of Medtronic, Inc., today one of the country's leading medical electronics companies, was a young electrical engineer in 1949 when he quit his job to form a medical equipment repair company with his brother-in-law, Palmer Hermundslie. In their 600-square-foot garage they built their servicing business and talked to researchers from medical equipment manufacturers who had ideas about better medical products but didn't know how to build them. In the mid-1950s, a leading pediatric cardiologist at the University of Minnesota, Dr. C. Walton Lillehei, approached young Bakken about designing a battery-powered pulse generator that would

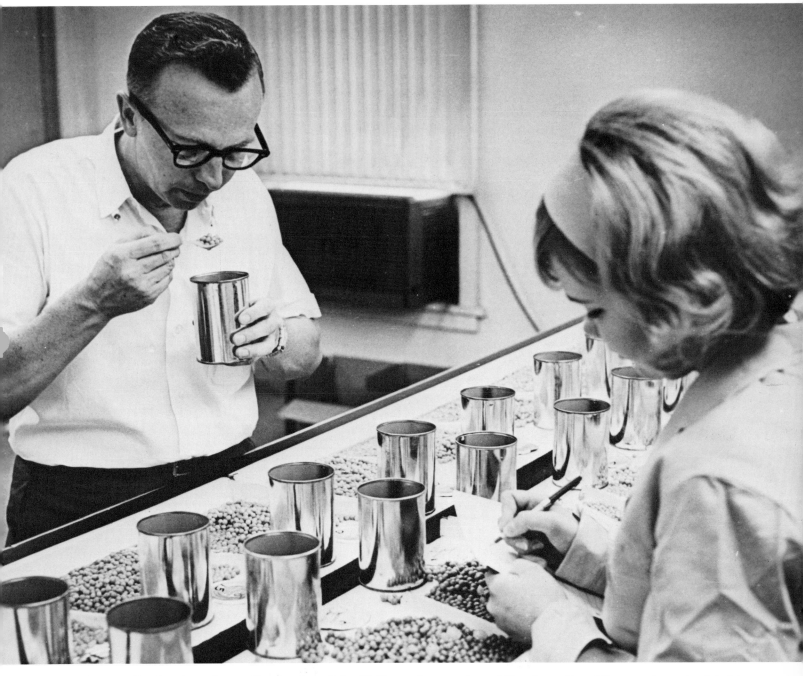

help pace abnormally slow heartbeats. By the time John F. Kennedy was elected President, Medtronic had outgrown its little garage and, with twenty-five employees, was refining the world's first implantable cardiac pacemaker. Over the next twenty-five years, more than one million Medtronic cardiac pacemakers would be in use by people around the world.

As the biomedical engineering industry gathered steam, there seemed to be no end to what the Minnesotan entrepreneurial mind could dream up. In Atlantic City, a tiny St. Paul company, Electronic Medical Systems, thrilled the 1961 American Hospital Association conventioneers with a prototype of a portable electronic device that could transmit electrocardiogram (EKG) information over the telephone. This was a breakthrough for rural hospitals, which had been sending EKG tests through the mail for analysis by cardiologists: the telephone transmission system could provide EKG evaluations for patients in four minutes instead of four days.

That same year a seminar in medical electronics was held for the medical staff of Minneapolis General Hospital by Whitehall Electronics and Epsco Medical—both

Even Minnesota ingenuity failed to find a machine that could match a person's ability to taste peas. Minnesota Valley Canning Company moved into the modern era of advertising in 1950 by changing its name to Green Giant. Now part of Pillsbury, Green Giant's quality control is still done by people. Courtesy, LeSueur Museum

181

small start-up companies in the Twin Cities. Whitehall demonstrated a patient care monitor that provided continuous and instantaneous readings of a patient's blood pressure, pulse, respiration, and temperature. If an emergency developed, alarms would immediately alert the nursing staff. Epsco showed a blood parameter analyzer that was said to provide a more complete and accurate analysis of important blood factors than had ever before been accomplished. The Bicom, a second breakthrough for Epsco, was capable of transmitting a patient's vital signs to remote locations without any wires.

The E.F. Johnson product line of 1960 was laid out for the camera. The early 1960s brought E.F. Johnson enough business to finance a new plant. The company has survived shifting economic times and remains a leading employer in Waseca in the 1980s. Courtesy, Waseca County Historical Society

Another biomedical engineering entrepreneur, Kenneth H. Dahlberg, helped put Minnesota on the world map as a leader in electronic miniaturization. In 1961, Dahlberg, then president of the Dahlberg Company, a subsidiary of Motorola which manufactured hearing aids, received a letter from the Argentine ambassador to Russia. The ambassador had read about the company's new "Miracle Ear," Dahlberg's dime-sized hearing aid, and wanted to know more about the product. Within weeks, he had ordered one for himself and had recommended them to his friends.

Miniaturization—particularly in the hearing aid industry—was highly competitive during the late 1950s and early 1960s. Eight Minnesota companies, including the Dahlberg Company, were developing and manufacturing tiny hearing product components for customers who wanted less cumbersome, easier to wear devices which played down the appearance of their hearing losses. Telex, a St. Paul-based company founded by Allen Hempel (inventor of the first wearable vacuum tube hearing aid) was a leader in miniaturized acoustical equipment, grossing $2.5 million in revenues during 1957.

Maico Electronics, Inc., a Minneapolis company, also manufactured miniaturized hearing aids and audiometers as well as electronic stethoscopes. The company showed $4 million in revenues for 1957.

As electronics became more sophisticated during the 1960s, and industries steadily discovered new uses for electronic technology, miniaturization became an art as well as a science. Miniature Instruments Corporation, a rapidly growing company in New Hope, was a high-volume manufacturer of miniature parts such as precision gears, shafts, pins, cams, and adaptors for computers and navigational equipment. In January 1961 the little company moved into a futuristic new plant at the Minnesota Science Industry Center in New Hope. An interesting feature of the plant was its white asphalt tile floors, which made it easier to find small parts when they were dropped.

But as the management of little start-up companies such as Miniature Instruments Corporation began to look around, they had questions about the state which had nurtured them. Many business decision-makers voiced concerns about high state taxes and unemployment compensation, workers' compensation abuses, and state policy leaders who didn't seem to care much about fostering business growth. Could business succeed and grow in Minnesota? It was a question that would persist through the decades to come.

Waiting for "George Somebody Else"

It was in 1954 that the Minnesota Democratic-Farmer-Labor party (DFL) overturned Minnesota's Republican administration for the first time in sixteen years by reelecting Senator Hubert Humphrey and electing Orville Freeman as the state's first DFL governor. The Democratic-Farmer-Labor party—made up mostly of urban Democrats and rural members of the Farmer-Labor party—was forged in the rhetorical fires of then 33-year-old Hubert Humphrey in 1944. In the 1954 election the DFL won most of the state's constitutional offices and it helped elect a liberal majority in the Minnesota House of Representatives. Labor groups, such as the Minnesota State Federation of Labor and the Minnesota State CIO Council, focused public attention on the need to change workmen's and unemployment compensation on behalf of workers, and to create better pension programs for union members. The continuing strength of labor accompanied by statewide discontent among the state's farmers resulted in Freeman's 1958 reelection and the election in that same year of a newcomer to the U.S. Senate—Eugene J. McCarthy.

Two years later, while business leaders all over the state grappled with a number of important issues, Minnesota Chamber of Commerce executives commissioned a study to determine whether the state was doing its best for the businesses that brought its people jobs. Released early in 1961, the study spoke of the "business climate" instead of the job environment. The members of the task force who spearheaded the report were careful to define their terms: ". . . simply defined, business climate is the net result of all outside conditions affecting the cost and manner of operating a business for the good of all concerned in our community. It's the ability of any firm to cover its costs:— meet its competition:—and still be able to operate at a profit."

In the true spirit of public relations, the business climate study was kicked off in St. Paul by a late-summer rally in 1960 in which the officials of forty-four Minnesota towns and cities and more than 600 business leaders were asked to take part. During the fall of that year, surveys were conducted throughout the state, asking business owners as well as chief officers of large corporations to rate the state in terms of its tax levies on businesses, its attitude toward labor, and its ability to create policy that would make expansion within the state possible, even appealing.

On the plus side, the results of the study reaffirmed that Minnesota was unusually abundant in its natural assets, such as iron deposits and rich agricultural lands; in its human assets and its skilled labor supply; and in its created assets, including 8,221 miles of railroads, 8,788 miles of state trunk highways, a waterway to the Gulf of Mexico, and a seaway through the Great Lakes to the Atlantic Ocean.

Business leaders in 1960 generally seemed to feel that labor relations within local plants were good and that employees and management were "getting along well." In fact, 45 percent of the business people polled said that labor relations within their plants were excellent, very good or good; only 2 percent said that labor and management had poor working communication. The tone of business's response to the question was guarded, however. Just two years before, steel mills on the Iron Range had been seriously affected by a strike that lasted more than 100 days. And at the Wilson Company, a meat-packing plant in Albert Lea, a bloody strike had been followed by a cavalcade of 6,000 union members from all over Minnesota who marched into Albert Lea with $50,000 in cash contributions and food donations for the strikers and their families. Still, business people felt that, overall, labor relations were good.

On the other hand, among the state's business debits were high personal property and inventory taxes (80 percent of those polled in 1960 complained that such taxes were too high); a state tax system that cried out for reform; and the growing political power of labor unions. (The study noted that "union activity in Minnesota politics has reached a point of serious concern," particularly in regard to unemployment and workers' compensation rulings.) As a result of labor's political influence, many business leaders felt that labor costs were becoming noncompetitive with surrounding states, and steel-plant management pointed to the cheaper costs of labor overseas, noting that Minnesota labor expenses had grown out of proportion.

Adding up all the problems, 30 percent of the business leaders polled said that they would expand their operations outside the state's borders. Of those companies that were expecting to expand within the state, most were firms with fewer than 100 employees. Noted the report: "This is something for every serious-minded citizen to contemplate."

The report noted also that 32 percent of those business people surveyed rated Minnesota's overall business reputation as poor, and it reminded its readers that the state could not afford to have a negative image when other states were on the lookout for ways to entice Minnesota companies to relocate.

"What had gone wrong?" the committee asked. "We have been leaving it up to 'George Somebody Else' and he has not been doing a very good job," the writers said. But it was the job of every citizen in Minnesota to think positively and to work hard for the state: "Jobs don't happen automatically! . . . every citizen should also be a salesman for Minnesota . . ." Concluded the report: "If we wait for 'Somebody Else' to do it, it will never get done."

But while business leaders were conducting this self-examination, labor was continuing to gain political savvy and influence across the state. It found willing ears in many of the top political leaders, who equated labor's voice with the voice of the people. While studies of the day showed that the approximately 375,000 union members in the state represented only 30 percent of the non-agricultural work force, to an outside observer the cities of St. Paul, St. Cloud, and Duluth appeared to be fortresses for an unbeatable labor army.

There was one thing that both labor and business did agree on: it was that labor had the power to upset the status quo through strikes and work actions. Sometimes the strikes were devastating, leaving a residue of bitterness behind. On April 12, 1962, for example, a strike was called by the fleet drivers' union of the *Minneapolis Tribune*. The next day, picketers were joined by members of the mailers' and typographical unions, and several other unions made it known that their members would refuse to cross the picket line. For the first time in nearly a century, the editorial voices of the newspaper were stilled. Production was shut down for 116 days. While the negotiators shuttled from one side of the bargaining table to the other, some news was carried over

Facing page: *Brown Printing pressmen posed with pride in front of their new roller press in about 1960. Brown Printing in Waseca grew rapidly on the wave of postwar prosperity as printers of magazines, fliers, and catalogues. Courtesy, Waseca County Historical Society*

local television stations. But before the presses began again on August 7, employees had lost more than $3 million in wages and 13,000 carriers and other distributors had missed out on $1.4 million in earnings.

The action of the fleet drivers had other far-reaching consequences. Not only were the *Tribune*'s circulation and advertising revenues damaged, but business activity throughout the Upper Midwest deteriorated. It was several months before the public's confidence in the newspaper was restored.

THE BITTER IRON PILL

Medtronic's pacemakers helped young patients as well as old. The University of Minnesota Medical School also benefited from the opportunity to pilot the new equipment. Courtesy, Medtronics, Inc.

Although labor boldly squared off against its opponents on the issues of wages, benefits, automation, and workers' compensation, it had an Achilles' heel. Up north on the Range, where the mining industry had once pumped high employment and dollars into the communities through its 400 mines, jobs and family security were now in question.

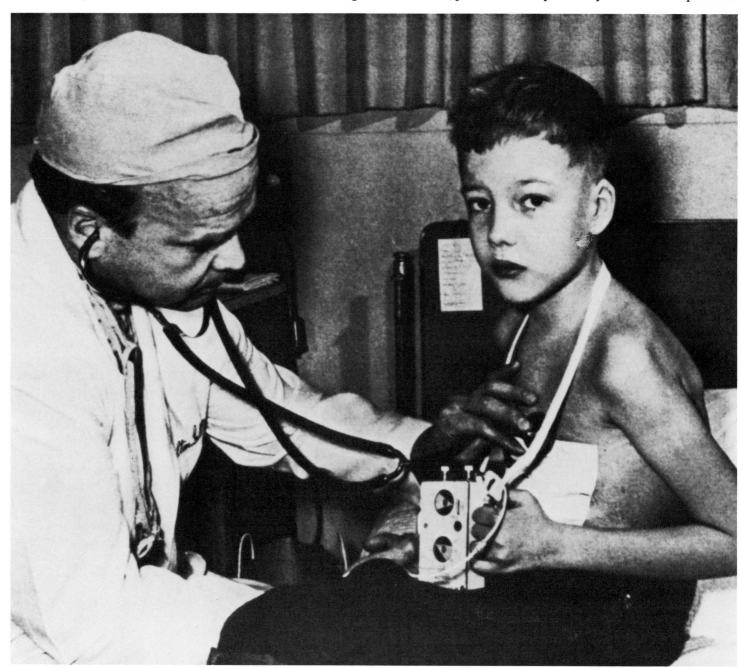

Between 1956 and 1966, 211 iron mines were shut down because they had exhausted their high-grade, economical-to-mine ores. Worse, mines in countries such as Canada and Venezuela were able to ship high-grade iron ore to the United States at competitive prices. Between 1950 and 1960 iron ore imports nearly quintupled. Mining management up on the Range knew that they would have to keep a tight grip on the prices of their ore if they were to compete in an international marketplace. For many, taconite seemed to be the best answer; taconite mining would bring the Mesabi Range back to health.

The taconite issue was hot up on the Range—as well as in the hallways of the Capitol—through the 1950s and 1960s. Taconite is a hard, fine-grained gray rock containing between 15 to 30 percent iron—a low-grade ore. Identified in the 1870s, taconite was studied in 1911 at the University of Minnesota's newly organized Mines Experiment Station and was considered a potential replacement when the high-grade ore played out. With state research funds, the problems of how to crush the rock were overcome. In 1951, the Reserve Mining Company and the Erie Mining Company announced plans to build a commercial taconite industry. High labor and production costs seemed the only remaining obstacles.

Optimism soared throughout the state. Not only was Reserve Mining Company building an open-pit mine that would produce more than 11 million tons of taconite a year, it would also build a primary crushing plant at Babbitt and a private railroad to transport the taconite across Minnesota to the shore of Lake Superior at Beaver Bay. The company was predicting that it would also build two new towns for about 5,000 people each, and each town would have the very latest in "modern homes, schools, medical facilities, sewage disposal plants, water supply systems, paved streets, recreation centers . . . stores and other modern conveniences."

People of the north country who could still recall the glory days of the early mining and timber industries in Minnesota began to hope that their families would soon see prosperity as they had never seen it before. By the early 1960s two commercial taconite plants and one pilot plant were in operation. Public policymakers—who were counting votes—searched for ways to help the iron mining companies further invest in Minnesota's labor pool.

Members of the legislature next turned to the taxes that had traditionally been imposed on mining companies. An old provision in the state's lawbooks had provided for a form of double taxation on iron mining companies and the ore they produced, and it was the legislature's idea to make certain that taconite (and other specified minerals, including copper and nickel) was not being taxed more heavily than other industries were.

Liberals in the state house had a difficult time deciding which way to bend: if they leaned to the right (no double taxation of mining companies), they would be conceding to the demands of big business; if they shifted left, they could use the extra tax revenues to help stimulate investments in the north that could change the course of the Range's economic future. Meanwhile, conservatives pointed out that iron mining taxes virtually supported the northern communities. In 1960, for example, mining companies paid 99.8 percent of the total taxes levied in the towns of Franklin and Fraser, 95 percent of the taxes in Coleraine and Taconite, and 64 percent in Hibbing. Mining company officials noted that they were reluctant to invest the large sums necessary to build and operate the plants in Minnesota because they expected that the state's policymakers would do to the taconite industry what they had once done to the owners of high-grade ore—legislate high taxes which would hurt potential profits.

In an uncomfortable coalition, both major political parties threw their weight behind the iron mining industry of Minnesota. The vote was eventually put to the people in the form of a "Taconite Amendment," which was intended to stabilize the taconite tax policy for twenty-five years and, it was hoped, invite new investments and expansion in the industry. But Governor Karl Rolvaag worried that public apathy would result in a "no" vote on the amendment, and he appointed Dr. Charles Mayo, chairman of the University of Minnesota's Board of Regents, to form a bipartisan publicity committee. The sole purpose of the committee was to ensure that the public understood how critical the Taconite Amendment was to the health of the state. On the publicity committee were an array of political stars, including former Governor Elmer L. Andersen, Lieutenant Governor A.M. "Sandy" Keith, and Attorney General Walter F. Mondale.

In subsequent months, more than 600 major state organizations rallied to support the amendment. Minnesota had never seen such publicity for an economic issue. Bumper stickers as well as television and radio announcements urged the public to vote "yes." Special taconite stamps were issued to help raise dollars as well as awareness.

But the media move of the year was still to come. In the middle of the campaign, the Ford Motor Company and the Ogelbay-Norton Company (a mine management company) announced that they would jointly begin the development of a taconite plant at the little village of Forbes; the company they would create to operate it would be called the Eveleth Taconite Company. The two parent companies were going to begin work on the plant, they said, because management was convinced that voters would go for the Taconite Amendment.

In their voting booths the public remembered to say yes to taconite by a whopping seven-to-one victory. Within days, the iron mining industry returned the favor. U.S. Steel agreed to spend $100 million on a taconite plant at Mountain Iron, and the Hanna Mining Company announced that it would build two plants, one at Nashwauk and another at Keewatin. Further, Erie Mining Company and Reserve Mining Company—the two original taconite players—said they would each expand their operations to the tune of another $80 million. Taconite shipments increased from 38.9 percent of the total ore shipped in 1964 to nearly 60 percent five years later. By 1970 more than $1 billion had been invested in the taconite industry. In the last five years of the 1960s, direct benefits to the state in the form of wages, supply and utility revenues, royalties and taxes amounted to between $125 and $150 million annually.

With the passage of the Taconite Amendment, the employment future looked good and both business and labor leaders were pleased with a job well done. In St. Louis and Lake counties, mining employment increased substantially, further linking the economy of the area to the fortunes of the mining industry. New secondary industries sprang up. A liquid oxygen plant at Babbitt built by Union Carbide Corporation, an American Brake Shoe steel casting plant at Two Harbors, a grinding ball production firm at Hibbing, and blasting agent plants belonging to Dow Chemical and Spencer Chemical at Biwabik were examples of second-string production that benefited from taconite production successes. As iron and taconite mining pumped dollars into the state's economy, leaders reveled in the thought that Minnesota had the capacity to produce 64 percent of the total national iron ore and taconite output.

But these heady days didn't last. Looming ahead were economic and environmental questions that would have to be resolved in order for Minnesota to maintain its hard-fought leadership in national taconite production. In a 1970 speech given to the Minnesota Commission on Taxation and Production of Iron Ore and Other Minerals by J. Kimball Whitney, then Commissioner of the Minnesota Department of Economic Development, the audience was reminded that another $1 billion needed to be invested in plants and expansions in order for the industry to reach a production capacity of nearly 62 million tons annually.

Additionally, there was some question about how much the taconite industry was actually able to increase employment on the Range. Metal mining employment reached a peak in 1957, when taconite-related jobs represented only 19 percent of the total number of mining jobs. In the years between 1958 and 1970, however, taconite employment rose threefold while metal mining jobs as a whole fell by nearly 28 percent. By 1975, of the 15,000 workers employed in metal mining, approximately 13,250 worked in taconite production. According to Commissioner Whitney, "... it is difficult to see

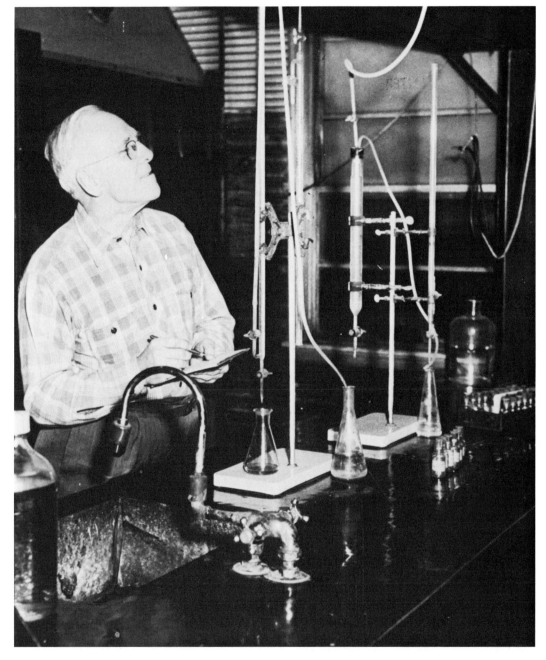

University of Minnesota engineer E.W. Davis worked for twenty years to find a way to process the hard Mesabi taconite into usable form. Davis found a solution just in time to keep the iron industry from collapsing after World War II. Courtesy, Iron Range Research Center, LTV Steel Collection

whether, in net, taconite development will be able to offset fully the decline in total metal mining employment resulting from the loss of direct shipping ores."

Increased competition from both domestic and foreign ore producers was another gremlin for the state in the early 1970s. Costs and quality were scrutinized by the steel companies and the wolf was always at the door as steel imports rose dramatically through the 1960s. In 1965 and 1968, for example, imports rose 61 percent and 57 percent respectively.

Closer to home, the public began to wonder if they had made such a wise decision in boosting the taconite industry. Minnesotans have long been proud of the crystal-clear quality of their lakes, and when Reserve Mining requested permission to draw water from Lake Superior for taconite processing, citizens grew concerned. They grew even more concerned when they learned that Reserve's Silver Bay plant was returning the processing water to the lake along with waste particles (tailings) created during taconite production. The lake around the Silver Bay plant turned a strange color—proof enough to most people that the tailings were polluting the water. In 1971 the federal government, as well as Minnesota and other states, sued Reserve Mining.

The public became frightened when scientists discovered that the tiny asbestos fibers contained in the tailings could be linked to cancer. Even more alarming was the discovery that the tailings had found their way into the Duluth water supply. After a hotly contested legal battle, Reserve was finally ordered to find an on-land waste disposal site. With the increased costs of converting to land disposal, Reserve Mining was caught in a bind, and it was a situation that would become very familiar through the next decade: how to balance the cost of doing business with the demands of conserving a very precious environment.

WHERE THE PRAIRIE MEETS THE SEA

Murmurs of disbelief could be heard as the speaker made his point, and he stopped for a moment to let his words sink in. Four hundred Minnesota businesspeople shook their heads and sat back waiting to be convinced. Handpicked personally by Governor Orville Freeman to attend a 1959 conference on the problems and potential of the Duluth area, these business leaders weren't in the mood for fantasy.

On the platform was Alex Freeman, a Canadian investor who was audacious enough to announce that the city of Duluth would make an economic comeback. Not only that, he said solemnly, he and his backers believed that, with a little help from sound business investment, Duluth's population would double by 1970. No one in the room held much hope that the north country would ever again have the commercial success it had enjoyed decades before in the glory days of the logging and mining industries. Yet the Canadian investor was pledging $100 million for development of the Duluth port area. His investment decision was based on the potential of the little city—a potential that could be realized in the form of the St. Lawrence Seaway.

As Freeman continued his presentation, members of the audience listened attentively as he talked about the profitability and timing of the venture. The St. Lawrence Seaway, a project that had been under construction since 1955, could bring Minnesota into competition with seaboard states. No doubt it would change the economic outlook for the Midwest, and it would add another critical resource to the state's business environment—inexpensive transportation for exporting the raw materials of the country's midsection.

The St. Lawrence Seaway project was the brainstorm of the Canadian government in the early 1950s. The Canadian government wanted to provide passage for large oceangoing vessels through the Great Lakes and to build major hydroelectric plants that would supply power to Canada's growing cities. Technically, the St. Lawrence Seaway is a 200-mile stretch of the St. Lawrence River between Lake Ontario and Montreal which, when developed, would lead to the opening of the entire 2,300 miles of the Great Lakes-St. Lawrence River waterway. By 1953 President Eisenhower had seen the wisdom of the plan and had elbowed the United States government into the action. Construction of the Seaway and power project began in 1955, and when the Seaway opened four years and $471 million later it included three major dams, seven new locks, and a number of canals. Additionally, the United States government spent another $65 million dredging major Great Lakes harbors to make them navigable for oceangoing ships. As a result of the Seaway project, major cities in the United States and Canada—Buffalo, Cleveland, Toledo, Detroit, Chicago, Milwaukee, Montreal, Duluth, Toronto—would be turned into seaports.

Back in Duluth, city planners, under the leadership of port Director Robert T. Smith, knew that the day of the Seaway was inching closer and that opportunity was about to come knocking at Minnesota's back door. Rallying business interest wherever they could, Smith and his co-workers created business confidence in the port and attracted significant investments in it. And they are credited with creating one of the

Facing page: *Inside a taconite plant the hard rock is crushed and ground and the iron is extracted with magnets, formed into pellets the size of marbles, and hardened with heat. The resulting taconite pellets contain twice the iron of the original rock. Courtesy, Iron Range Research Center, LTV Steel Collection*

best-planned harbors in the world. Designed to withstand heavy traffic, the Duluth harbor facilities included three major berths plus another marginal berth. The berth area was serviced by four railroad tracks, two tower floodlights, heating facilities, and pumps. According to an article in the premier issue of *Duluth Port,* a magazine created by the Seaway Port Authority of Duluth, one of the most spectacular equipment assets of the Duluth seaport of the day was the pair of ninety-ton gantry cranes which, in tandem, had a lift capacity of 180 tons—"the greatest one in the Great Lakes."

Private enterprise quickly responded to the Port Authority's development frenzy. F.H. Peavey and Company, for example, a Minneapolis grain handling company, announced a multimillion-dollar expansion of its harborside facilities so that it could handle the flood of grain expected to move through the port. Following Peavey's lead, twenty-one other grain elevator companies in Duluth and Superior modified their structures to match the projected increased need. At the same time, they formed the Duluth-Superior Grain Terminal and Exporters Association, which would help smaller companies learn the ropes of exporting.

In an all-out effort to prepare for the expected increase in grain exports, the Farmers Union Grain Terminal installed a special dump for unloading trucks carrying 600 to 650 bushels of grain per load. Trucks hauling grain were expected to come from as far away as Montana. At a number of grain elevators, including those owned and operated by General Mills, the Norris Grain Company, Capitol Elevator (a division of International Milling Company), Occident Elevator, and the Cargill Company, elevator loading spouts were raised to accommodate the ships, and grain slips were deepened to help increase each vessel's load.

When the first foreign oceangoing vessel reached the Duluth-Superior harbor on May 3, 1959, unofficially heralding the opening of the St. Lawrence Seaway, the citizens of Duluth kept their fingers crossed that prosperity was just around the corner. Blasting their horns, foreign ships from Britain, Liberia, Norway, Germany, Panama, and Denmark entered the harbor, eager for export grains. In languages that reminded many citizens of their parents and grandparents, sailors bargained for trinkets to carry home to their families thousands of miles away. By July, seventy ships bearing foreign flags had entered the Duluth-Superior harbor to pick up grain for shipment overseas. Skeptics who had not believed that Duluth would ever become a foreign port ate crow as new vessels crowded around the harbor waiting for berths.

The Seaway brought hundreds of new job possibilities to the north country: warehousing and cold storage, dredging, shipbuilding, and dry dock repair, as well as restaurants, cafes, hotels, movie theaters, stores, truck stops, and tourist attractions.

Even before Duluth had its sea legs as a foreign port, scores of trucks and trailer rigs filled with grain pressed their way into town, reminding citizens that the harbor would benefit the more than 15 million people living in the Upper Midwest. Lumbering around the edges of the city, five major railroad systems—the Milwaukee Road, the Chicago and Northwestern, the Great Northern, the Northern Pacific, and the Soo Line—hauled grain, bentonite clay, powdered milk, flour, honey, and farm machinery to the docks for export. Imported goods—including steel, ferrosilicon, wire, machinery, furniture, glass, granite, carpeting, autos, shoes—were hauled by railroad to waiting Midwestern factories and homes. In Minneapolis, Alexandria, and Park Rapids, a father could buy an English bicycle imported direct from the British Isles; camera buffs could snap wildlife photos with German cameras; coffee gourmets could grind beans that only months before had been growing on the mountain slopes of Colombia.

The opening of the Seaway was celebrated in a week-long festival between July 9 and 14, 1959, which was planned to demonstrate the impact the Seaway would have on every Minnesotan. On July 12, the governors from Montana, South Dakota, and Minnesota, and the U.S. Secretary of the Interior, Fred A. Seaton, dedicated the Duluth public marine terminal by pouring water collected from the seven seas of the world into the harbor. In an open-house celebration that lasted throughout the week, Duluth's industries showed off their new operations: the Duluth, Missabe and Iron Range Railway showed visitors how ore boats were loaded; the Northwestern-Hanna Fuel Company allowed guests to watch coal being unloaded from ships; the Soo Line freight house offered guided tours; and at the Nicholson Transit Company and Zalk-Joseph docks, people could see automobiles being lifted onto the docks and grain being loaded.

Along with all the noise, color, and bustle that the Seaway brought to Minnesota, it offered a new perspective on the world. Independent of the key seaboard cities, the state could play an important part in worldwide commerce. In fact, Duluth is 525 miles closer to Rotterdam and 225 miles closer to the Straits of Gibraltar and the Suez Canal

than is New Orleans. The distance through the Seaway between Duluth and Rotterdam is 492 miles less than the distance from Duluth to Rotterdam through New York, a route that formerly required 1,376 miles of more costly overland transportation.

Transportation costs had become a critical factor to shippers, who scrutinized their profitability margins in the fluctuating worldwide commodity market. What attracted many private shippers was the 40 percent savings they could realize by moving grain from Minnesota to the Netherlands through the Seaway. The *Duluth Port* reported that ships could carry wheat from Duluth to Rotterdam for 21.4 cents a bushel if they had return cargoes; the previous lowest charge was 35.3 cents. And there were other important advantages to Great Lakes shipping from Duluth. Because the cargoes were shipped directly overseas, less handling was required, and material packaging did not have to be as elaborate as was necessary when products were transported overland to the seaboard wharves.

Fitger's brewery was one casualty of the move to eliminate industrial discharge into Lake Superior. After nearly 100 years of brewing, Fitger's was closed by the state in 1969. Consumers of Fitger's beer and mixers maintain that the brewery served as a scapegoat when larger companies proved hard to control. Courtesy, Fitger's on the Lake

193

With tracks stretching into the heart of the Plains, bringing in ever-larger volumes of raw materials for export at the Seaway ports, railroad lines lowered their carrying rates. By the summer of 1959, some railroads had slashed their rates by as much as 25 percent.

Between 1959 and 1962, four groups of bulk commodities—agricultural products, bituminous coal, iron ore, and petroleum—constituted 75 percent of the tonnage transported on the Seaway. But grain quickly proved to be the shipper's gold, and the growth of grain shipments from Duluth-Superior directly overseas outstripped the most optimistic predictions. In 1958, one year before the Seaway had been completed, grain shipments from U.S. Great Lakes ports were about 100,000 tons, or 4 percent of the total U.S. grain exports for the year. Four years later, lake ports shipped 5.8 million tons of grain, or 18 percent of all U.S. grain exports.

On the rich farmlands of states within trucking or railroad shipping distance of

Grain traffic through the port of Duluth spurred more than the shipping and storage industries. The city benefited from expanded work opportunities, particularly pasta factories that processed hard North Dakota wheat. Courtesy, Northeast Minnesota Historical Center

the Twin Ports of Duluth-Superior, 75 percent of the country's wheat, 80 percent of the corn, 60 percent of the barley, and nearly 90 percent of the soybeans were harvested. Hard spring wheat from the Dakotas, Montana, and western Minnesota, which was valued for its high protein content, was shipped to the breadmakers of Europe. Durum wheat raised in the Plains States and used to make macaroni and spaghetti was sent overseas, as were corn, oats, rye, barley, and flaxseed for animal feeds and industrial uses. Soybeans were also becoming an essential staple in a number of different foreign industries. Soybeans, it had been discovered, could be used in making plastics, calking compounds, candles, paints, inks, mayonnaise, margarine, animal feeds, cosmetics, medical preparations, and even as a component in anti-knock gasolines.

But while the Seaway looked like the complete solution to the economic problems that had plagued the Duluth-Superior area for many years, it would not be able to

Construction of the St. Lawrence Seaway transformed Duluth into a world port. After 1959, foreign ships could pick up their cargo of Midwestern grain in the heart of the North American continent. Courtesy, Northeast Minnesota Historical Center

overcome some critical obstacles. For one thing, the Duluth harbor was only open eight months out of the year—from May through late November—and weather conditions often caused lengthy delays at lock and harbor entrances and in canals and channels. This unpredictability slowed shipments and caused headaches for the shippers. Cargoes shipped from Great Lakes ports to an overseas port such as Liverpool continued to arrive two to three days later than if they had been transported through the Port of New York. Further, the barge lines carrying grain from the central states to the Gulf port fought the Great Lakes shipping system with rate reductions of their own. Railroad companies, which frequently had some ownership interest in Mississippi River barge companies, also announced rate reductions on export grain moving from the Midwest to the Gulf. And early in 1961, several western rail lines reduced their rates on wheat that was moving from the Great Plains to ports in and around New Orleans. By 1963, export grain traffic at Gulf and Pacific ports not only had not been adversely affected by the Seaway, it was increasing, due in part to the reduced joint rail-barge rate packages. Duluth-Superior did attract some shipping business away from the Atlantic-side ports. The proportion of U.S. grain exported through Atlantic ports declined from 25 percent in 1958 to 13 percent in 1962.

Nevertheless, Duluthians and their neighbors in the taconite cities on the Range saw good fortune ahead as the 1950s pressed into the 1960s and the country was caught up in the Camelot mood of the Kennedy Administration. Expectations that tomorrow would be better than today made many voters forget how closely intertwined are industry and the land upon which it is built. Up ahead were more hard times for the region's businesses. But, for many, the rose-colored glasses of a temporary economic boom made the future difficult to see.

A pedestrian mall with trees and lights turned the central Minneapolis shopping district into a fantasy land. City residents responded by turning Nicollet Mall into a retailing bonanza. Courtesy, Minneapolis Public Library

INTO THE 21ST CENTURY

HOT DAYS IN VACATIONLAND

Minnesota businesspeople have a saying that most new enterprises quickly assume the shape of one of two animals: a cash cow or a cash hog. Cash cows generate revenues. Cash hogs gobble their way through profits. In the business world, cash hogs are either made into cash cows or they become corporate history lessons.

In 1973, Harvey Paulson, president of Scorpion—a manufacturer of snowmobiles in Crosby, Minnesota, and a subsidiary of Atlanta-based Fuqua Industries—had a heart-to-heart chat with Carl Patrick, president of Fuqua. Scorpion was a cash hog and both men knew it. When corporate economists predicted that sales of snowmobiles would slide because of the rising gasoline prices, Scorpion began to suffer even more. Patrick wanted to sell the company. But just before Scorpion was put on the public auction block, he agreed to give Paulson a hand in reshaping the company.

Although Paulson was a native of the Arrowhead vacation country and knew something about the way Americans spend their money on pastimes and special interests, he didn't feel confident that he could steer a snowmobile company through the changing economic times. But Paulson did thoroughly understand two-cycle engines and quality control. He also knew that if he could keep Scorpion running, his friends and neighbors would keep their jobs.

Paulson bought the company—liabilities, risk, and all—and joined the ranks of other entrepreneurs who believed that snowmobiles would revolutionize winter sports in snow country. They were encouraged by the proportions North American snowmobile sales had reached by 1971—something on the order of 500,000 units. Paulson figured that if he and his peers in the snowmobile business could steer around the OPEC oil embargo and the poor snowfall of 1974, open country might lie ahead.

There was fierce competition, however, among the snowmobile manufacturers in Minnesota. Sales in northern Minnesota, which was known internationally as the home of the snowmobile industry, were led by two separate companies that had been founded by the same man—Edgar Hetteen. In 1954, Hetteen chose Roseau as the site for Polaris E-Z-Go, an arm of Textron, Inc. In 1961 Hetteen founded Arctic Enterprises, the manufacturer of Arctic Cat snowmobiles, in Thief River Falls, a mere seventy miles from the Polaris E-Z-Go plant. Both companies were known around the world for building snowmobiles of durability and sleek design.

International Snowmobile Industry Association figures for 1978 (the best sales year for snowmobiles ever) showed that Minnesota was manufacturing 75 percent of the snowmobiles made in the United States and 43 percent of those manufactured worldwide. Nearly $100 million in revenue poured into the state as a result of the 1978 snowmobile sales.

It was also in 1978 that Scorpion allowed itself to be absorbed by Arctic Enterprises. With little capital for developing new product designs and promotions, Scorpion found that it could no longer withstand the competition from other snowmobile manufacturers. Arctic Enterprises, on the other hand, was thriving. Energized by its success, it stretched into new seasonal products such as the Wetbike—a water-borne motorbike.

After several dry winters in the 1970s, record snows during the winters of the early 1980s put Polaris E-Z-GO back on a solid footing. Courtesy, Polaris Industries, Inc.

It even added a marine-products division by acquiring Larson Industries of Little Falls, a manufacturer of fiberglass boats.

The decision for Arctic Enterprises to diversify into the summer recreation business was based on a new trend among consumers to "relax" as hard as they work. In 1965, a study by the Minnesota Outdoor Recreation Resources Commission (ORRC) had forecast a startlingly large increase in consumer demand for recreational equipment, facilities, and opportunities. The study had projected that between 1965 and 1976, public interest in summer camping would grow 276 percent, while participation in winter sports would jump 285 percent. In addition, better highway systems were already providing travelers with greater mobility, and a steady increase in per capita income made it possible for many people to enjoy recreational opportunities they had not dreamed of even a decade before.

Through the 1960s and the early 1970s, the recreation industry in Minnesota seemed to coincide with ORRC projections. The tourist travel dollar doubled during the 1970s, reaching nearly $900 million in 1972. Half of this total came from visitors from other states. In 1974, 2.5 million fishing licenses were issued and some 400,000 boats and canoes were registered in Minnesota. By the early 1970s Minnesota had 98 state parks, and in 1971 Congress added Voyageurs National Park, near the Boundary Waters Canoe Area, to provide more than 3,000 miles of open trails for hardier vacationers. In 1973 snowmobile lovers registered a record 300,000 snowmobiles.

Nevertheless, there was tough sledding ahead for the industry. Anticipating a record year, Arctic Cat went into the 1979-1980 season hyped up to have a record sales year with 600,000 snowmobiles ready for sale. But across the north country, snow refused to fall. By March, Arctic Cat management tabulated a 26 percent decline in sales and losses of $11.5 million. Nevertheless, hope continued to lead the company forward. Although Arctic Cat believed that such a dry year could never happen again, it reduced its available inventory of new snowmobiles by more than half in preparation for the 1980-1981 season. But the worst happened: again no snow fell. Arctic Cat's losses were estimated to be about $16 million for that fiscal year. On February 17, 1981, the company filed for reorganization under Chapter 11 of the Bankruptcy Act.

The company spent the summer of 1981 selling the remaining snowmobiles, service parts, and accessories under a court order that allowed the profits to be used for continuing operations. By the time the last 1981 product was sold, Arctic Cat could still claim 38 percent of the market share, even as the company was dissolved.

A number of companies considered buying the Arctic Cat plant, including John Deere, Suzuki, and arch-rival Polaris. In January of 1982, Polaris announced that it intended to acquire Arctic Enterprises, but the deal fell through. Certified Parts Corporation purchased Arctic's parts, tooling and licenses in May, while the remaining assets were slated for an auction to be held that summer.

A core group of former Arctic Cat employees attended that auction and purchased those components essential to starting a snowmobile factory. Under the name Arctco, Inc., the group pursued the financial backing of individual investors and their bank. When Thief River Falls received an Enterprise Zone Block Grant, the Arctco group gained momentum. The key to their financing was to obtain "irrevocable domestic letters of credit" from dealers interested in selling Arctic Cats. With guaranteed preproduction sales Norwest Bank backed the new venture.

The first year, Arctco had orders to build 2,700 new machines. Operating from a leased portion of the old plant, Arctco fulfilled all orders as promised. With the marketing slogan "The Cat Is Back," dealers sold out of the 1984 models as the company posted an after-tax profit of $600,000 on sales of $7.3 million.

As oil and gas costs and interest rates declined, sales continued to be brisk. Total sales for fiscal 1986 were over $25 million, with Arctco posting a profit of $1.9 million. Though below the figures from snowmobiling's heyday, recent Arctco sales have convinced even the skeptics that the Cat is indeed back.

But beyond the snowmobile industry's economic frustrations, a public relations problem was beginning to develop. Many people considered snowmobiles noisy and a nuisance. When Voyageurs National Park was designated a wilderness preserve by Congress, some people insisted that snowmobiles be banned from it. Later, a system of trails would be built to accommodate snowmobilers.

THERE IS NO "AWAY"

The proposed ban on snowmobiles in Voyageurs National Park was part of a larger issue. As more Minnesotans spent time outdoors—paddling canoes along the shores of lily-laden bays, stalking ducks in frosty sedges, following winter deer trails through the deep pine forests—they began to worry about the future of the land and the creatures living on it. Outspoken leaders turned to policymakers for help, asking for limits on the use of resources so that future generations would be able to appreciate the land's bounties as well. In a 1971 speech before the 67th legislature, newly elected Governor Wendell Anderson delivered a special message that reflected this rising concern for the restoration and preservation of the land. "We are no longer in a position to exploit our resources without regard to the immediate and long-range effects of that exploitation," the governor told the assembly. "As long as man remains in Minnesota, we will have to fight to repair and prevent his damage to the natural environment that sustains his life."

Anderson's formula disturbed people whose grandfathers had been lumberjacks and whose grandmothers had burned off prairie grasses and cut through the deep crusted sod. He told his audience that Minnesota's "environmental problems are primarily a result of our continuous failure to take into account the full consequences of our actions." This set the tone for the regulatory state government that was to come.

Anderson proposed an Environmental Policy Act that introduced the state's version of an environmental impact statement. He advocated that polluters be put on the defensive in the state's courts and prove that their actions were not polluting the air, water, land, or other natural resources. (Previous judicial policies had placed the burden of proof on the plaintiff.) Anderson contended that Minnesota required a statewide program of sewage treatment, and supported a proposed moratorium on the building of nuclear power plants as well as legislation that would control the level of waste discharges into state waterways.

The erosion of rich soil and pollution of the air, surface water, and groundwater worried every Sunday gardener who sifted dirt through his or her fingers and every individual who turned on the tap for a cold drink or whose breath was labored on a brisk walk down a city street.

A clash of wills between business and industry leaders and environmental activists over the question of environmental quality was inevitable. In Duluth, the question came to a head when giant U.S. Steel requested that it be granted a variance so that it could continue to operate its plant while updating antipollution facilities. Environmentalists sounded a warning, hoping that U.S. Steel would be forced to make the changes to its plant before further irreversible damage was done to Lake Superior. The corporation countered with concern for the jobs and lives of the 1,800 people who worked in the steel plant.

By the end of the 1970s, business and government leaders were wrestling with problems that had no immediate solutions.

Business leaders and environmental activists were squaring off over the hazardous-waste issue. Moving ceremoniously between the two camps, state administrators tried to find compromises that would appease both the public and the state's industries. What was clear to everyone—business person, policymaker, and ordinary citizen—was that it was easier to produce new technologies, chemicals, and products than to understand what would happen when they were unleashed upon the earth.

Hazardous wastes are defined as those industry by-products that are flammable, corrosive, and highly reactive when mixed with water, or that are toxic (which means that they can harm anything on contact). Over the decades, mammoth volumes of waste chemicals have been poured into barrels and stored underground. They include mutagens, which are suspected of causing genetic damage; teratogens, which cause birth defects; and carcinogens, which cause cancer. By the early 1980s, Minnesota industries—from major manufacturers to small metal-fabricating firms—were producing 174,000 tons of hazardous waste each year. Every day, management in major Minnesota businesses desperately searched for an out-of-sight, out-of-mind place for this waste.

In 1980 the Minnesota legislature passed the Waste Management Act, which created a temporary Waste Management Board and issued a directive that a hazardous-waste management plan be developed. In general, industry leaders were enthusiastic about the new law because they had been unable to find new, safe, and inexpensive places to dump waste products. They hoped for a government-sanctioned dump site within the state's borders, which would save on shipping costs. Small businesses, in particular, hoped for a state dumping site, burdened as they were by the escalating costs of shipping and storing.

But before long the questions became even more complicated. People diagnosed as having serious and even life-threatening diseases demanded that the businesses that had dumped wastes into the earth decades ago pay for personal damages. When boiled down, the question was much more simple than the answer: In what year should industries have known that their wastes would have a longterm effect on the health of people?

At the same time, the state's fund for cleaning up hazardous wastes was quickly depleting, and the need for hundreds of thousands of dollars for new clean-up projects was clear. In the early 1980s it was discovered that pollution sites in St. Louis Park,

Nearly every Minnesota town has a special celebration day each summer as well as a Fourth of July parade. Members of the Virginia High School Band keep busy all summer long. Photo by Laurel Cazin

The old Twin Cities rivalry pales in the light of the contemporary struggle between the cities and their suburbs. When the football franchise insisted on a covered stadium, Minneapolis usurped the location from suburban Bloomington. Lovers of outdoor baseball now have to go on the road to see a game under the night sky. Photo by Bruce M. White

New Brighton, and Arden Hills, surrounding the Twin Cities, were threatening the purity of the Prairie du Chien-Jordan aquifer—the groundwater reservoir that supplied fresh drinking water to most of the Twin Cities. The hazardous waste problem was now in every citizen's backyard.

To address both the personal liability and clean-up issues, a Minnesota superfund bill was introduced to the legislature in 1983. The superfund caused a major split between business leaders and the liberal administration of Governor Rudy Perpich, inciting Lewis Lehr (then chairman of 3M) to enter the fray. Of particular concern to business were the retroactive liability clauses in the bill, which made corporations liable for wastes dumped as far back as 1960. "We have testified in favor of such legislation and strongly support the clean-up provisions," Lehr wrote. "Please understand: 3M should be held responsible if we pollute the environment. But we should not be held liable to personal-injury suits relating to pollution that may have been caused by someone else's materials."

Public pressure did little to solve the disposal problems. The high-technology companies, of which Minnesota was so proud, were the hardest hit by stringent regulations for hazardous-waste disposal. Many continued to pay high transportation costs to have wastes hauled out of state.

Waste disposal sites of various sizes, shapes, and locations were proposed—each ardently rejected by people who lived nearby. No one was convinced that underground storage technology had progressed far enough to be fail-safe; and few people understood enough about above-ground storage to seriously consider it. A moratorium was placed on storage site selection between 1984 and 1986, until tempers cooled and advances in the industry were made.

The hazardous-waste issue touched another nerve among Minnesota's small-business owners. With the introduction of the superfund, insurance companies reviewed their business liability policies and decided that Minnesota businesses were simply too hot to handle. Policy costs soared and small businesses pleaded for relief to lobbying organizations such as the Minnesota Association of Commerce and Industry. In Osseo, a metal-plating shop owner complained that liability insurance rates were so high that they could put him out of business. "We are being condemned for acts that were accepted by society and government officials until the 1970s, when environmental issues became of greater concern to everyone," Art Joyner was quoted in a September 1983 article for *Corporate Report/Minnesota*.

The message got through to the legislature, and in 1984 an amendment that would limit third-party liability was introduced. The amendment got hung up in the house, but during a special session called by the governor it passed.

In its amended form, the superfund law more closely resembled the federal law after which it was originally patterned. While continuing to give the state a strong basis to pursue pollution violations, the amended law followed accepted principles of causation for liability cases. This fundamental change soothed business and industry leaders, and environmental protection ceased to be a major business issue.

WITHOUT A SINGLE VOICE

They're called the grandfathers of Minnesota business—3M, Honeywell, Univac (now Unisys), and Control Data. These companies began as tiny Minnesota snowballs and rolled into major avalanches by the 1980s. In 1981, these four companies employed more than 50,000 people out of a total state industrial work force of 325,000. They have been role models in the high-tech explosion. Young entrepreneurs have followed their leadership in risk-taking and creativity. Small companies were born and grew healthy in the nurturing climate that surrounded the success of Minnesota's top four corporate giants.

Entrepreneurs and venture capitalists have prospered hand in hand in Minnesota. Venturers have found fertile ground for products or technologies that are on the ground floor of an industry and show promise for early expansion. A rule of thumb for some venture capitalists in the medical field is that a start-up company must achieve $20 million in sales within the first five to seven years. Typically, venture capitalists seek returns of five to fifteen times the original investment within five years and 40 percent annual sales growth. Minnesota venturers boldly put their money on the line. In 1984, for example, venture capital firms raised more than $200 million, placing Minnesota among the top five states for the amount of venture dollars raised.

A case in point is Norwest Growth Fund (formerly Northwest Growth Fund, one of the oldest venture capital firms in the region) which in 1961 lured Robert Zicarelli from Chicago. Zicarelli liked Minnesota-bred companies and had already invested in Control Data and Memorex. With Norwest Growth Fund, he also affiliated with Cray Research, today a leading designer of large-scale scientific computers, and Network Systems, now a manufacturer of high-performance data communications equipment. In a little over two decades, Zicarelli's investments helped Norwest Growth Fund increase assets of $2.5 million into more than $85 million. Currently, Norwest Growth

Fund is considered one of the country's largest venture capital funds. The successes of winning companies such as Medtronic, Cray Research, and Network Systems continue to entice venturers.

Working against every venturer is the normal evolution of a business's growth. A high-technology venture investment can become a loser even before the product is ready for the marketplace.

Nevertheless, Minnesota's venture capitalists are the first-string supporters of new business in the state, and dozens of new companies have succeeded because the necessary dollars were pumped in when the going was the toughest. And new high-technology companies in the state have the added advantage of the research resources available through the University of Minnesota's Institute of Technology.

Although Minnesota was proving to be an excellent place to found a business in the 1970s and 1980s, many business leaders were losing confidence in the state as a place to expand their corporations. And business leaders discovered that they were no longer speaking with a unified voice in regard to business-related legislative issues. For manufacturing and construction companies, workers' compensation was a hot issue through the last half of the 1970s and into the 1980s. High-technology companies, on the other hand, were having a difficult time finding sources of ready growth capital.

The Minnesota State Fair marks the end of summer for thousands of people who would not miss attending for anything. Each visitor has his or her favorite event. Butter sculpting gives form to the products of local dairies while giving viewers a chuckle over the idea of wearing coats in the late summer heat. Photo by Bruce M. White

Middle-sized corporations were groaning under the weight of Minnesota's 12 percent corporate income tax, while larger corporations worried that high personal income taxes would keep top management candidates from coming to live in the state.

The issue that united small- and medium-sized companies during the 1970s and 1980s was workers' compensation. The first law relating to an employer's responsibility for injuries incurred on the job was enacted in 1887, and the first workers' compensation laws were passed in 1913. The original mission of the Minnesota workers' compensation act was to ensure that workers received speedy and effective economic compensation while recovering from their injuries. Workers' compensation coverage became compulsory for Minnesota employers in 1937 and quickly became a political football between business and labor. Through the years, as amendment after amendment was passed, labor hammered out such a comprehensive workers' compensation program that Minnesota's compensation rates were considered some of the highest in the country. In 1981, for example, the cost of workers' compensation insurance premiums for Minnesota's businesses approached $500 million.

Workers' compensation soon became the focal point of the problems facing businesses. Small manufacturing firms, such as high-technology companies, protested that lower workers' compensation rates could make the difference not only between profit and loss but in a company's ability to grow—and even survive—within the state's borders. In the late 1970s and early 1980s, the Minnesota Association of Commerce and Industry (MACI), business's strongest voice in the legislature, fought to limit the types of work-related injuries eligible for claims and to establish fairer guidelines for determining when payments should begin and the length of payments. MACI's goal was to ensure that vocational rehabilitation of employees would become a state objective. In 1979, an extensive review of workers' compensation yielded improved rehabilitation provisions.

Another major concern of the state's corporations was unemployment compensation. When the legislature met in 1982, the state's unemployment trust fund was $114 million in debt to the federal government. Within one year, the debt had nearly tripled. When the legislature met in 1984, it was determined that Minnesota had paid out more in unemployment insurance benefits than it had collected in taxes for seven of the previous ten years. Studying the issue, members of the Senate's employment committee agreed with business leaders that the state either had to get itself out of debt or incur penalties from the federal government. Suggested reforms included capping rate increases until the benefit structure had been reviewed, retaining a 1.5 percent per year limit on the employer's contribution escalator, and preventing wage credits from being granted to people who had been discharged from jobs due to misconduct.

During the 1984 legislature, labor and business factions settled down to negotiate a compromise bill that was to restructure the state's in-debt unemployment compensation system. The interests of both sides were clear. Labor would not allow any significant reduction in benefits to workers; business leaders were demanding lower taxes. As reported in the April 24, 1984, issue of the International Falls *Daily Journal,* the executive director of the Minnesota Business Partnership (a lobbying organization for business leaders) declared that "Minnesota is the only state we can see in this region in which our unemployment rate is well below the national average and our benefits paid above . . . our system pays out more than it should relative to other states." Business groups complained that Minnesota provided benefits to well-paid seasonal workers such as forest, construction, and shipping workers, that workers were paid for longer periods of time than in most other states, and that the amount of benefits was overly generous.

The 1984 bill that emerged was a typical compromise bill—loved by no one and a point of frustration for everyone. Business taxes would be increased by $274 million and benefit increases reduced $69 million from 1984 to 1988, thus sparing Minnesota employers the $360 million in federal taxes and interest charges that would otherwise be incurred in 1987 and 1988.

Despite the backing of such organizations as the Minnesota Retail Association, small businesses outside of the Twin Cities could not support the bill, taking with them the votes of a loose coalition of rural representatives known as the "Wood Ticks." Soon to follow was the support of Dayton Hudson, a major retailer and a provider of thousands of jobs in the Twin Cities metropolitan area; the National Federation of Independent Businesses; the Greater Minneapolis Employers Association; and a number of smaller chambers of commerce. Their complaint was that business lobbyists had not gone far enough in restricting benefit increases. The defeat of the 1984 bill was a turning point in the history of political battles between business and labor because it demonstrated clearly that business did not always speak with a single voice. The unemployment compensation issue would continue to boil.

Another issue, the corporate tax rate, had dismayed business leaders since the late 1960s. Despite reforms in the state's dual formula for corporate income tax—which meant businesses were no longer taxed for goods sold outside of the state—incorporated businesses continued to pay the fourth-highest corporate income tax rate in the country. Small-business owners fought for the passage of a graduated income tax plan—a battle still being waged in the 1980s.

Minnesota's product-liability laws have cut deeply into the hearts of a number of Minnesota's manufacturing companies during the last two decades. Because the judicial branch of the government redefined tort laws in favor of plaintiffs in the 1960s, corporate management felt stripped of its defenses against product-liability suits.

In 1979, for example, the state supreme court ruled six to two that Allis Chalmers was liable for injuries that a Beltrami County farmer suffered while operating one of the company's corn-harvesting machines. Although warnings in the owner's manual and on the machine said not to clean the machine while it was operating, the farmer attempted to remove corn that clogged the machine, losing most of his arm in the process. He sued, and Allis Chalmers lost the suit.

Reforms to state product-liability laws and correspondingly high rates for Minnesota companies have received considerable attention from MACI and other major business lobbying groups who have pressed for a statute of limitations for a manufacturer's responsibility for a product.

In the 1980s business property and casualty insurance rates began to rise in Minnesota, as well as in other states, as lawsuits between consumers and businesses multiplied. Yet for many insurance companies serving Minnesota businesses, significant rate increases could not offset their cash flow losses. To be profitable, many left the high-risk markets and focused on more traditional and predictable products such as automobile and homeowner insurance. Liability coverage options began to decrease for Minnesota's business management, and before long the public felt the effects of the insurance crisis as well.

Facing page: The Twin Cities has earned a reputation as a center for both traditional and experimental theater. The Heart of the Beast Puppet and Mask Theatre, which provides summer entertainment in the parks for children, is just one of many cultural opportunities in the Metropolitan area. Courtesy, Minneapolis Public Library

THE PICTURE CHANGES

Until the early 1950s, agriculture was both Minnesota's major money-maker and its largest employer. The land beneath their feet was what made a farming family's future promising. So, too, the land beneath the farmers' feet was what made the state's future secure. But population shifts, a decade of inflation and high interest rates, as well as a national policy to set agricultural commodity prices at artificial levels, radically changed the outlook for Minnesota's farming families by the 1980s. Added to the dismal formula was the fact that a strong U.S. dollar overseas had inhibited the growth of foreign commodity trading. In 1983, payments on interest were nearly 14.5 percent of all cash operating costs on the Minnesota farm. By 1984, 20 percent of Minnesota farmers were 40 percent in debt and one-third of the state's 45,000 full-time farmers were facing crippling cash-flow problems. According to an August 11, 1985, article in the *Minneapolis Star and Tribune,* the value of Minnesota farmland, after adjusting for inflation, decreased 40 percent, on average, between 1980 and 1985, and was equaled only by the declining value of assets such as farm machinery. Bankers faced with the odious task of foreclosing on family farms realized that the collateral value of land and equipment might not cover a farmer's debts.

By 1985, one-third of the state's farmers had debt-to-asset ratios of 70 percent to 30 percent or worse. A study by the University of Minnesota Agricultural Economics Department showed that in current dollars, Minnesota farmland fell from a statewide average of $927 an acre in 1984 to $686 by the following year. It seemed clear to everyone that the day of the traditional family farm in Minnesota was coming to an end. Forecasters predicted that 5,000 farms would be lost before the end of the decade and 10,000 more in the next decade, and that the impact of these changes in many parts of Minnesota would be devastating. As an indicator of financial industry anxiety, Norwest Corp. and First Bank System, the two regional bank holding companies in the Twin Cities, took quick steps to sell many of their rural bank properties in the Upper Midwest. Nevertheless, the two bank corporations carried loan portfolios that would

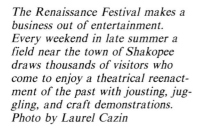

The Renaissance Festival makes a business out of entertainment. Every weekend in late summer a field near the town of Shakopee draws thousands of visitors who come to enjoy a theatrical reenactment of the past with jousting, juggling, and craft demonstrations. Photo by Laurel Cazin

3M's early commitment to research has allowed the company to create new products in response to industry demands. This ceramic fiber, which withstands heat up to 2,200 degrees Fahrenheit, will be used for heavy industrial fabrics and sleevings. Courtesy, 3M

continue to tie them tightly, and permanently, to the agricultural industry. Norwest, the largest commercial bank lender of farm credit in the north country, showed a loan portfolio in 1985 of $820 million—the second largest in the United States.

Throughout Minnesota, food processors, warehousers, and shippers were all affected by the pressures of farm industry changes. Large regional cooperatives such as Land O'Lakes, Harvest States, and Cenex reevaluated their operating systems and reorganized to better withstand the downturn. Life insurance companies, long a major source of mortgage financing, announced that they would wait until land prices went up again before financing any more farms. The American Council of Life Insurance, a major trade association for insurance companies, noted that life insurance companies had taken possession of Minnesota farms valued at $33.1 million during 1984. The pain of such foreclosures was felt throughout the state. Late in 1985, farmers' rights activist Jim Langman prepared his family for the loss of his 480-acre farm to Travelers Insurance, a Connecticut-based insurance company. As the sheriff stood on the courthouse steps in Glenwood to auction off the farm on behalf of the insurance company, tempers flared and 600 farmers stormed the little courthouse in protest. Organized by Groundswell, a grass-roots protest farm organization, the rally gave the Langman family a temporary reprieve.

Small agribusiness companies that once took their nourishment from surrounding farms are now looking across the oceans for new markets. Some, such as Hanska Seed in Hanska, are keeping afloat—even prospering—in the export business. In 1983, Hanska Seed sold 6,000 bushels of seed in its traditional domestic markets. But with the Minnesota Trade Office as an important resource, Hanska Seed was able to get leads on potential customers for their soybean and oat seeds. Selling two-thirds of the company's seed overseas, the little firm of ten people sold 38,000 bushels in 1984, doubled that number in 1985 and projected another year of similar growth during 1986, as the company sought new contracts with regional farmers to produce the highest-quality seed.

In the place of Minnesota-grown family farms comes the mega-farm: a consolidation of business acumen, capital, technology, and mono-cropping. By buying up acres of liquidated farmland and using purchasing and marketing clout, major farm corporations of 500 acres or more could be the key to Minnesota's ability to rank in the top five states for the production of food commodities such as corn, soybeans, sugar beets, oats, barley, peas, turkeys, milk and cheese, non-fat dry milk, and butter.

Technology has become the master of the farm—and of farm prices. The *Minneapolis Star and Tribune* reported in the August 11, 1985 issue that, by 1980, technology had made it possible to more than double the average cow's milk production,

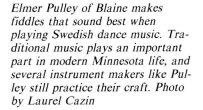

Elmer Pulley of Blaine makes fiddles that sound best when playing Swedish dance music. Traditional music plays an important part in modern Minnesota life, and several instrument makers like Pulley still practice their craft. Photo by Laurel Cazin

and the average acre of wheat produced and triple the amount of corn that it could produce thirty years ago.

But, as every high school freshman understands, a consistently growing supply eventually forces lower prices at the market. If demand doesn't follow supply, then farmers cannot make enough money to pay for the crops they produce. In the United States, price supports have filled the growing gap between the costs of production on the farm and the prices charged at the cash register. For Minnesota's farmers, price supports have been a necessary savior in this technologically-driven economy. Between 1982 and 1983, price support payments as a share of Minnesota total net farm income rose fourfold.

In 1890, nearly half of the state's population lived or worked on a family farm. Today, however, less than ten percent of its people make their living from the soil. Over the past fifty years, two out of every three farms have disappeared, and the backlash from this loss of farms has been felt deeply in the rural communities and small towns across the state. In the *Economic Report to the Governor,* 1987, it was noted that, for the first time, no county in Minnesota could boast that a majority of its income was directly generated from farming.

The fall-off in profitability of farming and mining is symptomatic of massive global changes that are beyond the control of communities, industrial regions, states, or even countries. Since 1980, the definition of a good business climate has been altered by new economic realties—shifting away from a regional market based on mass-production and low-skilled labor to an internationally based market which requires flexibility, adaptability, and ingenuity on the part of business management. To survive, many corporate decision-makers have had to come to terms with the fact that they must make incisive changes in the structure—even philosophy—of their corporations.

There is no better example of an ability to right a sinking ship than Control Data Corp. (CDC). Since its founding in 1957, the giant company had gathered a reputation as a company that gambled on wide diversity—that stretched itself—and then stretched again. Analysts on Wall Street were split on their opinion of CDC's founder, CEO and chairman William Norris. Norris believed that a business has an obligation to meet the social needs of its economic community. Under his leadership, CDC entered new arenas such as financial services and family farm- and inner-city support—programs that were only tangentially related to its main business: computer systems, peripherals, and data services. Some regarded Norris as an entrepreneurial leader, while others worried that the company was losing track of what it did best. So much so, the pundits noted, that the company was too encumbered to do well in the increasingly competitive international computer marketplace.

By 1984, CDC had begun to weaken. In the first half of 1985, the company announced a $14.8 million loss, while inventory towered at $900 million.

Troubles at CDC occupied front-page headlines for months as revenues in their disk-drive and peripheral businesses continued to fall. As Norris stepped aside in 1986 and Robert Price, former president and CEO at CDC took the reins, Minnesotans held their breath. Could the company reestablish itself as a major player? What would be the repercussions in the secondary supplier industries—those companies whose lifeblood had been CDC for twenty years or more?

The results of CDC's gradual rebirth have elements of both good and bad news for Minnesotans. The bad news was that CDC troubles sent serious shock waves through the Minnesota electronics industry. But the good news was that business leaders read beyond the headlines and learned a valuable lesson—that industries have to focus their attention on the technologies that will make them globally competitive, and not stray too far away from their core businesses.

Today, CDC still has considerable obstacles to overcome as it attempts to reassert itself in its primary markets. But the signs of recovery are noticeable. In 1987, CDC vigorously invested more than $400 million in research and development and it received

$100 million in federal government funding to develop computer system architecture, advanced circuit technologies, logic design, advanced packaging and cooling techniques, as well as mass storage technologies.

In the years following the 1981-1983 recession (which drastically affected the computer and electronics manufacturing industries) Minnesota employment remained fairly buoyant. In fact, between 1983 and 1985 the state's employment picture was brighter than the country's as a whole. Total employment in those years increased by nearly nine percent, compared with eight percent nationally. Employment growth was recorded in the services, manufacturing, and retail trade sectors. Significant statewide employment increases were also noted in finance, insurance, real estate, transportation, and communications industries.

Occupational projections prepared by the Department of Jobs and Training indicate that the state has a healthy outlook. Based on the state's entrepreneurial activity, forecasters predict that by 1990 there will be 242,900, or 12.3 percent, more jobs than were available in the state in 1980. Among the top growth occupations are sales, technical support, service, clerical, and managerial positions.

But it is the overall technical competence of its work force that is most attractive for Minnesota's future. The Twin Cities claims its rightful place as a high-technology corridor, ranking in innovation and manufacturing capability with California's Silicon Valley, Boston's Route 128, North Carolina's Research Triangle, and the Austin, Texas area. In 1985, Minnesota's high-technology corridor was the birthplace of more than 2,100 new companies, offering products in high-growth areas such as office and computing equipment, scientific instruments, and electronic components.

Minnesota is also known around the world as a place that fosters medical breakthroughs. In recent years, companies such as Medtronic, St. Jude Medical, Inc., Cardiac Pacemakers, Inc., Medical Graphics Corp., and American Medical Systems, Inc.—to mention a few—have made medical news in diagnostic and surgical implant technologies. Other growth corporations such as LecTec Corp., Scimed Life Systems, Inc., and Genetic Laboratories, Inc., have been prominent leaders in the research and development of pain control devices and in genetic engineering systems.

In 1984, Lee Berlin, chairman of the Governor's Commission on Medical Technology, was quoted in the May issue of *Mpls-St. Paul* magazine: "One of the best-kept secrets of the world is the incredibly quiet dynamic position of the innovative, medically oriented, industrial-university-financial-hospital complex in Minnesota," he said, calling the 250-mile stretch between Baudette and Rochester "Medical Alley." "This is truly the medical technological center of the world," said Berlin. He noted that the state manufactures more than half the world's pacemakers and hearing aids, and opined that Minnesota can claim more medical innovations per capita than any other place on the globe.

There is no doubt that Minnesota has bred an innovative, creative work force—one in which 72 percent of the working-age population is employed, compared with roughly 65 percent in the country. It is a work force that pinpoints problems and creates solutions. In 1985, in fact, Minnesota ranked fifth among the states for the number of patents issued for every million residents.

Innovative thinking has also helped the people of each geographic region of the state begin to cope with the effects of major industry changes in manufacturing. The central region (including St. Cloud) and the Twin Cities metropolitan area were the only regions in the state to increase their percentages of total manufacturing employment between 1976 and 1984, particularly in food manufacturing. The southeast region, including Rochester, lost jobs in industries such as lumber and wood products as well as in fabricated metals, stone, clay, and glass. On the other hand, the southeast gained more than 600 jobs in the chemical/petroleum industry, as well as in plastics, synthetics, and pharmaceuticals. Other important advances came in periodical production and general industry machinery, and there was a 55 percent increase between 1976

The Lutheran Brotherhood of Minnesota helped thousands of Hmong refugees take the plunge into American life. Once they adjust to modern urban living conditions, these Southeast Asian people enter the workforce with energy and dedication. Photo by Laurel Cazin

The Minneapolis Chamber of Commerce established the Grain Exchange in 1881 to handle the increasingly complex wheat trade. A century later this floor still buzzes with the trade that supplies Minneapolis mills. Photo by Laurel Cazin

and 1984 in the manufacture of office, computing, refrigeration, and other equipment. In the western areas of Minnesota, new jobs were created in electrical machinery production, and there were modest gains in employment for lumber and wood products, stone, clay, and glass manufacturing.

Diversification has been tougher in the northeastern part of the state, where the mining companies continued to announce shut-downs and layoffs throughout the first half of the decade. Between 1976 and 1984, more than 7,800 mining jobs were lost; today, only about 8,000 people have mining jobs. Small increases in jobs for lumber and wood products, printing and publishing, rubber/leather, fabricated metals, and machinery were not large enough to offset the employment losses of the early part of the decade.

Innovative thinking in Minnesota among policymakers as well as corporate leaders and the state's work force has expanded the state's reach far beyond the boundaries of the United States. In fact, a growing number of businesses are developing international linkages that are opening markets to them in the Orient, Europe, and Central and South America, as well as the Middle East.

At the same time, the leaders of these companies understand that Minnesota's economy as a whole is buffeted by national and international monetary and trade policies. When the United States lost its leadership role as the world's producer between 1960 and 1980, two of Minnesota's basic staple industries—agricultural products and iron ore—similarly lost position. It is critical, business decision-makers agree—that Minnesota never be caught in that defensive position again.

As Minnesota steps into the ring as an aggressive global competitor, headlines boast significant accomplishments. These are only samples:

Bio-Vascular, Inc., a medical device company in Roseville, breaks through world competition with an artery-graft device that can save the lives of thousands of coronary bypass patients who previously might not have been treatable.

Erwin Kelen, president and chief executive officer of DataMyte Corp., a

Minnetonka-based electronics company, leads the fight on behalf of American high-technology firms to discover how they can become competitive in a world where Japan and Germany are clearly technological ringleaders.

The Minnesota Software Association, Minnesota's major software trade group, lobbies legislators to help fund the Office of Software Technology, which provides advice and loans to Minnesota's 239 software companies.

LifeCore Biomedical, Inc.'s CEO, James W. Bracke, announces a successful stock offering in Great Britain, signaling a trend among smaller Minnesota-based companies to look toward Europe for equity financing.

Minneapolis-based Graco Robotics, Inc., a robotics company wholly owned by Graco, Inc., receives a $12.6 million order from Japanese automaker Mitsubishi International for a robot system. Mitsubishi will use the system in its Diamond-Star Motors joint venture with Chrysler in Illinois. The Japanese order is the single biggest order in Graco's sixty-one-year history.

BCE Development, a major commercial development company, opens Minnesota's thirty-seven story World Trade Center in downtown St. Paul.

Amador Corp., a computer-testing company in Taylors Falls owned by Control Data, becomes the first non-Japanese company certified by the Japanese to test computer products for electromagnetic pollution, opening Japanese market potential for U.S. computer manufacturing firms.

Medtronic's Activatrax, the first pacemaker in the world to detect body motion and regulate the heart rate accordingly, is giving heart patients new energy and stamina. "It's the difference between living and existing," says one recipient.

The Butler Brothers warehouse became Butler Square in the mid-1970s. This first successful adaptive use of a warehouse set the stage for the restoration of the entire Minneapolis warehouse district, which now throbs with the nightlife generated by successful restaurants and galleries. Courtesy, Hennepin County Historical Society

MINNESOTA ENTERS THE NEW CENTURY

It's been well over three centuries since Jean Nicolet put on his silk damask robe to celebrate what he thought was the opening of a new trade route between New France and China. He—and the men who followed him into the seventeenth century wilderness—understood the basics of a global economy. The forests, lakes, rivers, wildlife, rich soils, and minerals had the potential to yield commodities upon which to build trade.

Since that time, Minnesota's economy has lost some of its primordial ties to the land, but it has come to depend on what its people can provide—in accurately identifying problems, developing technological solutions, being flexible in adapting to world market changes, devising cost-effective methods of producing products and services, and having to compete in the far-flung marketplaces of the world.

This is a time of transition—when the rules of doing business and of being employed in Minnesota are changing—when the traditional tensions between labor and business must yield to new understandings—when public policymakers must think in marketing terms to create fair legislation that will help attract and hold growing businesses in the state—when educators must develop new programs to retrain people in new occupational areas—when academicians and business leaders must learn to talk openly to one another to ensure that young people understand both the theories and the reality of the business arena they are about to enter—when corporate heads must be willing to stop what they're doing and develop innovative approaches to strengthen employee productivity and build a competitive position both in their industries and in the international marketplace.

Minnesota's business began with the land. And like the glaciers before us, we have greatly changed the face of every natural resource we have touched. We hope that our new resources—brainpower, technological innovation, and flexibility—will be used with competence and clear vision, because these are the last gifts that our land can give us.

Keeping Minnesotans abreast of critical issues is the product of an enterprising St. John's University student. Minnesota Public Radio is now the largest listener-supported network in the country with six stations and award-winning programs in current events as well as the arts. Courtesy, Minnesota Public Radio

Facing Page: *This placid Minnesota Mississippi River backwater offers little hint of the water's mighty journey. Photo by R. Hamilton Smith*

The new Lincoln Center Building is reflected on a neighboring tower. Photo by Greg Ryan/Sally Beyer

Preceding page: Forest undergrowth blushes russet, gold, vermillion in the gathering fall, soon to yield to winter's cold, silver rest. Photo by R. Hamilton Smith

Above: *This Rush Creek Valley view graces an I-90 rest area near Winona. Photo by Kay Shaw*

Left:: *This fall study of secondary forest growth suggests the rich variety of trees common to Minnesota's North Woods. Photo by Kay Shaw*

Above: *A record late-July rainfall of ten inches swelled Minneapolis' usually gentle Minnehaha Falls to this booming cataract. Photo by Kay Shaw*

Above: *Winter's moods on Lake Superior range from capricious brutality to seductive beauty. Photo by R. Hamilton Smith*

Left: *Night steals across the lakes and islands of one of Minnesota's national parks. Photo by Matt Bradley*

Above: *No tree is more reminiscent of the North Woods than the elegant, supple white birch, delight of painters, canoe makers, and boys. Spring light graces these examples along the Big Fork River. Photo by Matt Bradley*

Left: *Humble fungi often achieve a kind of splendor in the North Woods, as here on a downed tree near Big Fork River. Photo by Matt Bradley*

Facing page: *The canoe holds a well-earned place of honor in Minnesota history and in the hearts of contemporary outdoorsmen too. This late afternoon scene might be anywhere in the Northland. Photo by Matt Bradley*

The Mississippi River catches the last of the day's color as the St. Paul skyline becomes a silhouette. Photo by Greg L. Ryan

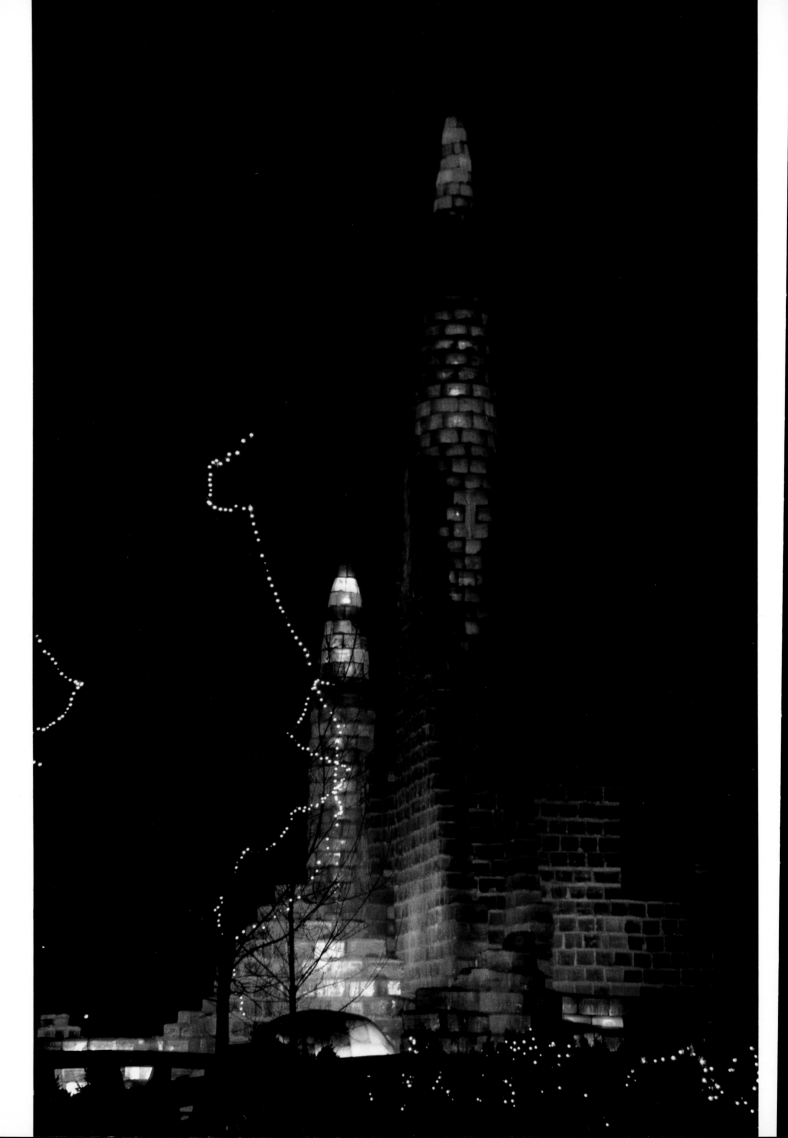

Facing page: *The lighting technician's wizardry transforms a St. Paul Winter Carnival Ice Palace into a fanciful vision. Photo by Leighton*

Left: *St. Paul's World Trade Center is among the most recent testimonials to the city's historic role in international commerce. Photo by Greg Ryan/Sally Beyer*

Below: *October 1987 was a great day for Minnesota baseball fans, and more than a few of them turned out to welcome the World Champion Twins in front of the Capitol. Photo by Kay Shaw*

Like many a sentinel along the lakeshore, Split Rock Lighthouse is part of Lake Superior's compelling history of navigation. Photo by Kay Shaw

The tranquil beauty of such scenes
as this late spring in southeast
Minnesota belies the complex haz-
ards of contemporary agriculture.
Photo by Greg Ryan/Sally Beyer

Above: *These twilight-clad farm buildings near Marine-on-the-St. Croix recall Minnesota's powerful agricultural tradition. Photo by Greg Ryan/Sally Beyer*

Right: *This Chicago Aeromotor Company exemplar spins near Beltrami. Courtesy, Rolland Hamrefa*

Left: *In Stillwater, crates at Aamodt's Apple Orchards promise plump pies, glowing cider, chunky sauce, and the unmistakable crunch of that first bite. Photo by Greg Ryan/Sally Beyer*

Below: *Sugar beets remain an important Minnesota crop, exemplified by this Beltrami harvest scene. Photo by Kay Shaw*

Facing page: *Summer turns the Como Park Conservatory in St. Paul into a riot of blooming color. Photo by Greg Ryan/Sally Beyer*

Right: *Emil Hastings' luminous oil painting,* Cornstalks, *brings to mind not only the enormous importance of corn to the state's economy but also the unique delight of fresh sweet corn on the supper table. Courtesy, Minnesota Historical Society*

Below: *On a fall afternoon drive on Highway 95, just north of Stillwater, if you stopped at Nelson's Roadside Stand you might see Indian corn like this. Photo by Greg Ryan/Sally Beyer*

Above: *Citizen's Bike Race com-
petitors are out in force on an
April morning. Photo by Greg
Ryan/Sally Beyer*

Right: *Speedskaters on Como Lake
push off at the start of a St. Paul
Winter Carnival race. Photo by
Greg Ryan/Sally Beyer*

Left: *The cheap thrill defined: snow tubing near Lake Calhoun on a snappy afternoon. Photo by Sally A. Beyer*

Below: *A four-man crew practicing on the Mississippi between Minne-apolis and St. Paul strokes past the Minnesota Centennial Showboat. Photo by Greg Ryan/Sally Beyer*

Above: *St. Paul's Winter Carnivals vie from year to year in icy grandeur, as in this soaring Ice Palace. Photo by Kay Shaw*

Right: *St. Paul's Winter Carnival has taken on a decidedly global zest in recent years, as attested by this 1987 Japanese creation. Photo by Kay Shaw*

Left: *Scandinavian influences abound across Minnesota. These children celebrate Norway Day in traditional folk dance. Photo by Kay Shaw*

Below: *TV Station KARE's fanciful float typifies the Minneapolis Aquatennial Torchlight Parade. Photo by Kay Shaw*

Above: *In this Howard Sprague painting, three of Alexander McDougall's innovative whaleback iron ore boats are depicted at the Duluth docks. From the mid-1890s for thirty years the efficient boats were workhorses of the Great Lakes iron ore shipping industry. Courtesy, Duluth, Mesabi and Iron Range Railroad*

Right: *Linking Duluth with Park Point, the Zenith City's Aerial Lift Bridge marks the entrance to one of the world's great harbors. Photo by Kay Shaw*

Left: *Burnished gold in the setting sun, a Northwest Orient Airlines Boeing 747 crosses the threshold at MSP, Minneapolis-St. Paul International Airport. Photo by Greg Ryan/Sally Beyer*

Below: *A Texan or a Sooner might claim this sunrise view, but it's really the Pine Bend Oil Refinery. Photo by Greg Ryan/Sally Beyer*

Right: *A Summertime Music Festival group delights an afternoon audience in St. Paul's Bandana Square. Photo by Kay Shaw*

Below: *Beneath the Ford Parkway Bridge passes a bit of reconstructed Mississippi River history—the Josiah Snelling excursion riverboat. Photo by Greg Ryan/Sally Beyer*

Above: *It's not all high culture at Orchestra Hall in downtown Minneapolis, as this glimpse of Peavey Plaza in summertime suggests.*
Photo by Greg Ryan/Sally Beyer

Left: *Norman Rockwell might have titled this St. Paul cyclist heading home with the greengrocer's best,* Balancing the Load *for a Saturday Evening Post cover.*
Photo by Greg Ryan/Sally Beyer

Right: *Its architectural statement as bold as any in America, Minneapolis boasts the Hennepin County Government Center Plaza area, the Pillsbury building just behind. Photo by Greg Ryan/Sally Beyer*

Below: *St. Paul's stately Union Depot eloquently echoes the enormous power of the railroads in a bygone era. Photo by Greg L. Ryan*

Above: *Few legislative halls assert the rich simplicity of the Minnesota House of Representatives Chamber in the State Capitol in St. Paul. Photo by Greg L. Ryan*

Left: *The grand effect of architect Cass Gilbert's 1905 dome for the Minnesota State Capitol in St. Paul endures. Photo by Greg Ryan/Sally Beyer*

To the first lumbermen in Minnesota, the pine forests looked like an
inexhaustible supply of timber.
Many farmers worked in the woods
in winter to earn cash to pay off
their land. They stacked the logs
by streams that would float them
to sawmills during the spring thaw.
Photo by William Roleff, Two
Harbors, Minnesota. Courtesy,
Minnesota Historical Society

MINNESOTA'S ENTERPRISES

What do we know about business in Minnesota? We know that right now—near the end of the 1980s—manufacturers account for 25.8 percent of the state's jobs, service companies 18.9 percent, retailers 9.54 percent, agriculture 4.28 percent, a surprisingly low figure in a state with so many farms, and mining, the industry that gave rise to so many great Minnesota fortunes, a nearly negligible less than one percent. We know that parts of the state are economically healthy, and that others, especially those that depend on mining and farming, are experiencing rough times. We know that over 80 percent of Minnesotans work in the private sector, and most work for companies with fewer than 500 employees.

We also know that Minnesota, heavily taxed, far from major markets, and buffeted by intemperate weather much of the year, has on the whole boomed in recent years, outperforming national business indicators in nearly every category. Various surveys, for instance, have placed Minnesota at or near the top on a per capita basis in generating new and fast-growing businesses. "Minnesota's magic touch," as *Time* magazine put it, is fueled no doubt by the 25 or so Minnesota venture-capital firms, one of the highest such figures in the nation. Many of those new businesses are second- and third-generation spin-offs, another marked Minnesota characteristic, of single companies born decades ago. Control Data Corporation, for example, begat an estimated 250 electronics firms, including the nation's entire supercomputer industry. Vision Ease gave rise to the 16 optical manufacturers that make the St. Cloud area one of the main sources of precision lenses in the nation. Medtronic, the pacemaker and medical devices company, started out in a garage as a collaboration between an engineering student and a cardiologist; now 350 Minnesota companies engage in the research and development and distribution of high-technology medical products. The list doesn't end there. The story has been repeated with hearing aids, processed foods, scientific measuring and controlling devices, printing and printing products, health management, and numerous other products and services.

On the other side of the coin, many Minnesotans tend to settle on one employer or career path and then stay put. Various surveys point to far less job mobility in Minnesota than in states with similar economic and educational profiles. Contradictory impulses? Maybe. Minnesotans seem to be abundantly willing to take risks. At the same time they appear to place a premium on job stability and security. Once someone figures out how to reconcile those two extremes, an important clue to the success of Minnesota's economy may be revealed.

Another Minnesota characteristic is the almost centrifugal impact the Twin Cities have had on the businesses and people of the rest of Minnesota, not to mention the neighboring states of North and South Dakota, Iowa, and much of Wisconsin. Few regions are as thoroughly dominated by a single metropolitan area (and in turn, few major metropolitan areas are as far removed from other population centers as the Twin Cities). The phenomena of the Twin Cities gives the Upper Midwest an economic focus that few other regions of the country can match.

But the size and importance of the Twin Cities sometimes overshadows—at least in the minds of some Twin Citians—the accomplishments of the many industry-leading businesses in Minnesota's smaller towns and rural areas. Indeed, the true genius of Minnesota business may reside outside the Twin Cities' limits. Nationwide, small town and rural economies have changed drastically in recent years. While nearly every American business has had to cope with a new set of economic realities, the shift has been greatest in non-urban areas, where the failures of just one or two businesses that couldn't keep up with the times can sometimes shut down a whole town.

The greater challenge of economic survival and prosperity in non-urban areas can sometimes call for a type of creativity that would seem revolutionary in urban areas. In Redwood Falls, for instance, a computer component manufacturer has managed to put in place one of the most sophisticated, Japanese-style manufacturing operations in the nation. In Alexandria, a packaging machine company assembles ingenious Rube Goldberg-like packaging devices, many big enough to fill a tractor-trailer, largely designed by graduates of the local vo-tech, who were using computer-aided design and engineering long before similar firms in big cities had even heard the terms. In tiny Warroad near the Canadian border, the distractions of the lakes and the hunting and fishing of the North Woods haven't hampered the growth of one the nation's leading window manufacturers. There are dozens of other examples of other companies firmly rooted in the Minnesota countryside that, without the benefits of easy access to transportation or big city capital, have managed to thrive in—and often conquer—their respective market niches. The owners and managers of these businesses will often acknowledge the odds against them and then go on to cite the one overwhelming advantage that none of their out-of-state competitors can match—the average Minnesota worker. Indeed, Minnesota employers are sometimes embarrassingly lavish in their praise of Minnesota employees. "We go in for national jobs, and we always have an edge," says one St. Cloud printer. "No other state can match our quality and productivity." Our people make the difference, is the endlessly repeated refrain, and while no one can really say with any certainty why, the underlying message is it's the fact that our people are Minnesotans that really makes the difference. Some of those same business people who have been tempted to move their operations to states where labor and government-imposed costs are lower are confronted with the biggest implication of such a move—the economic

sacrifice of moving from a state with the best-educated and arguably the most productive work force in the nation to another state that may offer everything but such a work force. That's an "off-the-balance-sheet" item for certain, but it's been compelling enough to keep many smaller and rural Minnesota economies healthy, which is definitely bucking a national trend.

When the nation looks at Minnesota, it can't seem to decide if Minnesota is just another quiet Midwestern state, a huge Lake Wobegon of quaint if unremarkable citizens, or the leading edge of social and economic trends that hold important implications for the nation's future. For example, during the recent flurry of national attention that attended the Minnesota Twins' successful World Series drive, it was entirely possible to pick up the same national publication and read one writer describe the area as typical Midwestern "flyover land," and elsewhere in the same publication, read another writer describing the Twin Cities as the pop music capital or advertising capital or this-and-that capital of the nation. Vanguard or enduring repository of traditional American values? Which is it? The pride and chauvinism of many Minnesotans may be a reaction to this ambivalence. It produces a peculiarly Minnesota type of defensiveness that leads people here to hoard statistical comparisons with other states as they wrestle with the problem of just what it is about Minnesota that produces such polar reactions.

Minnesota's secret may be that it manages to be both—solid and predictable in some ways, exciting and distinctive in many others. The organizations whose stories are detailed on the following pages have chosen to support this important literary and civic event. Many of these profiles illustrate how risk taking and vision can combine with a sense of tradition and the importance of deep, enduring values. That this business ethic can succeed so well is a tribute to the strength of Minnesota's sometimes mysterious, sometimes intangible, but always very real special qualities.

MINNESOTA CHAMBER OF COMMERCE

The Mesabi Range had grown to become the biggest source of iron ore in the world. Minneapolis and Duluth were first and second nationally in flour production. The state was at or near the top in lumber, dairy, and farm machinery production as well. In the previous 20 years the value of the state's manufactured products had increased from $76 million to close to $300 million. It seemed to the 11 businessmen who gathered at St. Paul's Carling Cafeteria in 1908 that the Minnesota business community needed organized representation.

Those informal meetings resulted in the formation of the Minnesota Employer's Association, a business lobbying group that gathered steam slowly but eventually became a major force in Minnesota politics. By the early 1940s the association counted 1,300 members. World War II interrupted its growth, which picked up again when Otto Christenson was hired to head the organization. Christenson was especially adept at dealing with the traditional party politics of the 1940s and 1950s; it is said that more legislation was negotiated at the Saint Paul Hotel than at the State Capitol.

The profound social, political, and economic changes of the 1960s brought an end to business as usual. In 1968 a new, broader organization was formed. Called the Minnesota Association of Commerce and Industry (MACI), the new group intended to concern itself with all facets of the state's economic well-being, including job creation, the environment, and education.

Under Oliver Perry, a respected consensus builder, MACI grew to include 2,800 companies by the middle of the 1970s and had a paid staff of 15. Its budget rose to $600,000.

Many business costs, including state income and unemployment taxes and contributions to the state's workers' compensation fund, skyrocketed. In some categories, the costs of doing business in the state were among the highest, if not the highest, in the nation. Many believed the deterioration of the state's business climate, which threatened to produce an exodus of businesses and jobs from the state, called for MACI to take a new, more aggressive turn.

When Perry retired, MACI's directors hired Winston Borden, an attorney and DFL legislator from Brainerd who had proved himself an effective political campaigner and powerful legislative leader. Borden made sure that MACI developed a high public profile and that its sometimes controversial views were widely disseminated. By the 1980s MACI had become one of the fastest growing organizations of its kind in the nation. Two statewide media campaigns that encouraged readers to write their legislators about proposed tax increases are considered by many to have played an important role in saving Minnesota individuals and businesses nearly $1.8 billion in new taxes. Recent statewide daily "Minnesota Business Viewpoint" radio broadcasts reach as many as 2 million listeners.

In 1986 it changed its name to the Minnesota Chamber of Commerce and Industry to reflect strong new alliances with community chambers of commerce. Today the chamber has 6,000 business members, a $4-million budget, and a staff exceeding 40.

Developments of the 1980s include the creation of both an influential political action committee and the Minnesota Chamber Foundation, contributing to educational excellence in Minnesota and developing important new corporate drug and alcohol abuse programs.

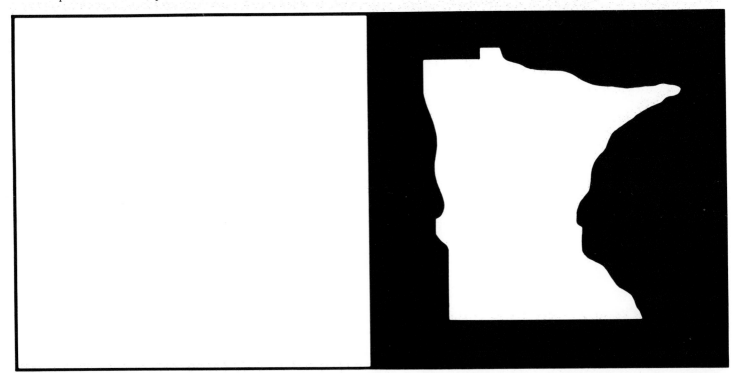

MINNESOTA CHAMBER

NORTHWESTERN BELL TELEPHONE

When Richard Hankinson, general manager of the Northwestern Telegraph Company in Minneapolis, heard of a remarkable new invention by Alexander Graham Bell called the telephone in 1876, his curiosity was naturally aroused. Hankinson saw to it that Minneapolis became one of America's first cities to have a telephone line installed. It ran from Hankinson's home to the old city hall. To demonstrate just how good the telephone connection was, Mrs. Hankinson, one of the city's leading sopranos, sang church hymns over it.

By 1878 Hankinson had formed the Northwestern Telephone Company. Its first actual telephone exchange in Minneapolis was constructed out of an old sewing machine stand and was located in city hall. There were 10 initial subscribers. Growth was rapid within the next two years; three miles of wire were strung and 700 instruments installed. St. Paul established an exchange, and by 1879 the two cities were linked.

As the telephone caught on, competing companies sprang up throughout the region, licensing the technology like Hankinson had done from the National Bell Telephone Company, later from the American Bell Telephone Company, and setting up local exchanges that were incompatible with other local exchanges. The competition became especially intense when the original Bell patents expired in 1893.

The succeeding decades were a time of consolidation and mergers within the new telephone industry. Customers were demanding an expanding and uniform service. In 1921 one of these growing regional telephone companies, the successor to the modest service Richard Hankinson established in Minneapolis, was incorporated as the Northwestern Bell Telephone Company. By this time there were more than 100,000 subscribers to the Minnesota exchange. When Northwestern Bell merged with the Tri-State Telephone and Telegraph Company 12 years later, what millions of upper midwesterners would know simply as the phone company was created.

In the decades since, Northwestern Bell has offered customers—today there are more than 1.3 million customers in Minnesota alone—every new advance in telephone technology, and in many cases has pioneered innovations, such as direct

Laying cable in the early part of this century was an arduous task, as this picture taken in downtown Minneapolis shows.

dialing and 911 service. The most momentous change for Northwestern Bell customers occurred on January 3, 1984, when AT&T's divestiture of its holdings in regional telephone companies went into effect, and telecommunications became more deregulated and a far more competitive industry. Northwest Bell joined with Mountain Bell and Pacific Northwestern Bell to form US WEST, Inc., one of the seven regional telecommunications companies formed after AT&T's breakup. Northwestern Bell has entered, along with US WEST, into emerging competitive and fully competitive telecommunications fields.

The changes in the organization, which has gone from a completely regulated monopoly to part of a market-driven *Fortune* 500 colossus, have been profound. For customers the changes have been major as well; many face options and choices never before confronted.

Northwestern Bell Telephone has managed to strengthen its basic commit-

ment to offering its customers a high-quality, fairly priced local service. With in excess of $5.5 billion invested in facilities locally to provide this service, the "phone company," in many ways, has not changed at all.

Today Northwestern Bell has installed a fiber-optic voice/data transmission system in the Twin Cities, consisting of a 96-fiber cable, with each fiber capable of carrying up to 6,048 voice conversations simultaneously.

DAIN BOSWORTH INCORPORATED

Dain Bosworth's success at understanding and responding to the financial needs of companies, communities, and individuals throughout the Midwest and Pacific Northwest shouldn't be so surprising. Today one of the nation's leading regional investment banking firms and one of the top 25 firms in the nation in municipal underwriting, Dain Bosworth has grown from a small regional investment banking and brokerage firm to form a single large company with all the assets and strengths of a major contender in financial markets. What makes Dain Bosworth different is that even through this growth and consolidation, the company never stopped acting like the regional and community-based financial services companies that came together to comprise it. The result is a financial services company with revenues of more than $100 million and 1,350 employees that manages to remain responsive to local finance and investment needs in dozens of widely spread communities. Those communities range from the Twin Cities to Seattle to Great Falls, Montana, with dozens of small and large cities in

Thomas M. Dale, Jr., is chairman and chief executive officer of Dain Bosworth Incorporated, now entering its 80th year of business.

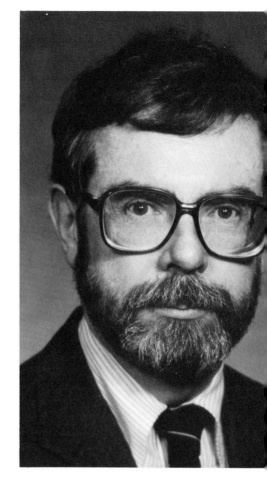

between—the communities where Dain Bosworth grew up.

The roots of Dain Bosworth were planted between 1909 and 1929 in four different cities by four separate companies. In 1909 Oscar Kalman opened the brokerage firm of Kalman & Company in the Pioneer Building in St. Paul. Seven years later and far from St. Paul, Bosworth, Chanute and Loughridge opened in the booming frontier town of Denver. In 1922 Quail & Company set up shop in Davenport, Iowa. The future foundation of Dain Bosworth was completed in 1929, when the municipal bond house of J.M. Dain and Co. was formed in Minneapolis. Eventually, time and several strong personalities would bring all four companies together.

Merill Cohen, who led J.M. Dain for 30 years, is often credited with starting the process that helped shape the present company. Under Cohen, J.M. Dain joined the New York Stock Exchange in 1955 and made headlines by paying the highest price for a seat since the Depression. Cohen also hired many of Dain Bos-

Richard D. McFarland is chairman and chief executive officer of IFG, Dain Bosworth's holding company.

Under president Irving Weiser, IFG has been repositioning itself into core industries.

worth's top management, including several who later became president.

One of those men, Wheelock Whitney, succeeded Cohen in 1963. Under Whitney, J.M. Dain engineered the key merger with Kalman & Company; later, the newly merged company bought Quail & Company and was renamed Dain, Kalman, Quail (DKQ). During the next decade DKQ acquired several other brokerage firms and reached a watershed in 1972, when the company went public with a national over-the-counter stock offering that sold 250,000 shares. Two years after the initial public offering, DKQ formed the Inter-Regional Financial Group (IFG) as a publicly owned holding company to acquire additional investment firms and help the company diversify beyond the Midwest. One of the first such acquisitions was in 1974 with Bosworth, Sullivan and Co. in Denver. For a time, the two firms were operated and managed independently. In 1978 the operations of the two firms were combined to form a new company which was renamed Dain Bosworth in 1979.

A few years later Dain Bosworth would look to the Pacific Northwest for future growth. By the early 1980s Dain Bosworth had established itself in several cities in Washington and Oregon. Dain grew to be a strong regional presence in the Pacific Northwest both through training and by hiring regional brokers and other investment professionals who were far more interested in working for a company with a history of regional community involvement than for large, centralized investment firms with few community ties.

That community presence is nowhere more evident than in the Twin Cities, where Dain Bosworth has had an incredible impact. As partner with government organizations and corporations, Dain has made significant contributions to the area's economy and infrastructure through bond placements, public stock offerings, and other investment services. Dain has managed, for example, initial public offerings or acted as investment banker for such companies as H.B. Fuller, Super Valu, Toro, Graco, The Tennant Co., Medtronic, and Minnegasco. During 1986 and 1987 alone, Dain raised over $2.7 billion for corporate clients.

On the public-sector side, Dain Bosworth has long acted as investment banker for the Minnesota Housing Finance Agen-

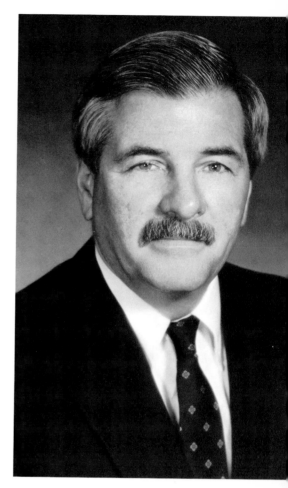

Fred Friswold, Dain Bosworth president, shares direction of the company with Dale. Under his leadership, important new markets have been developed.

cy, the St. Cloud Housing Authority, and the cities of Minneapolis, St. Paul, and Duluth. Dain packaged and underwrote bond offerings used to finance the Hubert Humphrey Metrodome, the new Minneapolis Convention Center, and the new Minnesota Timberwolves basketball arena. Dain has also put together bond offerings for Fairview Hospital, the Minneapolis Children's Health Center, HealthOne, and Methodist Hospital in St. Louis Park.

In the meantime, IFG, Dain Bosworth's parent, has become a diversified financial services company. Since its formation, IFG has acquired or created subsidiaries such as Midwest Life Insurance, Investment Advisors, IFG Leasing, Dain Corporation, a Minneapolis-based real estate investment services company, IFG Information Services, and Rauscher Pierce Refsnes, Inc., a Dallas-based securities investment firm. In recent years IFG has consolidated its holdings and sold its insurance, money management, and leasing units. Today Dain Bosworth, Rauscher Pierce Refsnes, and Dain Corporation are IFG's three main subsidiaries.

The Dain Bosworth of the 1980s and beyond is headquartered in the historic 26-story art deco Dain Tower in downtown Minneapolis. In addition to corporations and communities, Dain Bosworth serves 200,000 individuals through 41 offices in 12 midwestern and western states. Its hallmarks include corporate and public finance departments that are among the most active in the nation, and a research department that—in typical Dain Bosworth fashion—closely studies businesses and economic conditions in the different regional markets the company serves. That's only one aspect of many that makes Dain Bosworth so different. But as clients might tell you, it's one aspect of many that makes Dain Bosworth among the best.

The 26-story Dain Tower in downtown Minneapolis was built in 1929 as the Rand Tower and is widely admired for its historic art deco design.

LUTHERAN BROTHERHOOD

Most companies profess to having a mission. Some even claim they're out to make the world a better place. Lutheran Brotherhood, headquartered in downtown Minneapolis, is no exception. However, as a fraternal benefit society that provides insurance and other financial services to its Lutheran members throughout the United States, Lutheran Brotherhood is serious about its benevolent mission.

At the same time, thanks to far-sighted leadership and top management skills, Lutheran Brotherhood has become one of the largest and most successful insurance companies in the nation. Only in Lutheran Brotherhood's case, its success has a special meaning—a large portion of its operational gain is returned to its members to serve a variety of church, community, and other fraternal needs. In 1986 the nearly $28 million Lutheran Brotherhood distributed this way meant it had a church and community impact like few other companies.

Today, with about $20 billion of life insurance in force and more than $5 billion in assets under management, Lutheran Brotherhood is one of the nation's largest financial services operations. Measured by assets under management, it is the largest fraternal benefit society in the United States.

In its simplest terms, a fraternal benefit society is a not-for-profit, nonstock corporation that is owned by members with a lodge or branch system and a representative form of government, and that provides insurance and other financial and fraternal programs for its members. Lutheran Brotherhood offers its more than 900,000 members life and health insurance protection, annuities, mutual funds, other financial services, and numerous fraternal benefits that include scholarships, matching gifts to Lutheran colleges and universities, and funds to distribute to numerous church and community causes.

The story of Lutheran Brotherhood begins in 1917, a time of ferment for Lutherans in America. At the organizing convention of the Norwegian Lutheran Church of America (NLCA), held that year in St. Paul, three important Lutheran synods merged. Some lay and clergy leaders were concerned about finding a way by which NLCA church members could be supportive of one another and help "bear one another's burdens." Two delegates to the convention, J.A.O. Preuss and Herman L. Ekern, submitted a proposal for a Lutheran aid society that would offer life insurance to NLCA members. This

Lutheran Brotherhood president Robert P. Gandrud (left) and chairman Clair E. Strommen.

idea was opposed by some at the convention who believed insurance was in conflict with the belief, held by some Lutherans, that God would take care of his people.

Despite this opposition, the convention formed a committee chaired by the Reverend Thor Eggen to study the matter. From these deliberations emerged the Luther Union, a fraternal benefit society controlled by the NLCA, with a system of local units, and with Eggen as president. Luther Union was structured to remain close to the benevolent, education, and community activities of the church itself. It took another year, however, before the organization could meet the minimum requirements of Minnesota insurance laws, and on September 18, 1918, after receiving a license from the state, 506 contracts were issued.

In 1920 Luther Union reached an agreement with the Lutheran Brotherhood of America, an association originally formed to serve the social and religious needs of Lutherans in the military during World War I, to serve as its insurance auxiliary. That same year the young society changed its name to Lutheran Brotherhood and opened its membership to all Lutherans—not just those who were

The directors of the original Luther Union, which was formed in 1917.

T. EGGEN
President

H. L. EKERN
Director

J. A. O. PREUSS
Secretary-Treasurer

C. J. EASTVOLD
Vice President

LUTHER UNION
1917

INCORPORATORS

DIRECTORS

OFFICERS

H. G. STUB
Incorporator

J. N. KILDAHL
Incorporator

S. T. REQUE
Director

T. H. DAHL
Incorporator

G. M. BRUCE
Incorporator

Located in downtown Minneapolis, the Lutheran Brotherhood Building houses the society's 925 home office staff members and leases space to other firms. Completed in 1981, this 17-story, rose-colored building features an attractive greenhouse-style cafeteria and a 457-seat auditorium.

been named chairman of Lutheran Brotherhood's board of directors in 1922, Ekern established policies that made Lutheran Brotherhood an important part of Lutheran life. Despite the Great Depression, the society, under Ekern and Preuss, made mortgage loans to farmers and city dwellers and, among other moves, inaugurated a policy of lending money to churches at a time when Lutheran congregations found it difficult to borrow.

Preuss continued as chairman of the board until his death in 1961. Ekern was succeeded by Carl F. Granrud as president in 1951; he then became chairman of the board upon the death of Preuss. The Granrud administration was succeeded in 1967 by A.O. Lee as chairman and A. Herbert Nelson as president.

Following Lee's death and Nelson's retirement in 1970, Arley R. Bjella was elected chairman of the board and chief executive officer, and W.P. Langhaug was elected president.

In 1980 Langhaug retired and was succeeded by Clair E. Strommen, who served as president and later became chief executive officer. In July 1987 Bjella was elected chairman emeritus; Strommen, chairman; and Robert P. Gandrud, president of Lutheran Brotherhood.

New insurance and investment products have included health insurance, annuities, and mutual funds. Nearly all of Lutheran Brotherhood's 1,200 full-time representatives are registered to sell investment products distributed by the society's securities subsidiary.

Perhaps the best contemporary symbol of the society's success is its Minneapolis headquarters. When the 17-story building opened in 1981, it became an instant downtown landmark. With its planes of rose-tinted glass cascading toward a massive cylinder at the north front of the building, Lutheran Brotherhood's new home is both a functional business environment and a reflection of the spirit of the people inside—a spirit that combines caring, aid to Lutheranism, and excellence in business performance.

members of the Norwegian Lutheran Church of America.

Eggen proved to be an exceptional businessman during his 12 years as president. When he retired and was succeeded by Herman Ekern in 1929, however, Lutheran Brotherhood began to take off in important new directions.

Ekern had a long background in politics, fraternal societies, and insurance, including service as insurance commissioner for the State of Wisconsin. Along with J.A.O. Preuss—a former commissioner and governor of Minnesota—who had

PEAVEY GRAIN COMPANY

When Frank Hutchison Peavey's 25-year-old F.H. Peavey & Company filled America's first concrete grain silo in Minneapolis, Minnesota, it attracted quite a crowd—most standing at a safe distance because they were sure "Peavey's Folly" would explode. Grain storage containers were supposed to be made of wood—never mind that fires were frequent and insurance rates exorbitant.

But Frank Peavey knew that concrete silos were mandatory if agriculture was to grow. Such thinking had already earned him the title of "Elevator King" and poured the foundation for the Peavey Company, which through the next century was to become a large and diversified company engaged in food processing, grain merchandising and brokering, and specialty retailing.

Peavey's family were leading Minnesota citizens who left an indelible mark on the landscape and civic institutions of the Twin Cities. When Peavey died in 1901, his company owned nearly 450 elevators with a capacity of more than 10 million bushels. Leadership passed to his two sons-in-law, Frank Totton Heffelfinger and Frederick Brown Wells.

The acquisition of flour milling and distribution companies increased the company's market share. In 1969, a pivotal year, Fritz Corrigan was named chief executive officer, the first man outside the family to hold that position. Corrigan oversaw a decade of expansion and diversification. While flour milling and grain trading remained the company's chief business, it broadened through acquisition

Frank Peavey, founder of the Peavey Grain Company.

and internal growth to include marketing fertilizer, feed, and other agricultural items; commodity futures brokerage; specialty retailing in primarily smaller midwestern and Canadian agricultural communities; and consumer food processing, including not only flour-related products, but also packaged baked goods and the Home Brands line of jams and jellies.

When Peavey merged with ConAgra, it became the largest public grain trading company in the country.

Peavey Company went public in 1973; three years later it was a *Fortune* 500 company listed on the New York Stock Exchange.

In the 1980s, as agriculture and grain trading went through dramatic changes in the United States—many of them not entirely beneficial to either farmers or agricultural product companies—Peavey continued to change. The most dramatic was its 1982 merger with Omaha-based ConAgra, Inc., a giant diversified food-processing company. ConAgra's grain trading operation was then combined with Peavey's to form Peavey Grain Company, the largest public grain company in the country. The Peavey Grain Company continues to be committed to the American farmer and the agricultural community, and remains headquartered in a downtown Minneapolis landmark, the Peavey Building.

Even though ConAgra is an Omaha-based company, one thing that won't change is the civic influence Frank Peavey's descendants and the company he built have had on Minneapolis and St. Paul. Notable examples include Peavey Plaza, one of the jewels of downtown Minneapolis with its dramatic fountains and exquisite landscaping, located adjacent to Orchestra Hall. Peavey Plaza was a gift from the company to Minneapolis and its citizens in honor of Peavey's first century of service in 1974. Peavey's donation of land and buildings in Chaska, Minnesota, a Twin Cities suburb, to the College of Saint Thomas, allowed the college to open a satellite campus.

PARK DENTAL HEALTH CENTERS

Dentistry, a $35-billion enterprise in the United States, has been characterized by many health care analysts as a "cottage industry." Ninety-five percent of dentists today work in solo practices, and most group dental practices consist of two or three dentists at most. All of this despite economic trends that are making small dental practices, like many private medical practices, increasingly unrealistic. The situation is dramatically different in the Twin Cities, where Park Dental Health Centers, the nation's largest and most innovative group dental practice, has profoundly changed the delivery of dental care and, many would argue, considerably improved it.

A unique hybrid organization, PDHC is both a prepaid health maintenance organization participant through its affiliation with the St. Louis Park-based MedCenters Health Plan and one of the largest fee-for-service practices in the nation. And now, through a joint venture with American MedCenters called Dental Program Management, Inc., there is a management and consulting company to show dentists in other American cities how prepaid dental care can improve their practices, lower costs to health care consumers, and position dentistry in the forefront of creative change instead of trailing several years behind it.

Dr. Gregory Swenson is one of the founders and current president of PDHC. His notion of prepaid dental care began to form in the late 1970s after informal discussion with dentists in other parts of the country who were entertaining similar thoughts. At the time Dr. Swenson was part of a small group practice in Brooklyn Center. Swenson discussed his ideas with several colleagues, and a feasibility study was commissioned. Conclusion: The market was ready for the concept, but success would depend on several factors, including standardized procedures in all practice locations and a strong quality-assurance program.

Instead of trying to create a dental HMO from scratch, MedCenters Health Plan, Inc., a growing Twin Cities HMO, was approached. As a result, Park Dental Health Centers was formed in 1980, both as a prepaid dental plan for MedCenters members and as a fee-for-service group practice.

Today PDHC has grown into a network of 31 Twin Cities offices, serving

Park Dental Health Centers has become the nation's largest and most innovative group dental practice. Standardized procedures in all locations and a strong quality-assurance program have contributed to its success. Courtesy, Mel Jacobsen Photography, Inc.

more than 40,000 MedCenters members and several times that many fee-for-service patients. Dental Program Management and American MedCenters, MedCenters' parent company, are now in the process of bringing the dental HMO idea to other areas of the United States.

The internal program of greatest daily significance to PDHC is its quality-assurance program. The work of each dentist and dental hygienist is systematically reviewed by other colleagues within the organization for the purpose of accomplishing quality improvement. Within the past two years statistical process-control techniques used in business organizations are being applied to this quality review process. Also, PDHC is accredited by the Accreditation Association for Ambulatory Health Care, a national health care accrediting agency. This means that every three years PDHC is thoroughly evaluated by AAAHC and certified as provid-

Dental Management Program and American MedCenters are now in the process of bringing the Park Dental HMO idea to other U.S. cities. Courtesy, Mel Jacobsen Photography, Inc.

ing good quality dental care. PDHC is very proud of this achievement.

Based on the growth of PDHC, the idea of HMO-based dental care seems to be an idea whose time has come. There's little doubt that Park Dental Health Centers will continue to be an innovator in the years ahead.

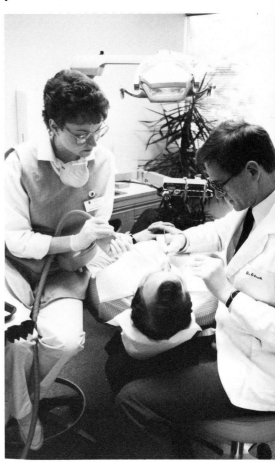

UNISYS

In 1986 Sperry Corp. and Burroughs Corp. merged to create a $9-billion information systems company, Unisys Corp. By capitalizing on the specialized market strengths each company brought to the merger, Unisys offers customers a broad range of solutions to meet their information-processing needs.

Unisys can trace its local roots to the drafty old barn of a factory on Minnehaha Avenue in St. Paul where Engineering Research Associates (ERA) set up shop in 1946. Formed to continue computer development work begun for the military during World War II, ERA was a catalyst for the birth of the high-technology electronics industry in Minnesota.

The nucleus of ERA was a group of scientists and engineers who had developed code-breaking machines for the U.S. Navy during the war. John Parker and his business associates located their new company in St. Paul because Parker owned a vacant building there large enough to accommodate the venture. The location proved to be perfect, as ERA was able to recruit talented engineering graduates from the nearby University of Minnesota.

Although the work environment was less than ideal—ERA employees frequently needed their coats and mittens indoors in the winter and worked shirtless for comfort in the summer—enthusiasm and a sense of exploration kept the pioneers going as they developed the technical advances that would build the modern computer industry.

Eager to prove itself as a problem solver, ERA took on the challenge of developing a general-purpose, stored-program computer for the U.S. Navy. In late 1950 ERA delivered the Atlas I, the first electronic computer of its kind. Later the company developed a similar device for commercial applications, the ERA 1101. Unisys still produces descendants of the ERA 1101 today—its 1100 Series mainframes.

In the early 1950s both ERA and Eckert-Mauchly, founded by J. Presper Eckert and John Mauchly, were purchased by Remington Rand. Eckert and Mauchly had created ENIAC, the first electronic digital calculating device. When Remington Rand merged with Sperry Corp. in 1955, its ERA and Eckert-Mauchly divisions became part of Sperry's Univac Division. In 1986 Sperry merged with Burroughs Corp. to form Unisys.

Today Unisys is the second-largest information systems company in the world, with the greatest concentration of

Operators monitor work activity performed by the large-scale Unisys 1100/90 System.

Unisys computer systems are subjected to testing and evaluation standards in preparation for shipment to customer sites.

its 90,000 workers worldwide in the Twin Cities area. Unisys is one of the leading industrial employers in Minnesota, with 12,000 employees in 21 facilities. The corporation produces innovative general-purpose computer systems and provides total information systems solutions for financial, public-sector, industrial, commercial, communications, airlines, defense, and federal markets. Unisys still has a building on the original Minnehaha Avenue site—its Computer Systems Division Midway facility—and continues to build on the foundation of excellence laid by ERA.

MEDTRONIC, INC.

When Earl Bakken was an electrical engineering student at the University of Minnesota in 1949, his sole connection to medicine was his wife, a medical technologist at Northwestern (Abbott-Northwestern) Hospital in Minneapolis. When doctors learned what Bakken studied, some of them sought his assistance in repairing electrical hospital diagnostic machines—bulky, based on vacuum tubes, and all too liable to break down.

From this relationship grew a company that was to have a revolutionary impact on Minnesota's economy—Medtronic, the world's leading supplier of cardiac pacemakers, an innovator in other biomedical areas, and the nucleus for Minnesota's vital biomedical products industry. An estimated 150 companies have evolved from Medtronic.

Medtronic started simply: Bakken recognized an obvious need, and with partner Palmer Hermundslie, set up a medical equipment repair company in a 600-square-foot garage in Northeast Minneapolis. Eventually they began making custom equipment for physicians and hospitals, and selling products made by other companies.

They became acquainted with Dr. C. Walton Lillehei, a pioneer in open heart surgery at the University of Minnesota, who was performing surgery on babies with heart defects. Electrical stimulation with pacemakers was needed to control the hearts of some children. The pacemakers were large and cumbersome with unreliable power sources that had to be plugged into a wall outlet. Lillehei turned to the young Medtronic to find an engineering solution. The result was the world's first external battery-operated pacemaker.

Dr. William Chardack and Wilson Greatbatch had developed an implantable pacemaker with a self-contained power source. Securing rights to manufacture the device, Medtronic began production in December 1960 and was on its way to becoming the world's largest manufacturer of implantable medical devices. Currently almost one in two pacemakers in the world is manufactured by Medtronic; more than 1.4 million Medtronic pacemakers have been implanted. One in four pacemakers implanted in the United States today is an Activitrax®, Medtronic's newest pacemaker that automatically adjusts its stimulation rate to a

Medtronic's first manufacturing facility was a 600-square-foot garage in Minneapolis.

patient's activity level.

Medtronic recently boasted revenues exceeding $500 million, a work force of some 5,000 people worldwide, and an unsurpassed distribution system that encompasses 85 countries, helping overseas sales grow to nearly 50 percent of revenues. The company's stock has been traded on the New York Stock Exchange since 1977.

The firm has branched out into a wide line of implantable medical devices, including mechanical and tissue heart valves and electrical stimulation devices for chronic pain. An implantable pacer-cardioverter-defibrillator system, a drug infusion system, and balloon angioplasty catheter are undergoing clinical studies.

Winston R. Wallin, chairman of the board, president, and chief executive officer, leads the company. Earl Bakken continues as senior chairman of the board.

Medtronic endowed a $2-million chair in Earl Bakken's name in biomedical engineering at the University of Minnesota and has been instrumental in efforts to develop a world-class biomedical engineering program at the university. Medtronic's mission is to contribute to human welfare by application of biomedical engineering in the research, design, manufacture, and sale of instruments or appliances that alleviate pain, restore health, and extend life.

Today Medtronic is the world's leading manufacturer of implantable medical devices. It helped spawn an industry that has become vital to Minnesota's economy.

NASH FINCH COMPANY

In 1885 Fred Nash, a young man from Vermont, opened a small candy and tobacco store in Devil's Lake, North Dakota. Soon he urged his brothers, Edgar and Willis, to join him. The North Dakota frontier was ripe with opportunity, young Nash figured. With hard work and gumption, the three brothers could probably make something of themselves.

The business world is full of stories of modest beginnings that become great endeavors, but few can parallel what happened to the little store the Nash brothers operated on the North Dakota frontier. That business would eventually become Nash Finch Company, one of the nation's leading food distributors and retailers with 17 distribution centers and a market that covers 24 states.

Right from the start the three Nash brothers established a pattern of innovation that continues to this day. Food retailing was as wide open in those days as the North Dakota frontier itself. Soon after Fred Nash was joined by his two brothers, two more stores were added in surrounding towns, including one in Grand Forks where the brothers moved their operation. After a carload of peaches arrived in town

one day without a buyer, the brothers bought it on the spot, a decision that was to have momentous consequences, and began traveling the surrounding territory taking orders from other stores.

They also hired young H.B. Finch for a princely $4-per-week salary. Finch was to be the first of three generations of Finches to head the giant that later became Nash Finch.

In the years following the turn of the century, as the railroads made shipping fresh food easier, the Nash brothers expanded into Crookston, Minnesota (where H.B. Finch was put in charge of a new operation called Finch-Smith Company), and began establishing warehouse operations close to small towns and rural markets. Between 1904 and 1912, 21 "fruit houses," as they were called, were built or purchased across the Upper Midwest, in Canada, and as far west as the state of Washington. A growing sales force traveled the region, going from town to town in open horse-drawn buggies, even in the below-zero chill of midwestern winters. The company had also entered the business of growing, packing, and shipping its own fruit through the purchase of orchards in Idaho and eventually in California, where the Nash DeCamp Company would grow to be a dominant supplier of fresh fruits and vegetables and a major

The Nash brothers and several employees in an early photo. Standing third from left is Willis K. Nash, and (also standing) fifth from left is Fred P. Nash. Seated is Edgar Nash.

contributor to the firm's later successes.

By 1921 the enterprise had set up headquarters in Minneapolis and officially incorporated as the Nash Finch Company in the United States and Nash-Simington Ltd. in Canada. By now it had 60 wholesale houses and a number of re-

Nash Finch's giant St. Cloud distribution center.

lated grocery, growing, shipping, and marketing operations. Fred Nash was named the company's president after the consolidation; when he passed away in 1926, H.B. Finch assumed his duties. During that same year an innovative employee ownership plan was established that would allow the firm to grow in the coming years without assuming large amounts of long-term debt. That pattern of giving employees opportunities to participate and grow with the company continues today.

When the Great Depression hit in 1929, Nash Finch was doing more than $35 million in sales and had established itself as one of the leading midwestern food distributors. The economic slump meant that the early 1930s would be years of survival for the company but little growth would take place. The year 1932 was the only year the organization failed to make a profit, however, and by the end of World War II, 427 Nash Finch sales representatives were calling on more than 35,000 retail establishments. But by then the nature of the food distribution business had changed.

Salesmen were calling on larger accounts while the company used catalogs to service its smaller accounts. That called for larger warehouses doing more volume and more competitive pricing. A huge change occurred for Nash Finch in the early 1950s with the purchase of 17 supermarkets, warehouses, and truck lines in Nebraska. That marked the beginning of the firm's retail supermarket business and transformation of the firm that would lead to the *Fortune* 500 giant of today.

The 1960s and 1970s were a time of tremendous growth for Nash Finch. Sales stood at $91 million in 1960; 10 years later they reached nearly $248 million. By 1980 that figure would top $987 million. Once exclusively a food wholesaler, Nash Finch in these two important decades would become diversified to include all important areas of the modern food industry—from growing and wholesaling to retail supermarkets. The concern itself would hardly be a household name, but its franchised or corporate-owned stores, including Jack & Jill, Piggly Wiggly, Family Thrift Center, and others, would be known to millions of consumers. Leadership would come from presidents W.E. Dietz, Harold B. Finch (H.B. Finch's son),

The interior of Nash Finch's latest Econo-Foods store in Iowa City, Iowa.

Thomas D. Hays, Thomas A. Riley, and today, Harold B. Finch, Jr.—the grandson of the man who along with the Nashes gave the company its start.

Nash Finch observed the centennial of its operation in 1985 with a train ride that crossed the original North Dakota territory. The company had much to celebrate. Sales most recently topped $1.5 billion, and the firm has just expanded into new regional markets, including the southeastern United States and Colorado.

The successes of its recent corporate strategies make Nash Finch optimistic about reaching its goal of $2 billion in sales by 1990. Much of that growth will come in markets the company has recently entered. At the same time Nash Finch appears to have never lost its commitment to providing employees with opportunities for personal and professional growth. The Nash Finch Scholarship Program, for instance, is now in its 12th year of providing scholarships to the children of company employees.

Despite the organization's size, the spirit that animated its founders on the North Dakota prairie 100 years ago appears to be the same spirit that is propelling the Nash Finch Company forward today.

ERNST & WHINNEY

By the beginning of this century Minneapolis and St. Paul had been transformed from the raw frontier towns of just a few decades earlier into economic powerhouses. The foundations of many of the great companies that shaped the region had been laid. Famous fortunes were already under way.

Naturally the area soon attracted the interests of a new type of professional called accountants; the activity had only been recognized as a profession in Great Britain less than a half-century earlier and fewer than 20 years earlier in the United States. In 1918 the young accounting firm of Ernst & Ernst, now Ernst & Whinney, became the third national company to open an office in Minneapolis.

Alwin C. Ernst and his older brother Theodore knew that American businesses had long outgrown the need for simple bookkeeping. In 1903 they founded Ernst & Ernst in Cleveland, Ohio. The two brothers pioneered a service-oriented approach to the new profession of accounting, an approach that emphasized using the practical application of accounting theory to show businesses their strengths and weaknesses. Their original philosophy was a forerunner for today's quality-conscious service environment. Growth was rapid, and soon Ernst & Ernst began opening offices in other cities.

When Ernst & Ernst opened its Minneapolis office, the company had penetrated only a handful of U.S. cities. The Minneapolis office was just the 10th of what would eventually become 120 offices nationwide. There were bigger cities, but Minneapolis had several factors in its favor, one that it was headquarters of the Ninth Federal Reserve District, recently created by the 1913 Federal Reserve Act. In addition to its growing importance as a financial center, the city had also become one of the nation's most important agribusiness centers.

The firm's instincts about the potential in both Minneapolis and St. Paul soon proved correct. The Minneapolis office was first headed by W.E. Fallberg, then B.T. Maer, followed by George F. Brewer. In order to keep up with a rapidly growing client base, Ernst & Ernst opened an office in nearby St. Paul in 1920, the first and, for many years, the only national accounting firm to have an office in both cities.

Ernst & Ernst's practice in Minneapolis began experiencing dramatic growth under the leadership of Harold C. Utley, who became managing partner in 1929. Utley brought unique qualities to

---

Today 25 partners lead the Minneapolis and St. Paul offices of Ernst & Whinney.

Minnesota's accounting profession, combining a zeal for high professional standards with his reputation for diplomacy. His impact is evidenced by the fact that the Minnesota Society of CPAs still presents the Harold C. Utley Award to the highest scorers on the state's CPA exam. As president of the Minnesota Society of Certified Public Accountants, Utley's skills as a mediator served him well. He worked hard to bring local and national firms together, recognizing the value that both offered to the Minnesota business community.

The professional and personal strengths of Utley helped expand Ernst & Ernst's list of clients. The firm's extensive services and resources were welcomed by companies that had to comply with complex Securities and Exchange Commission reporting laws established in the 1930s.

By the end of the 1930s many of the area's largest corporations had established relationships with Ernst & Ernst that continue today. Smaller companies also benefited from the services offered by the growing firm, earning Ernst & Ernst the respect of a large and diversified segment of the business community.

Utley left behind a legacy of community service and active involvement with civic and business groups that continues in the firm's Minneapolis and St. Paul

Edward L. Finn is the managing partner of the Twin Cities offices.

Pictured above are Willard J. Patty, Jr., managing partner of Ernst & Whinney's St. Paul location (left), and Edward L. Finn, managing partner of the Minneapolis location.

offices, evidenced by the offices' annual receipt of the chamber of commerce's Keystone awards.

During this period Ernst & Ernst had 34 U.S. offices. The need to serve a growing international business community brought about the affiliation of Ernst & Ernst with the prestigious English firm of Whinney, Murray & Co. Eventually the two firms combined to form Ernst & Whinney.

Harold Utley served as managing

partner until the mid-1960s. His successor, Thomas Spaeth, took over during a time when the accounting industry was changing. Firms were becoming, as one observer noted, "living, breathing, full-service organizations." Consulting services became increasingly important. Today Ernst & Whinney is one of the world's largest management consulting organizations.

The client base also grew to reflect the changing and expanding business world. In addition to its long-standing expertise in retailing, banking and financial services, transportation, and manufacturing, Ernst & Whinney began serving a growing number of high-technology, biotechnology, and health care companies—sectors that have shaped Minnesota's modern economy.

In the 1980s the Minneapolis office of Ernst & Whinney, under current managing partner Edward Finn (Spaeth's other successors included Robert Kelly and George Beck), has become one of the largest Ernst & Whinney offices in the Midwest, with specialized expertise in almost all practice areas.

In 1986 the St. Paul firm of Taylor, McCaskill & Co., Ltd., merged with Ernst & Whinney. The St. Paul office now has nearly 60 employees. Ernst & Whinney's national practice now includes

122 U.S. offices as well as offices in 75 other countries.

Today Ernst & Whinney in the Twin Cities reflects the complexity and diversity of the clients it serves. The firm offers audit, tax, and management consulting services, and has in recent years developed strong consulting expertise in health care, retail, information systems, manufacturing, and banking and financial services industries. The consulting practice's growth reflects the need of the firm's clients for an ever-increasing array of professional services.

After nearly 70 years of service to Minnesota business, Ernst & Whinney's Minneapolis and St. Paul offices have grown dramatically to become large, dynamic professional service organizations. These offices, through the dedicated efforts of their partners and employees, are committed to continuing their tradition of service to client needs, the community, and Minnesota business in general.

Audit and tax professionals at Ernst & Whinney's Minneapolis office use a microcomputer to provide service to clients. The firm's Twin Cities offices are in the forefront in applying computers to better serve the needs of the Upper Midwest's business community.

LAND O'LAKES

The cooperative tradition in agriculture has deep Minnesota roots. It is the state where many believe agricultural cooperatives—groups of farmers who band together to jointly market products through formal business entities—really got their start. Cooperatives help ensure higher prices for farmers and less profit for middlemen. They also give consumers a higher-quality, more stringently controlled product.

The cooperative spirit is so ingrained in Minnesota that by the second decade of the twentieth century the number of Minnesota dairy cooperatives alone numbered 620. But by then the sheer number of cooperatives and the way they pitted one small community against another was becoming counterproductive. Instead of working to benefit individual cooperative members, the intense competition was making market conditions tougher for everyone. Among those who saw this predicament clearly were John Brandt and William Harpel, who helped organize the historic meeting in St. Paul in 1921 of more than half of Minnesota's 622 cooperatives that formed the first statewide dairy cooperative—Minnesota Cooperative Creameries Assn.

Today Americans in every part of the country know this cooperative by the name it adopted five years later, Land

Land O'Lakes headquarters in Arden Hills, often called "the house that 250,000 farmers built."

O'Lakes Creameries, Inc., and its enduring and classic trademark, the Land O'Lakes Indian maiden, that has become among the most famous corporate symbols ever. Most also know it as a very big company. But even though its sales place it firmly among the *Fortune* 200, this cooperative, formed six decades ago, remains true to its original purpose—producing higher prices and better lives for

its farmer members, the people who own it and who now number more than 325,000.

The cooperative that eventually became Land O'Lakes was first concerned with getting its members a better price for their butter. Brandt, the cooperative's first president, traveled widely throughout the nation to convince grocers and distributors that this group of Minnesota dairymen produced a better product. When the name Land O'Lakes was adopted in 1926, Land O'Lakes butter became the first butter trademarked and marketed on a national basis. That was just the first of a series of marketing innovations that would allow the cooperative to expand its reach and its ability to serve its members, even through the Depression that loomed

John Brandt, a leader in the agricultural cooperative movement, served as Land O'Lakes president for 30 years.

Land O'Lakes quickly became known as the "nation's butter maker" and remains the leading marketer of butter today.

just a few years ahead. By 1929 sales, which now included turkeys, topped $52 million, and Land O'Lakes had become known as the nation's butter maker.

In the ensuing decades processing plants were built, other cooperatives joined the growing super-cooperative known as Land O'Lakes, and careful attention continued to be paid to the importance of marketing. Cheese, ice cream, eggs, meat, poultry, processed foods, and many other products were added to the Land O'Lakes line—all sold directly to retailers or distributors, with profits going right back to members. Especially important during those years was the establishment of Land O'Lakes Agricultural Services division, which was set up to provide cost-efficient products and services to members themselves, among them, the first successful milk replacer for nursing calves. By the end of the 1950s sales had reached $178.5 million. Ten years later sales had doubled again.

The past two decades have been times of the greatest growth for Land O'Lakes. Much of this growth has come through mergers with other large cooperatives. In 1970 the merger with Farmers Regional Cooperative (FELCO) greatly increased the company's agricultural services operations and expanded market opportunities. It also prompted the firm to change its name from Land O'Lakes Creameries to Land O'Lakes, Inc. Growth in sales in the 1970s were astonishing: By the end of the decade Land O'Lakes was a $1.4-billion company. Another historic merger—this time with Midland Cooperatives, Inc.—marked the early 1980s.

Land O'Lakes then moved into its beautiful new corporate headquarters and research center in Arden Hills, Minnesota—often called "the house that 250,000 farmers built." Important events of recent times for Land O'Lakes include a joint venture and later the acquisition of Schweigert Meats; the creation of Ag Processing Inc., a joint soy-processing venture; international business agreements in Ireland, Turkey, Japan, Costa Rica, and other countries; and the consolidation of several important milk-processing facilities with Mid-America Dairymen. Perhaps the most significant event was Land O'Lakes' consolidation in 1986 of its farm supply operations with those of another giant cooperative, Cenex, into a new ven-

Land O'Lakes conducts both plant and animal research at its 535-acre Answer Farm located near Fort Dodge, Iowa. The Answer Farm was designed specifically to help develop methods and products to improve farmers' productivity and profitability.

ture called Cenex/Land O'Lakes Ag Services. The move created a member-owned cooperative of national scale and is expected to position members of both companies to be more effective competitors in the international agricultural marketplace of the 1990s and beyond.

Today with more than $2 billion in sales, Land O'Lakes, the nation's best-known cooperative, is a company marked by both a great deal of pride and a renewed sense of commitment to improving the businesses of its members in an increasingly tough agricultural market. A New Spirit of Cooperation is the way Land O'Lakes characterizes its response to the challenges ahead. And though the trend is toward reducing duplication, pursuing greater efficiency, and obtaining greater marketing muscle—bigness, in other words—Land O'Lakes will continue to remain faithful to its original roots as an extension of its individual farmer-members.

The Land O'Lakes Foods Group and Meats Group manufacture more than 600 food items for consumer, food-service, and industrial markets. These foods range from familiar staples such as butter, cheese, and sandwich meats to food-service items such as cheese sauce and turkey products.

REMMELE ENGINEERING, INC.

Fred L. Remmele, an experienced tool and die maker born in Heilbron, Germany, found, in 1926 when he immigrated to Minnesota, machine shop managers disorganized and employees treated with little regard to their needs and interests. New ideas were allowed to founder, especially if they came from workers, whose potential contributions were great but were often ignored.

Remmele sensed a market opportunity for a company that could be run differently, one that emphasized employee participation and innovative management. Today that spirit continues to animate Remmele Engineering, Inc., the firm Remmele founded in 1949, and that has grown to be a relative giant in its industry, with revenues recently topping $38 million and a work force of 350.

In the decades since its creation Remmele Engineering has evolved into a company with three separate areas of specialization: factory automation equipment, short-run precision machining specializing in large parts, and long-run precision machining. The work is conducted at four separate facilities totaling more than 285,000 square feet.

The firm has been successful for a combination of reasons. For one thing, Remmele's growth closely corresponds to the growth of large Twin Cities-based companies that need a high-quality source for precision-made parts and automation equipment: "3M, Cray, Deluxe Check, FMC, Anderson Window, and others. Minnesota's vocational-technology edu-

Fred L. Remmele sensed an opportunity to build a company based on employee participation and innovative management.

cation system and the celebrated work ethic of its citizens also means Remmele has a work force that allows it to deliver the quality customers demand," a quality that is considered by many to be unsurpassed in its industry.

Another important contributor to the firm's success stems from Remmele's original notion about how such a company should be run, which has been strengthened by Ron Pfleider, Remmele's succes-

Today Remmele Engineering, Inc., is one of the nation's premier precision machining companies. It provides services to many Fortune 500 companies and produces revenues in excess of $30 million.

sor as president; Bill Saul, who succeeded Pfleider in 1976 and is now chairman; and current president Tom Moore. Remmele started one of the industry's first employee profit-sharing plans in 1956, an idea that was virtually unheard of at the time. Later the organization began an innovative apprenticeship program that helped attract young people into the industry.

Indeed, throughout the company's history, opportunities for employee growth and participation have been priorities. Corporate policies have helped ensure a motivated and highly-skilled work force, and at the same time have made important contributions to the communities that have helped it grow. Saul's formation of Minnesota Business for Excellence in 1981 illustrates these two concerns perfectly. The foundation awards cash grants to outstanding Minnesota schoolteachers "a form of merit pay way ahead of its time." Now more than 50 Minnesota companies contribute to the foundation, and in excess of $300,000 has been awarded.

Remmele has also led in technological innovation. Computers have become essential components in the four Remmele facilities and are in use in everything from inventory control to computer-aided design and manufacturing.

Remmele Engineering, Inc., facilities are as clean and technologically sophisticated as any high-technology industry. This pattern of reinvesting in facilities "and most important, reinvesting in its people" has created a company that is among the top in its industry.

CONTEL CORPORATION

City dwellers have long taken for granted modern telephone service, but people in small towns and rural areas often have not been so lucky. In the past, telephone companies that operated in urban areas—primarily the Bell System companies—had the market size and resources to continually adapt to the rapid pace of communications technologies. But hundreds of smaller telephone companies, many serving just a few hundred customers, frequently did not have the capital resources to provide the necessary improvements. But for rural customers in the Upper Midwest, however, that situation started to change in the 1960s, when the Continental Telephone Company was formed. And it continues to change to this day, as increasing numbers of rural customers boast of telephone service and communications access equal to that in urban areas.

Contel Corporation, as the firm is known today, was formed in 1960 by a group of investors and small telephone company owners to build a nationwide rural telephone network through the acquisition and consolidation of other small telephone companies. At the time many of these organizations were facing the impossible costs of converting to dial service for their customers, who even then were often still forced to route their calls through their local exchange operators. Minnesota was one of the first states to see a large number of local companies join the Contel system. The Minnesota Telephone Company, the Wanamingo Telephone Company, the Mille Lacs Telephone Company, and many other now-forgotten companies—20 in all—became part of the Contel system in its early days in Minnesota. The name given this new statewide phone system was Gopher State Telephone Company, which later became Continental Telephone of Minnesota, a member of the Mid-Central Division of Contel Corporation. The result of this unification was almost immediate improvement in telephone service for customers.

Contel Corporation quickly established a remarkable pattern of growth and diversification into communications-related businesses. In 1966 it became one of the youngest companies ever to be traded on the New York Stock Exchange. Today it is the parent organization to 27 individual telephone companies serving more than 2 million customers in 30 states. In addition to its telephone opera-

The Mid-Central Division of Contel recently moved into its new state-of-the-art facility in Mendota Heights.

tions, Contel, headquartered in Atlanta, has broadened into several other communications and information-processing areas, including satellite delivery systems. The result has been the emergence of a *Fortune* 500 company with nearly 22,000 employees.

In Minnesota, Contel started with 7,000 customers. It now serves more than 90,000 subscribers. In the areas it serves, Contel has steadily upgraded phone service, introducing rural customers to dial

Claude DeSanto is president of the Mid-Central Division of Contel.

service, eliminating party lines, and converting exchanges from analog to voice/data digital exchanges. Currently the Mid-Central Division, which includes Minnesota, Iowa, North Dakota, and South Dakota, has more than 800 employees and is based in a new state-of-the-art headquarters facility in Mendota Heights, Minnesota.

Deregulation of the nation's telephone system presents Contel's Mid-Central Division with opportunities as well as with great challenges. Customers now have options never before available, and consequently service has become the key to staying competitive. In the years ahead the Mid-Central Division of Contel, which has led the Contel system in customer satisfaction for four years running, should be in an excellent position to face such competition.

AMHOIST

American Hoist & Derrick (Amhoist), is a company used to doing big jobs. From Mount Rushmore to the Panama Canal and hundreds of other places around the globe, cranes and derricks manufactured by this century-old St. Paul firm have played a part wherever mountains needed to be moved. In the past decade Amhoist has faced its biggest job yet—restructuring out of the declining market for cranes and heavy construction. Mastering that challenge has not been easy; but today Amhoist is a diverse family of businesses with an attractive future.

The Franklin Manufacturing Company, Amhoist's precursor, was created in St. Paul in 1882 by Frank J. Johnson and Oliver T. Crosby, two St. Paul engineers. Despite the grand-sounding name, the firm was initially only one of many small repair shops that serviced the heavy equipment being imported into the state to work the iron ore mines and forests to the north. Both men soon realized, however, that the growing need for contractors and construction equipment represented a much greater market opportunity, and within a year had begun to manufacture a line of hand and horsepower hoisting equipment under a new name—the American Manufacturing Company.

Within two years American Manufacturing was making a wide variety of construction hardware and hoisting equipment. By 1891 American was selling heavy-lifting steam-powered and electrical hoists, and its sales territory covered many states. Growth was so rapid that within 10 years of its birth, a second distribution facility was opened in Chicago, and the organization's name was changed once again, this time to the American Hoist & Derrick Company.

As Amhoist the firm became the largest seller of lattice boom cranes in the world. Engineering advances kept Amhoist an industry leader. In 1938 the company set the record for lifting with a derrick that was rated at 250 tons. By 1976 a ship-mounted Amhoist crane would be lifting 3,000 tons and by 1987, 7,000 tons.

A watershed for Amhoist was reached in 1955, when revenues reached an all-time high of $25.9 million and John E. Carroll was named president. Carroll oversaw a series of acquisitions that would permanently change the nature of the organization. Under Carroll, and later under Robert P. Fox, who succeeded Carroll in 1973, Amhoist became a broadly diversified manufacturer, providing products and services to a wide variety of markets. By 1981 Amhoist's 13 separate units had sales that topped $500 million, with 50 percent still generated by construction-related equipment.

In the 1980s the dramatic evolution of Amhoist continued under Robert H. Nassau, who succeeded Fox in 1982. A

American Manufacturing Company's (American Hoist's) original plant at 459 North Robert in St. Paul, circa 1882.

slowdown in purchases of heavy construction equipment dictated a refocusing on profitable core business; the number of company units was pared to six, with construction equipment falling to less than 15 percent of revenues. Acquisitions made during the 1960s contributed increasingly larger percentages of Amhoist's total revenues. Two well-established St. Paul businesses, the Waterous Company, a manufacturer of fire-protection and water-distribution equipment, and Farwell, Ozmun, Kirk & Company (FOK), a distributor of wholesale hardware to its Trustworthy hardware stores and other mass merchandisers, became two of Amhoist's most important divisions.

Also of major importance are the Crosby Group, a manufacturer of fittings for wire rope that bears the founder's name, and Harris, a manufacturer of equipment for scrap metal recycling, solid waste compacting, and paper baling.

In its most dramatic move yet Amhoist divested itself of the crane division, selling it to the newly formed American Crane Company in 1987.

With Amhoist now returned to profitability, the firm continues to demonstrate that it can handle the big challenges.

The Amhoist tower in downtown St. Paul today.

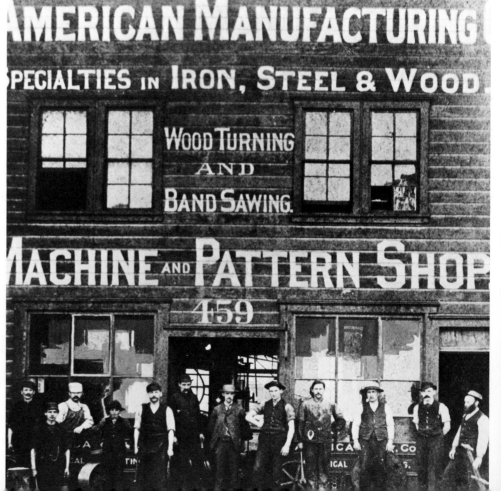

FIRST BANK SYSTEM, INC.

The collateral customers offered on the Minnesota frontier often consisted solely of a willingness to work. The Upper Midwest "might as well have been Timbuktu" to eastern bankers, but pioneer bankers had the faith to see that this new land had the capital it needed to grow.

Two such men, one on each side of the Mississippi River, left a legacy that today has become First Bank System, Inc. Parker Paine, a native of Anson, Maine, came to St. Paul in 1853 and created a private bank called Parker Paine and Company. At the time the only other bank in St. Paul was a general banking partnership that had been formed two years earlier. When Jacob K. Sidle, a native of York, Pennsylvania, opened a private bank with $10,000 in capital in Minneapolis with partner Peter Wolford in 1857, there were only a few private banks to serve the needs of a growing city of 4,500. Many banks would not survive the coming economic crisis, the Panic of 1857.

The banks of Paine and Sidle (Wolford soon dropped out) not only survived, but prospered. The period following the enactment of statehood in 1858 was a time of tremendous growth and consolidation for Minnesota banks. Paine's bank became the state-chartered Bank of Minnesota in 1862, and a year later, First National Bank of Saint Paul. By 1913 it had been purchased by James J. Hill and merged with Second National Bank, created in 1864 and one of St. Paul's largest banks.

Jacob Sidle's institution went through similar changes. By 1864 it was Minneapolis Bank. Two years later it became First National Bank of Minneapolis. By 1915 it had absorbed Nicollet National Bank and had merged with Security National Bank (and one of its directors went down with the Titanic).

During the 1920s bank failures reached epidemic proportions. In the Ninth Federal Reserve District alone, the number of banks declined by 70 percent between 1920 and 1939. The First Bank Stock Investment Company was formed by the First National Banks of Saint Paul and Minneapolis as a way to strengthen the worsening bank economy by buying majority interests in banks whose owners sought a strong financial partner, and to

Jacob K. Sidle opened a private bank in Minneapolis in 1857 that went on to become First Bank Minneapolis, which merged with First Bank Saint Paul into First Bank National Association on December 31, 1987.

help both institutions compete with Northwestern National Bank of Minneapolis' Northwestern Bancorporation, a bank holding company that was aggressively buying up banks.

Parker Paine founded the precursor to First Bank Saint Paul in 1853.

The new organization quickly discovered that its capital for acquisitions was insufficient and that many bankers wanted to remain active partners. First Bank Stock Investment Company restructured itself as a holding company whose principal subsidiaries were First National Bank of Saint Paul and First National Bank of Minneapolis. After a public sale of common stock raised $10 million, the company set out to acquire banks on an exchange of stock basis.

As a result of that union, First Bank System, Inc., the name adopted in 1968, became the nation's 15th-largest banking organization, with 65 banks and trust companies and assets exceeding $28 billion as of year-end 1986. It is one of the nation's most profitable "superregional" banking organizations with nearly 10,000 employees in six states. In recent years First Bank System has also emerged as the leading contributor to charitable causes of any banking organization its size in the nation. Since 1976 more than $50 million in grants has been awarded to hundreds of organizations. This investment in the communities it serves is strong evidence that First Bank System, Inc., retains the pioneer faith of its founders.

THE HOPKINS HOUSE

Hopkins, Minnesota, lies almost within the shadows of downtown Minneapolis, but Hopkins is not just a Minneapolis suburb. With its own distinctive neighborhoods, its own main street and central business district, its own traditions, and its own special atmosphere, Hopkins is a self-contained and highly appealing small city. Located in the heart of the Twin Cities metropolitan area, Hopkins offers its residents the best of two very different worlds.

The Hopkins House, a 165-room hotel and restaurant/conference center complex, shares this same split personality, which is partly why it has become such a Twin Cities institution. With the amenities and services to match any full-service Twin Cities hotel, and the relaxed and informal atmosphere of Hopkins itself, Hopkins House has become a favorite both for Hopkins residents and for those from around the metro area and well beyond.

That is partly what the nine investors who originally built Hopkins House back in 1963 had in mind. The nine, including Cal Olson, the hotel's first general manager, and Herb Mason, who is the only one in the original group still involved with the hotel, all lived in Hopkins,

Minnetonka, and other small cities on the western edges of Minneapolis. They wanted to build a facility that catered to both long-established and evolving characteristics of the area. Hopkins and towns such as nearby St. Louis Park and Golden Valley, for example, were home to a growing number of the nation's leading supermarket chains, food processors, and food distributors, companies such as SuperValu, Nash Finch, and General Mills. While this corporate population increased, the area was lacking in good places to eat for people who did not want to trek downtown. For that reason, when the original Hopkins House opened, its restaurants were the main attraction, while only 64 motel rooms were built.

Observers remember that the restaurants were full virtually from day one. Their popularity fueled the growth of the hotel side of the business. Thirty-six rooms were added in 1965; six years later a tower was built that brought the total

The Hopkins House offers the best of two worlds—the informal atmosphere of Hopkins with all the amenities of a first-class complex.

number of rooms to 165. The original group of investors bought other hospitality properties, including a restaurant in Golden Valley and the Breezy Point resort, and traded on the growing popularity of The Hopkins House by renaming them the Hopkins House Golden Valley and the Hopkins House Breezy Point.

The restaurant/hotel business is volatile, and during the 1970s and early 1980s The Hopkins House changed hands several times, leading to a lack of continuity in management. Today the Hopkins House has returned full circle with new owners Herb Mason, one of the original investors, and Dave Gravdahl, now general manager, who started out as a bartender at The Hopkins House back in 1963. The new team also includes operations manager Ray Duffy, who was a chef at the original Hopkins House.

Under Mason and Gravdahl nearly $2 million is being pumped into renovation and improvements. The renovation is designed to reinforce the two characteristics that have made The Hopkins House so successful in the first place—its relaxed, informal atmosphere and its ability to offer first-class, full-service amenities. The work is succeeding splendidly.

DELOITTE HASKINS & SELLS

In college football the Big Ten refers to a landlocked group of powerhouse teams whose conference leader appears each year in the Rose Bowl. But in the world of accounting and consulting the Big Eight can only mean one thing: the handful of giant firms that dominates the field.

In Minnesota, one of the oldest and largest of the Big Eight is represented by the regional office of Deloitte Haskins & Sells, which fields more than 26,000 employees in 400 offices worldwide. The Twin Cities branch employs more than 250 accountants, consultants, and support staff, offering services in accounting and auditing, tax consultation, and management advisory services, as well as expert consultation in small and growing businesses, mergers and acquisitions, computer applications, and more.

Deloitte Haskins & Sells got its start in Minnesota when the New York-based accounting firm decided to open a branch office to serve a growing number of clients in the area. The year was 1921. That first Minnesota branch office began with a single accountant, but began to grow almost at once with the acquisition of the established firm of Archibald F. Wagner.

The Minneapolis office continued to expand during the booming 1920s, shrank to a handful of staffers during the Depression, then rebounded after World War II.

Today in Minnesota Deloitte Haskins & Sells services some 350 clients in high technology, public service, manufacturing, real estate, and government. The firm is also a market leader in services for health care and health care providers. In recent years health care in Minnesota has become an increasingly competitive market. Gone are the days when a health care provider could offer care on a cost-plus basis. Deloitte Haskins & Sells is helping those providers become more cost efficient, particularly through better management of revenues and billing, expert advice and consultation on staffing re-

quirements, consolidation of services, and other issues vital to the health field today.

Deloitte Haskins & Sells' track record has enabled it to achieve a 146-percent increase in revenue in the past four years—without raising fees. It has also earned the firm customer loyalty: The company has the lowest turnover rate of any Big Eight firm operating in the Twin

Cities. For these and other reasons, the Minneapolis office has become one of the top 15 Deloitte Haskins & Sells offices in the world. The Deloitte Haskins & Sells office is led by Lynn V. Odland, who also has responsibilities for the Kansas City, Omaha, St. Paul, and Des Moines offices in his area and is a member of the Deloitte Haskins & Sells board of directors in New York.

The Deloitte Haskins & Sells office is led by Lynn V. Odland, who also has responsibilities for the Kansas City, Omaha, St. Paul, and Des Moines offices in his area and is a member of the Deloitte Haskins & Sells board of directors in New York.

AMERICAN LINEN SUPPLY CO.

George and Frank Steiner were an industrious pair. Sons of a traveling salesman, the two brothers helped supplement the family's income by taking a variety of odd jobs. George earned three dollars per week delivering clean towels to customers who paid one dollar a month for the daily service. In 1889, at age 15, George purchased the company for a grand total of $50.80. The arrangement involved a $25 down payment and an agreement to pay the balance of the owner's bill at a local drugstore.

The purchase was the beginning of the American Linen Supply Co. Continuing to operate under the name Lincoln Towel and Apron Supply Company, George soon found himself in a position where he could offer Frank a full partnership in the business. Handcarts gave way to green-and-white horse-drawn wagons that in the twentieth century gave way to the firm's hallmark green-and-white trucks.

In 1895 George went off to the boom town of Salt Lake City to open the company's first branch office. Shortly thereafter Frank set up an office in another boom town—Minneapolis.

In those early days of the business, washroom towels were a single loop of cloth hung on a roller. The first few users got a clean wipe; everybody afterward had to contend with a damp and soiled piece of toweling. Recognizing the aesthetic and sanitary shortcomings of such a dispensary, the Steiners set about devising the first ever continuous loop towel roll—a design so compact and efficient, it is still used today.

The purchase of a local laundry operation resulted in the establishment of corporate headquarters in Minneapolis. In 1914 the company added a second Minnesota plant in St. Paul. In 1925 American Linen Supply went international with the opening of a Canadian subsidiary. A year later the company moved into its current headquarters in the Steiner Building in downtown Minneapolis.

To ensure the quality of its linen products, American Linen founded its own textile-manufacturing business; it

By 1914 American Linen Supply Co. was operating out of this up-to-date plant in St. Paul.

later developed into the American Uniform Company.

American Linen Supply is a far different enterprise from the tiny laundry service purchased by George Steiner. The company has manufacturing units in the United States, Canada, and Europe. It owns more than 50 plants, employs 5,000 people, and serves in excess of 600,000 customers each week. Its line of products has expanded far beyond the clean towels customers received in 1889. The firm still cleans and installs hand towels, of course, but now also supplies industrial garments, hotel and restaurant linen, professional uniforms, and more.

One thing remains the same—the company is still owned and managed by the Steiners. Frank's son, George R. Steiner, is chief executive officer, while several other family members hold top management positions.

Today American Linen Supply Co. offers a wide range of services, including a clean room laundry facility. The facility specializes in providing high-tech and bioscience companies with sterile garments.

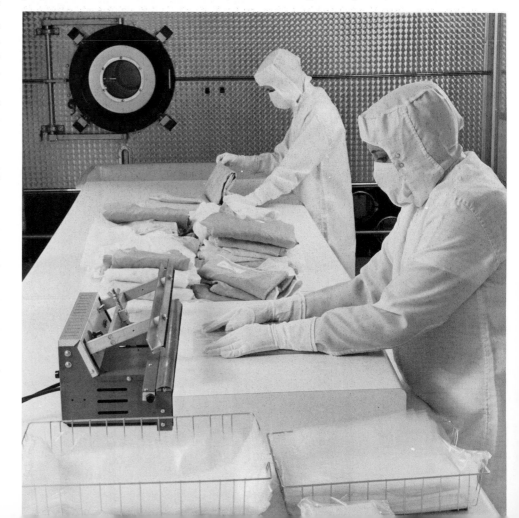

ATWOOD-LARSON

The grain elevators that dot the countryside throughout the Upper Midwest are more than a reminder of the area's small-town, agricultural roots. They are a vital link in the network of grain production, shipment, and processing that is still the region's primary industry. For almost 100 years Atwood-Larson, through its range of sophisticated marketing and management services, has helped keep that vital link healthy and strong even through economic bad times.

Atwood-Larson began life in 1889 when H.J. Atwood, an Iowa farm boy gone to seek his fortune in Duluth, started marketing feed for the draft horses working the mines on the Iron Range. In time Atwood went off into more profitable directions, assembling grain tonnage—concentrations of grain for shipment—for the railroads, a business that naturally led him into involvement with operators of track-side grain elevators and a move to Minneapolis, the new center of grain trading in the Upper Midwest.

In 1980 the firm entered a new phase of its existence when it became a wholly owned subsidiary of Con-Agra, a $7-billion diversified food company headquartered in Omaha. Despite this change, Atwood-Larson continues to serve country grain elevators, just as it has for almost a century.

Traditionally, regulating cash flow has been one of the major challenges for elevator operators, whose facilities, even today, form a vital link in the nation's agricultural supply network. Atwood-Larson helps its more than 90 full-service clients—a chain of country elevators spread throughout the Upper Midwest—with a cash-management account that provides working capital when the elevators need it.

Because most grain elevators are, in fact, small business enterprises, Atwood-Larson also provides the management expertise and marketing muscle small businesses generally lack. The company's management services range from budgeting assistance to help with long-range financing arrangements, to tax services, to traveling auditors.

On the floor of the Minneapolis Grain Exchange, Atwood-Larson sales representatives get the best price for grain supplied by Atwood-Larson clients. Elsewhere, at markets around the country, the company secures the highest bid for corn,

In 1889 H.J. Atwood started marketing feed for the draft horses working the Iron Range in Duluth. In time he ventured into other areas of business and became involved with operators of track-side grain elevators, which brought him and his company, now called Atwood-Larson, to Minneapolis, the center for grain trading in the Upper Midwest. Photo circa 1911

spring wheat, barley, oats, and oil seeds shipped by its customers to market.

While about two-thirds of Atwood-Larson's revenue is generated by its accounts with country elevators and trade in the commodities futures market, the firm also owns and operates a feed-production business. Its Ada, Minnesota, plant produces a line of special, high-grade feed primarily for performance horses, with racetracks, breeders, and private own-

ers as its customers. The company also produces steam-treated and vitamin-enriched feed grains.

When Atwood-Larson was founded, harvesting equipment was powered by draught animals, and crop quotations were kept in handwritten ledgers. Today farm equipment is driven by horsepower, not horses, and the complicated stream of numbers that comprise bids and prices is processed by computers. Atwood-Larson, like the clients it serves, has proven itself adept at changing with the times—and expects to go on serving clients for another 100 years.

On the floor of the Minneapolis Grain Exchange and in other markets, Atwood-Larson sales representatives secure the best prices for their clients.

NORTH AMERICAN LIFE AND CASUALTY COMPANY

Periodic structural changes in the economy—in particular those caused by the Depression of the 1930s, the two world wars, the sustained high rates of inflation of the 1970s, and the deregulation of the banking and financial market—have brought to the insurance industry a climate of constant competition. To remain profitable, life insurance companies have needed to devise new products and often revise methods of distribution.

Probably no organization has responded more creatively to these recurring challenges than North American Life and Casualty Company (NALAC), whose corporate symbol—the American bison—might be taken as a sign of its strength and resiliency. From incorporation to the present, the firm has been a leader in industry innovation for new product and marketing strategies.

NALAC was the creation of a group of Minneapolis businessmen who formed an accident and health company in 1896. Headquarters were several small rooms in the Plymouth Building. NALAC got into the life insurance business in 1912 and assumed its current name. Reincorporation made NALAC the first old-line legal reserve company in Minnesota.

After North American Life and Casualty Company was sold during the depths of the Depression to the Hoigaard family—better known today for its awnings, lawn furniture, and sporting goods business—the firm came into its own under the leadership of H.P. Skoglund, who served as chief executive officer for 37 years, from 1933 until 1970.

Under Skoglund, NALAC began to exhibit its flair for creative marketing and new product development. In 1949 NALAC and Investors Diversified Services entered into a joint marketing venture. The agreement called for the then relatively novel practice of permitting IDS agents to sell NALAC's decreasing term life policies to IDS mutual fund buyers. This venture continued for eight years, by which time IDS had formed its own life insurance company. The NALAC/IDS innovation helped push NALAC into permanent profitability and helped change it from a regional to an international company, with expansion into Canada.

During the 1950s NALAC grew at a rate that outstripped the industry average. The billion-dollar mark of life insur-

Under H.P. Skoglund, chief executive officer from 1933 to 1970, North American Life and Casualty Company (NALAC) moved into permanent profitability.

ance in force was reached in 1960. Three years later the company's stock was offered to the public for the first time. The $9.3-million offering sold out at once.

A milestone occurred in 1971, when Mutual of New York (MONY) purchased controlling interest in the firm. It was an industry first, as a mutual life in-

surance company had never before owned a stock life insurance company. The relationship proved profitable. Through joint-marketing programs, NALAC was able to underwrite products not offered by MONY and to sell them through MONY agents. The MONY/NALAC partnership yielded millions in new premiums for NALAC.

In 1979 MONY sold its interest in NALAC to the West German firm of Allianz Versicherungs-A.G. (Allianz), one of the largest insurance companies in the world. Headquartered in Munich,

Howard Barnhill, chief executive officer of NALAC and a consistent innovator in marketing and distribution.

Allianz maintains sales outlets through subsidiaries in many countries.

During the 1980s NALAC, based on its prior experiences with IDS and MONY, has pursued new agreements for joint marketing with other insurance firms that have proved innovative and profitable. Meeting other competitive marketing challenges, NALAC devised and implemented successfully a new way of selling its group health and disability plans. Instead of selling direct, NALAC appoints Third Party Administrators (TPAs), who hire and train their own agents, sell insurance, collect premiums, and pay claims.

As an industry leader in the TPA development, NALAC has been able to streamline the sale and administration of its health and disability business, handling less paperwork per dollar in premiums. Freedom from excessive paperwork has permitted NALAC to focus its creative energies on new products to meet changing demands. NALAC now offers a range of policies that are interest sensitive and pertinent to today's market.

Creativity and innovation have paid off. Today NALAC has more than 3,000 agents, brokers, general agents, and TPAs under contract. Its sales areas have been organized into five profit centers with four administrative divisions within the company as well. To keep abreast of changing technology and office automation, NALAC has made a major investment in new, increasingly more powerful computer equipment. Headquartered in its own building on Hennepin Avenue at Groveland Terrace, NALAC assets now top $800 million, and insurance in force exceeds $29 billion. Based on insurance in force, NALAC ranks in the top 4 percent of all life insurance firms. The A.M. Best Company, an independent analyst of the insurance industry, has awarded North American Life and Casualty Company an "A+ (Superior)" rating—the highest possible—for its financial condition and operating performance.

Lowell C. Anderson, president and chief operating officer of NALAC.

GOLDEN VALLEY MICROWAVE FOODS, INC.

Take America's apparently inexhaustible appetite for popcorn. Combine it with the ever-growing popularity of microwave ovens (market penetration: three out of five American homes). Add a single-minded commitment to developing foods specially designed for microwave preparation. Spice with significant social trends, such as the increase in the number of two-income households. Heat over a constant search for new and better products. Here you have the recipe for Golden Valley Microwave Foods, Inc., one of Minnesota's most remarkable success stories of the 1980s.

Like most overnight successes, Golden Valley experienced several lean years before hitting the big time. The company was founded in 1978 by James Watkins, who continues as chief executive officer, and a handful of backers. Watkins, who had worked with microwave products at Pillsbury, originally conceived Golden Valley to be a research and development and marketing company for microwaveable products, with actual production carried out by other businesses.

Golden Valley's first foray into the market—frozen entrées and soups—was less than a smashing success. The firm branched off into frozen microwave pancakes and—its bread-and-butter product line—popcorn. Both were sold through vending machines.

Growth was slow but steady the first few years of Golden Valley's existence. Eager for more rapid expansion, the company took a big gamble, deciding to compete head to head with industry giants in the retail grocery market. There may be no more competitive market than for packaged foods sold on the nation's grocery shelves. It is a field dominated by businesses with the money and marketing muscle to blow smaller competitors out of the water.

In this hypercompetitive world, surprisingly enough, Golden Valley Microwave not only survived, it prevailed. The introduction of Act II shelf-stable microwave popcorn was the beginning of the company's rapid growth. Using innovative packaging that allows more complete popping of the popcorn inside, Act II has helped the firm capture some 20 percent of the nation's estimated $350-million market for microwave popcorn. In 1985 Golden Valley licensed the packaging technology to General Mills, which sells

Founder James Watkins dedicated his company to developing microwave foods, and only microwave foods.

the product under its Betty Crocker Pop Secret brand name, further extending its market share. Together Golden Valley Microwave and Betty Crocker control almost 35 percent of the market for microwave popcorn, putting them just behind Orville Redenbacher, which leads the industry.

In 1986 the company took a decisive step to cure its chronic problems with undercapitalization by going public. From an initial price of $14, Golden Valley's stock soared to more than $36 a share in

only a few months' time, prompting *Fortune* magazine to put Golden Valley on its list of the top 10 new issues. The little company that took on the food processing Goliaths was not so small any more. From its inception Golden Valley's sales have roughly doubled every year. Sales in 1987 exceeded $90 million. Company officials expect that figure to top $130 million this year. And the firm now employs more than 400 people at three Twin Cities facilities.

One of the keys to Golden Valley Microwave's success has been its commitment to developing products specifically suited for microwave preparation, unlike other companies that market products that can be prepared either in a microwave or through conventional cooking techniques. Another key has been the firm's constant striving to develop new products or improve the ones it already markets.

Each year the company spends in excess of one million dollars on research and development. Collectively, its top management and research team hold about two dozen patents. Genetic engineering may seem an unlikely pursuit for a microwave food company, but Golden Valley is involved in that, too, in its search for a better-popping popcorn.

Marketed in grocery stores, vending machines, and also under private labels for other companies, Golden Valley's microwave pancakes represent only 10 percent of the firm's revenue. But the company is confident that this is going to change. Golden Valley points to a four-to-one preference for pancakes over waffles in restaurants across the country, even though the $200-million market for frozen waffles currently dwarfs the demand for frozen pancakes. With consumer acceptance of the superior flavor and quality of microwave pancakes, Golden Valley expects its product to perform as well as Act II popcorn.

But Golden Valley Microwave is not content simply to market microwave popcorn and pancakes. Future growth de-

Act II microwave popcorn has been the firm's biggest seller.

pends upon expansion into food categories previously thought unsuitable for microwave preparation. As the company searches for ways to brown and crisp foods in a microwave, its list of potential new products includes many of the top 200 foods Americans like most. As with popcorn and pancakes, Golden Valley's strategy will continue to be development of microwaveable versions of the foods we already like to eat.

So, if you step into the grocery store sometime soon and see microwave hamburgers or fried chicken, do not be surprised. They will probably have been developed by Golden Valley Microwave Foods, Inc., in which case you know they'll be as tasty as—well—popcorn.

GRAY, PLANT, MOOTY, MOOTY & BENNETT, PA.

Gray, Plant, Mooty, Mooty & Bennett, P.A., is the oldest continuing law practice in Minneapolis—and one of the most influential.

Starting with the one-man law office opened by Charles Woods in 1866, the firm has grown to more than 90 attorneys. It is well-known for its work in corporate, tax, and real estate law; in litigation; and for the leadership of its partners in legal and community service organizations.

In 1881 Charles Woods joined with William J. Hahn, a former state attorney general, to form Woods & Hahn. Two years later Joseph R. Kingman joined the firm, first as a clerk and apprentice while he studied law, and later as partner after he was admitted to the Bar. The small firm specialized in real estate work, as the city of Minneapolis was growing rapidly. Kingman's influence was so great that by the time he retired in 1950—and well afterward—the practice was known as "the Kingman firm."

By then Franklin Gray, Frank Plant, and John Mooty, three of the firm's current senior partners, were on board. Within a few years they were joined by Melvin Mooty and Russell Bennett.

A new era began when the firm moved to the Roanoke Building in downtown Minneapolis in 1955. By then the practice of law was becoming increasingly specialized, and the firm was growing rapidly. Already heavily involved in probate, estate planning, and real estate, the firm did increasing work in corporate, financial, and tax problems, and litigation. In 1984 the firm moved to its current quarters on two and one-half floors of Minneapolis' City Center.

Through its long history the firm has emphasized close working relationships among partners and associates to maintain the spirit of a smaller firm in spite of its growing size and influence.

With this growth came increasing prominence in corporate, real estate, antitrust, and product liability law, both on regional and national levels. For example, General Motors, a long-standing client, was successfully defended in three cases

Franklin D. Gray (right) and John W. Mooty (left), two of Gray, Plant, Mooty, Mooty & Bennett's senior partners.

arising out of lawsuits over the Chevrolet Corvair during the 1960s. Antitrust and product liability cases were argued and won for clients such as Du Pont and Westinghouse. At the same time the firm continued its tradition of real estate expertise in projects ranging from downtown office buildings to Southdale, the nation's first enclosed suburban shopping mall.

Today Gray, Plant, Mooty, Mooty & Bennett, P.A., ranks among the nation's top 500 law firms. It boasts one of the metropolitan area's strongest records of leadership in legal and community service organizations. Its attorneys have led the Minnesota State Bar Association, the Hennepin County Bar Association, the Federal Bar Association, and service organizations such as the Citizen's League, Legal Advice Clinics, the Minnesota Alumni Association, Rotary International, and the University of Minnesota Foundation. The firm's attorneys have served other organizations ranging from the Sierra Club to Fairview Hospital. Among the many traditions established over the firm's history, its commitment to community service is one of the strongest.

GROUP HEALTH, INC.

A quiet revolution began in Minnesota 50 years ago. A small group of forward-thinking credit union and cooperative leaders were concerned about the ability of the average person to pay for medical expenses. They knew that nearly half of all consumer loans were taken out to pay doctor bills.

To counter this hardship, which affected both consumers and medical professionals, they formed an organization called Group Health Mutual Insurance Company. Its goal was to offer prepaid health and hospitalization coverage.

Twenty years later the idea blossomed into one of the first health maintenance organizations (HMOs) in the country, and the first HMO in the Twin Cities. On August 1, 1957, Group Health opened its first medical center on Como Avenue in St. Paul. By today's standards (now half the population of the Twin Cities is enrolled in an HMO) the organization that opened that day was small; its membership was 2,000, and its medical staff consisted of one full-time and 12 part-time physicians.

It was not to remain so. Over the past 30 years Group Health's membership has swelled one hundredfold while its mission has remained the same: to provide high-quality convenient health care and to assist members in taking responsibility for their own health. Long before preventive medicine became a household term, Group Health members were benefiting from its practice.

Under the leadership of Maurice J. McKay, Group Health became a leading force in Minnesota health care. During his 22-year term as general manager of the organization (1960-1982), Group Health grew to more than 180,000 members and inspired the formation of other HMOs during the mid-1970s. With McKay at the helm, Group Health developed new concepts in health care delivery and financing—concepts that served as a model for other HMOs.

This legacy of innovation lives on. Recognizing that a full-term pregnancy is a child's best foundation for good health, Group Health instituted a Preterm

Group Health opened its first medical center in August 1957 and introduced the concept of comprehensive prepaid health care to the Twin Cities area. Today half of the population of the Twin Cities belongs to a prepaid health care plan, and the area is regarded as a national model for innovations in health care financing and delivery.

Birth Program to identify women at risk for premature birth and to prevent it. As a result of the program, Group Health members enjoy a premature birth rate that is 47 percent lower than the state average.

Group Health's staff of more than 240 medical specialists, representing 30 specialties, and dentists are all salaried. An additional 800 specialists in the community are affiliated with Group Health. The organization is unique in that its board of directors is composed entirely of member-directors elected by the membership.

In its range of services, marketing techniques, and facilities, Group Health, Inc., continues to provide Minnesotans with innovative and high-quality health care.

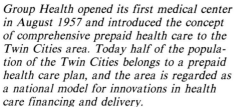

Group Health's tradition of innovation continues in such medical programs as its Preterm Birth Program. These babies overcame their mothers' high-risk status and were born full term and healthy. The program has reduced Group Health's rate of premature births to nearly 50 percent of the Minnesota rate.

LEEF BROTHERS, INC.

At the turn of the century the Glenwood area of the near north side of Minneapolis was a neighborhood with strong Swedish, Norwegian, and Finnish enclaves.

In 1908 a young man from that neighborhood opened his own industrial laundry plant. His company, the Minneapolis Overall Laundry, was the forerunner of Leef Brothers, Inc., the largest independent industrial laundry and rental supplier in the Twin Cities. As the company grew Harry Leef hired more and more neighborhood residents, and Leef Brothers became known as a family-oriented place where workers walked to and from the plant each day. Today this plant is a modern 88,000-square-foot facility.

But while the company was rooted in family and neighborhood, Harry Leef took pains to ensure that his facilities were the last word in cleaning. When he could not purchase equipment that could do the job, he would invent it himself, as with the Leef ironing and washing equipment that is still in use today.

Now in its 80th anniversary year, Leef Brothers continues the family tradition: Steve Leef, Harry Leef's son, assumed management of the firm in 1959 and has two sons working in the business with him. Many current employees are second- and even third-generation workers with Leef Brothers.

The company also continues its tradition of innovation and diversification. Leef Brothers helped to introduce "walk-off" entrance mats. These mats, which the firm continues to rent and service, have become common in office, commercial, and industrial buildings, although they were originally developed to reduce the level of dust and dirt in high-technology facilities.

Meanwhile, Leef Brothers' Garment Service provides convenient, cost-effective rental clothing for business and industry—everything from shirts, pants, and jackets to coveralls, lab coats, and executive attire. Other Leef services are industrial towels, chemically treated dust mops, washroom towel service, and a line of industrial cleaning products.

Through the decades Leef Brothers has been a leading innovator both in prod-

Harry Leef, founder of Leef Brothers, Inc., the largest independent industrial laundry in Minnesota.

Leef Brothers was one of the first commercial laundries to use giant all-metal washing machines.

uct uses and in equipment used at its plant in Minneapolis. In many instances equipment designed or improved by the company has been marketed to other industrial and linen supply services in the United States, Canada, and Western Europe.

To ensure a continuing stream of innovation, the firm operates a subsidiary called Production Design Products. This fast-growing young company develops equipment for initial use by Leef Brothers, then markets that equipment to the industry. A prime example of the subsidiary's inventiveness is the High Roller, a piece of equipment it developed that rolls en-

trance mats after cleaning.

Today Leef Brothers, Inc., employs 175 people in a Minneapolis plant located in the neighborhood where Harry Leef grew up, and another 50 at the recently acquired Fargo Laundry in Fargo, North Dakota. A fleet of almost 60 trucks services customers throughout Minnesota, North Dakota, and western Wisconsin with branch depots in St. Cloud and Waseca, Minnesota. The company has come a long way from those early days at the turn of the century. It has grown and prospered—but always, Leef Brothers, Inc., is proud to say, without ever leaving home.

Stephen D. Leef, president of Leef Brothers, Inc., continues in his father's tradition.

AERO SYSTEMS ENGINEERING, INC.

Few pieces of technology are as complex as jet engines, and few are subjected to as much abuse. Frequent testing of the tens of thousands of jet engines in use today is a matter of great concern to air carriers and aircraft builders alike. Few companies, however, have shown the willingness or possess the technical expertise to design, package, and sell integrated jet engine testing facilities—despite the potential size of the market.

But back in 1967 two engineers, Ray Richardson and Lars Broberg, decided that the market was too good to overlook. There was an opportunity, they figured, for a company that handled all phases of the complex process of designing and constructing jet engine testing facilities. Their gamble was the basis for St. Paul-based Aero Systems Engineering, Inc., which today has 167 employees and revenues that most recently topped $25 million.

Aero Systems, one of Minnesota's most unusual companies, has emerged in recent years as an international leader in the design, engineering, and construction of turbine engine test facilities. Aero Systems is one of Minnesota's most international small businesses. Its work force is multinational, its majority owner a holding company owned by the Swedish government, and its list of customers ranges from Areolineas Argentinas to Western Airlines.

Aero Systems, a company that now covers much of the world, began in the tiny confines of Ray Richardson's basement. It was formed in 1967 by Richardson and Broberg, both veterans of the same aviation engineering company, to design and build thrust stands for jet engines undergoing testing. Soon they were joined by fellow engineer Hans Widerstrom. The

An F100 gas turbine engine mounted into a company-built engine adapter and 120,000-pound thrust stand (overhead). This ASE testing equipment is shown installed in a depot-level post overhaul engine test cell.

new venture quickly moved to quarters in Bloomington. The three men had industry contacts enough to ensure some early business.

Three big projects got Aero Systems off the ground, including a huge contract for a thrust measurement and calibration system for the Airworks Corporation of Millville, New Jersey. Other early customers formed virtually a who's who of air

The Aero Systems Engineering, Inc., headquarters in St. Paul.

carriers, both commercial and military, and airline builders around the world. As Aero Systems grew its need for expansion capital led to the sale of a majority interest in the company in 1974 to a Swedish manufacturer of "hush houses" for jet engine testing. That firm later merged with Uddeholm, AB, a Swedish conglomerate. Uddeholm merged in 1981 with FFV AB, a Swedish holding company with diverse subsidiaries, many of them defense industries, that is wholly owned by the Swedish government.

As Aero Systems grew it formed several subsidiaries around the world, including ASE Texas, which between 1981 and 1984 built nearly $50 million worth of hush houses for the U.S. Air Force; ASE/SMA SARL, a joint venture with a French engineering firm; and ASE Europe AB, which has facilities in Sweden.

The company's growth is attributable to its increasing ability to provide automated turnkey systems that allow air carriers and manufacturers to test jet engines with speed and accuracy. While ASE has competitors, none can offer a similar range of expertise, from the design and planning of facilities to installation and training. In Aero Systems Engineering, Inc., with the installation of more than 190 systems to date, the Twin Cities area possesses one of the leaders in the aerospace field.

GOLLE & HOLMES CUSTOM EDUCATION

Once upon a time American business survived on raw material, instincts, guts, and luck. Those days are over. It still takes guts—and some luck—but more than ever success today depends on savvy—on the skills and knowledge businesses need in order to develop strategies and to position their products and services before their customers.

The proliferation of community education courses and generic training programs attests to a growing awareness of the fact that learning doesn't stop—cannot stop—when a person leaves school. If business is to grow, its people must be equipped to meet change and a never-ending stream of new challenges. In this new American business climate, Golle & Holmes Custom Education has created a new approach to adult learning and occupies a distinctive place in the training industry.

The custom education concept was initiated in 1970, when John Golle and Robert Holmes created a learning system for a major Wall Street investment firm. The system was designed to register new representatives and to train them in selling securities products and in sales management. The Golle & Holmes programs were so successful among the major securities firms that within five years the company held a 60-percent market share in

Ronald A. Boyle is Golle & Holmes' president and chief operating officer.

this area. Gradually the custom approach was applied in other industries—insurance, manufacturing, consumer goods, and agribusiness—with the same success. The Golle & Holmes Group grew until it

The center for Golle & Holmes Custom Education is located at 1600 West 82nd Street in Minneapolis.

consisted of five operating companies. Its success was recognized by the international community when, in 1985, Golle & Holmes Financial Learning Inc. was purchased by Longman Group USA, part of the British Pearson PLC, parent company of the London *Financial Times,* and the Lazard investment banking firm. The four remaining operating companies have since been merged into GHCE under the management of Ronald Boyle, president.

Golle & Holmes Custom Education has taken the custom design message to an ever-widening audience—pharmaceuticals, telecommunications, public transportation, insurance, professional and industrial associations, and airlines. In addition, multilingual professionals in London and Hong Kong deliver the GHCE custom design message to an international training audience.

GHCE clients are all drawn by the same interest—training programs that reflect their worlds and their needs. In the traditional approach to training an organizational problem is quickly categorized and labeled, and a training program addressing that general issue is applied. Sometimes it works; more often it is a temporary fix that fails. GHCE's approach to custom-designed training is far different. It calls for careful analysis of the actual situation and identification of possible

solutions. Training is developed from scratch and based entirely on the unique conditions of the client's industry. The clue to the success of GHCE lies in its responsiveness to its clients—in recognizing them as individuals with unique needs, in listening and observing without preconceptions. GHCE's development process ensures that client's needs are always met.

All GHCE projects begin with extensive research. Projects combine interviews with corporate and field personnel and experts in the area, observations of employees at work, group interviews with target audiences, analysis of existing training material, and formal surveys. This careful research yields an accurate picture of the training challenge, as well as rich details about the culture of the client's organization. In the final program, the in-depth knowledge gained during the research period will be reflected in the language, style, and scenarios used. GHCE achieves a level of real-life detail in its programs that astonishes its audience, who assume the programs must have been written by people within their own organization.

Once research is completed, GHCE begins to develop the training product. Development becomes a partnership between GHCE and its client. Client review and guidance is invited throughout the project, so that when the product is completed, clients have exactly what they need and what they want—quality training that will produce real change and growth in their organization. All materials are reviewed, revised repeatedly after client input, tested with target audiences, and professionally produced. The final products may be self-study texts, day-long to week-long seminars presented by people within the client's own organization, or entire curricula or systems of programs. All share a basic philosophy: Effective learning must refer to the learner's environment and create change not only in knowledge and attitude but in behavior as well.

GHCE's reputation for excellence and innovation is made possible through its organization. Unlike many generic training firms, GHCE can provide a broad range of services to assist in meeting all its clients' needs. Sometimes the first step is not training but changes in organization, job responsibilities, and human resources development. These needs can be

John T. Golle, one of the company's founders, serves as chief executive officer.

identified through GHCE's own Consulting Group. When it is time to develop training solutions, GHCE can turn to its design staff, one of the largest in-house design staffs in the country, with designers trained in applying the principles of adult learning in a variety of training vehicles. The staff also includes graphic designers, who create a visual identity for each program; computer experts, who de-

Robert Holmes, also a founder, acts as chairman.

velop computer-based instruction using GHCE's own authoring system; and media producers and writers, who create award-winning audiovisual components, from slide shows to videotapes.

GHCE's involvement with the client does not end with the completion of a project. The company provides support services to its clients by shipping materials, tracking student performance, and monitoring inventory levels. This ongoing concern for the customer has resulted in a prestigious client list marked by many long-standing relationships.

In the food products industry, for example, GHCE has designed *This is Your World* for the Kellogg Company. Developed over a span of several years, *This is Your World* is a comprehensive system that trains Kellogg sales representatives in every aspect of their job. The design of *This is Your World* and the relationship between Kellogg and GHCE allows both organizations to expand and modify the program to meet new challenges and to maintain Kellogg's industry leadership.

In agribusiness, GHCE has developed programs in many areas for Ralston Purina. Product knowledge, sales, and management programs produced by GHCE and delivered by Purina support Purina's dealership network both in the United States and abroad. GHCE and Purina have also worked in partnership to develop computer-based farm-management systems. These management systems use GHCE's skill in instructional design and Purina's knowledge of sound farm management to give farmers a new tool to help them survive tough economic times.

Over its 10-year association with NAPA, GHCE has focused on sales, financial management, and supervisory skills to give NAPA dealers unified training addressing all aspects of their business. These long-term projects are possible because GHCE is committed to the success of its clients.

Having spent the past 17 years acquiring the necessary knowledge, personnel, systems, and expertise, Golle & Holmes Custom Education has earned the right to become an invaluable partner in its clients' businesses. It stands now as an icon of a new breed of American business—customer focused, flexible, always committed to quality and innovation.

CAMPBELL-MITHUN ADVERTISING

Advertising is an evanescent industry. Agencies appear and disappear with great regularity. And those that do survive for a decade or more usually undergo so many changes of ownership and management as to be completely new businesses in all but name.

That is just one of the things that makes Campbell-Mithun such an exceptional advertising agency. Founded in 1933, the full-service agency is the 22nd largest in the country and the 25th largest in the world. Its annual billings exceed $400 million. Some of its major accounts include the Andersen Corporation, a manufacturer of quality windows; Dairy Queen, Inc.; General Mills; Toro; Land O' Lakes; 3M; and the Norwest Corporation.

Now for the unusual part. Not only has Campbell-Mithun been around a long time by advertising industry standards, but it has enjoyed remarkable stability as well, both in its accounts and its management. Continuity has been the rule, not the exception, at CM. In 56 years the company has undergone only three planned successions in its top management. Even more amazing in a fickle market, the firm retains its original three clients: Norwest, Land O' Lakes, and the Andersen Corporation.

How has Campbell-Mithun managed to prosper and remain stable for so long? In 1933 co-founder Ralph Campbell was office manager for the Minneapolis office of BBD&O. One factor that made him decide to go off on his own was a pending transfer to BBD&O's home office in New York. That likelihood led him to begin discussing opening an agency with Ray Mithun, a friend who had a newspaper background working in Mankato. The two men crafted an operating philosophy that remains in force to this day: "The only reason we exist is to help clients make a profit."

Over the years the agency has stuck by that philosophy, which in practice has meant finding creative solutions for a changing marketplace. The firm has proven adept at anticipating trends that will affect clients' business, and then devising creative ways of marketing services and products. Then, too, its advertising is the result of a fruitful collaboration with its clients—a collaboration based upon an understanding of key industries and the impact of change upon a client's marketing strategies.

Campbell-Mithun Advertising's long association with major food-processing and manufacturing clients has given the agency unparalleled expertise in new-product development. The list of products the agency has helped develop and introduce just in the past few years is long and varied: Golden Grahams and Oatmeal Raisin cereals for General Mills, soft margarine and Country Morning Blend for Land O' Lakes, Microwave Pizzas, Dairy Queen Blizzards, and new snow blowers for Toro, to name just a few.

DONOVAN COMPANIES, INC.

By 1918, 40 billion kilowatt hours of electricity were being produced in America. This growing new power was transforming homes, industries, and cities across the land.

The revolution usually stopped, however, beyond city limits. The nation's growing number of private utility companies did not think it would be profitable to extend service much beyond heavily populated urban areas. As a result, rural communities and America's farms were failing to benefit from the most important technological advance of modern times.

A young man named George Donovan helped bring about a change. Donovan was born in the town of Clinton, Minnesota, and had spent his early adult years installing telegraph and telephone wires throughout America for the company that would eventually become AT&T. The experience served him well when he saw the need to bring electricity to the countryside—and sensed an irresistible market opportunity. The Donovan Construction Company resulted, made up of Donovan himself and a handful of employees who strung electrical transmission lines to farms and small towns throughout the Upper Midwest.

By the 1930s his firm was also working on power plant construction, street lighting, and other electrical construction projects for some of the more than 2,580 publicly owned municipal utilities that had sprung to life during the previous decades. In 1938 George Donovan became involved in another type of energy by buying a natural gas plant that served the needs of the small town of Perry, Iowa. The Perry Gas Company gradually expanded into neighboring Iowa and Minnesota communities. In 1954 it became North Central Public Service, the corner-stone of the diversified energy organization that would be the Donovan Companies of the 1970s and 1980s.

Meanwhile the Donovan Construction Company was venturing into new construction markets—including, when America entered World War II, 110-foot wooden submarine chasers built in St. Paul and on Lake Champlain in New York. During the 1950s and early 1960s Donovan was involved in large construction projects that ranged from hospitals and office buildings to massive hydroelectric power plants and dams. The business, which included George Donovan's three sons, also continued to expand its natural gas distribution operations. Growth occurred both in the Upper Midwest and in Florida, where the company acquired Southern Gas and Electric Corporation. As the firm grew (revenues topped $40 million by 1965), George Donovan realized that the natural gas utility business would add the stability and predictability lacking in other areas. That strategy would provide the bedrock for the rapid growth of the late 1960s and early 1970s.

In 1969 all the various divisions of the organization were brought together under the name the Donovan Companies, Inc., and the firm went public, although the Donovan family continued to be majority shareholders and George Donovan's sons led the company. Within five years revenues topped $190 million. While other parts of the organization grew and the

The founder of what is today known as the Donovan Companies, Inc., George Donovan.

George Donovan recognized the need to bring electricity to rural America and began the Donovan Construction Company to string electrical transmission lines to farms and small towns throughout the Upper Midwest. Here an early Donovan electrical transmission power line crew works on an REA project in the 1930s.

company entered into real estate ventures (including the Holiday Inn near the Minnesota capitol), energy—primarily natural gas distribution—increasingly became the Donovan Companies' primary focus.

Today the firm's natural gas division serves nearly 50 communities in the Upper Midwest, as well as communities in Florida. Its strength in this area made it an attractive merger candidate for several major energy suppliers, including Midwest Energy Company of Sioux City, Iowa, which made an offer that was accepted in late 1985. Today, as a wholly owned subsidiary of Midwest Energy Company, the Donovan Companies, Inc., continues to bring energy to America's heartland.

KRAUS-ANDERSON COMPANIES

When Lloyd Engelsma bought out Matthew N. Kraus and Amos Anderson amidst the Depression in 1937, the assets of the company Kraus and Anderson had formed and that bore their name consisted of a pickup truck, a wheelbarrow, two employees, and little else apart from the modest goodwill the firm had created in its 10-year existence as a construction company that built mostly gas stations.

It may not have seemed an auspicious beginning, but Engelsma, a Hinckley, Minnesota, native who had been hired five years earlier by Kraus-Anderson as an office manager, estimator, and field supervisor, was known as an enterprising and ambitious young man. To get an idea of just how enterprising, consider what happened to Kraus and Anderson's little company after Engelsma took control: Today Kraus-Anderson ranks among the top 100 building contractors in the country, generating more than $370 million in building contracts annually; oversees the leasing and management of 75 properties from Minneapolis to Honolulu; and encompasses a dozen related enterprises, including insurance, mortgage underwriting, advertising, aviation, and commercial development.

The road to such a healthy and diversified corporation may seem an impossibly long one, but observers say that Engelsma's careful and steady guidance has made it a smooth course. Other things helped. When Engelsma bought the company the Depression was ending and World War II was brewing. Kraus-Anderson benefited both from the economic upturn and from important defense construction contracts. Between 1946 and 1950 revenues more than doubled, from $1.1 million to $2.8 million.

The suburbs began booming, too, and in the 1950s Kraus-Anderson became involved in many industrial and commercial projects, including some of the earliest Twin Cities shopping centers, one of which—Clover Center in Bloomington—marked the company's entry into property ownership and management. Important players in the firm's subsequent history were hired, including William J. Jaeger, Jr., now president and chief operating officer of Kraus-Anderson Construction Company, and in the 1960s Burton Dahlberg, currently president and chief operating officer of Kraus-Anderson Realty Company.

Kraus-Anderson's management team poses during the company's 50th anniversary celebration. From left are Burton Dahlberg, Daniel Engelsma, William J. Jaeger, Jr., Bruce Engelsma, and Lloyd Engelsma.

Building technology and the size of the projects Kraus-Anderson worked on rapidly escalated. Kellogg Square in St. Paul, Control Data World Headquarters in Bloomington, Point of France in Edina, Northwestern National Life and the Piper Jaffray Tower in downtown Minneapolis, the Amhoist Tower in downtown St. Paul, Lincoln Center in Dallas, Maui Hill in Hawaii—are all landmarks now and are only a few of Kraus-Anderson's completed projects. Most recently the firm completed the Canterbury Downs Racetrack in suburban Shakopee, Minnesota—three days ahead of schedule and only 15 months after being selected as contractor.

Today, on its 50th anniversary, the Kraus-Anderson shield extends to more than a dozen companies with close to 1,000 employees. In the years ahead the company intends to further solidify its position in real estate, construction, and supporting industries, continuing the course Engelsma, still chairman and chief executive officer of Kraus-Anderson Companies, established five decades ago.

Piper Jaffray Tower in downtown Minneapolis, constructed by Kraus-Anderson.

LAMAUR INC.

The year 1930 may have seemed a funny year to start a business, especially one that specialized in shampoos and hair care products. At a time when most Americans washed their hair with bar soap, hair care products represented a new and untested market. Products like cream rinses and conditioners were completely unknown. Then there was the Great Depression; it just did not seem to be the time for entrepreneurs.

Little of that mattered to Maurice Spiegel, a young Minnesotan with a degree in pharmaceutical chemistry tinkering in the labs of the Chicago Chemical Company. Spiegel was full of ideas, and he already had a specialty—beauty products. He also had a brother, Larry, with a business degree from the University of Minnesota. Maurice convinced Larry to join him in business. Maurice would research products in the basement of the family's Minneapolis home while Larry handled production and packaging. For a company name the two would diplomatically arrive at Lamaur.

Maurice Spiegel quickly developed a reputation as a product innovator, sometimes spending as many as seven days a week in the laboratory experimenting with new ideas. He is even better known today as chairman of the Lamaur of the 1980s—one of the industry's fastest-growing and most innovative companies,

a top-10 U.S. leader in hair sprays, shampoos, and conditioners. Recently Lamaur posted nearly $150 million in sales.

Lamaur's first products were permanent waving solutions, setting lotions, and cream cosmetics. Part of its growth in its early years was due to its insistence on marketing only quality products, which, along with the 1942 acquisition of a beauty salon distribution company, helped Lamaur establish a foothold in the growing professional salon market.

Maurice Spiegel's knack for developing the right new products at the right time also helped. In 1945 Spiegel introduced the first nondulling water-soluble hair spray. Lamaur later introduced solid creme shampoos, creme rinse concentrates, protein-based permanent waves and chemical permanent waves to replace the harsh electric waving machine treatment then used by salons, and the industry's first environmentally safe aerosol hair spray.

Spiegel's innovations helped Lamaur grow to a national manufacturer of its own brand-name products, including

---

Lamaur's 200,000-square-foot state-of-the-art facility in the Minneapolis suburb of Fridley. Lamaur Inc. is a national manufacturer of beauty products, from the Strata and Rusk styling aids for the professional salon market to the market-leading Perma Soft line of consumer shampoos.

Strata and, most recently, Rusk styling aids for the professional salon market, and the market-leading Perma Soft line of consumer shampoos that clean and soften permanent-waved hair without relaxing the curl. During the 1960s revenues skyrocketed from $7 million in 1961 to nearly $20 million by the end of the decade. A public stock offering in 1962 helped the company update its manufacturing operation, a process that reached a high point in 1970, when the firm moved into its new 200,000-square-foot state-of-the-art facility in the Minneapolis suburb of Fridley. Four years later Richard Spiegel, who had joined the corporation in the 1950s, was named president; his success at continuing his father's tradition of product innovation and creativity helped the company reach $40 million in sales by the end of the 1970s.

Growth and product innovation picked up even more steam during the 1980s. With one of the top research and development organizations in the industry, Lamaur has stayed in tune with changing trends in the hair care industry. Its Perma Soft line, introduced in 1984, has already doubled the company's share in mass-market hair care. Sales growth has nearly quadrupled since the decade began. After more than 50 years in the business, Lamaur Inc. emerged an industry leader.

NATIONAL CITY BANK

Wisecracks usually do not accompany the formation of an institution as solemn as a bank, but National City Bank of Minneapolis has been different right from the very start. In its first weeks of existence National City operated out of two rooms in the Sheraton Ritz Hotel in downtown Minneapolis, leading local wags to joke that here were the only bankers in town to run their business in a hotel bedroom. After two decades of growth and banking innovation—growth that has seen National City emerge as Minneapolis' fourth-largest bank and the seventh largest of Minnesota's 700 banks in terms of assets—no one jokes anymore.

When Selmer Jerpbak retired as chairman of the Richfield State Bank in Richfield, taking it easy was the last thing on his mind. He was intrigued by the opportunity of opening a new bank in downtown Minneapolis, where no national bank had opened in more than 40 years, even though the downtown business community had grown by almost exponential proportions. Jerpbak found the investors he needed in Dwayne and Lowell Andreas, two prominent Minnesota businessmen, who agreed to put up the lion's share of the $3 million needed to capitalize the bank. The Andreas brothers in turn were impressed with the abilities of C. Bernard Jacobs, an official of Continental Bank of Illinois in Chicago who was that bank's chief Upper Midwest representative. They asked if Jacobs would consider being chief executive officer of Jerpbak's new bank with Jerpbak as president.

Initially Jacobs declined, but the investors eventually proved persuasive, and in 1964 Jerpbak and Jacobs moved quickly to get the new bank off the ground. The institution's first headquarters was to be in the lobby and plaza of the Sheraton Ritz Hotel. Before work was completed, however, the new National City Bank set up shop in two guest rooms at the hotel—leading to innumerable jokes and a Xerox machine that had to be kept in a bathtub—and, after receiving a national charter, began taking deposits and making investments in commercial paper and Treasury bills.

When National City Bank moved into its official headquarters a few weeks later, it had already set out on a course designed to make it stand out among downtown banks. To achieve growth, officials of the new institution knew they would

In 1964 National City Bank had its grand opening and open house. Pictured (from left) are Julius Hendel, one of National City Bank's original directors; Arthur Naftalin, then mayor of Minneapolis; C. Bernard Jacobs, chief executive officer; and Selmer Jerpbak, president.

have to take a series of calculated risks. They did not intend to be all things to all people, but rather began to carefully target their customers and offer them distinctive services—services that did indeed set National City Bank apart from other downtown banks.

By 1966 National City had pioneered the full-service teller concept and had become the first Twin Cities bank to offer free checking. A year later National City astounded banks all over the world by being the first to lower its prime rate to 5.75 percent, a move duplicated by institutions such as Chase Manhattan a few weeks later. In later years, as National City began to grow dramatically, a Trust Department was formed and a series of firsts for the region, such as Money Market Checking, an Executive Line of credit that remains today one of the most innovative and extensive credit lines for executives and professionals, and other innovations were introduced. In the meantime Selmer Jerpbak had retired and was replaced as president by Edward C. Brown, Jr.

By 1972 National City Bank had be-

come the third-largest bank in Minneapolis and the sixth largest in the state in terms of capital—in a remarkable period of fewer than 10 years. Two years later, when National City reached the ripe old age of 10 years, the bank had assets of $188 million, with deposits at $144 million.

By then the number of National City employees had grown to 175, and the bank realized it needed larger quarters than its 14,000 square feet in the Sheraton Ritz. In a move that gave National City the physical presence downtown it had already established financially, the bank decided to lease much of the newly remodeled building that had previously housed the Federal Reserve Bank. The first three stories of the structure had been built in 1921; the top nine floors were added in 1957. After the massive remodeling project the facility was reborn as the National City Bank Building. At the same time the press began heralding National City Bank as the fastest-growing bank in Minnesota—an honor it held on to for many years to come.

Soon National City would expand again. National City Bank-Southdale was a new detached banking facility that was opened in 1978 after the institution had outgrown its other Edina location. Edward C. Brown, Jr., had retired as president, and James H. Hearon III was hired as his replacement. At the end of that same year National City's assets topped the $200-million mark.

National City Bank entered the 1980s with a reputation as an innovator, as a bank that consistently offered higher rates on savings products, and as a bank that responded quickly to changes in the financial marketplace. National City also became publicly owned in the early 1980s, when Archer Daniels Midland, the Illinois-based agribusiness giant that had received

Dwayne and Lowell Andreas' interest in the bank through a stock exchange, was required by legislation to divest itself of its bank holdings.

Today National City Bank con-

The original Federal Reserve Building in downtown Minneapolis now serves as the National City Bank Building.

Walter E. Meadley, Jr. (left), president and chief operating officer, and James H. Hearon III (right), chairman and chief executive officer of National City Bank.

tinues to provide innovative services to selected groups of customers. Current leadership comes from James Hearon III, who continues as chairman and chief executive officer, and Walter E. Meadley, Jr., now president and chief operating officer. Since National City's market niches include high-income professional achievers and fast-growing small and mid-size companies, the bank faces stiff competition. Even so National City has continued to grow during the 1980s, most recently showing assets of nearly $500 million and deposits of more than $350 million. It has become the business bank for middle-market companies.

That's a long way from $3 million and a suite at the Ritz, when National City Bank staked its future on innovation and service. The rest of the banking world may be catching up to that philosophy, but National City today is not willing to let go of its lead.

NUMEREX CORPORATION

For many American businesses survival in a tough global market—where foreign competitors often enjoy lower labor costs even while producing higher quality products—has forced a lot of American companies to adopt a different way of doing business. Computer-aided design and manufacturing, just-in-time manufacturing techniques, automation, and robotics are profoundly changing the American workplace.

Underlying all of these changes is an overwhelming need for precision and the absolute control of the manufacturing process. From prototyping and testing to mass production, parts must be made according to specifications—not most of the time, but 100 percent of the time. For many companies today there is absolutely no room for error. That is one factor that accounts for the growth of Numerex Corporation in recent years; it has more than quadrupled its sales since the beginning of the decade. Numerex is still small but it is assuming growing importance in a new field called metrology, which itself is becoming a critical component of the estimated annual $18-billion factory automation market.

Metrology is both the science of measurement and the name for the market into which Numerex sells its systems. Those systems include devices for measuring the dimensions and physical forms of one-, two-, or three-dimensional parts, from a supercomputer circuit board to a car door—any part or product, in fact, that must be made to fit with other parts. With Numerex equipment an electronic or optical probe passes over a part and measures tolerances at points along each of three measurement axes. The signals are transmitted to a microcomputer that compares the values to previously programmed specifications. The system improves accuracy and quality, and greatly reduces the time required for manual inspection. Such coordinate measuring machines (CMM) can inspect virtually any part and are used in a wide cross section of industries, from machined parts to aerospace components.

Numerex has been a leading innovator in the small but rapidly growing CMM field, and today competes successfully with the West German companies that previously dominated the field. Numerex products are even competitive in Japan, where it licenses its CMMs to a Japanese

Hans Sprandel, founder and president of Numerex Corporation.

manufacturer. A great deal of Numerex' success comes from the fact that its CMMs are simpler and less expensive than those of competitors, all the while performing at a level that sets industry standards.

Simplicity and innovation were what gave Numerex its start. In 1953 Hans Sprandel, a 17-year-old East German engineering apprentice, sprinted across the East German border with his widowed mother and his sister into the freedom of West Berlin. Six years later, after studying electrical engineering at a West German college, Sprandel emigrated to the United States and settled in New Ulm, Minnesota, the home of his American sponsor. Sprandel first worked as a janitor at a processed food factory and later used his engineering talent to get a series of jobs in the machine-tool industry. After several unsuccessful attempts to de-

sign and build new products, Sprandel founded Sprandel Tool and Engineering in 1972 in Watertown, Minnesota, to manufacture and sell an optical-inspection device for circuit boards of his own design.

Luck then played a part in the birth of Numerex. In 1974 one of Sprandel's customers needed an economical and easy-to-use CMM, which at the time was a complicated and expensive machine. Could Sprandel's company design and build one? Sprandel agreed warily. He felt intimidated by the cost and complexity of existing machines; simplifying the design and solving several key engineering problems would be required to meet the customer's request.

Sprandel's new CMM was an elegant device that consisted of a smooth granite worktable beneath a suspended granite arm or bridge that guided an electronic measuring probe over parts placed on the granite worktable. The probe was moved across granite guideways supported by nearly frictionless air bearings.

The use of granite, which constructing the CMM easier and less expensive than using steel, and the rest of the innovative design resulted in a machine that could measure tolerances to thousandths of an inch.

The rest of the industry quickly caught on. The design formed the cornerstone for Numerex Corporation, which quickly evolved from Sprandel Tool and Engineering when orders for CMMs began pouring in. Growth was modest at first, but by the time Numerex went public in 1981, American industry was beginning to realize the need for measuring devices like CMMs. With the rise of just-

The majority of parts manufactured today are less than one cubic foot in size. Responding to these manufacturers' needs, Numerex has developed the Minicoord coordinate measuring machine (CMM). The Minicoord is specifically designed to verify the dimensional integrity of small parts at an economic cost.

in-time inventory and manufacturing techniques, which required parts that flawlessly performed according to specifications, and statistical process control, an ongoing statistical procedure to test for quality, CMM technology began playing an important role in the competition to produce more economical, higher quality products. As the factory of the future became a reality, CMMs became a basic requirement.

Numerex participated through the simplicity and innovativeness of its products. One attempt to build CMMs with a customized built-in dedicated computer failed disastrously when the computer supplier did not come up with the required computer. Numerex then decided to stick with standard PCs from companies like Apple and Hewlett-Packard. The familiar technology, combined with Numerex' own custom-designed software, ensured a high degree of customer acceptance for the new products Numerex developed during the

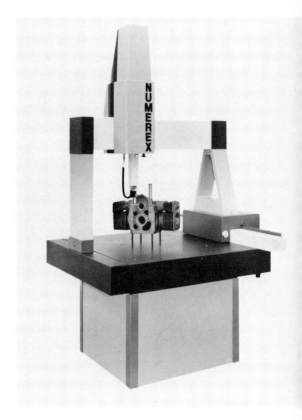

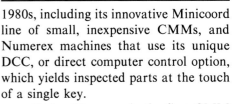

Numerex has introduced a new line of high-precision ceramic coordinate measuring machines (CMM) that dramatically improve the measuring capabilities for both large and small manufacturing companies.

1980s, including its innovative Minicoord line of small, inexpensive CMMs, and Numerex machines that use its unique DCC, or direct computer control option, which yields inspected parts at the touch of a single key.

Today Numerex is the first CMM manufacturer to use new high-technology ceramics in CMM construction. The ceramic material replaces the granite and produces machines that are even more "factory-floor hardened" than before.

Numerex' annual sales grew from less than $2 million in 1981 to a recent figure of close to $10 million. As measured by revenues per employee, its work force of 80 is among the most productive of any manufacturing company in Minnesota. Hans Sprandel continues to be the firm's sole product designer; a small support staff of engineers and software developers help turn his ideas into reality.

With such a strong presence in a market that is expected to grow rapidly in coming years, this innovative Minnesota company can look forward to a very bright future.

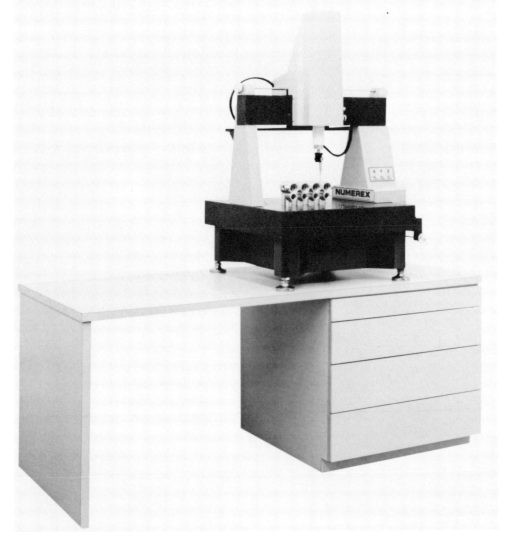

GNB INCORPORATED

Lytton J. Shields was just about unbeatable as a salesman. In 1906, when he joined a small parts distributor in Minneapolis, Electric Manufacturing Company, he knew that the demand for replacement parts for the automobile could only grow. He built an extensive regional network of dealers who sold one of the most profitable and important of all automobile replacement parts—batteries.

He did his job so well that by the time he was named president of Electric Manufacturing Company in 1911, he had won and then lost distributorships of three major battery manufacturers that opened their own direct branch warehouses once Shields had built up sales. Shields made a decision: If he was to have a future in the battery business, he would have to start making his own.

From that decision came GNB Incorporated, a company whose batteries today provide power for everything from nuclear submarines to electric golf carts. As the successor to several businesses, including National Battery Company, Gould-National Batteries, Inc., and Gould Inc., GNB's name may be unfamiliar. But GNB, with headquarters in Mendota Heights, is one of the world's largest manufacturers of lead-acid storage batteries, and is widely recognized as the leader in battery technology, and product development and marketing. Today GNB has more than 3,000 employees and 17 production facilities across the United States and Canada.

First Shields had to have a product. Initially, in 1916, the Electric Manufacturing Company sold farm-lighting batteries. To crack the automobile market, Shields had to start from scratch; the manufacturing techniques of other battery producers were closely guarded secrets. Thanks to the engineering skills of Carl Albrecht, later to become chief engineer, the art of casting battery grids out of lead was mastered. Despite setbacks, including a devastating fire at the company's factory in St. Paul's Midway district, the young firm began to grow. Shields was determined to compete on a national scale—one reason the organization changed its name to the National Lead Battery Company in 1921. By the early 1920s the factory was making as many as 350 batteries per day.

Going up against larger and more well-entrenched competitors was a monu-

mental task. By a bold stroke, however, Shields changed the ground rules.

In the 1920s Montgomery Ward was the nation's leading retailer. After waiting for three days in the lobby outside the office of Montgomery Ward's president, the legendary General Wood, Shields received an audience. Soon after General Wood visited National's St. Paul plant (filled with workers hurriedly hired to create the impression of a busy plant), Shields signed a contract with Montgomery Ward in 1922.

By 1930, after opening additional factories and making several acquisitions, National had captured 20 percent of the nation's automobile replacement battery business. That year Shields made another pivotal move with the purchase of the Gould Storage Battery Corporation of Depew, New York. This acquisition allowed National to expand its product line to include high-capacity industrial batteries.

In 1936, when sales reached an all-time high of $6 million, Lytton J. Shields died. His replacement by Albert H. Daggett, a business management specialist with a strong reputation as a problem solver, marked a turning point for the company. Marketing and production techniques became bolder than ever. The Kathanode battery, for example, introduced in the midst of the Great Depression when battery sales industrywide were falling, was a revolutionary product that offered buyers a lifetime guarantee. Sales soared, and the company made acquisitions and gained significant new contracts, including those that made it the supplier for Willys-Overland, developer of the Jeep, and Cities Service (now known as Citgo), with its nationwide chain of service stations.

National expanded rapidly during World War II. By the war's end sales had reached $25 million. In 1950, when the firm's name was changed to Gould-National Batteries, Inc., sales had more than doubled again. The decades that followed saw a burst of product development in the industry, with Gould-National continuing to lead the way. The demand for batteries skyrocketed. Gould-National's large market share in both the passenger car and diesel locomotive segments guaranteed tremendous growth. The firm also succeeded in gaining OEM contracts from Chrysler and Ford. Gould-National en-

Lytton J. Shields, GNB's founder.

tered the 1960s by embarking on an ambitious program of acquisitions designed to diversify and strengthen its position in both industrial and consumer products.

When Daggett retired and William T. Ylvisaker assumed his duties in 1967, Gould-National was a diversified, publicly held company with revenues exceeding $100 million. In the direction set by Ylvisaker, batteries became only one part of the company's total business, which would reach more than one billion dollars in sales. By then Gould-National had become Gould, and the firm introduced a number of new concepts in automotive and industrial batteries, including, in 1974, its Champion line of sealed, maintenance-free batteries.

In 1982, as part of the firm's move into electronics, all of Gould's battery-related businesses were consolidated into a separate, wholly owned subsidiary called GNB Batteries, Inc. Two years later GNB's president, Stanley N. Gaines, senior management, and a group of outside investors purchased GNB from its parent company in order to focus solely on producing and marketing the lead-acid storage batteries.

Late in 1987 Pacific Dunlop Limited, Australia's largest international manufacturer and marketer of consumer and industrial products, purchased controlling interest in GNB.

Today GNB relies on a reputation for quality and advanced research and development to maintain a competitive advantage. While automobile battery sales account for some 75 percent of the company's revenues, GNB is also the sole sup-

The Champion battery starts automobiles. The larger battery, used in multiples of hundreds, provides power for U.S. nuclear submarines.

plier of battery power sources for the U.S. Navy's nuclear submarine fleet, and was recently picked to supply batteries for the new Peacekeeper MX missile. GNB is also a leader in batteries for automobiles, recreational vehicles, fishing boats, heavy-duty trucks, electric forklift trucks for industry, and standby batteries for hospitals, telephone exchanges, and public power utilities.

GNB is also one of the nation's largest resource recyclers, operating the most technologically advanced lead reclamation and refining facilities to be found anywhere in the world.

By staking a claim on quality and innovation, pumping significant amounts into research and development, and maintaining Lytton Shields' marketing savvy, GNB Incorporated is a pacesetter in a $2.5-billion industry. It has developed and introduced more "firsts" than any other company in its field—a track record it fully expects to maintain.

GNB headquarters in Mendota Heights, Minnesota.

ANDERSEN CORPORATION

While helping fellow crewmen pry up tree stumps, the first English words Hans J. Andersen learned as a 16-year-old Danish immigrant were, "all together boys."

Since July 25, 1903, when Hans launched the Andersen Lumber Company (now the Andersen Corporation) with his sons, Fred and Herbert, on the banks of the St. Croix River, which separates Minnesota and Wisconsin, those three words have animated the firm's business philosophy, which Fred Andersen later termed The Magic Circle.

Now the world's most successful maker of windows and patio doors (roughly one billion dollars in annual sales), Andersen pioneered from the start a people-oriented way of doing business, as well as pioneering in products (43 patents), manufacturing innovations, and marketing. As one of the firm's 124 North American distributors puts it, "Andersen's dealings with employees, with the trade, and with the public have always been guided by only one criterion—the Golden Rule."

In 1914, when profit sharing was a revolutionary concept, Andersen launched a generous profit-sharing plan that to date has put more than an extra $310 million in its workers' pockets. This successful employee program, the third-oldest profit-sharing program in the nation, continues to work well today.

Through the years Andersen originated many benefits that were far ahead of their time, such as free life insurance, vacation with pay for factory and office workers alike, group hospital coverage, and a surviving spouse plan. In more recent times a scholarship program for employees' children was added, as well as a continuing employee stock ownership program completely financed by the firm—further evidence that Andersen sees its employees as working partners.

All of which leads to The Magic Circle. Fred C. Andersen, who took over the company reins following the deaths of his father in 1914 and his brother Herbert in 1921, once described The Magic Circle as having these key links: skillful, well-paid employees; good management, research, and an efficient marketing program; top-notch distributors and dealers, builders, and architects who believe in quality windows; and consumers who realize that "only the rich can afford poor windows."

These links, working "all together," have helped parlay the little 12-man business Hans Andersen established on the banks of the St. Croix into a phenomenon of the American building trade.

In 1903 Hans J. Andersen, a Danish immigrant, founded the Andersen Lumber Company with his sons, Fred and Herbert, on the banks of the St. Croix River. Today his firm is the world's most successful maker of windows and patio doors.

Fred C. Andersen, while working in his father's fledgling business, coined the company's business philosophy as The Magic Circle, otherwise known as the Golden Rule that links employees, management, and customers.

It was not chance that led Hans Andersen to choose the friendly valley of the St. Croix for his business venture. Lumbering was the area's principal industry, so the necessary raw materials were close at hand. In those days there was no such thing as a standard window size. Different states, and even different towns, followed local customs that varied all over the lot. Andersen single-handedly set out to standardize the sizes of windows and window frames—a venture that took years, but in the process enabled the company to gain the benefits of assembly line manufacture, long before Henry Ford introduced assembly lines to the automobile industry.

The original plant in Hudson, on the Wisconsin side of the St. Croix, had been outgrown by 1913 when new headquarters—now covering more than 50 acres of floor space—were established three miles upriver in Bayport, Minnesota.

Then and ever since, Andersen has followed a threefold policy: Make a product that is different and better, hire the best people and pay top wages, and provide steady employment as far as humanly possible.

Weather tightness and improved designs for beautiful windows have been at the root of Andersen's continued success in making products different and better. The multitude of patents that contributed to these results have been the brainchildren of a wide variety of individuals, from top management to factory workers and salesmen to research engineers. Fred Andersen himself was granted the firm's first patent—a locked sill joint that was the first in many steps toward windows that shut out the elements.

During World War I, while Fred Andersen and many employees enlisted for military service, the company filled orders for 200,000 window frames needed for Army barracks, then changed its production lines radically in order to turn out thousands of target frames and other wood products needed by Uncle Sam.

World War II saw Andersen become a major war plant, winning two coveted Army-Navy "E" awards for its

Andersen's Bayport plant employs 3,800 people.

versatility in setting up assembly lines to manufacture millions of ammunition boxes—more than any other U.S. supplier—as well as hundreds of prefabricated 16-square-foot Army shelters (called Stout houses), plus wooden chests

and military tool drawers by the hundreds of thousands.

Late in 1944 Andersen adopted its most widely known trademark, Windowalls®, when it was decided this name best reflected the company's leadership in creating window designs for the open look architects were seeking. Windowalls® were so weather tight they served as walls. Conversely, with Windowalls®, walls became beautiful windows.

Shortly after World War II Andersen created major news in the building world by pioneering the use of double-pane welded insulating glass, which for the first time effectively eliminated the need for storm windows. And in 1966, after an eight-year struggle that involved expensive research, testing, and modifications, the firm achieved a milestone by

Perma-Shield® combines the insulation of wood with the durability of vinyl. Shown is a cross section of a Perma-Shield® window. This type of window and door accounts for most of Andersen's billion-dollar sales.

reaching a dramatic goal that had eluded the entire industry—a low-maintenance window that also retains the important insulating properties of wood.

Wood provides insulation in both summer and winter, a key reason why Andersen has always been committed to its use. Wood, however, can be attacked by the elements, and wood needs to be painted—but not anymore. By using a process that eventually involved several patents, Andersen sheathed the wood elements of its windows and patio doors evenly with extruded hot vinyl—a revolutionary breakthrough trademarked Perma-Shield®. At first the vinyl sheath was used only on casement windows, gliding doors, and awning windows, but today its popularity has skyrocketed. Now most of Andersen Corporation's billion-dollar annual output is manufactured using the Perma-Shield® process. The Magic Circle is still weaving its spell.

CARLSON COMPANIES

Curt Carlson, founder, chairman of the board, and chief executive officer of the Carlson Companies, is the quintessential self-made man, the entrepreneur's entrepreneur. From the start of his first business more than 50 years ago, he has parlayed a simple idea—Gold Bond Trading Stamps—and a boundless appetite for hard work into a multibillion-dollar enterprise consisting of 75 separate corporations and realizing more than $4 billion per year in revenues. Over four decades the various enterprises that make up the Carlson Companies have attained an astonishing 33-percent-per-year compounded growth rate. Together those businesses have rocketed the Carlson Companies to the 14th-largest privately held corporation in the nation, making it one of the 125 largest U.S. firms in the *Fortune* 500 listing when compared to public companies.

Curt Carlson is a man who has never been satisfied with second place or a second-best performance. Despite his corporation's current size, he continues to stress the virtues of entrepreneurial thinking (and lots of hard work) for each of the Carlson Companies' separate operations.

As a result, the Carlson Marketing Group is the largest motivation company in the world; one of its constituent companies—E.F. MacDonald—is the cornerstone of this highly effective organization.

With the acquisition a few years ago of an important chain of retail travel agen-

Shown here is a model of the Carlson Companies' new world headquarters that will open in Minnetonka, Minnesota—just 10 minutes from downtown Minneapolis—in 1989.

Edwin C. Gage (left) serves as president and chief operating officer of Carlson Companies, and Curtis L. Carlson (right) is chairman of the board and chief executive officer; together they provide leadership for the future.

cies, Ask Mr. Foster, the Carlson Companies' Travel Group, through tremendous growth and acquisitions, now has emerged as the largest travel enterprise in North America with annual revenues of more than $2 billion.

The Carlson Promotion Group, the offshoot of the Gold Bond trading stamp business, is still a leader in the field of marketing promotions designed to enhance sales, increase profits, and capture customer loyalty for clients.

Throughout his long and successful career, Carlson has stressed the importance of achieving synergy among the many operations making up his business empire. Synergy is one of the key words to describe his decision to transform the Radisson Hotel Corporation into the fastest-growing upscale hotel company in the country. Under the dynamic leadership of Juergen Bartels, head of the Carlson Hospitality Group, the Radisson

Hotel Corporation has mushroomed, in only five years, from a regional chain of 35 hotels to a collection of more than 205 hotels worldwide, with 47,000 top-quality guest rooms and revenues in excess of $1.4 billion. This group also includes TGI Friday's, Country Kitchen restaurants, Country Hospitality Inns, and Colony Hotels and Resorts.

Contrary to the norm for entrepreneurs, Curt Carlson has always been a great believer in planning and careful growth. Even at the age of 73 he continues to think of the future and not the past. In Edwin "Skip" Gage, president and chief operating officer of the Carlson Companies, Carlson has ensured the continuation of his enterprises under able leadership well into the next century. At that time the firm will have a new home, too; 1989 is the year that the Carlson Companies are slated to move into the new world headquarters on the grounds of the Carlson Center, a 300-acre, $650-million "city within a city" that straddles the borders of Minnetonka and Plymouth. The move marks yet another milestone for a company whose 50-year history is one of unbelievable achievement.

IBM

In 1955 a group of Rochester business and civic leaders formed a nonprofit community development corporation called Industrial Opportunities, Inc. Their mission was to attract new business to the city, which was still largely dependent on the world-famous Mayo Clinic and the two hospitals that served it. IOI held a grand celebration at a downtown intersection to kick off a fund-raising drive to acquire the land and lay utilities for a new industrial park in the northwest corner of the city. There were speeches, the crowd was festive and excited, and a toy cannon was fired to launch the campaign.

Unbeknownst to members of the IOI group, company representatives and consultants were on a search mission. They were quietly scouting sites for a major new facility for the International Business Machines Corporation. Eighty midwestern cities had been explored. Few could match what Rochester offered—a highly educated work force, a good infrastructure and good schools, and certain intangibles, one being the civic-building enthusiasm that the new IOI seemed to have unleashed. Seven months later IBM's president, the legendary Thomas J. Watson, Jr., met with 40 Rochester business, professional, and civic leaders. That evening a banner headline appeared in the *Rochester Post-Bulletin*: "IBM to Erect Huge Plant Here; 1,500 to be employed by 1958." Manufacturing lines were soon set up in a building rented from IOI.

Ground was broken on the present 586-acre site in 1958. Three years later a development laboratory was established that would enable the facility to internally develop systems that would have a significant impact on IBM's growth over the past two decades.

By the mid-1980s more than 7,000 people would be employed at the IBM Rochester facility, one of the largest and most important IBM facilities in the world. And IBM would join the Mayo Clinic in shaping the destiny of modern Rochester, which has become, due to these two prestigious corporate citizens, one of the best educated and most prosperous small cities in the nation. IBM's economic impact on Rochester as well as on all of Minnesota is estimated to exceed $760 million yearly. Volunteer time and charitable contributions by IBM employees are also impressive, and most recently included more than 40 percent of Olmsted County's United Way donations.

IBM in Rochester is the largest Minnesota manufacturer outside the Twin Cities area and the state's eighth-largest private-sector employer. The huge blue-clad Rochester facility, with more than 3 million square feet of space, is the largest IBM facility under one roof.

IBM in Rochester grew to importance as the principal development and manufacturing facility for IBM's System Products Division, which develops small and intermediate-size general-purpose computing systems and data-storage devices for offices, small businesses, and department or division-size work groups. That market became immense with the computer evolution.

The Rochester facility's System/34, System/36, and System/38 products have become the industry's standard-bearers in mid-size computing systems. Throughout its growth IBM has been one of Minnesota's leading corporate citizens. Its contribution to the region's economy and quality of life continues to be a major reason Rochester has become known as one of the most attractive small cities in the nation.

The company was recognized in 1986, when the Minnesota Association of Commerce and Industry presented IBM at Rochester with the first Greater Minnesota Economic Development Award. The award is given to recognize contributions made by a Minnesota company to the state's economy.

Two views of IBM's facility in Rochester, Minnesota.

QUADION CORPORATION

When America entered World War II thousands of new companies sprang up around the country to supply products to feed the nation's gigantic war effort. Wilson Packing and Rubber, one such company, set up a little shop in Minneapolis to supply fabricated rubber parts for various types of armaments, including o-rings and gaskets for torpedoes being made by a growing firm across town called Honeywell, Inc. Within a year of its formation, Wilson moved to a new facility in St. Louis Park, that at 1,000 square feet was huge for a company its size.

The organization Wilson has become still makes rubber products, and still has a manufacturing facility in St. Louis Park. However, it has grown to include facilities in Litchfield, Minnesota; Cucamonga, California; Watertown, South Dakota; Mason City, Iowa; and Evreux, France. And its capabilities have expanded beyond rubber to include plastic as well as aluminum and zinc die casting at facilities in New Hope, Minnesota, and Singapore.

A new name, Quadion Corporation, encompasses these various divisions. "Quadion" refers both to the innovative four-lobed rubber seal that fueled the cor-

An overview of a press line at Minnesota Rubber's Watertown, South Dakota, plant, one of the firm's six manufacturing facilities.

poration's growth in its early years and to a four-part commitment to customers that has helped Quadion become one of Minnesota's fastest growing and most innovative privately held companies. The commitment is to on-time delivery, superior quality, cost-effective pricing, and superior customer service. Sticking to that commitment has resulted in a fourfold increase in revenues over the past decade to recently exceed $100 million and the emergence of Quadion as a leader in the markets it serves.

The story of Quadion really begins with Paul Dennison and George Carlson, the first of three generations of Carlsons to operate the company. Both men were entrepreneurs; Carlson was an inventor as well. He worked on early versions of today's modern electric toothbrush and, while an employee of General Electric, contributed to the development of the traffic light. During the war both men worked for Wilson Packing and Rubber; when the owner decided to sell, Dennison and Carlson jumped at the chance to develop their own business.

Renamed the Minnesota Rubber and Gasket Company, the operation continued to grow, although it was many years before it broke one million dollars in sales. A year after the purchase, a new 10,000-square-foot plant was built a few miles away. While the firm continued to specialize in gaskets and o-rings for industrial uses, it also broadened into producing molded rubber parts for such unlikely consumer products as hair curlers. But no matter what the product, the company established a reputation for meeting the customer's specifications, essential in this business.

That early reputation for quality, along with the development in the 1950s

Minnesota Rubber's Research and Development Laboratory performs various testing functions, including tensile strength tests on its rubber materials.

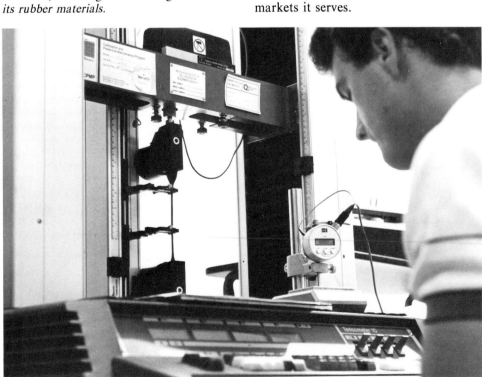

of an innovative type of o-ring, which the firm called the Quad-Ring® seal, helped Minnesota Rubber grow in the decades that followed. Growth was not spectacular—by the mid-1970s revenues only reached $25 million—but it was consistent, and the innovative Quad-Ring helped the company's reputation spread worldwide. Ordinary o-rings, used to seal flexible joints, are vulnerable to twisting and a loss of effectiveness under tough conditions. Minnesota Rubber's Quad-Ring, based on a four-lobed internal structure, could stand up to twice as much punishment as conventional o-rings. There were countless applications for this new type of o-ring.

When Paul Dennison died in 1955, George Carlson assumed control of the corporation as president. In 1957 he became chairman of the board when his son, Robert W. Carlson, was named president. At the same time "Gasket" was dropped from the company name, and various small divisions that had been operating independently were merged under the common Minnesota Rubber name.

Under George and Robert Carlson, Minnesota Rubber expanded sharply during the 1960s. The firm's St. Louis Park facility was expanded repeatedly. A new plant was opened in Watertown, South Dakota. That, too, was continually enlarged. Then tragedy occurred. On July 2, 1971, Robert Carlson was killed in a plane crash. A year later chairman George Carlson died. Luke Sewell, a longtime employee, replaced Robert Carlson as president, and he, along with surviving members of the Carlson family, took over management of the company.

In 1975, at Robert W. Carlson, Jr.'s, urging, Minnesota Rubber acquired Tool Products Company, a Minneapolis die caster of aluminum and zinc, and Carlson was named president of this new independent subsidiary. The acquisition of the $2-million organization, which was losing money at the time, marked a turning point for Minnesota Rubber. The diversification into die casting aluminum, zinc, and other materials opened up new business areas, and Tool Products later became a major contributor to Quadion's sales. Revenue from die-casting precision parts, many for demanding computer and high-technology companies, would grow to today's nearly $45 million. Tool Products also marked the beginning of Robert

Carlson's active role in the management of Minnesota Rubber, which culminated two years later when Carlson, assisted by David Koenig, who had helped Minnesota Rubber acquire Tool Products, bought out the remaining Carlson family members and assumed sole control of the firm.

Robert W. Carlson, Jr., who had worked for the company in one capacity or another since the age of 14, had clear notions about the kind of company Minnesota Rubber should become. He quickly set out to transform what had been a stable, modestly growing family business into an international leader in its markets.

Aggressive expansion plans launched in 1979 included a new plant in Iowa and a new corporate headquarters building adjacent to the original St. Louis Park plant. Late in 1981 Minnesota Rubber purchased Royal Seals Corporation, a California precision rubber parts molder, and strengthened its position in the rubber industry. In a move to better serve its major European customers, Minnesota Rubber acquired a plant in Evreux, France, in 1984. In February 1987 the firm designed and built a highly automated, state-of-the-art injection-molding facility in Litchfield, Minnesota. At the same time that Minnesota Rubber expanded to France, Tool Products built a new precision, automated die-casting plant in Singapore. The customer lists for these companies include many leading national and multinational firms, from the computer to automotive industries.

By the mid-1980s Minnesota Rub-

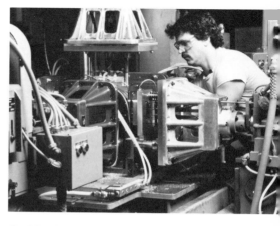

Tool Products is a high-speed, high-volume manufacturer of precision aluminum die-cast parts, with plants in Minnesota and Singapore.

ber had outgrown both its old industry image and its name. Quadion Corporation trades on the reputations of its predecessor companies (Minnesota Rubber and Tool Products) for quality, service, and innovative solutions, and the new organization's emergence as a dynamic leader in the markets it serves. Quadion's work force today tops 2,000, while sales are projected to increase at the same rapid pace established over the past few years. Quadion Corporation is a perfect example of what innovation and a commitment to quality can do for a business.

Quadion's corporate headquarters, built in 1979, sits adjacent to Minnesota Rubber's original plant in St. Louis Park.

ST. PAUL-RAMSEY MEDICAL CENTER AND RAMSEY CLINIC

St. Paul's tradition of excellence in health care can be traced to an old stone mansion that opened more than a century ago and grew to become St. Paul-Ramsey Medical Center. The handful of doctors, who once volunteered their time to care for the unemployed and working poor, has developed into a 160-member multispecialty group practice known as Ramsey Clinic. Today the medical center and clinic have formed a strong partnership with a national reputation for research, education, and pioneering work in the treatment of burns, trauma, and communicable diseases.

In 1872 Ramsey County purchased a 10-room mansion for $20,000 to house St. Paul's first hospital, City and County Hospital. For 11 years this facility was operated as an isolation ward for patients with contagious diseases and home for abandoned children. In 1883 Dr. Arthur B. Ancker was appointed superintendent by the county board.

When Ancker came to St. Paul, City and County Hospital had been expanded but was already inadequate. St. Paul had grown to exceed 100,000 people and was by then the 22nd-largest city in the country. City and County Hospital was desperately overcrowded and "saturated with the germs of disease," Ancker wrote. Ancker made it his life's work to expand and improve the hospital, using the considerable force of his personality to convince the city to make improvement after improvement.

At the start of Ancker's tenure, City and County Hospital consisted of two buildings with room for 25 patients. With a staff of four, including Ancker himself, the hospital cared for 350 patients an-

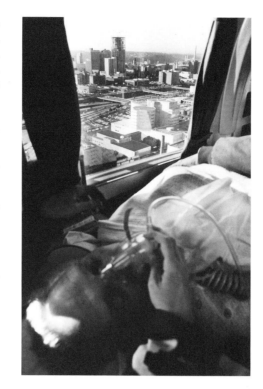

Life Link III, an air ambulance service, is jointly owned by St. Paul-Ramsey and two other Twin Cities medical centers. St. Paul-Ramsey and downtown St. Paul are in the background.

nually.

When the hospital celebrated its 40th anniversary in 1912, after 30 years of Ancker's guidance, it was the 10th largest in the country. With 12 buildings, 600 beds, 40 physicians, and 100 nurses, it served more than 5,400 patients annually.

The first ambulance was presented to the hospital in 1895 by a group of "charitable ladies." An anonymous donor bought the horses for the ambulance.

When Ancker died in 1923, City and County Hospital was the seventh largest in the nation and was renamed Ancker Hospital in his honor. Ancker physicians had helped eradicate many communicable diseases in St. Paul, and the city was known as one of the healthiest places in the nation. The hospital had also established a pattern of innovative treatment and was among the first in the nation to use X rays, to treat cancer with radium, and to initiate outpatient care.

In the late 1920s Ancker Hospital's Dr. Frederick Foley developed the catheter that bears his name and is commonly used in hospitals today. In 1935 Dr. John R. Meade established the first diabetes clinic. Innovations made at the hospital helped prevent the spread of infectious diseases and gave St. Paul the lowest infant mortality rate in the country in 1937. Twelve years later a heart surgery program was established. Most of these accomplishments were encouraged by superintendent Dr. Thomas Broadie, whose 30-year tenure proved nearly as fruitful as Ancker's.

When Ancker Hospital moved into a new, $16-million facility and officially became St. Paul-Ramsey Hospital in 1967, the foundations for the modern research, education, and treatment programs that give the institution its distinction had been laid.

Physicians who practice at the hospital were incorporated as Ramsey Clinic, which, together with St. Paul-Ramsey, is a subsidiary of the nonprofit Ramsey HealthCare, Inc. Both groups entered the 1980s as partners in providing outstanding health care. It has proved to be a fruitful partnership.

SCHOLL'S, INC.

Lorin John Scholl, better known as "Doc" to his friends, had been a bank teller and later a schoolteacher in his hometown of Chippewa Falls, Wisconsin, before he got the urge to seek his fortune in the nearest big city, St. Paul. Aided by a $2,000 loan from his stepfather, Scholl and his younger brother, Earl, moved to St. Paul in 1935, formed the World Products Distribution Company, and set up shop beneath an electric motor repair shop on Prior Avenue.

Doc Scholl was familiar with rural country stores. He knew they sold a little bit of just about everything but had no reason to stock many products in large quantities. Scholl was also familiar with "peddlers" or wagon jobbers, the small-time salesmen who plied the back roads of America selling merchandise to rural stores from the backs of their station wagons or trucks. World Products was intended to serve those peddlers with "carded" merchandise, products the Scholl brothers bought and then broke down into small quantities and mounted on cards that retailers could display behind their counters. The brothers established a foothold in the distribution business.

Earl soon discovered he did not like the pace of St. Paul and returned to Chippewa Falls. Doc stuck it out and, before his death in 1984, saw his operation grow into one of the region's premier distribution businesses, Scholl's, Inc., which currently distributes in 48 states, has more than 325 employees, and boasts almost $100 million in sales—a figure that in recent times has been growing by some 15

Lorin John "Doc" Scholl, founder of Scholl's, Inc.

percent per year.

Until the 1960s the firm, incorporated in 1956, had only a handful of employees. But as small-town general stores disappeared, Scholl's began to sell to discount chain stores with its own direct sales force. Fred Clark, who was hired as a shipping clerk in 1951, became the company's first salesman in 1961. By then the firm was distributing some 2,000 products, primarily health and beauty aids.

"Doc" (left) and Earl Scholl's (right) World Products Distributing Company has grown to become one of the Midwest's leading and most innovative distributing companies. Here the two brothers stand in front of their fledgling business, which was set up in an electric motor repair shop on Prior Avenue. Photo circa 1935

Scholl's was welcomed by growing, locally based discount chain stores, including Target stores, now one of the nation's largest discount chains. One reason was its pioneering use of "cost-plus" pricing. Instead of the manufacturer's suggested retail price minus a percentage, Scholl's charged retailers its own cost plus a percentage. The effect was lower costs and, since discounters were building business based on lower prices, the firm's approach proved a winning strategy.

Through a service program started in 1973, Scholl's bought, stocked, shipped, and set up products for retailers that saw the virtues of not having to warehouse and manage their own inventories. In the case of Dayton's Department Store, the company even supplied in-store personnel to do everything but man the cash registers.

By the end of the decade Scholl's had established itself as the area's leading distributor of health and beauty aids, as well as a growing presence on the national distribution scene. In 1979 a 124,000-square-foot facility was opened in Arden Hills, a St. Paul suburb, and a 56,000-square-foot facility was added near Los Angeles, California, in 1983. Doc Scholl sold the business to his children— Michael, Tim, Dan, and Patricia. Tim and Dan Scholl are actively managing the company today.

Through the diversification of both its customer base and its product mix, Scholl's, Inc., has become a specialist in product distribution with national capabilities. And the company's unswerving dedication to customer service remains its greatest strength.

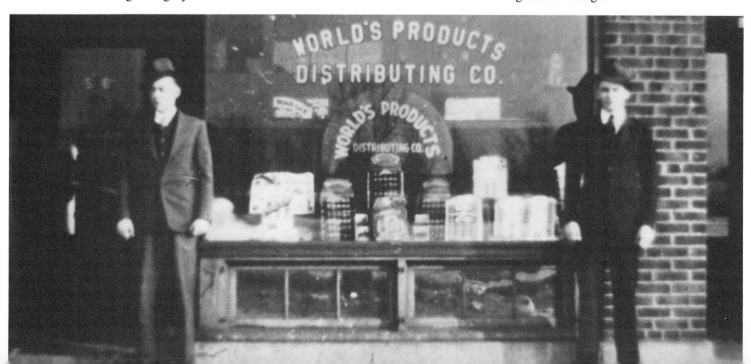

SLUMBERLAND, INC.

When Kenneth Larson took over Slumberland stores in the early 1970s, the Twin Cities-based specialty retailer was trying hard to put a little distance between itself and the competition.

Started by E.G. Graham and his son, James, in 1967, Slumberland originally set out to be an all-purpose mattress store, specializing in complete low-cost packages that included bedframes, inner springs, mattresses, mattress pads, even pillows and sheets. Later sleep sofas were added, and in the early 1970s Slumberland became a dealer for La-Z-Boy recliners.

It was a very competitive business. Statistics showed that consumers bought a mattress perhaps once every seven years, so massive amounts of advertising to attract consumer attention were essential. Because of the time span between purchases, few customers have the knowledge or expertise to be an informed buyer. It was felt they would turn first to a firm (store) they could trust.

Soon after he bought the Grahams' interest in 1971, Larson instituted a guarantee policy that caused a stir. Slumberland guaranteed that its prices were the lowest in the area by matching prices found elsewhere for the same merchandise within 30 days. Slumberland also guaranteed that customers could not buy the wrong mattress, sleep sofa, or recliner by offering a full refund or an exchange within a week of purchase if customers believed they had made the wrong choice. Finally, Slumberland offered a full year guarantee on material and workmanship—even if the manufacturer offered none. Slumberland's guarantee brought

customers, and was quickly copied by other speciality retailers.

Slumberland's decision to specialize in sleep sofas proved to be very important as living areas in new homes, condominiums, and apartments began to shrink to keep up with rising construction costs and interest rates. Consumers began buying sleep sofas not as a luxury to be used on rare occasions, but as a necessity that used shrinking living spaces more efficiently. Today sleep sofas account for more than one-third of all sofas sold. Recliners began to match the changing lifestyles as consumers started spending more to increase the comfort of their homes and less on outside entertainment in a phenomenon that has been dubbed the "cocooning" of America.

By placing a premium on customer satisfaction and narrowing its focus to capitalize on these emerging trends, Slumberland has grown steadily in recent years. Today there are nine company-owned Slumberland stores in the Twin Cities area and 15 franchised stores in cities in the Upper Midwest. In the Twin Cities, Slumberland has the leading market share in several sleep and rest merchandise categories.

Slumberland has worked hard to establish a high comfort level through the expertise and professionalism of its store personnel, its trend-setting guaranty policy, and in other ways. Recently, when a Twin Cities mattress retailer went bank-

---

Slumberland's nine company-owned and 15 franchised sleep stores place it among the top 10 specialty home furnishing store chains in the United States.

Slumberland president Kenneth R. Larson.

---

rupt, Slumberland offered to honor any deposits made by consumers with the out-of-business chain. The gesture enhanced Slumberland's credibility and helped build customer loyalty. Slumberland's size and its narrow specialization has also made it a major account to many of its suppliers; the preferred pricing treatment it receives is frequently passed on to its customers.

The firm's $27.7 million in sales in 1986 placed it among the top 10 specialty home furnishing stores and chains in the United States. Slumberland, Inc., continues to prosper from lessons it learned long ago: Offer the highest quality and place a premium on customer service and success is bound to follow.

FINGERHUT CORPORATION

By using precisely targeted mailing lists, merchandisers can hone in on consumers with just the sort of buying preferences it takes to sell their products. Add increasingly sophisticated computerization and automation techniques and you have a phenomenon that has revolutionized retailing, with direct mail, according to some recent estimates, accounting for as much as $13 billion in sales.

Some say the revolution began with Manny and William Fingerhut. In 1948 the two brothers began making what for the time was an innovative new product—seat covers for automobiles—out of their family-run sewing business. Not satisfied with simply selling their product to car dealers, the brothers began searching for a way to reach their market more directly. The solution: Go directly to the customers by obtaining automobile registration lists and offering their product for sale, without middlemen and middlemen markups, directly through the U.S. mail. The impulse produced a company that grew to what the recent bestseller, *In Search of Excellence,* called "maybe the ultimate niche company. By tracking customers and customer profitability, virtually every individual customer is a separate market segment." That concept has translated

into a six-year string of 20-percent annual compounded growth and most recent annual sales of more than one billion dollars.

During the early 1950s only clear plastic seat covers were offered. Important innovations included some of the first free gift and free trial offers. As the company began adding products to its line in the 1960s, its growing and carefully maintained mailing lists of existing customers provided an important base for expansion. That expansion was accomplished through an increasing number of products the firm manufactured in its own facilities and offered, without middlemen, at low costs to consumers. Revenues increased dramatically. The company's initial public stock offering in 1969 was a tremendous success.

The 1970s saw several important changes that set the stage for the Fingerhut of today. By early in the decade Fingerhut was offering in excess of 40 products through solo direct-mail campaigns, but the growth curve began to flatten and share prices fell. To keep the company moving ahead, long-term strategic planning was initiated. Catalogs and new products were introduced as Fingerhut phased out of manufacturing and became strictly a distributor instead. The

firm also began more precisely segmenting its customers and creating different appeals for different tastes. By the end of the decade Fingerhut had regained its momentum as the pioneer and innovator of direct mail—so much so that in 1979 the giant conglomerate American Can Company made a successful offer for the corporation of $20 a share—up from a share price of $1.75 during the mid-1970s.

During the 1980s Fingerhut became one of the largest and most profitable subsidiaries of Primerica Corporation—the new name of American Can, which reflects its new identity as a financial services company.

Fingerhut is one of Minnesota's largest corporations, and it is an all-Minnesota company, with 10 facilities and all of its nearly 5,000 employees in the state. A 3,000-person operation in St. Cloud makes it the largest employer in that part of Minnesota. Today the company is run by a professional management team, including William C. Johnson, chairman and chief executive officer, who has guided the firm through its greatest growth.

Fingerhut is sometimes called the world's best direct marketing company, an assessment that raises little disagreement.

PRESS ON INCORPORATED

When Press On Incorporated wrote a creed, it began with "Press on, for nothing in the world can take the place of persistence." There were a few other things that were important to the history of the Stillwater automotive graphics company as well, including luck, talent, good salesmanship, a friendly bank, an ample pool of dedicated and high-quality employees, and a manufacturing contract with a famous corporate neighbor called the 3M Company. But sheer, dogged persistence helped Press On become, in a little more than a decade, one of the St. Croix Valley's largest and most respected employers.

Such persistence was required during Press On's early days, when the company's office consisted of a camper backed up to an old chicken coop, and owners, new employees, relatives, and friends helped construct the firm's first manufacturing facility, and later sometimes worked around the clock getting out the company's first orders. Today Press On builds the latest addition to its complex of buildings on the site of the old chicken coop, and contemplates a future as, among other things, the major supplier of decaling and custom die cutting to 3M's huge Automotive Systems Division.

Press On came about through an unusual partnership of three Washington County men. In the early 1970s Jim Torseth was a young university graduate with a degree in business management,

Press On's original offices consisted of a camper connected to an old chicken coop.

and a strong entrepreneurial aptitude nurtured while working for his family's graphic arts business. Neal Skinner began working for the Torseth, Inc., while a sophomore in high school. Like his friend, Jim Torseth, Skinner did many odd jobs and learned about the screen printing business from the bottom up. He was soon running presses and had become familiar with the technical end of operating a screen printing business.

Both men had ambitions. Torseth, Skinner, and Oscar Kern, a Washington

Press On's 65,000-square-foot Stillwater facility is almost always being expanded.

County farmer and entrepreneur, met and began discussing the development of a screen printing business. Torseth knew the business and could handle general management, pricing, and sales. Skinner had the technical knowledge and manufacturing leadership to buy equipment and get the operation off the ground. Oscar Kern was impressed with the two young men and became a partner, helping to arrange the financing and contributing a great deal of accumulated business wisdom.

Press On was incorporated in 1974. After a grueling winter and spring of construction, with Torseth, Skinner, and new employees pitching in along with the general contractor, Press On's first building was ready for business in 1975. The company's first order took eight hours to prepare and print and netted Press On a total of $275.

The firm's original business plan called for it to seek work from a wide variety of commercial customers with many different screen printing needs. The company had persistence, with Torseth and Skinner frequently camping out in the new building to carefully check press runs. The resulting high-quality product helped generate an increasing number of referrals. Early customers, many needing point-of-purchase displays, included Andersen Corporation, Winnebago, and Steiger tractor.

During that same year Jack Whaley and Steve Meyer, both managers with 3M's Decorative Products Division, visited the Press On facility, the beginning of a long and fruitful relationship. 3M, based in nearby Maplewood, was in the business of supplying U.S. carmakers with screen printed automotive graphics. The operation was growing, and 3M needed a source of high-quality product. Press On was asked to bid on several 3M jobs and was soon awarded a contract to print a design for Chrysler's Dodge Dart. 3M, which had built its reputation on quality and was a demanding company to work for, was impressed. By 1976 Press On had outgrown its original building. Two years after it was conceived, the firm's work force had grown to 100.

Press On grew as 3M's demands for its products grew. In the late 1970s new custom presses were installed, and Press On began to concentrate almost exclusively on supplying 3M with automotive graphics, one of the most spectacular being the phoenix in flight that graced the hood of Pontiac's Firebird. Press On also acquired one of Oscar Kern's businesses, Kern Collectibles, a small company that specialized in limited-edition giftware. By the end of the decade two more buildings had been constructed, and Press On's work force had reached 175.

Press On's growth in the early 1980s was interrupted by the recession and high interest rates that dampened demand for new cars. Kern Collectibles provided much-needed cash flow, but Press On was still forced to shrink its work force, though only temporarily, which was extremely painful for a company that had built up a deep family atmosphere. The firm became determined to be one of the highest quality suppliers in its industry. Rigorous quality improvement programs were developed, and the company began adopting innovative Just-In-Time manufacturing techniques. Torseth and Skinner, who had bought Kern's interests in the operation, also became determined to seek an even closer affiliation with 3M. One obvious advantage of working with a company like 3M would be the job stability Press On would be able to offer its employees.

Press On had taken over management of 3M Decorative Products Division's Product Distribution Center by 1981. Three years later the relationship with 3M paid off spectacularly, when Press On was awarded a 15-year manufacturing contract to print exclusively for 3M. The firm employed 290; a year later the figure reached 342. Products improved while operations became more efficient. Press On became an early leader in Just-In-Time manufacturing. The close relationship with 3M was symbolized by the design and technical development centers 3M established with 3M employees adjacent to Press On's Stillwater facility.

A sixth Press On Incorporated facility, with more than 65,000 square feet of space, is scheduled for completion in early 1988 and will help the company consolidate its custom-designed automotive graphics operations. Press On has also become an active promoter of the St. Croix

Press On Incorporated president, James W. Torseth.

Press On Incorporated senior vice-president, Neal H. Skinner.

River Valley, whose people have helped it become one of the area's largest private employers. Back in the cold January days when Jim Torseth and Neal Skinner were building their first facility, they knew persistence would pay off. But they probably could not have guessed just how well.

GRACO INC.

Once a quiet family-owned business, Graco Inc. has become one of the world's premier manufacturers of fluid-handling equipment and systems. The applications for the technology it has pioneered seem endless.

Consider, for instance, that Graco equipment squeezes tomato paste onto millions of frozen pizzas, or that Graco pumps oil and lubricating fluids into millions of cars, or that it applies paint to homes and business and industrial installations, or that it helps give cars made around the world their high-gloss finishes, most recently through sophisticated robotics. By successfully exploiting a growing number of applications, Graco's performance in recent years has been remarkable. Sales have nearly doubled since 1982, and stock prices have risen accordingly. Graco's market niche may be specialized, but that doesn't stop that niche from being huge. Today Graco is one Minnesota company that clearly proves what being a market leader means.

In addition to being the world leader in fluid-handling technology, Graco is a leader in robotics. Here, Graco robots work in the Ferrari plant in Italy.

Graco's original plant was located here at 10th and Marquette in Minneapolis.

All of this seems a long journey from that winter's day in Minneapolis in 1926, when Russell Gray, at the time a parking lot attendant, figured there had to be a better way to lubricate cars than by using hand-operated grease guns, especially when the temperature had dropped as low as it had that day and grease was impossible to move.

To meet that need he developed a grease gun powered by air pressure. Favorable reaction from service station owners and an automobile market that

was clearly growing led Russell and his brother, Leil, to form a business to market Russell's new grease gun. The result was Gray Company, Inc., which generated sales of $35,000 during its first year of operation.

During the next two decades Russell and Leil guided the company through sustained growth, primarily with lubrication pumps for automobiles. Russell was said to be the inventive force behind the firm; Leil, as the company's first president, provided the business acumen.

By the start of World War II Gray Company was doing one million dollars in sales. The firm responded to the new demands and opportunities presented by America's rapid defense buildup with a variety of new lubricating products. When the war ended management realized it could apply its fluid-handling expertise in many other areas than just automobile servicing.

By 1948 the company had found another foothold with its first paint pump, and a year later had introduced a direct-from-drum pump for heavy-duty industrial fluid handling. By the mid-1950s the Gray Company would continue to be a leader in automobile servicing, but would also become established in paint spraying and finishing, food handling, cleaning, and literally hundreds of different industrial fluid-handling applications areas. While still a small enterprise, sales rose to $5 million and the work force grew to 400.

With the development of the airless spray gun in 1957, which made Gray Company the market leader in spray coating and painting, and the death of Leil Gray in 1958, the Graco of today began to take shape. Harry A. Murphy, Gray's successor, served for four years, and on his retirement David A. Koch assumed leadership of the company. Koch set out to strengthen the firm's commitment to its constituencies, which he believed included the community in which it was based as well as customers and employees, by aggressively expanding the corporation. When Gray Company went public in 1969 and changed its name to Graco, sales stood at $33 million.

Graco reached the $50-million mark two years later, a little less than 50 years after the sale of its first grease guns. Significantly, Graco had by then acquired H.G. Fischer & Co., an electrostatic paint-

Leil Gray (top) and Russell J. Gray (above) founded Graco Inc in 1926.

ing equipment manufacturer, and dramatically boosted its position in the automotive finishing industry, which was even then replacing hazardous and wasteful air-atomized painting with environmentally cleaner and more efficient electro-

static painting. Growth continued as well; by the decade's end Graco, through solidifying its position in existing markets and entering new ones, would pass $100 million in sales. Important decisions had also been made—including the decision to make significant strategic investments in finishing technology—that would set the stage for even greater growth in the 1980s.

Today Graco defines its basic mission as "service to people through profitable growth." Both objectives seem to be keeping up with each other. Graco has become a world leader—with nearly one-third of its sales coming from overseas—in systems that move, control, deliver, dispense, and apply fluids in commercial and industrial settings.

In the automotive finishing area, Graco systems now include robotics, a field Graco entered in the early 1980s and patiently developed even as other companies dropped out of the robotics race. Graco's finishing division is one factor that has driven the firm's recent increase in sales, and Graco is today one of the few profitable U.S. manufacturers of robots. Successes in the company's other three product areas have also contributed to sales that have nearly doubled in the past five years. Most recently Graco reported doing more than $225 million worth of business. Investors and industry watchers expect a similar pace in growth to continue in the years ahead.

Graco also has a nearly unparalleled record of corporate citizenship. It sets standards in a state where standards are high to begin with. Much of it can be tied to chairman and chief executive officer David Koch. In 1975 Koch (while president of the Greater Minneapolis Chamber of Commerce) was instrumental in forming the Five Percent Club—a small group of Minnesota businesses that pledged to contribute 5 percent of pretax profits to nonprofit community causes. Today dozens of Minnesota's businesses have followed Koch's lead, and the idea has spread to include more than 1,600 companies nationwide.

Graco Inc. has shown that patient investing can lead to sustained and profitable growth while allowing a firm to live up to its obligations as a partner in community development. As it has most recently shown with its investment in robotics, such a strategy has undeniable benefits.

GENERAL MILLS, INC.

The history of General Mills, Inc., one of Minnesota's largest and most famous companies and one of its leading corporate citizens, is characterized by what many within the company like to call "change and continuity."

The firm's mix of businesses and its strategic thinking have been altered in response to market conditions several times, and the company has gone through periods of real change. At the same time its fiscal responsibility, its concern for employees and the community, and its emphasis on being the quality leader in its marketplaces have given General Mills a rock-solid continuity that has underpinned its entire six-decade history.

While Betty Crocker, Wheaties, Cheerios, and other General Mills products and symbols may seem enduring, General Mills is world famous for its new product development and marketing skill and has become a magnet for national business and marketing talent. Change and continuity—the recipe has served this Minnesota giant well.

It started in 1886 with an entrepreneur named Cadwalader C. Washburn, who was one of the first to recognize that through innovative milling techniques midwestern spring wheat could be milled to match winter wheat in color and baking qualities. Washburn's advances helped establish Minneapolis as the nation's leading milling center. Washburn was joined by John Crosby, and the Washburn Crosby Company was formed and export markets established. Washburn Crosby flour won a gold medal at an international exposition in 1880 and the Gold Medal label was born, leading the market ever since.

Eight years later James Stroud Bell became the first of three generations of Bells to lead the company. Over succeeding decades many of General Mills' world-famous consumer food products were introduced. Especially important was the creation of Betty Crocker as a corporate symbol; she initially began as a pen name for the consumer affairs department. Through acquisitions and internal growth the company—whose name was changed to General Mills in 1928—was the largest flour miller in the world at the time of its inception.

Numerous products were added to the firm's packaged food lines, including the first Betty Crocker cake mixes, as part of a shift from a commodity-oriented busi-

By the early 1920s the Washburn Crosby Company had established a brand name that would later become known throughout the world.

ness to one that emphasized consumer products. General Mills aggressively diversified during the late 1960s and early 1970s, and acquired numerous nonfood companies. In the 1980s General Mills took on a tighter strategic focus, divesting several businesses to concentrate on consumer foods and restaurants, its two highest areas of growth and profitability.

Today General Mills is one of the largest and most innovative consumer foods producers in the world. Its Red Lobster restaurants are the nation's largest dinner house chain, and it has a substan-

General Mills' corporate headquarters. The building contains an extensive art collection of nearly 1,200 pieces.

tial presence in specialty retailing with Talbots and Eddie Bauer. Many key leaders have served General Mills, including General Edwin Rawlings, James P. McFarland, E. Robert Kinney, and H.B. Atwater, Jr., current chairman and chief executive officer. General Mills has 66,000 employees, and sales exceed $5.2 billion annually.

Throughout its history General Mills has demonstrated a commitment to the communities that have helped it grow. General Mills is often cited as a corporate model for the nation. In recent years, through the General Mills Foundation and employee involvement in community programs, the company has taken an activist role in community and economic development.

Through these efforts, and through its record of growth and profitability, General Mills has had a beneficial impact on Minnesota that can be matched by few other companies.

BOKER'S, INC.

Stamping may be an unfamiliar term to many, but this manufacturing process is essential to nearly every industrial market segment. Basically, stamping involves using a combination of technologies to shape metal and plastic into component parts for industries, from high-tech electronics to heavy manufacturing. Minnesota, with its strong vocational education tradition and its heritage of highly skilled workers, has long been a national center for the precision stamping industry. It maintains a strong position today thanks to companies like Boker's, Inc., one of the state's oldest and largest precision stamping firms and a business that has built an enviable reputation for quality and reliability in an industry that is increasingly demanding both.

Boker's was formed in 1919 when Vitus Boker, a young Danish emigrant and a skilled machinist, set out on his own and created Boker Manufacturing Company with his son John in the basement of their Minneapolis home. Initially Vitus Boker intended to build the company around its first products, an envelope folding machine and a small hand check protector. Soon, however, the enterprise began generating more revenue from manufacturing prototypes and custom parts for automated machinery. As the word spread that Boker Manufacturing could produce high-quality, short-run, stamped metal parts, the demand for its services quickly outgrew Boker's basement. The business would outgrow two subsequent manufacturing spaces until it settled on Snelling Avenue in Minneapolis in 1939. The war years brought increasing

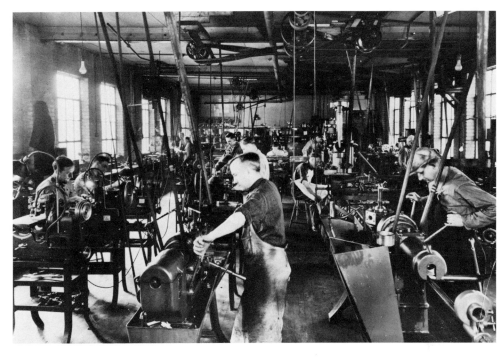

A scene from Boker's original facility on Washington Avenue in Minneapolis. Photo circa 1930s

business from defense contractors, and the pace continued as the company adjusted to the postwar consumer economy.

In 1968, after the facilities on Snelling Avenue had been expanded four times, eventually encompassing more than 50,000 square feet, Boker's, Inc., entered its modern era when it was purchased from the Boker family by four employees: William Tedlund, Joseph Basara, Chester Engquist, and Joseph

Today metal stamping at Boker's has become a highly sophisticated operation.

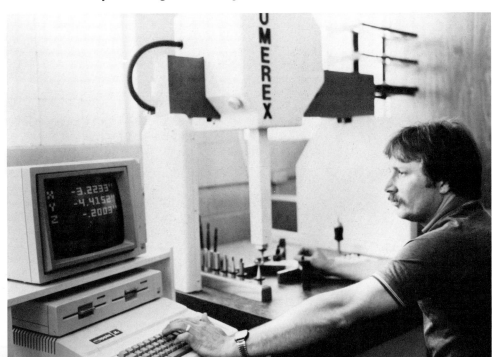

Kantorowicz. Tedlund and Basara continue to guide the company today.

In recent years the work force has grown to more than 100 employees, many highly skilled tradesmen, some of whom have been with the firm for decades. Today Boker's specializes in short-to medium-run stampings, in quantities as small as 25 to those exceeding 100,000. The company also maintains extensive secondary operations, including welding facilities, which enable it to provide its customers with assemblies and subcomponents.

Another distinguishing characteristic of the firm is its inventory of more than 2,000 different types and sizes of materials. Boker's has also emerged as a major supplier of nonstandard washers and spacers, and can provide customers with millions of different options with no tooling charge in most cases.

Boker's trades on a reputation for quality and on-time delivery built up over its nearly seven decades of existence. Both characteristics have become crucial in today's stamping industry. Foreign competition, the near-obsession with quality of many U.S. manufacturers, and the adoption of just-in-time inventory techniques that require the frequent delivery of small orders are putting tremendous pressures on many metal-stamping companies. With its traditions and its history of excellence, Boker's, Inc., should be one metal-stamping company that continues to prosper.

LIBERTY DIVERSIFIED INDUSTRIES, INC.

Jack Fiterman came to this country in the late nineteenth century as a young boy with his father to escape village life in Czarist Russia. As an adult he followed another family member to Minneapolis, and in 1918 started a company, buying and selling new and used wooden boxes, crates, burlap bags, and other containers. Fiterman operated out of the back of his house. It was hardly a glamorous or booming business, but Fiterman was grateful for the opportunities and freedom this new land presented him. He thus named the business Liberty Carton Company. Now Liberty Diversified Industries (LDI), it has been built by subsequent generations of Fitermans into one of Minnesota's biggest and most respected family-held corporations, with recent sales exceeding $140 million.

While New Hope-based Liberty Diversified still sells boxes, it has grown into one of the nation's leading manufacturers of corrugated fiberboard, plastic packaging, and storage products, as well as office and business equipment and materials handling equipment. The idea behind the company is roughly the same as in its early years—serving the packing, shipping, and storage of America's businesses with a steady stream of new and innovative products. When Liberty created a mail-order subsidiary to market its corrugated fiberboard office products, the door was opened to becoming a leading supplier of office and business equipment as well.

LDI's corporate headquarters, located in New Hope, Minnesota, is also home for Safco Products Company and Fidelity Products Company.

Jack Fiterman built his business slowly; his sons and grandsons, especially Ben Fiterman, who began working with his father in the garage behind the family's Minneapolis home in 1937, built the company to its present size. By the time Jack Fiterman retired in 1955, heavy wooden boxes had been replaced by corrugated fiberboard boxes. Because corru-

The 350-foot-long corrugator has made Liberty Carton Company a leading corrugated manufacturer in the Midwest.

gated material was inexpensive and flexible, it could be used to create new products that were far more than just packing containers.

Liberty recognized the opportunity, and in 1957 bought equipment to shape corrugated blanks into products it could call its own. As a manufacturer the firm began to grow quickly. The next big step was the installation of a huge two-story, 350-foot-long corrugator in the 1970s, allowing the company to be a completely self-sufficient manufacturer. Today Liberty Carton has two manufacturing plants and warehouses in six states.

When Liberty Carton acquired the ability to make its own corrugated products, it looked not only at the packaging field, but also to the office supply market. Even in the early 1960s, when the company was still small, Liberty had placed a premium on researching market needs and developing innovative new products. One early example was a corrugated fiberboard file box, an inexpensive and convenient way to temporarily or permanently store office records. Liberty tried office supply distributors, but also tried to sell the file box itself through a small direct-mail operation set up in 1961.

Jack Fiterman's backyard box business has evolved into one of the nation's largest container corporations.

Called Fidelity Products Company, the direct-mail operation grew from receiving three or four orders a day, based on a mailing of 2,500 brochures that had been hand addressed by Ben Fiterman's daughter, Serene Simon, to one of the nation's leading business-to-business direct marketers. Today Fidelity mails more than 10 million catalogs and brochures annually, selling a complete line of office products and industrial supplies.

When customers began asking for Fidelity products in traditional retail outlets, Safco Products Company was formed. It offers a complete line of office and graphic arts storage products, including Liberty's innovative corrugated products, through office supply stores, wholesalers, and retail outlets. It has become a leader in its industry, helping LDI become one of today's fastest growing office supplies manufacturers.

By 1970 Liberty had grown to a $10-million corporation. The Fiterman family was as deeply involved as ever. The Fitermans' extended family included Liberty's growing number of employees. Ben Fiterman's son, Mike, joined the company in 1970 and eventually became chief executive officer. Bernice Fiterman, Ben's wife, also played an important role, joining the firm soon after their marriage in

the 1940s to become a major player in handling the company's finances.

Two strategic acquisitions in the 1970s helped the firm's sales grow nearly eightfold by the end of the decade. Shamrock Industries, an innovative, high-quality plastics injection-molding operation, was acquired in 1972 to give LDI the ability to offer a wide array of plastic products. It has grown dramatically and

Mike Fiterman (standing) is president and chief executive officer and Ben Fiterman is chairman of the board of LDI.

today is one of the Midwest's largest plastics injection molders, with products that include plastic packaging, housewares, furniture, building products, and custom-manufactured products. The acquisition of Valley Craft Products in 1979 allowed LDI to move into fabricated metal products as well. A small, high-quality Lake City, Minnesota, manufacturer of materials handling equipment, Valley Craft has since tripled in size and entered LDI's expanding office and business supply market.

By the 1980s LDI offered its customers products made of corrugated fiberboard, plastics, and metal. Integrating the three produced a diversified yet focused full-service manufacturer of storage and packaging products, office supplies, and materials-handling equipment. A continued heavy investment in new product development kept the company a step ahead of changing marketplace needs. In 1984 LDI, through its subsidiary company, Southern Diversified Industries, Inc., and its Western Diversified Industries division, began manufacturing corrugated plastic, a unique fluted-core plastic sheeting. Marketed through LDI's Diversi-Plast division, this innovative material creates additional solutions to customers' needs.

Growth has been especially strong during this decade, with sales rising from $75 million to nearly twice that figure today. LDI now has 20 manufacturing/marketing divisions and more than 1.2 million square feet of manufacturing, warehouse, and distribution facilities located in seven U.S. states with an employee base of more than 1,200.

Growth has been largely dependent on Liberty Diversified Industries' ability to create new products to satisfy its expanding customer base while maintaining the strong customer service orientation that Jack Fiterman established so long ago. But that growth could never have taken place without the hard work and dedication of the employees who are the real LDI family. Some of the employees have been with the company since it began manufacturing in 1957, and many have brought other members of their families to LDI to be part of, and contribute to, the LDI success story. Based on the recent evidence, Liberty Diversified Industries' string of successes should continue in the years ahead.

ROBINSON RUBBER COMPANY

A framed quotation from British philosopher John Ruskin hangs on the wall above Brad Robinson's desk. It reads: "There is hardly anything in the world that men cannot make worse to sell for less, and people who consider price alone are this man's lawful prey."

Over the decades manufacturing quality products has basically been the story of Robinson Rubber Company, a New Hope custom manufacturer of molded rubber components for industry. With 47 employees and nearly $4 million in annual sales, Robinson Rubber is not a huge company, but it is one of the most consistently profitable in its industry and has always upheld a reputation for quality and consistency. When parts are for companies such as IBM, Du Pont, 3M, and others, those latter two characteristics are all that matters.

The reasons for Robinson Rubber Company's success are reflected in traditions established by the firm's founder, Ralph Robinson, Brad Robinson's father, who began phasing himself out of active management in the 1970s. Perhaps Ralph Robinson's most important legacy has been the long-term retention of employees in an industry marked by turnover. Achieved by a history of generous benefits and wages, the committed and skilled work force, motivated with a real stake in the company, has given Robinson Rubber the quality advantage it has needed to compete in an increasingly competitive industry.

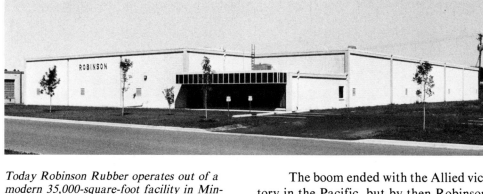

Today Robinson Rubber operates out of a modern 35,000-square-foot facility in Minneapolis. It supplies custom rubber products to numerous Fortune *500 companies.*

Ralph Robinson also showed a great deal of innovation in responding to changing market conditions. Initially Robinson Rubber sold tires and serviced cars from the chamber of commerce garage in downtown Minneapolis—that was the location where Ralph Robinson started by pumping gas in the early 1930s. Toward the end of the decade Robinson started recapping tires as well.

At the time tire recapping (applying new tread to worn-out tires) was not in great demand, but soon after Robinson got into the business World War II came along and changed everything. The rapid Japanese conquest of Southeast Asia rubber-producing countries and the priority needs of the defense industry slashed the rubber supplies available for new consumer tires. Soon Ralph Robinson found himself with nearly 100 employees and a 24-hour-a-day operation.

The boom ended with the Allied victory in the Pacific, but by then Robinson was firmly entrenched in the rubber goods business. With the market for recapping tires dwindling, Robinson bought equipment to begin manufacturing custom rubber products for industrial use, including a rubber-mixing machine with a 75-horsepower motor, which the city of Minneapolis thought might be too industrial for the commercially zoned area where Robinson was located. That prompted a move to a 15,000-square-foot facility in St. Louis Park, the former home of a bankrupt cookwares manufacturer, and eventually, when the facility was outgrown, Robinson moved to its current modern, 35,000-square-foot facility in early 1975.

Under Brad Robinson sales have doubled in the past decade, and he has continued the traditions established by his father—steady and controllable growth, an emphasis on employee welfare, and, above all, the focus on quality that Robinson Rubber Company's customers demand.

Ralph Robinson's business mushroomed when World War II cut off the supply of rubber for new tires. Recapping tires became a 24-hour business.

PELLA PRODUCTS, INC.

The small town of Pella, squarely in the middle of the flat and fertile farmland of central Iowa, is not your typical farm town. Pella is known for windows. Its reputation for windows extends from coast to coast. Nearly $300 million worth of windows bearing the Pella name are sold each year.

Home owners, builders, and architects who have come to respect the Pella name might be a little surprised to discover that Pella Products' offices do not actually make windows. Rather, the windows are made by the Rolscreen Company, the little-known manufacturer based in Pella that got into the business 70 years ago and went on to revolutionize the window industry. Pella does sell windows—that is, the independently owned companies around the country use the Pella name and market Rolscreen products.

Pella distributors stay closely attuned to their local markets and help the Rolscreen Company keep in step with consumer preferences. Rolscreen, in turn, provides its Pella distributors with a steady stream of new and innovative windows. Pella distributors then customize and service Rolscreen products, and those companies that do a good job of it have become, especially in recent years, growing and successful.

Pella Products, Inc., based in Minneapolis is one of the oldest and largest distributors. The firm has 74 employees with sales growing at better than 20 percent per year (recently almost $13 million). Pella Products, Inc., has eight Window Stores in the Twin Cities area and a new 85,000-square-foot showroom/warehouse/custom manufacturing facility in the midway area.

The firm's success is largely due to the three generations of Johnsons who have owned and operated the company since it was formed 60 years ago. In the early 1920s Lloyd Johnson, an Iowa farmer, came to Minneapolis to seek his fortune. His specialty was selling and installing home-insulating, weather-stripping material for windows and doors. One of his first products was the rolscreen, a type of bug screen that could be rolled up into a box mounted at the top of the

A Pella Products showroom. Pella Products, Inc., has eight Window Stores located in the Twin Cities area.

Curtis W. Johnson (left), chairman of the board, and Ronald W. Johnson (right), president of Pella Products, Inc.

window.

Johnson's business became tied to Rolscreen Company, and it grew as the Rolscreen Company grew. In 1946 Curtis Johnson, Lloyd's son, took over the business. He became chairman of the board when his son Ronald became president in 1980. As Rolscreen Company grew and expanded the number of windows it manufactured, its independent distributors adopted the name Pella, which soon became synonymous with quality and innovation.

In the 1980s, as the window business became both more profitable and more competitive, Pella Products, Inc., opened its innovative Window Stores—retail showrooms located in primarily upscale suburban shopping areas. These stores allowed consumers to buy direct or see ideas they could suggest to their architect or building contractor.

The changing nature of the business required Pella distributors to become both sophisticated marketers and custom manufacturers. Under the Johnsons, Pella Products, Inc., in the Twin Cities has emerged as one of the largest and most successful Pella distributors. Pella's commitment to customer service and Rolscreen's commitment to product quality have produced a winning combination.

INCSTAR CORPORATION

By 1975 Dr. Arnold Lindall, a physician and Ph.D. in biochemistry, was getting tired of packing up his research in endocrinology and carting it off to wherever research grants were available. Lindall had taught and performed research at several Twin Cities medical institutions and had built a private practice as an internist. He knew of several diagnostic tools he could use in his practice if only they were commercially available at an affordable cost. Like many of today's scientists who have become entrepreneurs, Lindall chafed at the restrictions and uncertainties of publicly funded research.

The result was Immuno Nuclear Corporation, now INCSTAR Corporation, which Lindall formed in 1975 with $150,000 raised from 15 local backers. The company, which pioneered several diagnostic products using radioimmunoassay (RIA) technology, quickly became one of the most promising biomedical technology start-ups in Minnesota. RIA technology uses low-level radioactive isotopes to measure certain hormone and peptide levels in a patient's serum sample, indicative of a disease state or tumor. INCSTAR quickly established a reputation for quality as well as leading-edge technology. A public stock offering in 1978 sold out quickly, and by the following year the new company had topped one million dollars.

INCSTAR grew into a more professionally managed organization that focused on marketing and long-term strategy as well as on research and development. Growth during the 1980s has been modest and steady, with sales rising from $4 million in 1982 to more than $5 million in 1984.

Recent changes included reorganization of the marketing department and changes in key management, including the board's replacement of founder Lindall as president and chief executive officer by Dr. Orwin Carter, a physical chemist who had previously held several senior positions in biomedical technology firms. Today the company offers a growing line of diagnostic products and is aggressively exploring new clinical and research market niches. New marketing ventures include a recent agreement with Sandoz, the mammoth Swiss pharmaceutical firm, to develop diagnostic test kits to monitor the drug cyclosporin, the life-saving immunosuppressant that has

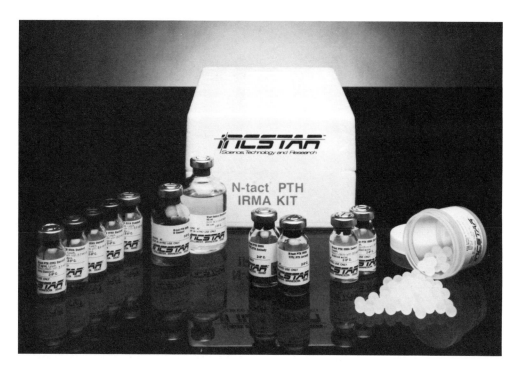

INCSTAR's new N-tact PTH kit is used in hospitals and labs to measure hormone levels in a patient sample that may be indicative of a disease state or tumor.

largely made successful organ transplants possible. International sales, managed by Boston-based vice-president/International Marketing Jacques Bagdasarian, have also become an important growth factor; the company today derives half its revenues from overseas customers. Total sales in 1988 could reach $12 million.

The firm became INCSTAR in 1986 in anticipation of immunoassays no longer relying on radioactive isotopes and to reflect its expanded line of diagnostic tools. INCSTAR recently broke ground for a needed addition to its Stillwater facility that will double its production space. Coupled with a significantly increased commitment to research and development, the potential of INCSTAR as one of the most productive and exciting biomedical technology firms in Minnesota may finally be realized.

INCSTAR's corporate headquarters is located in Stillwater, Minnesota.

UNITED TELEPHONE COMPANY

When a group of eight Minnesota telephone professionals formed the Pioneer Telephone Company in April 1927, they had no idea that their fledgling firm would someday be an important part of one of America's major telecommunications corporations, United Telecom. The road to success has taken a dedicated team effort of both management and nonmanagement employees, often in very trying circumstances.

The company's early years in St. Paul were marked by rapid growth, as Pioneer acquired no less than a dozen smaller telephone companies in nearby rural and suburban areas. Then the Great Depression occurred, forcing Pioneer to lower rates and lose customers. Banks all across the state were closing, tying up company funds needed for service improvements and restricting sources for new funds. Pioneer was forced to enact cost-saving measures that included reducing salaries and moving its general offices to the small town of Waconia.

By the late 1930s the outlook had improved: The company installed new telephones, granted wage increases to employees, and even purchased a vacated bank office building in Waconia. World War II brought new turmoil. The firm was proud of its high-quality service to outlying areas, but employees were joining the war effort in droves, delaying new lines and service improvements. Financing these improvements was also a problem, as the bulk of available funds was being channeled to the war effort.

When the war ended, E.E. Patterson and H.B. Crandell purchased stock control of the company in 1945; the fortunes

A supervisor keeps a watchful eye on her operators during the early days of Pioneer Telephone, the predecessor of United Telephone Company. Photo circa 1925

of the company were on the rise once again. Patterson's expertise in raising funds through bond placements proved invaluable in financing long-needed service improvements and a plant rehabilitation program. The new owners hired H.R. Bollinger, a noted Wisconsin telephone executive, to manage the firm.

The 1950s and early 1960s saw the Pioneer network extend across the entire state of Minnesota and even North Dakota through the acquisition of other independent telephone companies. Numerous

United Telephone of Minnesota provides service to many rapidly growing areas neighboring the Twin Cities.

major service improvement programs were implemented and customer service improved.

By 1967 it was evident that the company needed a new financial partner with substantial resources to enable the continuation of service improvement programs. In 1968 negotiations with United Telephone System were completed, and Pioneer, along with its 17 subsidiary companies, became Pioneer-United Telephone Company of Minnesota.

The Pioneer-United merger proved ideal. Pioneer became part of the Northern Division of United Telephone's Midwest Group, and has made several unique contributions to the parent firm, including its nationally recognized training programs and wide-ranging experience with all types of customer service. Today United Telephone Company of Minnesota, headquartered in Chaska, serves more than 90,000 customers in 85 communities across the state.

United Telecom, the parent corporation, has annual revenues of more than $3 billion and assets exceeding $6 billion. Its subsidiaries, including United Telephone System, North Supply, and US Sprint (owned jointly with GTE), provide local and long distance telephone service, telecommunications equipment, and a variety of related products and services.

Today United Telephone is well-positioned to maintain its proud history of serving the communications needs of Minnesota.

Historical information provided by Ken Larson, retired UTC Northern Division vice-president.

ZYTEC CORPORATION

When the little-known Zytec Corporation was recently ranked as Minnesota's 20th-largest high-technology company by a regional business magazine, it shared the list with such heavy hitters as Control Data, Honeywell, Cray Research, and others. That's quite an accomplishment for a firm that has only existed formally for a little more than four years. That is only one of the things that makes Zytec one of Minnesota's most unique and—if recent trends are any indication—most uniquely successful high-technology companies.

Zytec makes custom power supplies for computers, telecommunications equipment, medical diagnostic machines, and other sophisticated products. Its production facility is in the southwestern Minnesota town of Redwood Falls, where it employs nearly 450 people and is by far the town's largest employer. Its corporate headquarters and engineering staff of 90 are based in the Minneapolis suburb of Eden Prairie. Recent sales of $45 million ranked it nationally as the seventh-largest concern in its industry.

Zytec owes its existence to Control Data Corporation, where it was originally set up as an operating unit in 1966 to provide power supplies for Control Data computer peripherals such as disk drives. In the 1980s, when Control Data began altering its strategic planning, the company decided it no longer needed a captive power supply operating unit. Instead of seeking an outside investor, Control Data turned to three of its executives and offered them the opportunity to buy the operation. Ron Schmidt, Larry Matthews, and John Steel agreed to the leveraged buy out and assumed control in January 1984.

The first years of Zytec were turbulent. While the firm booked $66 million

The leaders of Zytec Corporation (from left) Ronald D. Schmidt, chairman, president, and chief executive officer; John M. Steel, vice-president of marketing and sales; and Larry J. Matthews, vice-president of engineering.

in sales in 1984, virtually all of it continued to come from Control Data. When Control Data drastically reduced its orders in 1985, sales fell sharply, and the new owners of Zytec, which included a substantial number of employees invited to invest in the company, worked hard to

With a client list that includes such businesses as AT&T, Hewlett Packard, and Kodak, Zytec Corporation is one of Minnesota's most successful high-technology companies. Here lab technician Mike Anderson tests power supply.

find new customers. The effort began to pay off in 1986 and 1987, and Zytec's dependence on Control Data was reduced appreciably.

By then Zytec was in the midst of fashioning a brand-new corporate culture—one that emphasized increasing efficiency through employee participation and competing in a tough marketplace by placing a premium on quality. One result is a client list that grew to include companies such as AT&T, Hewlett Packard, Northern Telecom, Sun Microsystems, Kodak, and others. Another is a remarkable return to profitability.

Zytec still remains a modestly sized company, but it has successfully implemented a number of cutting-edge production and management techniques that have reduced costs and won it a reputation as one of the most innovative and quality-conscious businesses in its highly competitive industry.

Strong programs to promote employee participation and ownership and a commitment to doing business with other Minnesota companies distinguish Zytec. It replaced its Far Eastern suppliers of circuit boards in favor of Hibbing Electronics Company, one of the few recent success stories on Minnesota's economically depressed Iron Range. It has also become the economic mainstay of Redwood Falls.

Zytec Corporation may not yet have a lot of history behind it, but by most measures it appears to have a lot of history ahead.

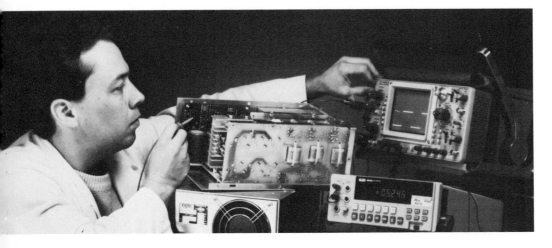

ANDERSON TRUCKING SERVICE, INC.

Trucking has been Harold Anderson's life since the age of 15, when he hauled loads of gravel for his family's road construction business near the little town of Isle, Minnesota. His love for the trucking industry has never left him. And, while the trucking business may be a lot more complicated today than it was then, in a sense Harold Anderson is still behind the wheel. Only today what Anderson is driving, along with son Rollie, is one of the nation's top 100 trucking companies—Anderson Trucking Service, Inc., which has emerged as one of America's biggest and most innovative trucking firms and one of St. Cloud's leading employers.

St. Cloud is frequently called The Granite City. Granite quarried by companies in the area has clad the exteriors of buildings in cities across the nation. When Harold Anderson graduated from high school, he took a job hauling granite for one such outfit—the Cold Spring Granite Company. After serving in World War II as an Army Air Corps pilot (he flew 29 successful missions over Europe), Anderson returned to become manager of the firm's fleet of trucks. Because St. Cloud's growing granite business needed increased hauling capacity, Cold Spring Granite encouraged Anderson to set up an independent trucking fleet.

Anderson Trucking Service, Inc., began operations in 1955 with two drivers, an old wooden warehouse, and authority from the Interstate Commerce Commission (ICC) to haul granite and stone products. It ended its first year with revenues of $95,000. In addition to his love for trucking, Anderson had a great deal of business sense. Within seven years

Anderson Trucking Service has built a national reputation for hauling large and complex equipment.

Anderson Trucking received additional operating authorities, was serving 48 states, and posted revenues of close to one million dollars. By the end of its first decade Anderson Trucking emerged as a diversified trucking company with 21 separate ICC authorities and another 10 soon to be added. In addition, it had established a network of truck terminals around the country, each linked by teletype to major shipping agencies.

Harold and Rollie Anderson represent two generations of leadership at Anderson Trucking Service.

In 1969 Harold Anderson purchased the Alaskan K&W Trucking Company, a milestone in the expansion of Anderson Trucking and the beginning of the most extensive Alaskan transport network in the industry. Two years later Anderson installed one of the first computer-assisted dispatching systems in the industry. That same year Rollie Anderson joined the business.

Much as his father did in his father's company, Rollie had worked in the loading shed, the trailer shop, and other areas during the summer. By the time he joined the firm he had received a business degree from the University of Minnesota, served in the Air Force, and been named one of the Outstanding Young Men of America. He has since become vice-president of Anderson Trucking and president of K&W Trucking. Daughter Barbara is also involved in the company, managing the Contractor Services Department. Another son, Jim, chose not to enter the family business and instead serves as a minister.

The past decade has seen Anderson Trucking Service, Inc., diversify even further and establish a national reputation for specializing in hauling large and complex equipment. While deregulation has rocked the trucking industry by removing most restrictions on hauling and increasing competitive pressures (the number of companies in the industry has more than doubled since 1980), Anderson has aggressively expanded since the beginning of the decade.

FAEGRE & BENSON

John B. Faegre and John C. Benson knew each other well when the Minneapolis law firms they worked for merged in 1922. The two men had met on the football field in 1909, when Faegre's University of Minnesota team walloped Benson's Hamline University. Faegre and Benson later were classmates at the University of Minnesota Law School. Eventually they gave their names to Faegre & Benson, one of the oldest Twin Cities law firms in continuous practice. With more than 200 lawyers and offices in Minneapolis and Bloomington, Minnesota; Denver, Colorado; and London, England, the firm is also one of the region's largest and most respected legal establishments.

Faegre & Benson is the lineal descendant of Cobb & Wheelwright, a Minneapolis law firm opened by two transplanted New Englanders in 1886. Albert C. Cobb was the son of a prominent Maine lawyer. John O.P. Wheelwright was the namesake of the Reverend John Wheelwright, who came from England to the Massachusetts Bay Colony in 1636. Both men were classmates at Maine's Bowdoin College. Their Minneapolis law firm quickly prospered, and over the next 25 years Cobb & Wheelwright represented many leading businesses in the rapidly expanding city.

Albert Cobb had a reputation as an outstanding business and banking lawyer representing Northwestern National Bank of Minneapolis and later Northwest Bancorporation, both of which he served as a director. John Wheelwright had a general practice and was involved in the firm's litigated matters. In 1912 a third partner, John I. Dille, joined the firm, and soon John Benson was hired away from the Minneapolis Legal Aid Society.

John Dille left the practice in 1919 to join another law firm composed of George Hoke, Claude G. Krause, and John B. Faegre. Three years later Dille retired, and his partners joined his old firm, where John Benson was now a partner. The merger brought together Faegre and Benson, and set the stage for the next act in the firm's history.

Bart Faegre was known for his personal warmth and considerable wit, establishing a strong reputation defending personal injury suits for James J. Hill's Great Northern Railroad. Under Albert Cobb's mentorship, Faegre became a leading business and banking lawyer, suc-

John B. Faegre (1887-1986) (top), and John C. Benson (1890-1986) (above).

ceeding Cobb on the boards of both Northwestern National Bank and Northwest Bancorporation. John Benson was known as a business trial lawyer and a genial conciliator in adversarial situations.

In 1930 the firm moved into the Northwestern Bank Building and actively aided Northwest Bancorporation and other clients through the economic minefields of the Great Depression. The 1930s also saw the firm add a number of bright, hard-working young lawyers, including Paul Christopherson, a graduate of Carleton College and a Rhodes Scholar;

Robert J. Christianson, son of a Minnesota governor and brother of a justice of the Minnesota Supreme Court; and Paul J. McGough, who developed the firm's insurance practice, which grew to significance when the litigation explosion created the need for experienced trial lawyers. In 1940 the firm adopted its present name of Faegre & Benson.

After World War II the firm continued to grow with the addition of John S. Pillsbury, Jr., Rodger L. Nordbye, and George D. McClintock, Jr. In addition to Northwestern National Bank, the firm represented a growing number of major corporations, including *The Minneapolis Journal* (later *Star Tribune*), The Dayton Company (later Dayton Hudson Corporation), Archer-Daniels-Midland Company, Northwestern National Life Insurance Company, The Pillsbury Company, and various charitable and nonprofit organizations such as the Archie Walker Trust, Walker Art Center, and Abbott Hospital.

Paul Christopherson and Robert Christianson headed the firm through the 1960s and 1970s—decades that saw a dramatic increase in the use of the legal system to regulate conduct, resolve disputes, and determine reparations. Along with Paul McGough, Hayner N. Larson, Everett A. Drake, Armin L. Johnson, Donald L. Robertson, Wright W. Brooks, and other members of the firm, Christopherson and Christianson realized they were laying the foundation for a firm that could meet the many challenges of the years ahead, and by the early 1960s Faegre & Benson was regularly visiting law schools to recruit talented young men and women to continue the firm's high standards of professionalism and expertise.

Christopherson retired in 1980 and Christianson died unexpectedly in 1981. By then the next generation of leadership was in place at Faegre & Benson, a generation that reflects both the size and wide-ranging scope of the firm. The firm continues as counsel to Norwest Bank Minnesota and Norwest Corporation through James A. Halls and Paul T. Birkeland; Gerald T. Flom and Gale R. Mellum head corporate and securities counseling; James Fitzmaurice and John D. French head its extensive litigation practice; John S. Holten and Thomas M. Crosby, Jr., head public law and real estate; George E. Harding and

James M. Samples head employee benefits and labor and employment law; and John E. Harris and John K. Steffen head the firm's trust and estate and tax practices.

One of the firm's greatest recent challenges came from an unexpected source—the Thanksgiving Day fire that roared through the Northwestern Bank Building and virtually destroyed the firm's offices in 1982. In an effort that attracted national attention, Faegre & Benson was open for business the following Monday in the IDS Center. Later the firm moved to the Multifoods Tower, where it awaits completion of the new Norwest Center. Faegre & Benson will be a major tenant in the 57-story center when it opens in 1988, just a few days short of the firm's 102nd anniversary.

Many outstanding lawyers have contributed to Faegre & Benson over the course of the past century. The common thread is the firm's mission—to provide creative legal services of the highest quality on a timely, responsive, and cost-effective basis. The firm's practice has been to allow individual professional and personal development to the maximum extent possible, and to actively encourage involvement in the cultural, educational, and political affairs of the community. Commitment to those principles has allowed Faegre & Benson to grow and prosper, preparing the firm for its second century.

The Northwestern Bank Building during the 1982 Thanksgiving Day fire. Faegre & Benson offices were located on the upper floors.

The Norwest Center will be located on the site of the old Northwestern Bank Building. Faegre & Benson will occupy eight floors when the center opens in 1988.

NORTH CENTRAL LABORATORIES, INC.

By the late 1960s it was becoming apparent that due to the accelerating pace of medical technology, large centralized medical laboratories could do many kinds of testing more efficiently and more cost effectively than physicians and clinics—and, in many cases, even hospitals. Large central laboratories could also achieve the economies of scale needed to justify the acquisition of the emerging automated and highly expensive test equipment.

James Stang saw all of this clearly, but he also realized that if such a system intended to serve widely dispersed outstate locations, one key element would be needed—an extensive and efficient courier system. Stang, a St. Cloud medical technologist, formed a team of physicians and medical technologists to build such an operation in St. Cloud, 60 miles from the Twin Cities. The year was 1969, when the medical testing business was beginning to boom, but usually only in large urban areas, where competition was often intense. Medical direction was provided by Dr. Robert Fedor, a pathologist and one of several physicians in the shareholders group of North Central Laboratories.

Meanwhile, a similar lab had been formed in St. Paul by a group of pathologists, many practicing at St. Paul-Ramsey Medical Center. Central Regional Pathology Laboratories P.A., located in St. Paul's Central Medical Building, performed testing similar to North Central Laboratories. One important exception was Central Regional's tissue pathology work. There were enough similarities, however, for the two groups to begin discussing a merger. When it finally happened in the early 1970s, the St. Paul group became a minority shareholder in North Central Laboratories, which took over much of Central Regional's testing operation. Central Regional's tissue pathology work was spun off as a separate entity, which retains the Central Regional name today and provides services to North Central Laboratories.

North Central Laboratories continued to grow during the 1970s, but with growth came a series of problems. Financial controls proved to be inadequate, and the lab may have been performing too many different types of tests for its own good. The result was overexposure, unrealistically high sales projections, and worsening financial problems—finally resulting in a Chapter 11 filing. After the

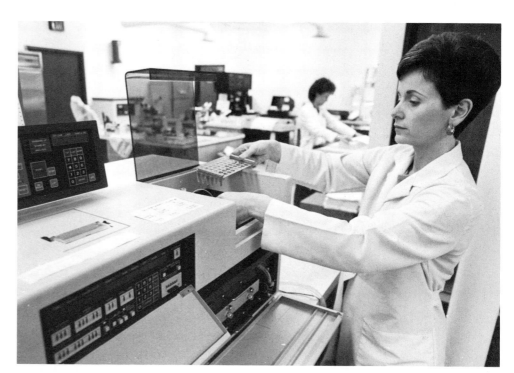

North Central Laboratories' advanced technology and sophisticated equipment combines with the expertise of certified medical technologists to assure quality results.

board reorganized and elevated controller Jack Matzke to president, he successfully brought the firm through a long bankruptcy procedure, and growth resumed on an upward track.

By the end of the 1970s North Central resumed its expansion, beefing up its innovative courier system and gradually acquiring the instrumentation and exper-

tise needed to compete as a major regional medical testing lab. The board was wrestling with the problem of what direction the company's future should take. Should it continue as a primarily outstate service, or should it try to penetrate the larger Twin Cities market as well? The question was resolved when the St. Paul group bought out the St. Cloud shareholders and resolved upon a course of expansion. Under Matzke's direction, all of this would be accompanied by careful financial controls.

North Central Laboratories entered

Servicing the five-state area with 36 vehicles logging more than 13,000 miles daily assures North Central Laboratories' clients receive written reports within a 24-hour period.

the 1980s with plans to go public. It was a time of tremendous change in health care: Technology was constantly improving; but these improvements came at a price, and concerns about health care costs were mounting. A public stock offering raised the capital needed for North Central to buy a five-acre parcel of land in a St. Cloud industrial park and build a state-of-the-art high-volume laboratory. The federal government's new cost-containment DRG reimbursement program for health care costs made the testing services offered by laboratories such as North Central more attractive. The result for North Central was dramatic growth and increasing penetration of the Twin Cities market. Revenues would increase from just exceeding $2 million per year at the beginning of the decade to more than $7 million in 1987.

Today North Central has become the largest independent medical laboratory headquartered in the Upper Midwest. Its St. Cloud lab, which offers more than 900 routine and esoteric tests, has a staff of more than 200 and operates around the clock. More than 900 clients, including physicians, medical clinics, hospitals, nursing homes, and veterinarians are served in a five-state region. Auto-

mated analytical equipment and computers provide high-quality, rapid-response (in most cases, less than 24 hours), high-volume testing and reporting. Testing services include clinical chemistry, immunochemistry, serology, cytology, hematology, immunohematology, microbiology, virology, parasitology, toxicology, endocrinology, and urinalysis. As many as 30,000 individual procedures are performed each day. North Central's courier fleet of 36 vehicles logs more than 13,000 miles a day.

In May 1985 Charles Arndt replaced Jack Matzke, who died of a heart attack, as president and chief executive officer. Medical direction is provided by Dr. John Uecker, a pathologist and president of Central Regional Pathology Laboratory. North Central's main St. Cloud laboratory is augmented by two speciality laboratories and four patient drawing stations in the Twin Cities area.

Recent acquisitions have played a significant role in the company's growth. With the acquisition of SERA, Inc., North Central expanded into nationwide markets with such specialized services as allergy and spina bifida testing. A major expansion of the firm's sales and marketing organization helped it strengthen its position in both regional and national clinical testing markets. North Central has upgraded its computer system to enhance its ability to telecommunicate test results direct from its labs to hospital and physician offices.

Medical testing itself is changing. Low-cost and efficient medical testing is a concern to many Americans and national businesses. Tremendous changes are anticipated, changes that will not be without controversy. North Central, which has demonstrated that it can provide the quality that health care professionals require, is in a position to evolve with its markets.

The use of state-of-the-art computer equipment and software allows the customer service staff at North Central Laboratories rapid information retrieval for optimum customer care.

TELEX COMMUNICATIONS, INC.

Telex Communications, Inc., has a low profile with Minnesotans, but many industry groups are very familiar with this Bloomington-based company. National Football League coaches, for instance, use Telex headset intercom systems to communicate with their coaching staffs. Referees are using Telex wireless mikes to announce penalties and calls while TV and radio announcers keep in touch with the field and provide commentary through Telex headphones and boom-mic headsets.

Entertainers, television newscasters, ministers, and many others also use the same Telex technology. Meanwhile, high in the air, pilots communicate with air traffic control centers using Telex headsets that are designed to transmit voices clearly in high-noise environments. People with hearing impairments gain access to the world of sound with Telex sound-enhancement products and its pioneering hearing aids—innovations that have spawned a Minnesota hearing aid industry that by some estimates produces as much as 60 to 70 percent of the hearing aids Americans wear.

Today Telex Communications, Inc., is a subsidiary of The Telex Corporation, a company originally formed in Minnesota but now headquartered in Tulsa, Oklahoma. Its other major subsidiary is Telex Computer Products, Inc., also based in Tulsa, which manufactures terminals, printers, private branch exchanges (PBXs), and other integrated voice/data information systems products. Both subsidiaries contribute to a company that has become, through acquisitions and internal development, a *Fortune* 500 leader in its markets, with recent revenues topping $840 million.

The complex history of Telex begins in Minneapolis in 1936 with Allen Hempel, the Upper Midwest sales representative for a now-defunct hearing aid manufacturer. Hearing aids at the time were essentially carbon-excited headphones. Users had to haul around suitcase-size units powered by huge dry storage batteries. Many people with hearing impairments preferred to do without.

In 1936 Hempel saw an electronic vacuum tube hearing aid. The unit was much smaller, lighter, and produced infinitely better sound quality. This first truly portable electronic aid had been made by a brilliant young engineer named

This 1936 Telex hearing aid was hand carried and battery operated.

Ralph Allison, who only the year before had founded the Audio Development Company (ADC). Allison built a few of these aids only for the local market. Hempel recognized the potential, approached Allison, and they soon concluded an agreement under which Allison manufactured the hearing aids and Hempel sold them nationally. Hempel named both the product and the sales company Telex. Allison immediately

Hearing aid pioneer and Telex founder Allen Hempel.

started with the design of a truly wearable vacuum tube hearing aid, introduced in 1937. The aids sold well, leading Telex to establish its own manufacturing shop in the historic Fawkes building at Hennepin Avenue and Loring Park.

Sales grew, and in 1940 Telex moved into a new laboratory that contained some of the most advanced research and development equipment available.

When America entered World War II, Telex and a handful of other companies pioneered in the miniaturization of electronics that contributed much to the war effort. Telex turned out hundreds of thousands of compact radio and telephone earsets. By the early 1950s sales of products that stemmed from the war, including headsets, pillow speakers, and other products, eclipsed hearing aid sales for the firm, incorporated in Minnesota as Telex, Inc.

In 1959 Allen Hempel decided to retire and sold his interests in Telex to a group of Minnesota investors headed by A.J. Ryden. One objective of the investors was to use Telex as a vehicle for acquisitions, and these followed quickly, six in all in 1960 and 1961. Included was Waters Conley Company, a Rochester, Minnesota, phonograph manufacturer that had started business in 1909 as a camera manufacturer.

With its acquisition of Inteledata, Telex entered the relatively new computer field, forming a Data System Division to build mass-storage disk files for companies such as General Electric. The division was later spun off and is today's successful Data Products Corporation.

In 1962, in an acquisition that would permanently change the nature of the company, Telex acquired Midwestern Instruments of Tulsa, Oklahoma. Founded in 1950 as an instrument manufacturer by M.E. Morrow, it had gone on to develop products using magnetic recording technology, then had grown through acquisitions, including the 1956 purchase of Magnecord, a pioneer of professional and commercial magnetic tape recorders. Telex and Midwestern became a company with revenues of more than $30 million.

It also suffered a split identity; that problem was resolved when a group of board members headed by Morrow won control of the firm and moved its headquarters to Tulsa. The company's dual

Telex first leased space in the Minneapolis Fawkes Building.

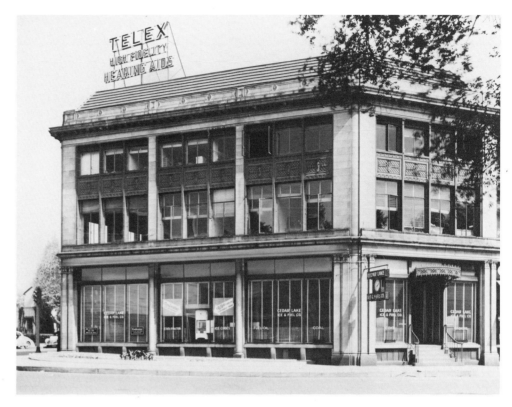

nature hampered growth, with the original hearing aid and headset operation plus the electronic recording and amplification business languishing while the parent company pursued computer and information-processing businesses. Investor Roger Wheeler took control in 1965 and instituted a company-wide reorganization with Telex Computer Products, based in Tulsa, and Telex Communications, based in Minnesota, both under The Telex Corporation.

Wheeler hired Stephan Jatras as president in 1965 (named chairman in 1981), and named Ansel Kleiman to take charge of Telex Communications. Then the company set out on a path of planned and careful growth. Telex Communications has since grown from annual sales of some $2 million and a work force of only 70 people to a company approaching $100 million in annual sales and a work force of approximately 1,500, staffing facilities in Bloomington, Blue Earth, Glencoe, Le-

Telex Communications is today part of The Telex Corporation, a fast-growing Fortune 500 communications company.

Sueur, and Rochester, Minnesota, and Lincoln, Nebraska.

Several businesses were acquired and incorporated into Telex Communications: Viking of Minneapolis tape recorders, HyGain antennas, Turner microphones, and the former Education Divi-

sion of the Singer Company. Telex Communications is a leader in diverse fields varying from high-speed tape-duplicating systems and hearing aids to communication antennas, audiovisual projectors, headsets, and wireless microphone systems.

NORTHLAND ALUMINUM PRODUCTS, INC. (NORDIC WARE®)

Twice a year an informal group of marketing managers, engineers, and sales people get together for an eight-hour new product brainstorming session at Northland Aluminum Products, the maker of Nordic Ware® cookware. Product ideas ranging from outlandish to ingenious are presented for consideration. Rules include "no laughing at someone else's idea." Many ideas will be tested and prototyped. Six or seven will finally make it to market.

Northland Aluminum is a 40-year-old family business that in its own quiet way has emerged as one of the Twin Cities' most innovative companies: the Bundt® baking pan; the first microwave carousel (Micro-Go-Round®); the first microwave pressure cooker (Tender Cooker®); the first self-cleaning gas barbecue grill; an ice cream maker that does not need salt, ice, or electricity; a stove-top popcorn maker, and so on. These new products are partly responsible for a company that recently topped $70 million in sales. In that sales figure is 17 percent of the microwave cookware market; Northland is number three in an industry of more than 40 manufacturers.

Northland began to take shape in 1946, when two brothers, H. David and Mark Dalquist, began a business in the basement of a Minneapolis home to provide custom plastic parts for local manufacturers. After modest growth and the construction of a small manufacturing shop, the two brothers shifted to the consumer market and began making specialty cookware from cast aluminum. The items, familiar to any Scandinavian, included a Rosette Iron, Ebelskiver Iron, and a KrumKake Iron. The company grew out of this small but comfortable niche when, in 1949, it purchased a Minneapolis firm called Northland Aluminum Products, a small cookware manufacturer that made griddles and steak platters.

By 1964 sales had reached one million dollars annually. Northland became one of the original 12 licensees of Du Pont Teflon, and began making a Bundt® pan for a Minneapolis Jewish women's society, which used the replica of the old German "kuglehof" pan as a fund-raising promotion. Eventually it attracted the attention of The Pillsbury Company, which was beginning to market a new idea, the packaged cake mix. Pillsbury introduced its Bundt® Cake Mixes in 1972 and offered buyers a discount on a Nordic Ware Bundt® pan. Soon Northland was shipping nearly 30,000 Bundt® pans per day. The success of the Bundt® pan gave Northland the confidence—and capital—to expand, without the need to go public.

When the microwave oven began to change America's cooking habits, North-

The Bundt® pan, an innovation in cookware.

land was one of the first small cookware manufacturers to aggressively court this market. It proved its talent for innovation once again with its famous Micro-Go-Round® automatic food rotator by solving the tricky engineering feat of shielding metal machinery from microwaves. Nordic Ware® also recently introduced a series of revolutionary self-cleaning gas barbecue grills.

Northland's growth has outperformed the industry average by a wide margin. Today the work force stands near 500. Nearly 10 percent of sales are foreign. Northland Aluminum Products, Inc., is considered the "new idea company" in a competitive and constantly changing industry. The Nordic Ware® name is recognized for quality, dependability, value, and innovation.

An aerial view of Nordic Ware's international headquarters in St. Louis Park.

HEALTHEAST

Midway, Mounds Park, St. John's Eastside, St. John's Northeast, St. Joseph's, Bethesda Lutheran, Divine Redeemer—for decades the diverse, proud neighborhoods of St. Paul have been served by these religiously affiliated, high-quality, primary care hospitals.

They were sources of holistic care and comfort. These hospitals kept their independence, while many Minneapolis institutions were merging into ever-larger hospital corporations. Today the parent companies of these St. Paul hospitals and their vast array of health care services have merged their identities into HealthEast. Virtually overnight it became one of the largest health care companies in the Twin Cities. HealthEast has been one of the region's most dramatic health care developments in a decade marked by almost constant change. The organization has brought together former competitors—each with long histories and traditions, different religious affiliations, and separate medical staffs, boards, and administrations—into a single health care company that promises to permanently change the health care industry in St. Paul.

The initial formation of HealthEast can be traced back to the early months of 1986. The Baptist Hospital Fund, which owned Mounds Park and Midway hospitals and Health Resources, the parent company of a number of diversified services, and the two St. John's hospitals consolidated several services at Mounds Park and St. John's Eastside, two neighboring hospitals on St.Paul's east side.

The original HealthEast offered a glimpse of what could be achieved through cooperation. An expanded HealthEast with more St. Paul members could consolidate management, set common strategies, allocate capital effectively, negotiate better group contracts, and in all probability offer better health care to St. Paul citizens—without sacrificing the special qualities of the parent organizations.

Industry observers were astonished at how quickly it came together, especially since the original sponsors of HealthEast agreed to create a single medical staff,

Today HealthEast provides a wide range of traditional family health services along with the latest in technological advancements in medicine.

The HealthEast family includes hospitals, nursing homes, home care, a physician referral/information line, child care, health and fitness services, medical transportation, housing options for seniors, and more.

board of directors, and administration, relinquishing much of their autonomy. In the fall of 1986 the Baptist Hospital Fund, Health Resources, and Bethesda Lutheran Medical Center formed the expanded HealthEast. St. Joseph's and Divine Redeemer Memorial hospitals joined the corporation in 1987. Today HealthEast provides a full spectrum of traditional family health services, including hospitals, nursing homes, home care, a physician referral/information line,

child care, health and fitness services, medical transportation, housing options for seniors, and more. It is the largest network of health care services in the East Metro area. HealthEast provides consumers a continuum of health care and wellness services that can be used throughout their lives—both in sickness and in health.

HealthEast has more than 5,000 employees, exceeds 900 affiliated physicians, operates more than 1,400 beds, and generates in excess of $220 million in annual revenues. Half of all patients admitted to a hospital in St. Paul are admitted to a HealthEast hospital. Even in a state noted for its pioneering innovations in health care, the transformation of competing St. Paul health care organizations into HealthEast was remarkable.

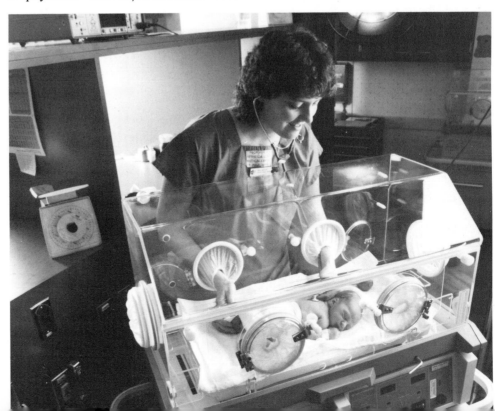

DYCO PETROLEUM CORPORATION

All during the 1950s and 1960s imported oil was plentiful and cheap, and there was little economic incentive to tap into new areas of America's vast oil and gas resources. By 1968 America was consuming more oil than it was adding to its domestic reserves. Reliance on imports was creeping steadily upward. Occasionally a wildcatter or a lucky entrepreneur made it big with an oil or gas strike, but for most individuals the risks of domestic oil and gas

A Dyco Petroleum rig drills into the many potentially productive formations in the Anadarko Basin in western Oklahoma and the Texas Panhandle.

exploration outweighed the rewards. But oil industry insiders knew things were bound to change.

Jaye Dyer, founder and president of Dyco Petroleum Corporation, was one such insider. By the time Dyer, who was trained as a geologist at the University of Oklahoma, moved to Minneapolis to take charge of Apache Corporation's Canadian oil exploration at age 34, he had a decade of experience in the domestic oil and gas industry. Dyer was among many in the late 1960s who were troubled by America's imbalanced energy situation.

They knew that energy prices were bound to rise, spurring domestic production and presenting tremendous opportunities both for individual investors and for oil and gas companies. The trick was to bring the two together.

Dyer and other Apache associates developed an innovative investment program at Apache they called Operation Upturn. The program planned for rapidly increasing individual investor participation in Apache's oil and gas exploration programs. Dyer began thinking about forming his own oil and gas exploration company—a company that would specialize in raising outside investor funds for exploration and production to supplement its own. The result was Dyco Petroleum Corporation, formed in 1971 by Dyer and two brothers, Minneapolis businessmen N. Bud and Harold Grossman. The new venture started with $10,000 in cash, two employees (Dyer and Ron Wade, an associate at Apache), and great expectations. A million-dollar debt guarantee by the Grossman brothers allowed the new enterprise to begin its investor programs in earnest.

Since then Dyco Petroleum has become one of the nation's premier investor-based oil and gas exploration and production companies. In 1976 Dyco became publicly held and five years later was listed on the New York Stock Exchange. More than $500 million has been raised from individual investors through public partnerships to find and develop domestic oil and gas reserves, primarily in the rich Anadarko basin of Oklahoma and the Texas Panhandle, where Len Williams heads Dyco's Tulsa-based operations headquarters. Two characteristics have contributed to Dyco's growth: Its investment programs have always been clear and plainly stated, and it was one of

Jaye F. Dyer, founder, president, and chief executive officer of Dyco Petroleum Corporation.

the first companies in its field to use an independent underwriter to place its investment offerings. Dyer and Williams developed a unique set of operational objectives and proportioned mix of high- and low-risk drilling designed to preserve the investors' capital and provide a competitive rate of return. In Dyco's case, the formula has been an unusually successful one.

In 1985 Dyco merged with Diversified Energies, Inc., the parent of Minnegasco and other companies. The move created a leader in natural gas distribution, energy exploration, and energy measurement. In response to open access deregulation of natural gas pipelines, Dyco created its own marketing division, Dyco Gas Marketing, in 1987.

Through it all, Dyco Petroleum Corporation has remained true to its long-standing commitment to keep its operating costs low while generating maximum benefits for its investors, one reason why Dyco has remained a leader in the complex and constantly changing oil and gas industry.

SKARNES, INCORPORATED

Most companies celebrate when they get a big order from a new customer. Skarnes, Incorporated, a small Minneapolis company that sells and services materials-handling equipment, has learned that it is time to start celebrating only when the second order comes in. That means that one essential component of Skarnes' business strategy—service—has paid off. The result in Skarnes' case is repeat business from a customer list that includes most of the major Twin Cities manufacturing firms. The company has grown and prospered for more than six decades.

Materials handling has changed dramatically in recent years. Computers and automation have increased both the efficiency and complexity of materials-handling systems. But certain aspects of the industry have not changed at all since Reubin Skarnes started the business in 1923. The most important is the need to understand the specific needs of customers and to provide a solution.

Reubin Skarnes reportedly had the mind of an engineer, although he had received no formal engineering training, and was able to quickly grasp the needs of the manufacturing customers he called on. He started Skarnes, Incorporated, in the back room of his brother's hardware store; the first company he represented was the Chicago Rawhide Company, which sold leather belting and rawhide gears. The business remained small, with Skarnes spending much of his time on the road until World War II stimulated manufacturing and increased the demand for materials-handling equipment. After the war Skarnes moved the operation to its present location on Franklin Avenue near the bluffs of the Mississippi River in Minneapolis. By then he was representing numerous lines, including Skarnes' own ROL-A-LIFT hand trucks, an idea Skarnes had bought in the 1940s and used his natural engineering skills to improve greatly.

In 1956 Skarnes was hit with a personal crisis that threatened to wreck his business. An automobile accident left him unable to call on customers as doctors told him he would never walk again unassisted. He turned to his future son-in-law, Tom Wanous, and to his nephew, John Kilby. Both men agreed to enter the business and proved quick learners. Reubin Skarnes confounded his doctors by regaining the use of his legs. The business continued to

grow until Skarnes' retirement in 1961, when he sold the business to Wanous and Kilby.

Under Wanous and Kilby, and most recently under Tom Wanous since John Kilby's retirement, Skarnes continued to be a small, service-intensive company that registered steady growth by expanding the lines it represented and increasing its customer base. Today 13 major lines are represented, and Skarnes can offer its customers virtually any materials-handling solution. Most recently, computerization and automation have swept the materials-handling field, and Skarnes has continued to stay abreast of the latest developments. Large and technologically sophisticated automated materials-handling systems are installed for customers, thanks in part to Skarnes' own staff systems engineer. Skarnes has also installed a computer system capable of interfacing directly with

Reubin F. Skarnes started his self-titled materials-handling business in 1923; he retired in 1961.

Tom K. Wanous, the current owner and president of Skarnes, Incorporated.

customers' computers.

The result is that while the industry and Skarnes, Incorporated, itself are undergoing tremendous change, one longstanding Skarnes characteristic remains constant—service.

PARK CONSTRUCTION COMPANY

As a young man, Charles Ludwig Carlson started his career as a coachman for a newly rich family that lived on Minneapolis' Park Avenue, a street that aspired to greatness. It was the late nineteenth century and the new city's youth was apparent beyond Park and 22nd Street, now a core city neighborhood, which at the time demarcated the city from the miles of farmland, lakes, and forests beyond.

Carlson was a combination of stable groom, delivery man, and private driver. He began thinking of ways to start his own business, especially after the birth of his first child in 1888. Horses and hauling were what he knew best and, luckily, in the city at the time there was a growing demand for drayage, the transporting of goods by a low, strong horse-drawn cart without fixed sides.

In 1890 Carlson formed the Park Avenue Transfer Company, which transported household goods, small freight from the new Minneapolis train terminal, ashes, and everything else the new drayman could fit into his one-horse express wagon. Headquarters was a barn around the corner from Park Avenue, and many of his customers were residents of the avenue.

Charles Carlson's family grew much faster than his business. By 1903 he had seven children, with Walter, the oldest, followed by Alvin and Bennet. That same year Carlson's beloved wife died. Two months later Carlson himself died. The seven Carlson children were left with-

Today the Park Construction Company is still owned and run by the Carlson family, and serves as one of Minneapolis' premier heavy industrial general construction firms.

out support. Out of the tragedy grew one of the region's most unique family businesses, which today is headed by a third-generation Carlson. Walter Carlson, age 15, and Alvin Carlson, all of 11 years old, vowed they would not only keep the family intact, but also would run their father's business. Thanks to the efforts of a Minneapolis attorney and the support of an uncle and aunt, the Carlson boys managed to do just that.

Charles Ludwig Carlson's firm, the Park Avenue Transfer Company, which he founded in 1890, transported household goods, small freight, and anything else that could fit into a drayage wagon like the one in this picture. Photo circa 1913

Walter and Alvin, and later Bennet, took their father's Park Avenue Transfer Company and began transforming it into the organization it has become today. They quickly expanded to general freight hauling and later made their services available to the excavating business. That move marked the first step in the evolution of Park Construction Company, which today moves a lot of earth as one of the area's premier heavy industrial general construction firms.

In the 1930s the brothers invested in earth-moving equipment after several years' experience in road-grading projects. Soon the Carlsons abandoned hauling altogether and changed the firm's name to the Park Construction Company (even though they had long since moved their operations away from their old Park Avenue neighborhood). Contracts for the various federal Works Projects Administration projects proved to be lifesavers during the years of the Great Depression. In the 1940s Park worked on a new innovation called drive-in theaters. During the 1950s the company gradually evolved from being a subcontractor to prime or general contractor status. By the 1960s Park was ready to tackle large construction and grading projects, including water-treatment plants, big road-paving projects, golf courses, power plants, and dams and excavations of all kinds.

Today, under chairman Richard Carlson and president and chief executive officer Duane Prairie, Park Construction Company has become a general contractor of national scope. A full-time work force exceeding 300 includes a fully staffed office in Denver. Recent work has ranged from massive flood-control projects to the excavation and utilities installation at Minnesota's new Canterbury Downs Race Track.

SHERATON NORTHWEST

If location, timing, and image are the three factors that most often lead to success in the hospitality industry—as many claim—Sheraton Northwest in Brooklyn Park may be a textbook example of how to build a hotel/meeting complex and make it work.

When Sheraton Northwest opened in 1974, the northwestern Twin Cities area was sparsely developed and populated. Today it is one of the fastest growing spots in Minnesota. Sheraton Northwest, one of the first hotels in the area, can now count at least 10 competitors within a five-mile radius.

The hotel's banquet and meeting facilities were put to early use serving the needs of companies that began moving into the area in the late 1970s and early 1980s—a list that reads like a who's who of Minnesota high technology. At the same time the growing number of home owners in Brooklyn Park, Brooklyn Center, Maple Grove, and other burgeoning communities needed a place to eat, drink, and enjoy themselves. Sheraton Northwest provided the option. And while the southwestern and Mexican architecture and interior furnishings may have struck some as improbable in Minnesota, the warmth and fun it produces became an immediate hit with patrons. The right place at the right time with the right amenities—that's been the story of Sheraton Northwest.

George Bleecker, the developer and original owner of Sheraton Northwest, has never been accused of being a visionary, but his instincts were obviously impeccable. Bleecker got together a group of Minneapolis investors in the early 1970s to form a partnership to develop a hotel and meeting facility on the then-unfinished I-94 corridor in Brooklyn Park

The pool area, with its adobe-style enclosure, is just one of the many amenities offered by Sheraton Northwest to its visitors.

that would eventually connect downtown Minneapolis with the northwestern suburbs and Saint Cloud, forming the nucleus, Bleecker figured, for an eventual burst of development.

As a newspaper account reported at the time, Bleecker also recognized "his limitations in complicated fiscal matters," and hired Bart Boyer to handle financing the complex and John Okerstrom, a hospitality industry veteran, to manage the new motel. Both men would be instrumental in Sheraton Northwest's success. When Bleecker retired from the business in 1985 and sold his interests to a limited partnership headed by Okerstrom, Boyer, and Donn Erickson, Sheraton Northwest had

Southwestern and Mexican architecture and interior furnishings distinguish Sheraton Northwest from its competitors in the northern suburbs of the Twin Cities.

undergone several modifications and improvements, although it never strayed far from the Mexican theme. Among its many distinctions were its two indoor courtyards, the pool area and the Fountain Court for meetings and receptions, and its live entertainment, which included the first ever appearances by the Jets, a band from nearby New Hope High School who later went on to pop stardom.

Under the new management team many of the Mexican furnishings were replaced by lighter and more elegant Southwest American decor. All 214 guest rooms and suites were completely renovated. An executive wing was established with its own indoor courtyard. The motel's main dining room was also upgraded from El Gallo Rojo to Charley Goodnight's, which began serving a menu of imaginative American and southwestern fare.

Today the Sheraton Northwest, with 250 employees and revenues in excess of $5 million, has become something of a Twin Cities landmark. Few other landmarks are so much fun.

DAHLBERG, INC.

Hearing loss is gradual, painless, and all too often simply accepted as an inevitable consequence of aging or disease. That may be why only 4 million of the approximately 22 million Americans who are estimated to need a hearing aid actually have one. The nature of the hearing aid industry itself is a disorganized and sprawling collection of more than 50 small U.S. hearing aid manufacturers and as many as 7,000 retail outlets. Educating the public is one of the industry's biggest needs.

Dahlberg, Inc., a venerable and pioneering Minneapolis hearing aid manufacturer, has been tackling these problems with strategies that are virtually unique to the industry. Dahlberg may be remaking the industry itself. The process began in 1983, when the Federal Trade Commission lifted a 10-year-old consent decree that banned exclusive dealer distribution within the hearing aid industry. Dahlberg, a respected, 40-year-old company, seized that opportunity to act. "Going for Broke" is how one industry trade publication characterized Dahlberg's strategy.

Dahlberg is attempting to make

Dahlberg's Miracle-Ear Centers revolutionized the hearing aid business. The system of franchises and company-owned stores contributed to a sales explosion in the 1980s.

buying a hearing aid as easy as buying eyeglasses. That strategy involved conversion of its network of independent dealers into unique Miracle-Ear® Center franchises, most located in highly visible retail centers, and an aggressive marketing campaign. It was something completely new to the hearing aid industry, and the results have been remarkable. Dahlberg, which posted revenues of fewer than $10

Building hearing aids is labor intensive and technologically sophisticated. Dahlberg has facilities in Minnesota, Arizona, England, and Australia.

million at the beginning of the decade, will top $50 million and expects to near $100 million within a few years.

Kenneth H. Dahlberg founded the company in 1948. A St. Paul native, he

was building a career in the hospitality industry when World War II began, at which time he became an aviation instructor at an Army Air Corps base near Phoenix, Arizona. Dahlberg shipped out to fly combat missions over Europe where he downed 15 German planes, was shot down twice, escaped both times, and finally spent five months in a German prisoner of war camp after being shot down a third time. When the war ended Dahlberg returned to the Twin Cities and met Allen Hempel, owner of Telex, Inc. Hempel convinced Dahlberg to join his company, and Dahlberg went to work as Hempel's special assistant.

Three years later Dahlberg struck off on his own, using the expertise he had gained to form his own hearing aid company. Dahlberg, Inc., also made products for the hospital industry, including portable paging units for doctors and nurses, remote-control music distribution systems, and private bedside speakers. Within 10 years Dahlberg had a $4-million company and the attention of corporate suitors; Motorola Corporation bought Dahlberg out. When Motorola began divesting its consumer operations five years later, Dahlberg bought back the hearing aid division.

Dahlberg became involved in national politics through the presidential campaign of his old friend, Barry Goldwater, culminating in his role as midwestern chairman of the 1972 reelection campaign of Richard Nixon and as a member of the National Republican Finance Committee.

During the early 1970s Dahlberg and other major hearing aid manufacturers had begun building networks of exclusive geographical dealerships. In 1972 the Federal Trade Commission called these exclusive dealerships anticompetitive and broke up the distribution systems of Dahlberg and others, saying in effect that manufacturers had to sell to anyone who claimed to be in the retail hearing aid business. That action, according to many, guaranteed that companies in the industry would remain small and that strong marketing systems like the one Dahlberg was attempting to establish would never materialize. One result was that the industry grew little during the 1970s, and lost much of its U.S. market share and nearly all of its export business to foreign competitors.

Kenneth Dahlberg, founder and chairman of Dahlberg, Inc.

Ken Dahlberg satisfied his strong entrepreneurial instincts by backing new companies with venture capital. He continued to nurture his own company as best he could, and took it public in the late 1970s. By 1980 sales had reached $10 million.

After much controversy the FTC changed its mind about exclusive dealerships in 1982. Dahlberg was ready. K. Jeffrey Dahlberg, Ken's son, spent much of his life working for the company and is credited with much of the success of Dahlberg's bold new marketing strategy, which in reality harks back to the work done establishing a dealer network before the FTC action.

The process involved converting Dahlberg's sprawling network of independent dealers into a carefully structured system of Miracle-Ear franchises and company-owned stores. Through its Miracle-Ear Centers Dahlberg hoped to project a uniform and professional image by using state-of-the-art marketing methods. Dahlberg could pump large amounts of training and marketing dollars into its retail outlets without fear that they would be used to sell competitors' products.

It was a risky strategy for a small company. Dahlberg's existing distribution system could have been plunged into chaos and the firm was required to spend huge amounts ($6 million in 1985) on marketing for a company its size. Dahlberg had to acquire a new set of management and selling skills as it shifted from primarily a manufacturer to one that was just as much a retailer. Sales rose rapidly, as did selling and administrative expenses—from $4.6 million in 1982 to exceed $11 million two years later.

Ken and Jeff Dahlberg's payoff for taking their four-decade-old company and running it through the entrepreneurial paces of a brash start-up corporation was a fivefold increase in sales since 1980 and the prospect of soon becoming the leading company in the hearing aid industry. Miracle-Ear Centers now span the country, and more than one in 10 hearing aids sold is a Miracle-Ear. Dahlberg now employs more than 1,500 people and has manufacturing facilities in Minnesota, Wisconsin, Arizona, Canada, Australia, and England.

Jeff Dahlberg, eventually named president and later chief executive officer, resigned in 1986 to start a business leading other companies through the franchising process. While much of Dahlberg's history is recent, certain things remain the same, including a tradition of technological innovation (Dahlberg, Inc., built the first in-the-ear hearing aids in the 1950s), and a commitment to words Ken Dahlberg wrote on a napkin as he pondered a strategy for his new business soon after its inception: ". . . to help every person suffering from man's oldest incurable disease, that silent, painless destroyer of human communication . . . deafness . . . rendering this service with dignity and devotion to client and community."

A Dahlberg hearing aid.

LAKEWOOD PUBLICATIONS

Lakewood Publications in Minneapolis has goals that cover the usual objectives of serving its customers better than its competitors do and generating stable profits, but they also talk about "surrounding" the markets Lakewood serves and keeping business "simple and fun."

Lakewood surrounds its markets by providing the professional audiences who read its six publications with business- and career-building tools that are virtually unique in the publishing industry, including seminars, conferences, newsletters, and customized market research. Lakewood keeps its business simple and fun by encouraging an open and fulfilling corporate culture that would be the envy of companies many times its size. One result of these two policies has been a decade of growth, a preeminent position in the markets it serves, and, most recently, the merger of the organization with the giant Canadian communications firm, Maclean Hunter, Ltd.

Lakewood's origins are surprisingly recent. In 1960 Tom Nammacher, Lakewood's founder, scraped together enough capital to launch *Airport Services Management* (ASM) magazine when he discovered that there was no professional trade publication for the general aviation and airport industry. As ASM grew, Nammacher acquired or launched new professional trade publications, including *Potentials in Marketing* in 1968, which has since become the leading new-product tabloid for the huge promotion marketing industry.

Nammacher also hired a 26-year-old advertising manager named Jim Secord, who would develop a close working partnership with Nammacher and eventually become Lakewood's president and chief executive officer.

By the 1970s Lakewood had formulated the concept of surrounding the markets it served with new and innovative products and services, including a computerized sales lead referral system for *Potentials* advertisers. In 1976 Lakewood purchased *Training,* which has become the leading and most widely respected publication for professionals in the training and human resources development fields. *Training* soon led to a series of conferences, seminars, and exhibits organized by a division within the company called Lakewood Conferences, including the premier conference and trade show

The interior of Lakewood Publications.

held each year in New York City, which draws more than 10,000 human resource professionals from around the world.

New publications and further innovations followed in the 1980s, including *Recreation, Sports & Leisure,* a new-product tabloid for recreation professionals who manage recreation facilities; photography magazines, which serve the professional photography market; and *Lakewood Research,* which supplies market research to Lakewood's publications, as well as to such outside clients as

The Lakewood Building in downtown Minneapolis, formerly the home of WCCO Television, is being remodeled into a premier office/retail center.

AT&T, IBM, and the American Management Association.

It took 15 years before Lakewood's sales topped one million dollars in 1975. By the middle of the 1980s revenues were closer to $15 million, and Lakewood's associates numbered more than 100.

Lakewood Publications has recently changed dramatically. After years in cramped leased quarters in downtown Minneapolis, Lakewood bought the former home of WCCO Television and transformed it into a publishing environment that has attracted national attention. Tom Nammacher decided to sell his interest in the company he founded, and a search was on for a compatible partner. Such a partner was found in the billion-dollar Maclean Hunter, whose goals and philosophy closely match Lakewood's own. With the tremendous resources of this new partner backing it, Lakewood's future appears even brighter than its past.

BERNE SCALE COMPANY

When a truck loaded with chickens hits a bump on the highway and all the chickens fly up in the air, does the truck weigh the same as it did before it hit the bump?

For a solution, "Newton's Apple" producers turned to Berne Scale Company, a 27-year-old, scale sales, rental, and service organization in St. Louis Park. Berne Scale designed a test involving an electronic scale, a large platform, and a radio-controlled model helicopter. The experiment was performed on television: The truck does indeed weigh the same.

In one way or another that is what Berne Scale has been doing for most of its existence, although its customers are more frequently the likes of 3M, Control Data, Unisys, Cargill, and other major Minnesota manufacturers whose needs for scales are numerous and surprisingly diverse. Berne Scale focuses on keeping up with advances in scale technology and helping customers find solutions to weighing problems. The company offers customized scales for virtually every application by mixing and matching modular components—both for outright sale and rental. While such a customer-service orientation can consume a lot of energy, in Berne Scales' case, it has resulted in a sixfold increase in sales in less than a decade.

Owners Chris Berne and Jim Rannow, Chris' brother-in-law, may have hit on such a strategy simply because they did not have enough business background to know any better. Don and Harriet Berne, Chris' parents, started the business then known as Berne Equipment Company in their southwest Minneapolis home in 1961, after Don had worked as an Upper Midwest sales representative and branch manager for a major scale manufacturer. While Chris had always been involved in some aspects of the business, he majored in Russian studies at the University of Minnesota and was not planning to enter his family's business immediately upon graduation—if at all. Then Don Berne suffered a heart attack in 1977, and Chris found himself soley in charge at the tender age of 23. Jim Rannow, a part-time employee and a geography major at the University of Minnesota, gradually began assuming some of Chris' duties, since Chris was often working 80-hour weeks. This working relationship proved to be mutually rewarding, and Chris and Jim decided to become co-owners of the company upon Don's retirement. The name

Don Berne, founder of Berne Scale Company.

was changed to Berne Scale Company at that time.

The scale industry was being transformed by the microelectronics revolution that was picking up speed during the late 1970s. Scales based on computer chips could handle infinitely more applications than mechanical scales. New manufacturers were springing up almost daily. In an industry that had once been dominated by three giant manufacturers, with nearly 80 percent of the U.S. market, there were now dozens of companies, many offering highly specialized products.

Both Berne and Rannow realized that the uses of scales would explode—if users recognized those applications and could turn to a supplier with the experience and expertise to accommodate them. Hence the focus on customer service, innovatively mixing and matching modular components to meet highly specific weighing needs. The firm maintains a large rental department that today offers hundreds of scales for customers with occasional needs such as year-end inventory. The expert service department provides factory-trained maintenance and repair service. Today Berne Scale Company has 14 employees and represents the lines of more than 40 manufacturers.

Jim Rannow (left) and Chris Berne (right) demonstrate the transition of scales from mechanical to electronic.

M.A. MORTENSON COMPANY

Quiet competence has been the hallmark of the M.A. Mortenson Company for three decades as it has grown into the largest general contractor in Minnesota. Establishing and maintaining the confidence of many of the Midwest's finest corporations, Mortenson has built upon a base of repeat clients to establish itself as a national leader in construction and construction management. From the contemporary Radisson Plaza VII Hotel and Office Building in Minneapolis to the renovations at St. Paul's historic Landmark Center, Mortenson has also been one of the most important players in the recent building renaissance in the Twin Cities.

Construction runs in the Mortenson family. When M.A. Mortenson, Sr., founded the company in 1954, he was trading upon a tradition of excellence and pride in a job well done that was passed on to him by his father, a Scandinavian emigrant who brought an "Old World" sense of craftsmanship to his work. In its first year M.A. Mortenson's new company secured 15 contracts worth $424,000 and made a modest profit. The company has been profitable ever since, and its dollar volume of construction contracts has increased steadily each year.

Much of Mortenson's growth is due to M.A. Mortenson, Jr., who took the foundation his father laid and helped create a construction firm of national scope. With a degree in civil engineering, he joined the company in 1960, assembling the management team that now operates the company. This team collectively represents more than 200 years of construction experience and provides progressive innovative direction, establishing the Mortenson reputation for quality workmanship and ability to meet its clients' expectations.

By 1974, 20 years after its creation, M.A. Mortenson Company was listed by *Engineering News Record* (ENR) as one of the top 400 contractors in the United States. It broke into the nation's top 100 firms in 1981, and in recent years the annual volume of the company's revenues has exceeded $500 million.

The result of Mortenson's steady, controlled growth is its ability to deliver services that consistently meet the chang-

M.A. Mortenson Company, the largest general contractor in Minneapolis, has built a national reputation with the successful completion of projects such as the massive Intermountain Power Project in Delta, Utah.

ing needs of the construction market. Mortenson has successfully completed virtually every type of project, for many of the nation's most prestigious developers. In Minneapolis alone, Mortenson has built many of the city's most architecturally distinguished projects, including the striking Lincoln Centre, the 57-story Norwest Center, and the jewel-like Conservatory on Nicollet. These buildings have been praised for their high quality of craftsmanship. The construction manager on the $100-million Minneapolis Conven-

tion Center, Mortenson brings to each project a level of construction competence—from safety to steel erection, from concrete to EEO—that only a traditional family-owned business could present to an owner.

Mortenson's dedication to the highest quality construction has fostered a reputation for honesty and integrity in its business practices. These attributes have paved the way for Mortenson's progress, especially in the areas of negotiated contracts with many national firms, the successful acquisition of public bid work, and in the demanding field of health care construction. Mortenson has consistently produced projects on time and within budget. It is this type of performance that has made it the contractor of choice for

The Conservatory is the high-fashion focal point of Minneapolis' downtown Nicollet Mall.

Northwest Airlines, Lutheran Brotherhood, Cenex, IBM, Trammel Crow, and others who have selected it to build corporate headquarters or major corporate office facilities.

In the public sector, Mortenson's expertise in the competitive bidding process has led to its work on large public building projects that range from the B-1 Bomber Support Facility in Rapid City, South Dakota, to the Minneapolis V.A. Replacement Hospital, the largest public building contract ever constructed in Minnesota.

Mortenson has also served the health care industry for more than three decades with the successful completion of more than 100 health care projects, totaling nearly one billion dollars. Just as impressive as its completion record on health care projects is the continuing relationships that have been established with prominent leaders in the health care industry, such as Abbott/Northwestern and Fairview Community hospitals. National hospital projects range from the huge Tripler Army Medical Center in Honolulu, Hawaii, to the University of Minnesota Hospital Renewal Project, a portfolio of experience few builders in the nation can match.

A large measure of M.A. Mortenson Company's recent success has been due to a diversification—geographically and in the services offered. The firm established a full-service regional office in Denver in 1982, and by 1987 that office had grown to become the largest Denver-based contractor. Building on the success of the Denver operation, Mortenson duplicated the concept with regional offices in Seattle and Tampa. To support its role as Minnesota's leading construction firm, the company also opened district offices in Rochester and Grand Rapids. These regional and district offices were part of a divisional strategy, transforming Mortenson into a diversified, national construction company, capable of successfully undertaking major products anywhere in the country.

Through expansion, addition, and acquisition, Mortenson has also diversified its range of services offered to its clients. The firm has built upon its expertise in the completion of large energy and processing facilities to formally establish a Heavy/Industrial Division in 1975. Mortenson Development Company was formed in 1980 to serve the real estate development needs of clients. Three years later Mortenson acquired Construction Management Services, Inc., a prominent Minneapolis construction management firm responsible for such notable projects as the Hubert H. Humphrey Metrodome, the Hennepin County Government Center, and Orchestra Hall to strengthen its construction management capabilities. This diversification has enabled M.A. Mortenson Company to service all aspects of the construction market, including general contracting, construction management, design/build, and development services on projects ranging in cost from less than one million dollars to more than $150 million.

Mortenson's capability, experience, and philosophy have proven particularly significant in recent years, especially as many projects are built on a design/build or fast track basis and the contractor assumes major importance for coordinating both design and construction. Mortenson's people, the cornerstone of the company's success, have developed a strong reputation for being hard working, professional, and energetic. Their talents, covering all facets of modern construction, are combined into a team of professionals that has one goal: the success of the project.

The M.A. Mortenson Company continues to build upon its traditions, reputation, and people to perform up to the standards of excellence that are embodied in its corporate mission:
—To operate its business with quiet competence.
—To construct facilities meeting its clients' expectations for quality, schedule, and budget.
—To conduct its business activities with complete integrity and fairness.
—To foster teamwork and opportunities for personal growth.
—To perpetuate its company through service based on the highest ethics.

One of the most architecturally distinguished projects on the Minneapolis skyline, the 57-story Norwest Center is another M.A. Mortenson Company highlight.

The Minneapolis Veterans Administration Hospital represents the largest single contract ever let by the V.A. at that time.

EBERHARDT COMMERCIAL REAL ESTATE

Eberhardt Commercial Real Estate is one of the major players in the building renaissance that has transformed the Twin Cities in recent decades. Eberhardt works behind the scenes—buying land, securing financing, finding tenants, managing properties, and consulting on a myriad of commercial real estate matters—not for itself, but for owners, developers, and institutional investors. Its reputation for the quality and expertise of its people and their dedication to serving clients has helped Eberhardt become one of the leading real estate services companies in the region.

Walter C. Nelson joined the firm in 1939 as a junior partner and later became its owner and president. The original company was established in 1935 by Alex Eberhardt to manage rental properties for institutional investors. Nelson acquired the firm after Eberhardt's death in 1951.

Under Nelson's direction, the Eberhardt Company began to change dramatically. Diversifying throughout the 1950s and 1960s, Eberhardt grew from a property management company to one that offered a full range of real estate services, including mortgage banking, real estate sales, and consulting. After Nelson was elected president of the Mortgage Bank-

The Eberhardt corporate headquarters in Edina.

Walter C. Nelson (left), former chairman of the board. James W. Nelson (right), president.

ers' Association of America in 1958, Eberhardt made the decision to develop its commercial mortgage banking activities. Eberhardt also acted as a residential land developer during those years, with two dozen residential subdivision developments located in Twin Cities western suburbs.

During the 1960s the wide ranging real estate expertise of the growing company became attractive to an increasing number of institutions, real estate investors, and developers; Eberhardt often serves as a middleman in major developments. It represented Dayton Hudson in the acquisition of the property that was developed into Ridgedale Center, a regional mall in Minnetonka. Eberhardt identified and purchased more than 8,500 acres that McKnight family interests developed as the planned community of Jonathan. Eberhardt also acquired the land for the Minneapolis Institute of Arts and other Minneapolis developments. Walter Nelson played a major role in the development of Minneapolis' Nicollet Mall as president of the Minneapolis Downtown Council. New employees who

helped structure these complicated deals included William S. Reiling, who would later become owner and chairman of Towle Real Estate; Bob Morris, an alumnus of Arthur Anderson who became the company's chief financial officer; and James W. Nelson, Walter's son, who joined the firm in 1965 and was named president in 1976 when his father became chairman of the board.

When Eberhardt moved into its new Edina headquarters in 1970, the synergy among its various operations became apparent. While it continued as a full-service real estate company, it also began to specialize in marketing financing packages for commercial developments, brokering land and buildings for individuals and corporate clients, consulting on a wide range of real estate transactions, and managing and leasing commercial, retail, and residential properties.

Eberhardt Commercial Real Estate participated in the new Conservatory retail/office complex in downtown Minneapolis. The firm helped assemble the land, bring together the development partners, arrange financing, and lease the retail portion of the $75-million project. Eberhardt's role was one of performing for the developers behind the scenes, but its contribution was significant.

HEALTH RISK MANAGEMENT, INC.

Information has become one of the most important commodities in today's economy. Consumers gather it so they can compare brands and prices before making a purchase. And companies do likewise when making purchasing decisions on a larger scale—let's say, for the steel that goes into automobiles.

Only one major industry exists without that common kind of exchange of information between the buyer and the seller. It is health care. And that is where Health Risk Management, Inc. (HRM), comes in.

In 1977 the founders of the Edina-based company, Dr. Gary T. McIlroy and Marlene Travis, owned a medical testing laboratory serving doctors and hospitals in Minnesota and nearby states. McIlroy is a pathologist trained at the Mayo Clinic, and Travis is experienced in the business management and communications aspects of medicine. With more than 15 years apiece of experience in the medical field, they had long recognized the information gap in the industry.

They started solving the problem by extending their lab services to the general public. Healthstyles, their first HRM program, used lab tests to tell people more about the status of their health and what could be done to improve it. HRM provided worksite training and health promotion programs as follow-up. Employers bought Healthstyles because they knew the value of employing healthier people: fewer sick days, increased productivity, and lower health care costs.

Costs soon took precedence. A well-publicized national study said health care costs were out of control, and as a business expense were so high that they interfered significantly with the ability of U.S. corporations to compete in the world market.

The problem is lack of information. Consumers have no access to information about what their medical choices are. There is no way to compare prices beforehand because that information is not available to the general public either. The employer providing health insurance coverage for employees is not in much better shape. HRM accepted the challenge, applying analytical skills, medical knowledge, and the latest computer technology to the task.

Today large corporations, unions, and other employers nationwide can count on HRM for information that the health care consumer needs in order to contain costs. HRM's staff has grown to include scores of doctors and nurses, along with experts in medical economics, epidemi-

---

Dr. Gary McIlroy and Marlene Travis transformed a medical testing laboratory into one of the nation's leading health care cost-management companies.

ology, biostatistics, computer science, medical records, utilization review, health benefit plan design, claims administration, employee communications, and health promotion.

HRM doctors and nurses in all the major medical specialties review with each patient's doctor the reasons for a proposed hospital stay. They also negotiate the doctor's fee and the hospital's charges in advance. Never before has this type of information been available in time to make the health care consumer more aware of his or her choices. Clients may employ HRM as a contracting intermediary. HRM experts then would negotiate with hospitals to guarantee more competitive rates in exchange for incentives that steer the client's employees their way.

In addition, a division of medical data experts decode every medical claim by computer and show the employer where the past year's money went, also pointing out which hospitals and doctors were more efficient. This information and HRM's interpretation help the employer design a better benefit plan. A related service can track current claims throughout the year.

HRM's clients together spend billions of dollars each year on health care. HRM reduces their expenditures significantly without compromising the quality of care that their employees receive.

CHERNE CONTRACTING CORPORATION

Anthony Cherne started a plumbing and heating supply company in the little town of Buhl on Minnesota's Iron Range in 1916. Customers included schools, homes, and businesses, whose needs were usually quite simple. Cherne's business philosophy was just as simple: respect for working men, a strong belief in the union movement, paying suppliers on time, and not going into debt—honorable and straightforward objectives, but hardly the kind of thinking that might set the business world on fire.

Simplicity is often powerful, and Cherne's clear ideas about how to run his business were enough to transform it into Cherne Contracting Corporation, one of the region's leading full-service contracting firms. In past decades Cherne Contracting established itself as a national leader in the construction of fossil fuel and nuclear power plants, paper mills, and ore-processing plants. Most recently Cherne has diversified into many new areas of mechanical, electrical, and civil construction. Through all of this growth, it has never lost sight of Anthony Cherne's levelheaded approach to business.

Anthony Cherne's business expanded slowly during the first two decades. After a few years of growth that mirrored the growth of the Iron Range during the early part of this century, Cherne opened a second plumbing and heating contracting operation in Ironwood, Michigan. In 1928 Cherne expanded to Chicago, where the downtown Loop was undergoing tremendous commercial development and the demand for mechanical contracting work was high.

Anthony Cherne (left) and Albert Cherne inside one of the company's first big construction jobs, the White Pine Copper project, in 1954.

The boom was cut short by the Depression, and Cherne was forced to close the Chicago operation in 1931. The firm managed to maintain some prosperity, partly as a result of mechanical work needed by such federal government relief programs as Civilian Conservation Corps camp construction. When America entered World War II, Cherne and similar companies found themselves expanding dramatically as Army barracks, hospitals,

Cherne's 100,000-square-foot Minneapolis headquarters was completed in 1984.

and other buildings began sprouting up across the country. As Cherne expanded it began tackling larger jobs; in 1949 the firm received its first big contract to do the mechanical work for a mining operation in Michigan and left the residential market entirely.

During the 1950s Cherne's office and engineering staff exceeded 50, and its contract labor force of skilled craftsmen frequently swelled into the hundreds to meet the requirements of major contracts, such as the Reserve Mining Taconite Plant in Silver Bay and Michigan's White Pine Copper Mine. Although headquartered in Ironwood, Cherne was bidding for jobs from coast to coast.

Cherne became large and confident enough to bid successfully for massive fossil fuel and nuclear power plants. In 1964 it moved its headquarters to Minneapolis, where it recently erected the 100,000-square-foot building that houses it today. By then Albert Cherne had succeeded his father as president, although Anthony Cherne continued to be involved with the company into his eighties.

In the late 1970s Cherne Contracting Corporation began to diversify into other contracting areas through acquisitions. Now under president Gary Ratcliffe, a 14-year veteran of the company, and Al Cherne, chairman, Cherne has become a turnkey, full-service contracting company with a permanent engineering, field, and office staff of 160. That is a long way from a plumbing supply business on the Iron Range.

TOWLE REAL ESTATE COMPANY

Innovation, dedication, and professional personal service continue to be the trademarks of Towle Real Estate Company's growth and success. The people of Towle have evolved over the firm's 78 years from generalists to specialists capable of doing the most sophisticated transactions. The Minneapolis-based company has a staff exceeding 200 and is positioned to satisfy all commercial real estate needs.

The Towle-Jamieson Company was created in 1909 by George E. Towle, a North Dakota banker, and Thomas A. Jamieson, a Minneapolis real estate broker, to act as a mortgage loan correspondent for the Prudential Insurance Company of America, the first of many relationships the firm would establish with major national financial institutions. Insurance companies were the principal source of money for farm loans, and Prudential was one of the largest in the industry. Prudential was also underwriting commercial and residential mortgages in Minneapolis.

The Great Depression in 1929 forced Prudential to foreclose on many of the loans in its portfolio. Towle-Jamieson in turn became increasingly involved in property management and sales, and changed its name to Towle Mortgage Company. By then Jamieson had died and Walter G. Wallace, hired in 1920, became secretary/treasurer. The company was already beginning to diversify.

When Prudential decided to open its own Minneapolis office, it provided the impetus for Towle to seek other investors for its mortgage loans, including Connecticut Mutual and Lincoln National Life. George Towle died and Walter Wallace became president. Darrel M. Holt, who had been in the real estate business in Fort Wayne, Indiana, was hired as sales manager. By 1951 Wallace and Holt had purchased all of the company's stock from the Towle estate and were equal owners of the firm.

Wallace retired in the early 1960s and Darrel Holt became president of the company. Wallace, who was a trained accountant, had the solid business instincts to carefully lead the organization through the growth years of the 1940s and 1950s. Holt, with his selling experience, would establish a level of excellence in sales and property management. During the 1960s the company passed the $200-million mark in mortgage servicing and amassed

Three generations of leadership at Towle Real Estate: Walter G. Wallace (above left), Darrel M. Holt (above), and William S. Reiling (left).

a property management portfolio exceeding 3 million square feet.

William Reiling acquired part ownership of the company in 1973 and became president, with Holt advancing to chairman. Reiling began to enlarge the business, increasing the emphasis on providing a broad spectrum of services to other real estate professionals and the large financial institutions that now dominate much of the commercial real estate market. Reiling established a participatory management style that would allow the company to grow beyond the limits sometimes found in businesses owned and managed by one or two individuals.

Today, under president Mark Reiling, Towle Real Estate Company is the largest locally owned real estate service firm in the Midwest. Its services include commercial real estate brokerage, mortgage banking and financing, property management, insurance, and appraisal consultation and syndication. The diversification reflects the expertise of the men who founded the company and made it grow.

MARVIN WINDOWS

Warroad, Minnesota, is an unlikely place to find one of Minnesota's most innovative and fastest-growing companies. Located 350 miles from the Twin Cities on Lake of the Woods, which separates much of northern Minnesota from Canada, Warroad is tiny (population 1,800); far from markets, suppliers, and transportation routes; and locked during much of the year in the icy grip of the area's legendary winters. The hunting and fishing and forests are great, but other towns like Warroad have seen their young people move to big cities and their economies shrink in recent years.

Warroad's difference has been supplied by Marvin Lumber & Cedar, better known throughout the world as Marvin Windows, the world's largest manufacturer of custom windows and a leader in a multibillion-dollar industry. Marvin's story is inseparable from the people of Warroad, who are not the typical product innovators and market leaders. "We're so far up in the boondocks, we didn't know any better," a retired sales manager says of the string of innovations that have built Marvin into a $200-million and rapidly growing company.

Even back during the 1940s George Marvin was troubled by the lack of opportunity rural areas like northern Minnesota presented young people, including four of his sons who were returning from World War II. Marvin had come to Warroad in 1904 to establish and operate a grain ele-

The Marvin Lumber and Cedar Company in its infancy. The business produced railroad ties, pulpwood, and even World War II ammunition boxes before it began manufacturing windows nearly 50 years ago.

vator for his Canadian employers, who figured that Warroad might make a good grain shipment point. A few years later the firm thought better of the move, and tore the elevator down plank by plank and moved it to Saskatchewan. George Marvin stayed, purchased Warroad's lumberyard, and opened Marvin Lumber & Cedar Company.

In the following years George Mar-

The same care goes into handcrafted Marvin windows today as it did when the company first began to manufacture them. Alice Qualey, Susan Geiger, and Caroline Searles put on some finishing touches in this photo taken in the late 1950s.

vin expanded his business. He built his own grain elevator and later started a pulpwood and railroad tie brokerage business. He started selling hardware, feed, and seed. By the 1940s Marvin's business was still small, with only eight employees (including son Bill, who joined the company after receiving degrees in agronomy and agricultural economics from the University of Minnesota), but it was diversified and profitable. What kept it going was George Marvin's prodigious capacity for work and a commitment to running a viable business in northern Minnesota, with its attractive North Woods outdoor life-style.

When Bill Marvin joined the company, Marvin Lumber expanded into window making, but in a strictly minor way. Harry York, Marvin's lumberyard manager, was an experienced craftsman and talked Marvin into buying equipment for making window frames—mostly to keep

himself busy during the slow winter months. The firm also used the equipment during World War II to make food containers and ammunition boxes for the war effort. Like many businesses at the time, Marvin Lumber saw its work force increase dramatically—to nearly 50.

Bill Marvin began wondering what would happen when four of his younger brothers who had gone off to fight the war, plus the many other young men from the area, returned. He and his father, George, knew that most young people would prefer to stay in the area, but in the booming postwar economy that was taking shape, the jobs and opportunity would be elsewhere.

Bill realized that making windows was probably the only aspect of business that did not rely on the local economy. Windows could be sold to larger markets—markets that would expand dramatically when the war ended. By concentrating on windows Marvin might just be able to offer a reason for Warroad's young people to stay.

In the next two decades Marvin Windows grew steadily. Warroad's distance from major markets forced the company to operate a little differently than other manufacturers. Since railroad connections to Warroad proved inadequate to ship a growing number of units reliably, Marvin became the first window manufacturer to establish its own truck fleet and ship windows directly to distributors and dealers. Marvin was also the first manufacturer in America to ship window units to dealers completely set up and ready to install, the first to use wood-bead glazing instead of putty glazing, and one of the first to make double- and triple-glazed windows for cold climates. All have become standard industry practices today.

Bill Marvin became president and numerous other members of the second generation joined the company. Today a third generation of Marvins is involved. The company was able to grow and prosper, many say, largely due to the ingenuity and work ethic of people in Warroad and the surrounding area, many of them farmers used to being self-reliant jacks-of-all-trades. Above all, Marvin Windows became a Warroad institution, inseparable from the town itself.

When a fire destroyed the under-insured Marvin plant in 1961, Marvin re-

Marvin plant workers prepare custom round tops for shipment. In 1981 Marvin Windows reintroduced the all-but-extinct round top to the market.

ceived offers from a number of U.S. and Canadian cities that were eager to provide subsidies and incentives to get Marvin to relocate. The company never even considered it, members of the Marvin family say. A new plant was built in Warroad, and the firm continued to grow. By 1970 Marvin Windows employed nearly 200 people, almost all of them from Warroad. A decade later the work force had swelled to 875, and sales reached nearly $44 million per year.

The period of the company's greatest growth, however, began in the 1980s at a time when the U.S. construction industry hit a slump. By then Marvin had staked out a niche as a custom window manufacturer, a company that made windows to order and specialized in architecturally unusual and custom windows. (Today the firm makes more than 5,000 standard shapes of windows.) In 1981, for instance, Marvin reintroduced the old-fashioned round-top window, a style that had virtually disappeared decades ago. The company's willingness to accommodate customer needs, and its innovative reintroductions of older-fashioned windows, appealed tremendously to the burgeoning market for restorations and renovations that boomed during the 1980s. Sales also continued strong in lower-cost, more standardized windows. The result was a period of growth that nearly tripled the work force to more than 2,500 and saw sales exceed $135 million in 1986.

In 1981 the company opened a sec-

ond plant in Tennessee, partly to get closer to new markets in the South and partly because employment was so high in Warroad that there were virtually no workers left to employ. Today both Warroad and Marvin Windows are undergoing a boom. Marvin manages to be a company that doubles its revenues every two to five years, while maintaining such paid holidays as Deer Monday, which falls on the opening of the deer hunting season.

Warroad is building schools, churches, and residential dwellings. All in all, it appears to be exactly what George Marvin had in mind.

Located in Warroad, the Marvin plant presently employs more than 2,500 people and is a mainstay of the area's farm-depressed economy.

McGLYNN BAKERIES, INC.

James T. McGlynn had never baked so much as a bread stick, but that did not stop him from opening a downtown Minneapolis bakery that quickly became six, then a wholesale baking company, and today, in a new form under McGlynn's descendants, one of the fastest growing baking companies in the nation.

McGlynn opened his first bakery at 408 Marquette in downtown Minneapolis in 1919. McGlynn figured that a "window bakery," with the kitchen in view of passersby, would be a natural addition to the busy downtown. His hunch paid off; in just a few years McGlynn had six such bakeries in the downtown area.

McGlynn decided he had better know something about baking and enrolled in a vocational training course at Dunwoody Institute. McGlynn bread, entered under a fictitious name, earned a third-place ribbon in the bread baking competition at the Minnesota State Fair.

By the time McGlynn's son, Burton, joined the business in the late 1940s, McGlynn Bakeries had 11 downtown shops and several wholesale routes. Business was limited, however, by the fact that few people went downtown on weekends. McGlynn installed a bakery in a converted bus (complete with a self-leveling oven of his own invention), and created the nation's first known traveling bakery. McGlynn's Trav'l Bake attracted a lot of

attention, including a story in *The Wall Street Journal,* but was short lived.

McGlynn's other innovations were much more successful—the first use by a commercial baker of vitamin-enriched unbleached flour, the first gluten bread for diabetics, and even the first weight-reducing formula to be approved by the American Medical Association. Dietine is still popular today, manufactured by Sandoz Pharmaceutical Corporation.

Burton bought his father's interests in the company in 1956, and two years later sold it to a commercial bakery that catered to the restaurant industry. In 1962 the Applebaums' supermarket chain asked McGlynn if he would lease space in a new type of supermarket/discount store complex that Applebaums was setting up with the Dayton Company's new Target chain of discount stores. One of the nation's first bakeries to operate as a department in supermarkets and department stores, McGlynn's growth was rapid. Michael McGlynn joined the company right out of college in 1972, later to become president. McGlynn opened a 12,000-square-foot central bakery to help keep up with the demand, and the innovative, fast-growing McGlynn Bakeries, Inc., of today was born.

In the early 1980s Applebaums' corporate parent, G. Weston, Ltd., of Canada, asked the company to develop a French-style bakery/café for the new super-size grocery stores it planned. The café concept eventually failed, but the bakeries, called A Taste of France and supervised by Dan McGlynn, were a huge success. The popularity of croissants led McGlynn to buy three large European croissant-making machines. A Taste of France branched out into a full line of breads, pastries, and frozen dough products, growing from nothing in 1982 to $40 million in 1986. The 3 million croissants McGlynn makes each week are shipped to all 50 states and some foreign countries.

Today McGlynn operates in-store bakeries and bakery departments in more than 100 stores. Its work force has grown to exceed 900. The strong vo-tech system in the Twin Cities area has helped ensure a supply of talented bakers, and the firm's tradition of paying its employees at the top of the scale has kept turnover low. James T. McGlynn's spirit of innovation has helped McGlynn Bakeries, Inc., become one of the fastest growing major baking companies in the nation.

McGlynn Bakeries became one of the first in the nation to operate as departments in supermarkets and department stores.

ST. JOSEPH'S MEDICAL CENTER

The Benedictine Health System's St. Joseph's Medical Center in Brainerd uses the acronym QUEST to describe the values that form the foundation of its mission: the Quality of a big-city medical center in this small, central Minnesota resort community; Unity of purpose; the Empathy, or loving quality of concern, the staff brings to patient care; St. Joseph's commitment to Christian Service; and the long Tradition of the Sisters of the Order of St. Benedict of caring for the sick.

St. Joseph's has become one of the most important Minnesota medical centers outside of the Twin Cities area. As a regional medical care facility, St. Joseph's offers a full range of medical services—from home health care to the latest inpatient medical technology—that residents of central and north-central Minnesota might otherwise have to travel long distances to receive. Meeting the needs of its patient population, which includes both seasonal and year-round residents, many of them elderly, poses special challenges. St. Joseph's has been successfully meeting those challenges.

St. Joseph's quest began in 1897, when the Sisters of St. Benedict took over management of a hospital that had been started many years earlier by a central Minnesota medical pioneer, Dr. James Leaworthy Camp. Dr. Camp had opened his first Brainerd hospital in a renovated boardinghouse. Its 15 beds primarily served accident victims of the booming northern Minnesota logging industry. After several moves, the Lumberman's Hospital Association settled on St. Joseph's present location. There the Sisters of St. Benedict became instrumental in caring for a growing number of patients. In 1901 the religious community bought the hospital building from Dr. Camp and Dr. J.A. Thabes, Sr. The two physicians stayed on to form the nucleus of the hospital's medical staff. Eventually St. Joseph's became part of the Benedictine Health System, a holding company established by the Duluth Benedictine Sisters to support several Benedictine medical institutions in northern Minnesota.

As a Benedictine institution, St. Joseph's grew to become one of the area's largest and most important health care facilities. A two-story addition built in 1902 served as the main hospital building until 1953, when a new hospital was built just south of the original building. St. Joseph's

opened a $10-million addition in 1984 and remodeled the 1953 structure.

The hospital made a strong effort during the 1970s to attract new physicians to the area and increase the number of medical specialties it offered. To meet its commitment to being a regional medical center, St. Joseph's began developing programs seldom found in rural areas. Today St. Joseph's offers care in 18 medical and dental specialties, one of the largest home health care programs outside the Twin Cities, outpatient surgery and physical therapy, a full range of mental health services, and cutting-edge medical technology that includes a CT scanner.

St. Joseph's also maintains a tradition of being strongly ecumenical. Joint

St. Joseph's Hospital as it looked when completed in 1902. This facility served as the main hospital building until 1953.

ventures have been established with groups such as Lutheran Social Services and the Brainerd Medical Center. St. Joseph's also operates a reference laboratory widely used by many central and northern Minnesota hospitals and clinics. Throughout its history St. Joseph's Medical Center has drawn on the strength and determination of its entire community to meet its long-standing quest.

St. Joseph's Medical Center today, a regional medical center that serves the residents of central and north-central Minnesota.

SCHERER BROTHERS LUMBER COMPANY

When the Minnesota logging industry was at its peak during the years between the 1870s and World War I, the Mississippi River was a primary waterway for hundreds of millions of trees. Great rafts of logs, some carrying in excess of 20 million feet of lumber, were floated down the Mississippi to Minneapolis, just north of downtown, where lumberjacks would sort out these log rafts into the chutes of their proper owners.

But much of the lumber never got that far. Log jams, which were frequent, often drove lumber down into the soft sand of the river bottom. There the lumber rested, millions of board feet of it, often for decades, until it was retrieved by deadheaders like Clarence and Munn Scherer. Deadhead lumber referred to these forgotten logs embedded in the river bottom long after the Minnesota timber boom had ended.

Deadheaders like the Scherer brothers used flat-bottom scows and long poles with sharp metal ends to pry the lumber out of the river's soft embrace; the wood's natural buoyancy, even after years of being submerged, usually caused the logs to rise to the surface. The logs were

The first permanent office building of Scherer Brothers Lumber was here in northeast Minneapolis in the early 1940s.

no longer prime lumber, but they were good enough for framing and sheathing lumber. The slabs of bark were sold as firewood. The sawdust was used for insulation in the great block-ice houses.

When the Scherer brothers began their careers as deadheaders, the Depression was raging and, faced with few other opportunities, deadhead lumber was a source of income. Scherer Brothers Lumber Company still occupies the land where Clarence and Munn began their deadhead lumber business, only now the brothers are Clarence's sons Roger and Gary and Munn's sons Michael and Gregory.

The original lumberyard has ex-

panded to 13 acres, with 250,000 square feet of buildings, and while the business is still lumber (no longer of the deadhead variety), Scherer Brothers also sells all sorts of materials to building contractors as well.

One of the leading Twin Cities manufacturers and distributors of building supplies, the firm has more than 300 employees and recent sales of nearly $85 million. Clarence and Munn's business has come a long way from poking in the mud of the Mississippi River for deadhead lumber.

Scherer Brothers really got its start when Clarence and Munn, who were originally farmers in western Hennepin County, bought a half-interest in a deadhead lumber business in Minneapolis in 1929 for $240. Within a few weeks the brothers decided to give up farming and bought out the yard entirely for not much more. For several years the brothers eked out a marginally profitable business.

Then, in 1933, when the brothers were experiencing especially trying times, a builder/contractor pulled into the Scherer Brothers lumberyard and bought out the entire inventory of deadhead lumber to help shore up the foundation of the new First National Bank tower in St. Paul, which was being built on ground overlooking the Mississippi that turned out to be much softer than expected. That transaction provided a much-needed shot in the arm, and soon the company moved to a new location on the banks of the Mississippi River near the historic Grain Belt Brewery.

The brothers' philosophy was simple: Do as well as the past year, with a little left over for needed improvements. One improvement was an investment in a

Munn and Clarence Scherer were prospering young mill owners when this picture was taken in 1940. The brothers started in the business by selling deadhead lumber, lumber that had been recovered from the bottom of the Mississippi River.

saw to remanufacture odd sizes of lumber. That allowed the firm to prosper during World War II, when Twin Cities defense contractors needed a large variety of custom-sawed pieces of lumber, and the company could sell every piece of lumber it could get its hands on (which, during years when lumber was being rationed, required all of Clarence's skills of persuasion). When Munn returned from the war, he found a business that had nearly 30 employees and was no longer selling deadhead lumber.

After the war Scherer Brothers' growth was fueled by the boom in home construction. The company developed a reputation for being especially sensitive to the needs of small contractors. Clarence and Munn did not want to become overdependent on a few big housing tract builders. They extended both credit and friendship to a growing number of small contractors who specialized in custombuilt, higher-quality homes. This tradition, even after Scherer Brothers began to become a major company, continued and has helped cement its reputation as a quality building supply manufacturer and distributor.

The firm also began manufacturing the finished mill work that many of its customers needed. Today, under the name Pinecraft Windows, Scherer Brothers manufactures many of the windows in new home construction and renovation in the Twin Cities.

During the 1950s and 1960s Scherer Brothers continued to do "as well as last year," plus quite a bit more. Sales topped $3 million annually by 1960, and the company continued to expand its Minneapolis

John Reiser, a young sawyer of the 1980s, inspects the square of a carriage and saw. This is the same rig used in the start of the company in 1930.

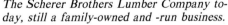

lumberyard. When Clarence Scherer died in a tragic automobile accident in 1974, the firm's sales had reached $12 million. When Munn retired in 1979, sales were closer to $25 million.

By then a second generation of Scherers had begun working for the company. Today Roger Scherer is president; Mike Scherer is vice-president/operations; Gary Scherer is vice-president/finance; and Gregory Scherer is vice-president/personnel and marketing.

The sprawling Scherer Brothers complex includes milling and woodcrafting shops where Pinecraft products are made, drafting studios, a display room, a retail hardware store, and, of course, one of the region's largest inventories of lumber. The staff includes a full-time sales contracting staff of 20; a seven-man city desk, one of the largest in the industry; six full-time estimators; and dozens of skilled craftsmen. Scherer Brothers also owns Truss Manufacturing Company in Albertville, Minnesota, which was created in 1976 to satisfy Scherer Brothers' growing demand for wood trusses for roofs, and the Medbery Yard in New Brighton, Minnesota, which was purchased in 1985 and currently has sales of $12 million to $15 million per year.

Clarence and Munn Scherer had a reputation for keeping the business simple. Today some of the same simplicity remains. Even though Scherer Brothers Lumber Company has become a major business, it still caters to the same quality-oriented small contractor Clarence and Munn knew so well. And it's still very much one of Minnesota's most successful family businesses.

The Scherer Brothers Lumber Company today, still a family-owned and -run business.

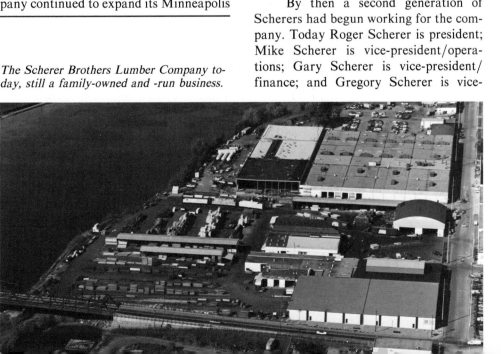

OTTER TAIL POWER COMPANY

Otter Tail Power Company, headquartered in Fergus Falls, Minnesota, serves northwestern Minnesota, eastern North Dakota, and northeastern South Dakota. Included is some of the richest farmland in America, as well as rolling western rangeland; hundreds of clear, cool lakes; and vast pine forests. Its diverse customer base includes homes, farms, commerce, and industry—in all, a population of a quarter-million people living on 50,000 square miles.

It has 800 employees, and its 15,300 stockholders live in all 50 states and many foreign countries. The company has grown significantly, with revenues rising from $80 million in 1977 to more than twice that a decade later. At the same time it has emerged as a national leader in productivity growth according to studies by the National Association of Regulatory Utility Commissioners (NARUC).

The company served its first customers in 1909 with electricity from Dayton Hollow Dam on the Otter Tail River. More dams were built to take advantage of the river's 300-foot drop across Otter Tail County. In an entrepreneurial frenzy, high-line was built, and Otter Tail hooked up town after town. By 1919, 44 towns were being served; 10 years later the count was 314. Most towns already had electricity, but Otter Tail's hydroelectricity was less expensive and offered 24-hour service. "Towns clamored to get on the Otter Tail," according to Thomas Wright, son of Vernon A. Wright, who was one of the company's founders and the first president.

Thomas followed as president and then Vernon's youngest son, Cyrus. In 1961 Albert Hartl became president, the first appointment of someone outside the Wright family to head the company.

As proud as Otter Tail is of its heritage, it's even prouder of the people it serves. Like the company, they are pure Americana, living in small towns—Fergus Falls, the largest town it serves in Minnesota, is barely 12,000—with early American values. Like the land, they are strong, resourceful, and genuine. By tradition, Otter Tail managers think like customers and act accordingly. In the 1930s Vernon Wright cut rates—as well as his own dividends. The NARUC data also shows that of the 113 largest investor-owned electric utilities in the nation, Otter Tail ranks at or near the top in rate

John MacFarlane, president of Otter Tail Power Company

stability.

When the company's 75th anniversary rolled around in 1984 the company wanted to thank its customers as one would a revered friend and neighbor. A famous entertainer was hired to conduct a series of free concerts and social events in 14 division headquarter towns. About a fourth of Otter Tail's customers accepted the invitation, a phenomenal turnout for so large a company. Their thank-you notes filled three scrapbooks.

Otter Tail serves a quarter-million people in an area the size of Wisconsin.

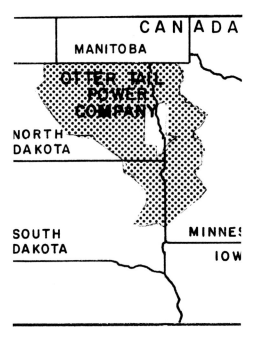

President John MacFarlane and board chairman Robert M. Bigwood are in charge now, and they're keeping Otter Tail personal and caring. In electric service that means keeping electricity prices, reliability, and safety comparable to anywhere in the nation. This is accomplished through modern equipment, skilled employees, joint ownership of lignite-fired steam plants and transmission lines, interconnections between electric systems, power pooling, sale of surplus capacity, and least-cost purchases.

In outstate Minnesota, caring also means leadership in community service and in community development. All Otter Tail employees are encouraged to work toward community goals, and they have a commendable record. At the corporate level, area development specialists have been on the payroll for several decades. More recently Otter Tail has signed a contract with an industrial development consulting firm that will assist local leadership.

An uncommon entrepreneurial spirit created Otter Tail Power Company and caused it to grow. It is that entrepreneurial spirit, propelled by the momentum of more than three-quarters of a century, that will lead Otter Tail into the future.

ALAMCO WOOD PRODUCTS, INC.

When the Weyerhaeuser Corporation, the giant Washington-based wood products company, decided to divest itself of many of its wood-processing operations in the early 1980s, there were inevitable casualties, including the firm's Albert Lea, Minnesota, plant. The plant made glued laminated structural timber, often referred to as glulam. While profitable, the plant no longer fit Weyerhaeuser's strategic focus. With reluctance, Weyerhaeuser decided to shut the plant down, and in August 1982 the 60 workers lost their jobs.

There the story would have ended if not for the courage and tenacity of 10 former plant employees. The employees, led by Russell Wulff, had spent most of their adult lives in the business, with more than 250 collective years of experience in laminated wood products. They were not about to let the business die. With the assistance of the Small Business Administration, State of Minnesota economic development programs, and local lending institutions, the group came up with a plan to purchase the plant from Weyerhaeuser and reopen it in 1983 as Alamco Wood Products, Inc. Today the business has re-

turned to its former levels of production. It is one of the most unusual success stories of its kind in recent Minnesota history.

The plant that was reborn as Alamco has a long and interesting history. Before it was purchased by Weyerhaeuser in 1960, the plant was owned and operated by Rilco Laminated Products, Inc., which was incorporated in Minnesota in 1939. Initially Rilco's products were used for farm building construction. The process of laminating wood involves taking individual boards and putting them together with moisture-resistant adhesives, creating the beam, arch, or other product being manufactured. In a sense it's "a sawmill run backward." Because glulam utilizes all the advantageous properties of wood while liberating wood from the limitations of size, shape, and natural defects, Rilco's products soon found uses in many types of construction, including churches, schools, shopping centers, homes, electrical power distribution, noise walls, and

Alamco revitalized Weyerhaeuser's laminated wood products plant in Albert Lea.

bridges. In 1954 the present 134,000-square-foot facility in Albert Lea was built.

Alamco Wood Products, Inc., was incorporated in Minnesota in September 1982, shortly after the announced closing of the facility by Weyerhaeuser Company. By the end of the year negotiations with Weyerhaeuser and all the financing arrangements had been completed, and Alamco was ready to begin operating. The initial work force consisted of the new owners themselves, who often had to double up on duties, including staffing both the front office and the sprawling production facility behind it. Within a year Alamco's work force had grown to 40, then to 60 the following year, and finally to 75 today. Revenues recently topped $6 million. Local ownership revitalized the operation, and today Alamco is a midwestern leader in laminated wood products with customers nationwide. Much has changed since the Weyerhaeuser days, but today Alamco Wood Products, Inc., carries on the Rilco and Weyerhaeuser tradition of quality and customer service. That means jobs for Albert Lea and a positive influence on the city's economy.

FARIBAULT WOOLEN MILL CO.

A century ago nearly every midwestern town of any size had its own woolen mill. There were dozens of mills scattered throughout Minnesota, using the wool of sheep raised in their surrounding areas to make everything from flannel under-clothes to Army blankets. Many of the flocks of sheep are gone, and most of the mills have disappeared as well, victims of changing times and competition from the huge weaving mills of the East Coast and the South, where transportation was bet-ter and labor costs cheaper.

Faribault Woolen Mill, a 123-year-old Faribault institution, is perhaps the Midwest's most famous and successful survivor. Faribault's products—nearly all of which are wool blankets, lap robes, and close variations—are known throughout the world, from the high-fashion confines of Bloomingdales in New York City to the pages of the L.L. Bean catalog. Faribault succeeded by finding a small but profit-able niche that larger mills were overlook-ing—the market for premium-quality wool blankets—and applying a liberal dose of creative marketing. The result is one of Minnesota's oldest and most inno-vative family-run businesses.

The Klemer family has run the com-pany since its beginnings. Carl Henry Klemer was a German-born cabinet-maker who moved to Minnesota in 1857. Eight years later he purchased a wool carding machine and began carding wool from the flocks of sheep that were then abundant around the Faribault area. Klemer was soon carding 12,000 pounds of wool a year, and by 1877 the new Fari-bault Woolen Mill Company had four looms and was among dozens in Minne-sota that were making cloth, flannel, and blankets.

Klemer's company grew slowly, helped along by his sons Henry and Ferdinand. Frank Klemer, Henry's son and one of five Klemers to serve as presi-dent, reported many years later that the mill's early decades were characterized by "plodding along slowly, feeling our way, letting others experiment with new ideas before they were adapted by us." Such caution kept Faribault in business as the industry changed in ways that were not beneficial to small mills like Faribault.

Those changes were to prompt Fari-bault to focus on a strategy that first con-tributed to its survival, and later to its strong growth from the 1960s on. Under Walter Klemer, Ferdinand's son, and Edward Johnson, the first of several gen-erations of Johnsons to work for the com-pany, Faribault decided to specialize in high-quality wool blankets and forsake the cheap synthetic materials and mass production that transformed the textile in-dustry in the decades before and after World War II.

In 1965 the town of Faribault mounted a citywide celebration to toast the 100th anniversary of its oldest contin-uous employer. Today Faribo Blankets, the company's trade name, are sold by most of the nation's top department stores, by high-quality direct-mail companies, and as promotional premiums and spe-cialty advertising products. Faribault also operates two successful retail stores; one is located right down the road from the mill and has become something of a tour-ist attraction.

More than 1.5 million pounds of wool per year are woven into premium blankets at Faribault Woolen Mill Co. The 170-person work force represents more than a century of labor peace. Cur-rent president Richard Klemer is the fifth Klemer to fill that role. The mill in Fari-bault is truly a Minnesota institution.

An early photograph taken about 1895 shows mill workers standing outside the original Faribault Woolen Mill.

LAKE CENTER INDUSTRIES

C.W. Whittaker brought Lake Center Industries to its current home of Winona in 1948. His interest in the company stemmed from its contract with the Chrysler Corporation to supply the automaker with half of all its foot dimmer switches for headlights on new cars. In 1951 Whittaker sold the firm, then Lake Center Switch Company, to James Henderson and Andrew Charles, who moved Lake Center into new quarters. That year the business employed 10 people, who operated out of 8,000 square feet of space, manufacturing just one product, for a total of $300,000 in sales.

In 1955 the Guy F. Atkinson Company, a San Francisco-based multinational construction firm, became a general partner in Lake Center Industries. In 1983 Atkinson purchased the company outright; Lake Center is now a division of Atkinson.

During the 1950s and 1960s Lake Center operated as a designer and manufacturer of parts for the auto industry. Its list of products increased year by year: clips for chrome moldings, interior lamp assemblies, and heater switches. By 1973 the firm had sales of $31 million and a work force of 1,300, making it the largest employer in Winona.

During the 1970s the market for consumer counter-top appliances mushroomed. Lake Center Industries entered that market in 1973, when one of its engineers created a model for an electric coffee maker, which the company sold to Norelco.

Lake Center was just as successful in this endeavor. Soon it was designing and manufacturing parts for corporations such as Norelco, Whirlpool, and Clairol. Lake Center designed, developed, and produced Norelco coffee makers, hamburger cookers, Clairol makeup mirrors, and sunlamps, as well as parts for major appliances manufactured by Whirlpool. By 1976 employment peaked at 1,930, and revenues exceeded $64 million per year.

But then the bottom fell out of the counter-top appliance market. Norelco built its own parts plant and took its business away from Lake Center Industries. The company's fortunes plummeted. By 1983 revenues fell to 1973 totals, and employment fell to a little more than 800.

The firm redirected its attention and research energy back toward the auto-

David Keller, president of Lake Center Industries, has helped steer the company to a new area of growth.

motive market. But with gas prices soaring and recession settling in, the 1981 car industry was also slumping, and Lake Center had to expand its range of parts. In short order its engineers designed new kinds of washer/wiper switches, temperature-control systems, headlamp switches, and turn signal assemblies for domestic automobiles. Its parts are used on products for Chrysler, Ford, and General Motors.

The company continued to develop its trade in parts for major appliances. Electronic and electromechanical parts from Lake Center are used in the manufacture of business machines, computers, and Sears and Whirlpool refrigerators. Lake Center does not simply make parts; as a full-service contract manufacturer, it also designs, tests, packages, and transports products.

Today 90 percent of Lake Center's revenue derives from the automotive market. Sales have rebounded up to more than $80 million in 1986. The firm operates seven plants in locations throughout southern Minnesota and southwestern Wisconsin and employs some 1,800 people.

Lake Center Industries stresses its philosophy of working with customers to assure that all parts meet performance and quality standards.

Products manufactured by Lake Center Industries: top left, electronic climate-control system; top right, electronic refrigerator-control module; center, custom switches; bottom left, smoke detector; and bottom right, electric motor actuator assemblies.

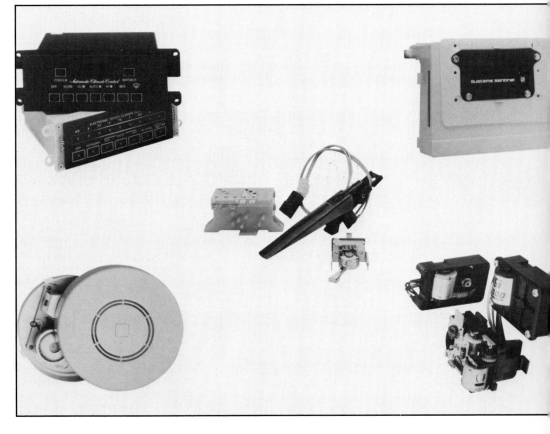

MAYO CLINIC

When the Civil War broke out, William Worrall Mayo, an English-born country doctor from Le Sueur, found himself the examining surgeon for the First Enrollment District of southeast Minnesota, which was headquartered in a little town called Rochester. After the war Mayo stayed in Rochester and began developing a prosperous practice.

W.W. Mayo had an extraordinary desire to serve. He was president of the state medical society, served in state government, and was mayor of Rochester. An ardent defender of the underprivileged, he passed this commitment to serve on to his two sons, William and Charles, who very early in life knew they wanted to be doctors. William received his medical degree in 1883 and returned to Rochester to join his father's practice. Charles did the same five years later. This closely knit family "group" practice marked the genesis of Mayo Clinic, today the most widely known and respected medical institution in the United States and, quite possibly, the world.

W.W. Mayo began to involve himself more in public service activities. The practice grew quickly as Charles' and William's reputations as surgeons spread. The Mayos began a close relationship with Saint Marys Hospital, which opened in 1889 with a total of 27 beds. As their fame spread, their family practice outgrew the family.

The Mayos invited other physicians to join the practice and started the first private group practice of medicine in the world. The first was A.W. Stinchfield from nearby Eyota. In 1895 Christopher Graham joined. Melvin C. Miller, Henry S. Plummer, Edward Starr Judd, and Donald C. Balfour completed the original partners. Each man had different areas of specialization, and they worked closely together to complement the patient care each could offer.

An increasing number of physicians began visiting the operating rooms at Saint Marys Hospital to watch the proceedings and listen to the Mayo brothers. By 1907 the term "Mayo Clinic" was commonly used. That year 5,000 patients would register to see Mayo doctors.

In 1914 the first building ever designed for a group medical practice was completed and officially called the Mayo Clinic. That same year the partners saw 30,000 patients. In 1919 the Mayo

Dr. William Worrall Mayo (center) and his two sons, Dr. Charles H. Mayo (left) and Dr. William J. Mayo (right), practiced medicine with a commitment to the underprivileged. Their family practice evolved into what is today the internationally known Mayo Clinic.

brothers deeded all assets of Mayo Clinic to a charitable organization they created. In 1923 the partnership organization was replaced by a voluntary physicians' association administered by a board of governors. All proprietary interests ended, and the entire staff became salaried.

Mayo Medical Center, the world's largest private medical center, currently employs more than 14,200 people in

The Mayo Clinic complex in downtown Rochester.

Rochester, at Mayo Clinic, Saint Marys Hospital, and Rochester Methodist Hostal. All are governed by the Mayo Foundation. Mayo educational and research programs are among the most productive and renowned in the world.

In recent years Mayo has introduced its approach to health care to other parts of the country. Mayo Clinic Scottsdale (Arizona) and Mayo Clinic Jacksonville (Florida) are linked by a unique satellite telecommunications system to the Rochester clinic, which is currently undergoing its greatest building construction program ever. Close to one billion dollars is being spent on new facilities. Mayo Clinic, whose team of doctors and scientists now numbers more than 900, has clearly positioned itself on the cutting edge of health care while maintaining the simple and noble traditions of the Mayo brothers.

METHODIST HOSPITAL

Methodist Hospital will celebrate its 100th year of health care in 1992 as a leader in combining quality and cost-effective care. The hospital spent its first 67 years in downtown Minneapolis until its move in 1959 to its current site in St. Louis Park.

The hospital began when a prominent Methodist churchwoman convinced Sarah Harrison Knight, a wealthy Minneapolis widow, to endow a facility to care for the sick poor of the area. Mrs. Knight gave freely of her time and money, and the result was the 1892 opening of the 34-bed Asbury Hospital on the corner of Ninth Street and Elliot Avenue in Minneapolis.

The new hospital was filled to capacity almost from the beginning, and planning soon began for a larger facility. Over the next 20 years expansions brought the number of beds at Asbury to more than 250. During that same period construction was begun on a separate facility to house and train nurses.

Asbury's finances in those days were always precarious, and in 1921 Mrs. Knight agreed to lease the hospital to the Veterans Administration. When the lease ended, rather than move back to its original building, Asbury remained in its "temporary" headquarters. A new facility was clearly needed, but the Depression and World War II made raising the capital an almost impossible task.

In the 1950s, after years of planning for a new hospital, the board of the then-Asbury-Methodist Hospital made a bold decision: to locate a new hospital in the western suburbs, where there were large numbers of people in need of health care, but no nearby hospitals to serve them.

Methodist Hospital today has 2,000 employees and more than 700 physicians on its medical staff, who practice in nearly 60 specialties and subspecialties. In addition to its 45-acre St. Louis Park facility, Methodist operates a clinic in Eden Prairie and rehabilitation centers in several western suburbs, including Hopkins and Golden Valley.

The hospital affiliated in 1988 with the LifeSpan organization, which is the parent corporation for Abbott-Northwestern Hospital and Children's Hospital in Minneapolis. This allows Methodist to continue its leadership position in serving the southern and western suburbs of Minneapolis.

The institution's list of achieve-

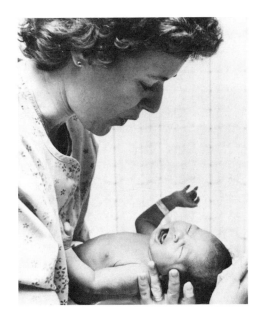

A Methodist Hospital nurse cares for a baby born at Methodist Hospital. There were 3,213 babies born at Methodist in 1987 and the hospital has ranked as the second-largest birthing center in Minnesota since 1984.

ments and noteworthy programs is lengthy. Methodist was the first community hospital in the Twin Cities to receive accreditation as a Comprehensive Cancer Care Center by the American College of Surgeons and now has the second most active cancer program in the Twin Cities area. In 1984 its hospice program was the first in Minnesota and the third in the country to be accredited by the Joint Commission on Health Care Organizations. Methodist also developed one of the

nation's first computerized tumor registries. And the hospital's participation in the National Cancer Institute's clinical research studies ensures that its patients receive the most current treatments available.

The institution also was an early pioneer in same-day surgery, services to senior citizens, and comprehensive rehabilitation programs. Methodist's Senior Connection provides referrals ranging from housing to health care and nursing visits.

The hospital also offers a full range of cardiac care, including laser-enhanced angioplasty and open heart surgery. Methodist's 24-hour emergency department is one of the busiest and most comprehensive in the area. In addition, the hospital serves the five-state region as an information and referral center for the American Parkinson Disease Association.

Methodist Hospital enters the 1990s with the same concern for quality and accessibility that has characterized its first 100 years. What ties it all together is a philosophy about caring for people that has stood the test of time and has created one of Minnesota's premier medical institutions.

Methodist Hospital's modern campus is located in the heart of the Twin Cities' western suburbs, just 15 minutes from downtown Minneapolis (in the background, upper right).

MICO, INC.

MICO, Inc., of Mankato is a composite of two companies that merged after World War II.

The original MICO was a Mankato-based manufacturer of machined parts, many of which had been used by the military during the war. In the immediate postwar years the company acquired the patent rights to a product that would forever determine the shape of its business—the two-stage power brake cylinder.

The production of automobiles for civilian use had been suspended during World War II, and the postwar period brought a natural explosion of pent-up de-

mand. Not only did consumers want new cars, they wanted new cars with new-fangled accessories like power brakes. The demand for MICO's product was, understandably, very high among automakers.

Meanwhile, the A.T. Hansord Company of Minneapolis, which, among other

---

MICO, Inc., is located in North Mankato, Minnesota, approximately 80 miles southwest of the Minneapolis-St. Paul area. The increased demand for quality MICO products has dictated the need for several expansions since MICO's founding in 1946.

things, operated car dealerships, formed a new organization called Minnesota Automotive Inc. It was in the business of selling and distributing automotive products, including the MICO power brake cylinder. In early 1947, a little more than a year after it was formed, Minnesota Automotive acquired all of MICO's stock. Two years later the two companies were merged. Minnesota Automotive continued as the corporate name, with MICO as the brand name—a situation that prevailed until 1982, when the company name was changed to MICO. At the time of the merger, MICO had a product line

of nine different items, 45 full-time employees, and annual sales of approximately $300,000.

After his discharge from the Navy, G.J. "Mac" McGrath went to work for National Starch, moving on from there to a position as sales manager for Minnesota Automotive. After A.T. Hansord's death, McGrath and a partner, Sonny Wischnik, purchased Minnesota Automotive from the Hansord estate. In 1962 McGrath bought out Wischnik and a subsequent partner; today MICO is a closely held corporation headed by McGrath. Several of his sons are active in senior management.

As American industry grew in the past 40 years, so did demand for MICO products. From automotive products the firm branched out into the material-handling and construction equipment industries, developing brake systems for a wide variety of vehicles and equipment.

Its power brake cylinder was the mainstay product of the company until the acquisition of patent rights on the brake lock, a one-way check valve that utilizes service brake systems to provide a dependable supplemental parking brake for heavy vehicles.

In subsequent years the organization added the MICO portable liquid transfer pump, caliper disk brakes, multiple disk brakes, air/hydraulic actuators, quadrigages, new variations on the brake lock, pressure intensifiers, brake actuators and valves, and many other hydraulic brake components. One of its newest growth areas is in the sale of full power

brake systems for off-road construction equipment. The power brakes in passenger cars and most trucks utilize a "power assist" system. Full power systems use an all-hydraulic system capable of braking 300-ton construction vehicles with no more effort than it takes to stop a subcompact. Because so much of MICO's production is custom built, there is no way to determine the market share of its more than 2,000 products. But in certain product lines, such as brake locks (which account for 25 percent of the company's overall sales), MICO is the sole supplier in the United States, and enjoys a 20-percent share of the caliper brake market for off-road vehicles. Among its customers are Clark Equipment Corporation, Bendix, John Deere, Allis Chalmers, General Dynamics, FMC, Caterpillar Tractor Company, and many more. The firm has approximately 700 OEM customers, 700 transfer pump accounts, and 1,300 jobbers and distributors serving the auto aftermarket. MICO products are distributed worldwide.

Over the years MICO has been headquartered in three different locations, all in the Mankato area. The

---

MICO West was organized in 1965 in the Los Angeles, California, area to serve as a manufacturing and assembly operation to cover the western states. MICO West has just recently moved into a new facility in Ontario, California.

company began life in an old street barn on Front Street in Mankato. Expansion prompted a move to a Patterson Avenue facility in 1963. When that headquarters was flooded out two years later, the firm looked for a site on high ground. It found just that at its present headquarters in North Mankato, occupied by the company since 1974. In 1965 MICO also organized Almico, Inc., located in Los Angeles, to serve as an assembly and manufacturing operation for the western states. In 1979 the name was changed to MICO West. MICO West is now a divisional operation of MICO and is headed by Mark McGrath. His brothers, Brent and Dan McGrath, serve as secretary/treasurer and vice-president, respectively.

As a completely integrated manufacturing and sales company, MICO controls all elements of its production process, from raw materials to finished products. It is still a leader in the design and manufacture of hydraulic brake systems, cylinders, actuators, and locks for numerous industries, including mining, forestry, airport ground support, agriculture, construction, transportation and utilities, material handling, oil and gas, and more.

To maintain that leadership position, MICO, Inc., uses sophisticated computer-aided design. Its CAD systems mean that MICO engineers in Mankato and California can offer customers prompt response to their product needs. The company has historically enjoyed a 10-percent growth rate. Sales in 1988 are expected to exceed $20 million.

VARITRONIC SYSTEMS, INC.

The success of a start-up company depends upon a number of factors, including a marketable product, entrepreneurial skill, and the availability of venture capital. The brief but so far successful history of Varitronic Systems, Inc., is a case in point—and a textbook illustration of why Minnesota is such a hospitable place for start-ups.

Headquartered in Minneapolis, Varitronics produces electronic lettering systems that enhance the quality, professionalism, and effectiveness of business communications. Their broad marketplace includes professionals in a variety of disciplines from architecture and engineering to sales, marketing, and office administration to medical services and real estate. It was founded in February 1983 by Scott Drill and G.L. Hoffman. Two years earlier Drill had left his position as director of international sales for Kroy, Inc., the Minnesota company (now located in Arizona) that pioneered lettering machines, and went to work for the Conklin Company, a local chemical products firm, where he met Hoffman. Management problems at Kroy, coupled with dealer dissatisfaction with corporate policies, led the two men to conclude that the market was ripe for a Kroy competitor and Varitronics was founded.

The first step was to design a product, and they hired a California consultant to organize a design competition. The winning prototype was the work of the father/

Varitronics' first product, the Merlin® lettering system and its lettering discs (left), and the Merlin Express®, introduced in December 1986, and its font cards. Both products generate type on adhesive-backed tape up to one-half inch high.

son team of Tom and Larry McGourty of Paso Robles, California. The machine they designed was faster than the then-current Kroy lettering product, and would cost less to produce and sell.

But even though they were design rich, Drill and Hoffman were capital poor. They pitched in $18,000 of their own money on the project, and raised an additional $100,000 from relatives and friends. But if they were to succeed, they needed a cash infusion from outside sources.

Varitronic Systems' co-founders are (from left) Scott Drill, president and chief executive officer, and G.L. Hoffman, chairman.

Capitalization for the venture got a big boost in the fall of 1983 when Varitronic Systems signed a contract with Gestetner International, a giant British office supply firm. In exchange for guaranteed sales of 9,000 units per year, Gestetner, which had been a private-label distributor for Kroy, got exclusive rights for foreign private-label distribution of the new line of lettering machines.

Production delays caused the contract, with an estimated annual value of $6 million, to be rescinded. But at the time it made it possible for Drill and Hoffman to approach venture capitalists with a fair degree of success.

And succeed they did. In 1983 the pair raised $1.2 million in venture capital. A private offering early the following year brought in another $1.4 million. In September 1984 Varitronics obtained yet another $2.5 million in backing. Most of the money came from Minnesota investors.

Varitronics premiered its first lettering system in April 1984. The Merlin® produces high-quality lettering on an adhesive strip. Weighing less than 30 pounds, it offers eight different type sizes up to one-half inch high and more than 30 different type faces—which can be changed by replacing a disc approximately the size of a 45-r.p.m. record.

Faster and easier to use than competitive products, the Merlin was shipped in quantity in December 1984. Varitronics realized nearly $8 million in sales the following year.

Varitronics always envisioned its initial product as the beginning of a family of lettering machines and accessories. The Merlin was quickly followed by the Merlin Jr, a smaller, less expensive version of the Merlin. Varitronics' Merlin PCI allows users to interface the Merlin with IBM or IBM-compatible personal computers.

Its biggest success to date has been with the Merlin Express®, introduced in December 1986. This high-speed, compact lettering machine weighs only 10 pounds and has optional battery operation. The Merlin Express was the first lettering system available to use thermal transfer imaging technology, a heat process commonly used in facsimile equipment.

Instead of using discs like the Merlin, the Merlin Express has font cards that house a single type style and size, including upper- and lower-case letters, numbers, and symbols. About the size of a 35-millimeter slide, font cards are available in more than 20 type styles from six to 36 point.

The next member of the Merlin Express family was introduced in the spring of 1988. The Merlin Express XT® prints letters up to two inches high on an adhesive strip—a size particularly desirable for a wide range of signage and graphics applications.

Merlin lettering has a diverse range of uses: headlines for presentations, proposals, or newsletters; names for identification badges; titles for overhead transparencies; lettering for charts, graphs, or engineering drawings; as well as numerous labeling projects.

Worldwide the firm estimates that it now has a 75- to 80-percent share of the keyboard lettering market. To service that market Varitronics has developed a multitiered distribution system that includes a network of independent dealers, distribution through other office equipment firms, and private labeling under other company names. Domestically it has a network of more than 200 independent dealers that handle the full line of the firm's products. Varitronics also sells through Harris/3M and Gestetner

Corporation, both leaders in the office equipment supply business. The company has private-label agreements with GBC (General Binding Corporation), which sells Varitronics products through 50 branches, and Chartpak, the leading dry transfer lettering company, which sells Varitronics lettering systems through a network of 60 dealers.

Internationally Varitronics markets its products through 20 key distributors, many of which sell the equipment under their own names. In Europe Varitronics is handled by 3M, Gestetner, SOFT, a French firm, and others. 3M and Gestetner also sell Varitronics equipment in Australia and East Asia.

With the introduction of new products, Varitronics continues to grow vigorously. Sales for 1987 topped $26 million, a 38-percent jump over the year before. In 1988 the company projects another big boost, to $40 million. Its long-range goal, according to Scott Drill and G.L. Hoffman, is to top the $100-million mark by 1992. At the moment Varitronic Systems, Inc., employs 160 full-time and some 60 part-time employees. The company is headquartered in St. Louis Park and recently added a 60,000-square-foot assembly and distribution facility in Brooklyn Park.

Merlin lettering enhances the appearance, professionalism, and effectiveness of business communications from overhead transparencies and meeting materials, to newsletters, name badges, and labeling projects.

Many businesses, such as architectural and engineering companies, have numerous uses for Merlin lettering—proposal covers, engineering drawings, title blocks, file folders, and scheduling boards.

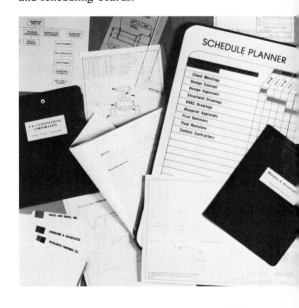

CHANDLER-WILBERT VAULT CO.

Henry F. Chandler was a man of many and diverse interests, and during the years following World War I his occupations ranged from hotel operator to owner of a private detective agency.

In 1922 the "jack-of many-trades" settled upon an unusual and little understood career that would, through the ensuing years, grow into a successful family industry—the concrete burial vault business.

Chandler began his enterprise as The Perfected Burial Vault Co. with the original plant located at 372 Howell Street in St. Paul, Minnesota. Business thrived, and within three years a larger plant facility was established on Selby Avenue in St. Paul. Fifteen years later the present plant was built at the intersection of Highway 36 and Hamline Avenue in Roseville, Minnesota.

Henry Chandler established himself as a hard-driving, autocratic manager who did it "his way" and one who had mastered the art of pinching the proverbial penny. Soon, however, Henry realized he could not operate the business alone, and in 1931 his son Wesley "Bud" Chandler joined the firm to assume the responsibilities for the company's sales, collections, and deliveries.

During the years of World War II Henry Chandler's health began to fail, and in 1945 his son Bud tendered an offer to buy the business. Despite his weakening condition, however, Henry was still the hard-headed, one-man band, and responded to son Bud's offer by Western Union Telegraph. The essence of the telegram was simply, "You're fired, and clear out your desk immediately!"

Time and cooler heads prevailed,

and within weeks Henry Chandler had agreed to sell the firm to Bud for $230,000. Doom merchants predicted that Bud would never be able to pay off the loans, but those were people who knew little or nothing about the man.

Because Bud Chandler possessed the innate gifts of vision, tenacity, and basic business sense, he disproved the predictions of the cynics, and by 1955 the business was his, free and clear. Under Bud Chandler the organization changed its name to Chandler-Wilbert Vault Co.—a name that reflected the firm's agreement to manufacture the Wilbert brand-name burial vault as part of a national franchise structure that today includes more than 300 manufacturers and distributors in the United States and Canada.

As a visionary, Bud Chandler immediately sensed the need to expand Chandler-Wilbert's manufacturing locations in order to increase sales. The weight and bulk of a concrete burial vault, coupled with the critical importance of providing timely delivery and service, makes it extremely difficult to transport the products over long distances. This inspired Chandler to expand his market by opening new plant sites, and in 1945 the growth began with a plant in Mankato, Minnesota.

Today the firm owns 16 manufacturing operations in Minnesota, Wisconsin, and North Dakota, and serves a distributorship in Aberdeen, South Dakota. These widespread operations have enabled Chandler-Wilbert to emerge as the dominant burial vault manufacturer in the markets it serves. Standing as one of the largest Wilbert franchises in the country, the organization's sales have steadily increased through the years to the point

Chandler-Wilbert was originally called the Perfected Burial Vault Company. The name was changed in 1945.

where it now employs nearly 150 people. Also, in recent years the company has expanded into other precast concrete products such as steps, curbing, wall panels, and so on; however, the majority of its revenue is still derived from burial vaults.

During the 30 years that Bud Chandler ran Chandler-Wilbert Vault Co. he transformed it from a seat-of-the-pants operation into a modern, progressive organization. At various times in his career he served as chairman of the Moundsview Town Board, president of the St. Paul Kiwanis Club and St. Paul Jaycee's, and as King Boreas of the St. Paul Winter Carnival.

Upon Bud Chandler's untimely death in 1972, the reins of the company were taken over by his wife, Lucy Chandler Lake and, benefiting from her business acumen and management skills, the company has continued to grow and prosper. Lucy Chandler Lake continues to serve as chairman of the board and chief executive officer.

Henry Chandler ran a number of enterprises, including a hotel, before starting the Chandler-Wilbert Vault Company.

Wesley "Bud" Chandler bought the company from his father in 1945.

Lucy Chandler Lake has run the company since her husband Bud's death.

HUBBARD MILLING COMPANY

In the 1870s southern Minnesota was becoming one of the world's leading producers of spring wheat, a fact that did not escape the attention of George M. Palmer and R.D. Hubbard, two Mankato entrepreneurs. With so much wheat growing around the city, Palmer proposed a new flour mill to Hubbard, and the two men became partners in the Mankato Mill Company (forerunner of the Hubbard Milling Company), which was legally incorporated in 1878 and began processing flour in 1879.

At first the firm used an actual millstone, but soon moved on to newer technology, re-equipping the mill with steel rollers. From the start the operation used a patented purifying device and thus was able to put a high-grade product on the market. The organization's leading retail brand, Mother Hubbard, and its commercial product, Hubbard's Superlative, became known as some of the best flour products for home or bakery use.

In 1928 the company began what would prove to be a long and profitable history of diversification when it embarked on the manufacture of Hubbard's Sunshine All-Purpose Concentrates, nutritionally fortified high-class livestock feed to be used by farmers in conjunction with their homegrown feed.

In 1946 Ogden P. Confer joined the company that had been cofounded by his grandfather, George M. Palmer, nearly 70 years earlier. Twelve years later he became president, and then chairman of the board and chief executive officer.

Under his leadership Hubbard Milling rapidly expanded and diversified its line of products. In 1946 the firm had a single flour mill and two feed-plant operations. Its sales volume that year was $8 million. Today Hubbard is a multistate, diversified, and highly profitable organization with sales of some $250 million per year.

Through acquisitions such as the Feed Division of Archer-Daniels-Midland in 1960, Vigorena Feeds in 1963, and the Tri-State Milling Company in 1970, the company has expanded its animal-feed business. The firm has acquired a dozen feed-milling and grain-handling operations throughout the Midwest. With the 1964 purchase of Altura Rex Turkeys Inc. of Altura, Minnesota, it launched Hubbard Foods Inc. The company has diversified into cattle feeding, leasing,

Ogden P. Confer, Hubbard Milling's chairman of the board, has been with the company since 1946.

printing, insurance, and the restaurant business. With the acquisition of four pet food manufacturing plants in 1986 and 1987, the firm also emerged as the world's largest producer of private-label pet food.

Today Hubbard Milling Company has more than 20 manufacturing and sales facilities throughout the Midwest and employs more than 1,000 people. In 1982 Hubbard Milling constructed a computerized pet food manufacturing facility in LeSueur, Minnesota, one of the most modern in the country. A new animal-feed manufacturing mill, constructed in Mankato in 1985, has received recognition throughout the industry as the most technologically advanced computer-driven manufacturing facility for animal feeds in the United States.

Looking toward the next five years, Hubbard Milling Company has set the most ambitious goals for expansion in its 109-year history. The company will build on its three core businesses—animal feed, turkey production, and pet food—and actively seek growth opportunities in these areas, while not overlooking diversification into new ventures unrelated to that core.

Hubbard Milling was one of the first companies to produce feed supplements. This 1947 display was the firm's introduction of special feed concentrates.

H.B. FULLER COMPANY

H.B. Fuller Company has long been concerned with the right formulas. Formulas for the adhesives and chemicals that have fueled its growth. Formulas for reshaping itself as its markets and world conditions changed. Formulas for tempering ambitious growth objectives with a humane and supportive work environment and a determination to have a positive impact on the communities it serves. Judging by the evidence on the firm's 100th anniversary, those formulas have worked; for example, Fuller broke into the ranks of the *Fortune* 500 and was named one of America's best 100 companies to work for.

Harvey Benjamin Fuller was a self-starting, risk-taking, man with visions of succeeding with new products and inventions. Fuller dreamed of building a company with a new type of glue that would be convenient, economical, and so versatile it could serve homemakers and manufacturers alike. His research and development took place on top of his kitchen stove, where he "cooked" new compounds in search of the right formula. In the meantime he made a living repackaging and selling an existing product, Fuller's Premium Liquid Fish Glue. Fuller's glue proved popular enough to enable him to set up a storefront operation on Franklin Street in Chicago. Fuller became restless. Chicago was already an old and established city. Fuller was betting that the opportunities in the newly established State of Minnesota were greater.

In 1887 Fuller settled in St. Paul and quickly began producing new products for the fast-growing Upper Midwest. He developed a paste made with flour to capitalize on its cheap supply in what was then becoming the flour milling capital of the nation. The product sold well to paperhangers who had been forced to mix their own.

In 1887, with $600 put up by three lawyers, Fuller opened a modest manufacturing plant on Robert Street in St. Paul and incorporated as the Fuller Manufacturing Company. His products consisted of whatever the market seemed to need: ink for city schools, bottled laundry bluing, paste made to order for paperhangers, and adhesives for a growing number of manufacturing customers, including printers, bookbinders, box manufacturers, as well as just ordinary citizens with things to mend or put back together.

By the beginning of the twentieth

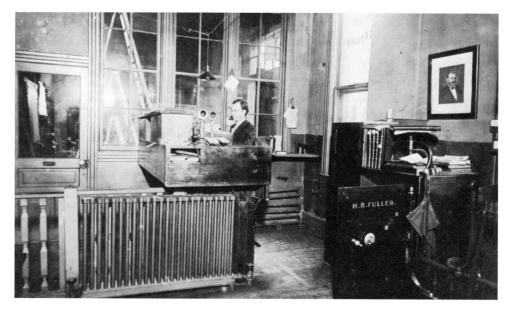

N. Clinton Stork in his office at the H.B. Fuller Company at 186-190 West Third Street. He had two telephones, one for St. Paul and one for Minneapolis. Photo circa 1908

century Fuller reached sales of $10,000 per year on the success of new products such as a dry wall cleaner that could be mixed on the job and thus eliminated the spoilage problem that had plagued previous cleaners, and a dry paste that could be shipped easily to distant customers. Fuller also dabbled in products that had nothing to do with adhesives or cleaners, including an adjustable scaffolding for painters and paperhangers.

This 1908 photo shows an interior view of the H.B. Fuller plant at 186-190 West Third Street and three of its employees (standing, left to right) Clint Stork, Joe Voudell, and Alex Mierva.

As the company grew new employees were added, including Harvey Benjamin Fuller, Jr., whose special interest was advertising and marketing Fuller's growing list of products, and Clint Stork, who soon became a jack-of-all-trades—from bookkeeper to shipping clerk—and a key figure as the company grew in the years ahead. By 1915 the firm announced plans to reincorporate to reflect its new size and its expanded work force. Stock valued at $75,000 was issued. Harvey Sr., Harvey Jr., and Clint Stork were named officers.

During World War I the demand for glue for the canning industry skyrocketed. With the war's end, however, the market slumped and prompted the company to go after bigger and more promising targets, especially the industrial adhesives market. A young chemist named Ray Burgess was hired to create new products for industrial applications. H.B. Fuller, Sr., died, and

Harvey B. Fuller, Jr., became president. In the meantime Ray Burgess, despite primitive lab tools and secondhand equipment, began to develop a long string of new products. Twenty-nine different stock adhesives and dozens of different custom formulas were sold during the 1920s. By 1929, the eve of the Depression, sales would reach an all-time high of $157,000.

H.B. Fuller survived the Depression and even managed modest growth. But the early 1930s were important for another reason—the hiring in 1934 of a young man from Michigan named Elmer Andersen as an advertising and sales promotion specialist. Within three years Andersen became the company's sales manager. Andersen had a different and very ambitious way of looking at things, which would have a profound impact on the firm.

By World War II H.B. Fuller Company had cemented its reputation as a small innovative organization that paid close attention to its customers' needs. Warehouses were established in Utah and Texas to better serve customers in growing western and southern markets. Ray Burgess developed a new type of adhesive for canning labels that solved the handling problems of the unwieldy gum then in use. It soon found a market in all 48 states. Richard E. Smith, another H.B. Fuller chemist, developed an adhesive that kept labels on beer bottles even when they were cooled in ice.

There were setbacks, including the

In 1907 these workers demonstrated the strength of the scaffolding developed and patented by Harvey B. Fuller I, (fifth from left). N. Clinton Stork is fourth from the left.

defection of three key employees that represented the company's entire sales force, and a downturn in the canning industry; but Andersen took over all sales calls, blanketing Fuller territory.

More unsettling was a stroke suffered by H.B. Fuller, Jr., in 1939. In his mid-fifties and ailing, Fuller wanted out. But a meager offer by a rival firm hardly

Fuller delivery trucks circa 1916. N. Clinton Stork is sitting in the Ford that he made collections from; he was also the company's first bookkeeper.

seemed a fitting way to conclude the business his father had started 50 years before. Elmer Andersen made a counter offer.

Andersen decided that Fuller should try to double in size every five years—which required 15-percent annual sales increases. The key to reaching such a figure was decentralizing manufacturing operations. High freight charges made it hard to be price competitive in markets where adhesives were already being manufactured by local companies.

This thinking marked the beginning of a pioneering expansion strategy that would see H.B. Fuller Company open autonomous branch plants in Kansas City, Cincinnati, San Francisco, Chicago, and two other cities during the 1940s. Managers in these cities would be free to operate in their own style, responding to the needs of their markets in a way no centralized manufacturer could. Fuller became the fourth-largest adhesives manufacturer in the country by 1950, with sales of almost $2.5 million.

The company Harvey Fuller started had been extraordinarily good to Andersen, Ray Burgess, Clint Stork, and others. It had allowed them to explore the limits of their potential. Fuller seemed to embody some distinctive qualities, not the least being its ability to help its employees prosper.

In an effort to define what made Fuller special, Andersen and others developed a corporate philosophy that has remained to this day. Andersen believed that a corporation owed much to those who helped it prosper—customers, employees, stockholders, and communities. Incentives seemed to be the engine of the firm's growth. Major programs such as employee stock ownership, year-end bonuses, and early profit-sharing plans were launched. When Fuller began giving a day off with pay for each of its 150 employees on their birthdays in 1950, it was an idea remarkable enough to make *The Wall Street Journal*.

During the 1950s the company experienced numerous acquisitions of new plants and operations, including a Canadian subsidiary and a sales office in the Bahamas. New products, 600 adhesive products in all, pushed sales to $10 million by 1959. That same year H.B. Fuller Company began to reorganize. Its operations outside Minnesota had been run as separate affiliated companies. Now the firm began to convert these operations into geographically based divisions. The corporation's new size and rapid growth made some degree of centralization necessary.

Elmer Andersen achieved an objective he had revealed to Harvey Fuller long before—to serve in the state legislature. Elected as a Republican in 1949, it was the start of a dual career for Andersen. He

The H.B. Fuller building on West Third Street (later to become West Kellogg Boulevard) and a large billboard that advertises Fuller Stixo paste, which continued to be produced in small quantities until the early 1980s.

The office at 186-190 West Third Street in 1931.

held office for 10 years while continuing as president and chief executive of H.B. Fuller Company. In 1959 Andersen decided to put politics aside and return to the company full time. The Republican Party in Minnesota had other ideas, however, and at the party's urgings Andersen ran for governor in 1960 and won.

Al Vigard, who had been with H.B. Fuller Company since World War II, replaced Andersen as president. The firm had 14 adhesives plants, 3 speciality plants, and 8 warehouses, and was beginning to aggressively expand into overseas markets. In 1962, on the company's 75th anniversary, sales reached a record $14.2 million. That year Andersen lost his bid for reelection and soon returned to H.B. Fuller as the company's first chairman of the board.

By then Fuller was in the process of reshaping itself. The system of nine autonomous regional units that set their own pricing policies and devised their own product formulas was replaced by a more centralized corporate structure. Fuller's customers, many by now quite large, were demanding a greater degree of product and pricing uniformity. Fuller had also become a national and international marketer with more growth potential than ever and was contemplating a public stock offering to fund expansion. A public stock offering would also give H.B. Fuller Company employees, who were heavily invested in the organization, an opportunity to maximize the value of their holdings.

The results of the change were dramatic. Two years after the reorganization sales reached $24.7 million. The 1968 public stock offering sold out on the day it was offered. The next year earnings rose a remarkable 64 percent.

Fuller began to emerge as an international company during the 1960s. Joint ventures were established with Malaysian, Australian, Nicaraguan, and Argen-

tinean partners. H.B. Fuller Company became the majority shareholder in Kativo Chemical Industries, a holding corporation for 10 Central American companies. The expansion was part of a continuing product diversification and an ongoing search for new markets. By the end of the decade, sales topped $40 million.

In April 1971 Tony Andersen, Elmer Andersen's 35-year-old son, became H.B. Fuller's fifth president. Dave Durenberger was hired as Fuller's legal counsel. Durenberger would be instrumental in developing the firm's expanded community affairs programs during the 1970s.

H.B. Fuller Company was one of the first to join the Five Percent Club of Minnesota businesses that contributed 5 percent of pretax profits to community projects. Fuller also established an employee-staffed Community Affairs Council, and later similar councils were established in communities where the firm had operations. The councils would identify and channel company resources into pressing community issues. Fuller's programs and procedures would come to be called national models for corporate involvement. Durenberger, who spearheaded many of these efforts as director of corporate affairs, harbored a dream similar to Elmer Andersen's to serve in public office. It culminated in 1980,

when he was elected to the United States Senate.

Tony Andersen realized that in order for the firm to maintain its traditional 15-percent annual growth, certain strategic changes would be required. Two of the most important were expanding its range of products beyond those related to adhesives and becoming an important player in the vital European market. Acquisitions would advance this strategy. One of the most important was the purchase in 1974 of a leading West German manufacturer of special waxes for a variety of industrial applications. By the end of the decade Europe accounted for 37 percent of sales.

During 1974 H.B. Fuller Company, in a major reorganization, replaced its regional structure with a structure of specialized divisions that developed products for specific industries. That same year the firm reached the watershed mark of $100 million in sales.

In 1975 H.B. Fuller Company bought Paisley Products—the same organization whose offer 41 years earlier had spurred Elmer Andersen to action. As the firm ended the decade, it was saddened by the deaths of Clint Stork and Jim Watt.

George Svoboda, an early H.B. Fuller Company driver, stands by a load of Fuller pastes. George went to Cincinnati when a plant opened there in 1944.

Watt began his career with H.B. Fuller as a chemical engineer and ended up in charge of U.S. operations. This was also a time of unparalleled growth. Strategic planning had led Tony Andersen and his management team to focus on a strategy that combined market-driven business units that vigorously explored new growth opportunities with an integrated, nationwide manufacturing and marketing effort. Sales in 1980 were close to $300 million.

H.B. Fuller began the 1980s as a diversified, technology-based manufacturer with a reputation for strong and innovative new product development. The importance of research and development was evidenced by ground breaking for the organization's $16-million Willow Lake Research Center, the largest investment the corporation had ever made. Since the decade began H.B. Fuller Company has acquired seven U.S. and four international companies, which tripled its European sales and made it among the top five adhesives manufacturers in Europe. Each foreign acquisition continued to be staffed by nationals, who were encouraged to assume ownership in the firm.

In 1987, with sales exceeding a half-billion dollars and an international work force of more than 4,500 employees, H.B. Fuller Company expects to keep growing and selling new business opportunities in growing markets.

MEDCENTERS HEALTH PLAN
PARTNERS NATIONAL HEALTH PLANS

MedCenters Health Plan, one of the oldest and most successful health maintenance organizations in the state where HMOs got their start, is a name familiar to nearly everyone in Minnesota. What many Minnesotans may not know is that MedCenters is now part of Partners National Health Plans, a joint venture by The Aetna Insurance Company and VHA Enterprises, the nation's largest private insurance companies and one of the nation's largest health care corporations. The combined strengths of the two organizations, namely the pioneering HMO management skills of MedCenters and the financial depth and marketing clout of Partners, have produced an HMO distinguished by its concern for quality and its cost efficiency.

In 1972 St. Louis Park Medical Center, a large multispecialty Twin Cities clinic, formed MedCenters Health Plan, a nonprofit health maintenance organization managed by physicians affiliated with the clinic. At first the new HMO—set up by doctors for doctors—was a novelty in the health care world. The clinic soon developed a reputation for being conservative and quality conscious—the same approach that later would be shared by

most successful HMOs.

MedCenters Health Plan was designed to see if employers in the Twin Cities area shared this philosophy. It may have been the early days of HMOs, but the advantages of the MedCenters approach proved attractive to many employers. Soon MedCenters became established as one of the area's leading HMOs, and one of the few based on the multispecialty teamwork approach to medicine. Eventually 18 of the area's 21 largest employers would be offering their employees MedCenters coverage.

Meanwhile, other important multispecialty clinics in the area became part of the MedCenters systems. The most important addition took place in 1983, when the St. Louis Park Medical Center merged with the Nicollet and Eitel clinics to form the Park Nicollet Medical Center. MedCenters would later add Comprehensive Medical Care and other large physi-

The divisional headquarters for Partners National Health Plans and headquarters for MedCenters Health Plan are located here in the Minnesota Center in Bloomington, Minnesota.

cian affiliations to its list of participating providers.

As the growth of prepaid health care exploded in the 1980s, MedCenters' board made some important strategic decisions. A management company called American MedCenters, Inc., was formed in 1984 to provide administrative and long-term planning support to the growing MedCenters Health Plan system. The new organization would be owned by the Park Nicollet Medical Center and the public through a stock offering. Two years later the board sold American MedCenters to Partners National Health Plans, a joint venture of VHA Enterprises, a subsidiary of Voluntary Hospitals of America, and Aetna Insurance Company.

Partners was designed to create a national network of hospitals and physicians to provide quality health care at negotiated rates.

To Minnesotans who still know their HMO as MedCenters, little has changed. The quality and care of more than 1,200 MedCenters Health Plan physicians is just as high as ever—only now MedCenters seems ready to be just as successful in the decade ahead as it has been in the past two decades.

APV DOUGLAS MACHINE, INC.

Arnold "Bud" Thoen always liked to tinker with mechanical castoffs and scraps lying around his parents' Douglas County farm. His cousin, Paul Anderson, lived across the lake and shared Bud's mechanical aptitude. The boys were putting together working miniature tractors, threshers, and other farm implements.

It was a fixation neither would ever outgrow, eventually resulting in Douglas Machine Corporation of Alexandria, now APV Douglas Machine, an internationally renowned builder of specialized packaging machines with recent sales of more than $16 million and a work force of 300.

As a young man Paul Anderson got a job with a Minneapolis manufacturer of packaging machines. Later brother Vern and cousin Bud worked for the same company. In 1964, when Thoen heard that a one-person machine shop in Alexandria was for sale, he jumped at the chance to move back to Douglas County and scraped together enough money for a down payment on the shop. With his wife, Pat, doing the bookkeeping and working as a legal secretary to help support the business, Thoen opened the Douglas Machine Company. The first year Thoen did small machining jobs and just barely broke even. The following year he got his first big job, a conveyor for the Curtis Candy Company of Chicago, mostly because it appeared to be a difficult job, and established companies were not interested in bidding on it. Vern Anderson and Frank Chan, now a longtime Douglas employee, worked part time to help Thoen build the $6,000 machine. Soon the company got a second order.

By 1966, after the firm received an order for a $30,000 machine for the De-Soto Chemical Company, Thoen and Vern and Paul Anderson teamed up to incorporate as the Douglas Machine Corporation. As the organization grew, employee benefits grew along with the addition of a strong profit-sharing program, and even a company chaplain on call to counsel employees would reflect the three partners' Christian beliefs.

What the company today calls "The Douglas Difference"—a stronger commitment to excellence in its machines and the quality of its people than to profits—meant that Douglas packaging machines came to be regarded as among the best in the industry. Douglas Machine was among the first packaging machinery

companies in the United States to invest in sophisticated computer-augmented design and engineering; today its engineering department, with 14 computer-augmented design work stations, is as advanced as any small corporation's anywhere. Douglas continues to grow in all departments with the use of 30 computer work stations.

Douglas grew to become one of the top five companies in the corrugated packaging machinery industry, with equipment installed in most U.S. states and in countries around the world. Sales have been especially strong since the beginning of the 1980s, when Douglas moved into its present 82,000-square-foot facility. Revenues have more than doubled in the past three years alone.

Recently Bud Thoen retired from active duty at Douglas and now runs Palmer Industries, an electrical wire fastener manufacturing operation Douglas acquired in 1982. Vern Anderson is presently Douglas' chief executive officer,

The officers of APV Douglas Machine are (from left) Bud Thoen, retired president; Vern Anderson, chief executive officer; and Paul Anderson, executive vice-president.

while Paul Anderson serves as executive vice-president.

Another change came in 1986, when Douglas agreed to be acquired by APV Holdings, Ltd., a $1.3-billion British holding company that specializes in baking, food-handling, and packaging equipment. APV Douglas Machine, Inc., will be operated autonomously with access to the financial clout of the British giant. The Douglas Difference will continue to give this quiet Minnesota giant its competitive edge.

After moving from the original 1,200-square-foot building in 1966, Douglas Machine Corporation, through several expansions, has grown to its present 82,140-square-foot building.

CLOW STAMPING COMPANY

Merrifield does not seem to be the kind of place to conduct a thriving national and international business, especially one in the fiercely competitive metal-stamping and metal-fabrication industry—an industry composed of thousands of companies making custom metal parts for manufacturers of electronics, industrial, and transportation equipment.

Offshore competition and the quest for quality have raised expectations to exacting levels. An 80- or 90-percent acceptance rate of just a few years ago is no longer good enough; now the true competitors in the industry are expected to fashion perfect parts nearly 100 percent of the time—and they are expected to deliver those parts when they are needed. Merrifield's Clow Stamping has emerged as just such a competitor, even though similar companies are most usually located in or near major transportation and labor cen-

ters. Clow's secret? An unrelenting commitment to quality, including one of the industry's first uses of statistical process control, and a stable and skilled northern Minnesota work force that may be one of the state's best kept secrets. The result is growing revenues, which recently topped $8 million, and a list of blue chip customers that range from IBM to Mack Trucks.

Everett Clow had been a tool and die maker for years before he decided to open his own metal-stamping business back in 1970. At first Clow operated out of a small building in St. Louis Park. His wife, Gladys, handled the books. Growth was slow but steady, and after several moves to bigger quarters within the Twin Cities area, Clow Stamping was billing a few hundred thousand dollars per year for a

Everett (left) and Gladys (right) Clow, founders of Clow Stamping Company.

small but growing number of customers, among them Control Data and Xerox. In 1973 Clow contemplated expanding again and discovered an existing small manufacturing facility for sale in Merrifield, a hamlet 10 miles or so north of Brainerd.

The move to Merrifield removed Clow from the distracting hustle and bustle of the big city and introduced the company to the factor it feels has most contributed to its success—the dedicated and hardworking people of northern Minnesota. In an industry characterized by rapid employee turnover, Clow's employees average six or seven years with the company. In turn, Clow Stamping has tried to provide its employees with an unusually high level of benefits, including wages that are competitive with similar firms in the Twin Cities.

Clow's ability to attract and keep skilled workers helped it develop a reputa-

tion as one of the highest quality short-to-medium run metal fabricators in the business. As Everett Clow's sons, Reginal and Ric, joined the business, growth came quickly. In addition to its 40,000-square-foot Merrifield facility, which is currently being expanded, Clow also operates two smaller facilities. A 12,000-square-foot plant in Monticello does finishing work for parts fabricated at Merrifield and serves as a distribution center. A plant in Pequot Lakes specializes in buffing and grinding.

Today Clow Stamping has 120 employees, a field sales force of 45 independent manufacturer's representatives, and

Inside Clow's Merrifield plant. Clow has built a reputation as one of the highest quality metal fabricators in the industry, in large part due to its northern Minnesota work force.

a strong reputation as a "ship-to-stock" quality leader in its industry. Recent acceptance rates for Clow parts reached 99.6 percent, while its on-time delivery record stands at 94 percent. Clow has shown that a firm does not need a big-city base to thrive in the metal-fabrication business. Dedicated people and the ability to offer quality are what gives Clow Stamping Company its edge.

BANG PRINTING COMPANY

By some estimates, the commercial printing business is the third-largest industry in Minnesota, employing an estimated 50,000 people. One of Minnesota's most interesting—and in recent years, most successful—printers is found not in the Twin Cities, but much farther to the north, in the heart of the state's beautiful North Woods.

Bang Printing, just outside of Brainerd, has become a leading sheet-fed (as opposed to roll-fed) printer by offering customers, some found as far away as California and New York, an unusual level of service for a small-to-medium run printer. With its own complete binding facilities—a rarity for printers even many times its size—Bang, under the recent ownership of John Kurtzman, has evolved a distinctive formula for success. Bang's in-house bindery allows it to maintain complete control over the finished printed product, while the skill and dedication of Bang's northern Minnesota work force adds an extra dimension of quality. One result has been an almost fivefold increase in revenues since the beginning of the decade.

Bang remains one of Brainerd's oldest and largest private employers. It was born in 1899, when E.E. Beard, a newcomer to the area, started a commercial printing business and a Brainerd daily newspaper, *The Arena*. Ten years later Beard's paper was purchased by R.M. Sheets and renamed *The Brainerd Journal Press*. When Sheets died suddenly in 1936, the paper was sold to Ralph R. Cole and Ralph E. Lindberg. Shortly after World War II Ray Bang, a restaurant and nightclub owner, became a partner with the two men, and eventually bought his partners out, but not before the partnership had purchased the area's oldest newspaper, *The Brainerd Tribune*.

By 1951 Bang realized that the area was oversupplied with newspapers and sold his newspaper operation to *The Brainerd Dispatch*. Now strictly a commercial printer, the company was renamed the Brainerd Press, and later Bang Printing. The firm grew slowly but steadily through the next two decades, specializing in catalogs and boxes for food-

Bang Printing's old facility was located in the 500 block on Front Street.

service firms. By the early 1970s the company attracted the attention of a much larger printer, Volkmuth Printers of St. Cloud, which bought Ray Bang out in 1973. Volkmuth, in turn, was acquired by the giant Webb Publishing Company of

St. Paul in 1979. Bang Printing was the only part of their holdings the Volkmuth family decided to keep, and they hired Dennis Johnson to run the operation.

Two years later John Kurtzman, a real estate developer, teamed up with Dennis Johnson to make a successful bid to buy the company from Volkmuth. Kurtzman contributed financial expertise to Johnson's years of experience in the printing business. The two men decided to upgrade the facilities and expand the company's sales force. Under Kurtzman and Johnson, Bang Printing moved to a new 80,000-square-foot building on the outskirts of Brainerd and invested in state-of-the-art printing and bindery equipment.

With Dennis Johnson's untimely death in 1985, John Kurtzman became the sole owner and president of the firm. Under Kurtzman and operations manager Jim Lorentz, Bang Printing Company has emerged as an important player in Minnesota's printing industry. Revenues recently topped $6 million, and today Bang employs 80 people. The skills and commitment of Bang's northern Minnesota work force have played a key role in the firm's recent success.

This artist's rendering depicts the floor plan of Bang Printing's new 84,000-square-foot facility.

CONTINENTAL MACHINES, INC.

The sons of Julius Wilkie inherited much of their father's fascination with the tools that make machines. Leighton Wilkie, the oldest son, took his father's knack for building innovative machine tools a huge step further, and matched it with instinctive marketing and organizational skills that may have been even more innovative.

The result was Continental Machines, Inc., one of the nation's leading machine tool builders and one of the world's largest manufacturers of metal-cutting band saws, a machine Wilkie first developed and that has since gone on to become a worldwide standard. Continental, which today includes a large and growing hydraulic equipment division, is also one of Minnesota's most uniquely structured companies. Most of its products are marketed through the Illinois-based DoAll network of companies, also controlled by the Wilkie family.

As Leighton Wilkie's enterprise grew, he developed a unique vision of separating manufacturing from marketing, both to encourage growth and to retain the flexibility of running Continental as a privately held business. Wilkie's instincts proved spectacularly successful.

Julius Wilkie, the son of European immigrants, turned a childhood aptitude into the Wilkie Machine Works in Winona in the early 1920s. With the assistance of his four sons, Wilkie made specialty tools, with an emphasis on tools used for reconditioning automobiles. In 1928 the firm moved to Minneapolis and was renamed Continental Machine Specialties, Inc. Soon after, Julius Wilkie died, and his four sons took over the business.

In the late 1920s the Wilkie Machine Works moved to Minneapolis and became Continental Machines, Inc.

Leighton built on machine tool technology advances made by his father and invented a unique method of making light dies for short-run metal stamping. The machine, a metal-cutting band saw, cut rapidly through metal, removing inside sections in a single piece and leaving clean edges. It replaced a laborious and expensive process. Called the DoAll band saw when it was introduced in the early 1930s,

An aerial view of Continental's Savage plant. Continental has grown to become one of the Minnesota River Valley's largest employers.

it had a profound impact on the die-making business. Sales skyrocketed from $115,000 in 1935, when Wilkie and his wife traveled to sales presentations around the country with a DoAll machine hitched behind their car in a trailer, to exceed $7 million 10 years later.

Leighton was determined to see that management stayed lean and flexible. Marketing and manufacturing facilities were opened in the Chicago suburb of Des Plaines, while a huge facility was built in Savage, Minnesota, the present home of Continental Machines, Inc., which is now a separate corporation and the primary supplier of DoAll products. Regional sales companies were also formed to sell DoAll products in retail stores.

Leighton Wilkie also believed that working conditions and employee benefits that exceeded industry averages were another essential ingredient. Profit sharing, paid vacations, health benefits, group insurance, and even free beverages during twice daily breaks, became part of the Wilkie formula.

Continental Machines, Inc., and Continental Hydraulics, a subsidiary formed in 1961, grew to become one of the Minnesota River Valley's most important private employers. To date, more than 100,000 DoAll band saws have been sold; many sold decades ago are still in operation. Continental intends to remain the leader and is developing new machine tool technology, including computerized numerically controlled metal-cutting machines and water jet saws.

DETECTOR ELECTRONICS CORPORATION

In the fire protection and management field a "friendly" fire, such as one found in a power plant boiler, burns at a steady and carefully controlled rate. An "unfriendly" fire, such as those that have been known to flash through oil refineries, mines, and munitions plants, can wreak immense damage within a fraction of a second.

Worldwide, a handful of intensely specialized companies are dedicated to protecting people and equipment from these instant large fires with sophisticated and surprising technology. Detector Electronics Corporation has grown to be one of the best in the high-hazard industrial-protection market, and has become one of Minnesota's most successful foreign exporters. Detector's success can be measured by its virtually complete worldwide market share in ultraviolet (UV) flame detectors, and by its growing prominence in hazardous gas-detection technology and sophisticated burner management systems. Detector's UV flame detectors can detect a flame and trigger a flame-suppression system in less than 11 milliseconds—roughly 5 percent of the time it takes to blink an eye.

Detector's founders, William Crosley, T.E. Larsen, and Alan H. Petersen, had more than 50 years of combined service at Honeywell when they negotiated the rights to a Honeywell-developed UV high-hazard flame-detection system in the early 1970s. Honeywell had decided not to pursue the market, but to Crosley, Larsen, and Petersen, that very same market looked big enough—provided they could sell their UV fire detector on a worldwide basis. The tiny new start-up had an aggressive export orientation. Within a few years of its creation, Detec-

Detector Electronics boasts the most complete line of fire- and gas-detection equipment in its industry. The company installed tens of thousands of its ultraviolet detectors worldwide.

tor was doing more than half of its business overseas. Eventually it received the coveted "E" Award and the "E" Award with star from the State of Minnesota for its outstanding record of competing in world markets.

At first, Detector's main market was the oil industry, whose facilities at the time were mostly protected by slow-responding thermal detectors—little more than the sprinkler systems found in many office buildings. The company set out to upgrade existing UV technology. It made a huge breakthrough in 1975 with a patented technique it called Optical Integrity, a system that monitored the sensitivity of its UV detectors, particularly the clarity of the glass window that covered

Nestled in the southwest corner of Bloomington, the Detector Electronics headquarters facility houses 80,000 square feet of research and manufacturing activities.

the UV detecting element and which could be obscured by dust and grime. Optical Integrity made Detector's products the most reliable and technologically advanced in the industry.

A public stock offering in 1982 and a new 80,000-square-foot headquarters and research and manufacturing facility in Minneapolis gave Detector the impetus it needed to enter more segments of the high-hazard detection field. The company entered the decade determined to diversify beyond its single UV flame-detection product line, even though it was considered the best in the industry.

Through acquisitions, Detector entered the market for combustible and toxic gas-detection and large industrial computer-based burner-management systems. The acquisitions enabled Detector to become one of the few companies able to offer a full line of high-hazard detection products. Growth reflected this new market strength: Sales doubled during the 1980s, and Detector's work force grew to exceed 250. In 1987 Detector agreed to be acquired by Graviner Ltd., a British company in the fire-detection and suppression field, giving Detector Electronics Corporation access to an even bigger world market and creating an international force in fire protection.

PATRONS

The following individuals, companies, and organizations have made a valuable commitment to the quality of this publication. Windsor Publications and the Minnesota Chamber of Commerce gratefully acknowledge their participation in *From This Land: A History of Minnesota's Empires, Enterprises and Entrepreneurs.*

Advantek, Inc.
Aero Systems Engineering, Inc.*
Alamco Wood Products, Inc.*
American Linen Supply Co.*
Amhoist*
Andersen Corporation*
Anderson Bros. Construction Co. of Brainerd
Anderson Trucking Service, Inc.*
APV Douglas Machine, Inc.*
Atwood-Larson*
Bang Printing Company*
Bauer Electric Inc.
Berne Scale Company*
Boker's, Inc.*
Campbell-Mithun Advertising*
Carlson Companies*
Chandler-Wilbert Vault Co.*
Cherne Contracting Corporation*
Chicago Tube & Iron Co. of Minnesota
Clow Stamping Company*
Contel Corporation*
Continental Machines, Inc.*
Dahlberg, Inc.*
Dain Bosworth Incorporated*
Dalton Gear Co.
Deloitte Haskins & Sells*
Detector Electronics Corporation*
Donovan Companies, Inc.*
Dyco Petroleum Corporation*
Eberhardt Commercial Real Estate*
Ernst & Whinney*
Faegre & Benson*
Faribault Woolen Mill Co.*
Fingerhut Corporation*
First Bank System, Inc.*
H.B. Fuller Company*
General Mills, Inc.*
General Security Services Corporation
GNB Incorporated*
Golden Valley Microwave Foods, Inc.*
Golle & Holmes Custom Education*

Graco Inc.*
Gray, Plant, Mooty, Mooty & Bennett, P.A.*
Group Health, Inc.*
HealthEast*
Health Risk Management, Inc.*
The Hopkins House*
Hubbard Milling Company*
IBM*
Incstar Corporation*
Kraus-Anderson Companies*
Lake Center Industries*
Lakewood Publications*
Lamaur Inc.*
Land O'Lakes*
Leef Brothers, Inc.*
Liberty Diversified Industries, Inc.*
Lutheran Brotherhood*
McGlynn Bakeries, Inc.*
Helen L. McNulty
Marvin Windows*
Mayo Clinic*
MedCenters Health Plan Partners National Health Plans*
Medtronic, Inc.*
Merrill Corporation
Methodist Hospital*
Mico, Inc.*
Midwest/Osakis Telephone Company
M.A. Mortenson Company*
Nash Finch Company*
National City Bank*
North American Life and Casualty Company*
North Central Laboratories, Inc.*
Northland Aluminum Products, Inc. (Nordic Ware®)*
Northwestern Bell Telephone*
Numerex Corporation*
Otter Tail Power Company*
Park Construction Company*
Park Dental Health Centers*
Peavey Grain Company*
Pella Products, Inc.*
Press On Incorporated*
Pro Engineering Inc.
Quadion Corporation*
Remmele Engineering, Inc.*
Robinson Rubber Company*
Rochester Sand & Gravel, Inc.
St. Joseph's Medical Center*

St. Paul-Ramsey Medical Center and Ramsey Clinic*
Scherer Brothers Lumber Company*
Scholl's, Inc.*
Sheraton Northwest*
Skarnes, Incorporated*
Slumberland, Inc.*
State Bond Companies
Teleprint, Inc.
Telex Communications, Inc.*
Towle Real Estate Company*
Tursso Companies Inc.
Unisys*
United Telephone Company*
Varitronic Systems, Inc.*
Zytec Corporation*

* "Minnesota's Enterprises" in *From This Land: A History of Minnesota's Empires, Enterprises and Entrepreneurs.* The histories of these companies and organizations appear in Chapter 9, beginning on page 247.

BIBLIOGRAPHY

Note: The following is a selective bibliography of sources used in this book. For further resource materials, contact your local reference librarian.

Agricultural Marketing Service. *Impact of the St. Lawrence Seaway on the Location of Grain Export Facilities.* Washington, D.C.: Government Printing Office, 1960.

"A Growing Problem." *Don Larson's Business Newlsetter.* (August 1, 1983):14-15.

Albertson, Don L. "Sister Kenny's Legacy." *Hennepin County History.* 37:1 (Spring, 1978):3-14.

Anderson, Antone. *The Hinckley Fire.* New York: Comet Press Books, 1954.

Anderson, Governor Wendell R. "Special Message - Restoring and Preserving Minnesota's Environment." Address to 67th Minnesota Legislature. St. Paul: April 1, 1971.

Andrist, Ralph K., ed. *The American Heritage History of the 20s and 30s.* New York: American Heritage Publications, 1970.

Appel, Livia, and Theodore C. Blegen. "Official Encouragement of Immigration to Minnesota in the Territorial Period." *Minnesota History Bulletin.* 5 (August 1923):167-203.

Appelbaum, Arlene. "Talented Entrepreneurs Help Minnesota Grow." *Minnesota Business* (August 1981) 32-37.

Atkins, Annette. *Harvest of Grief.* St. Paul, Minnesota: Minnesota Historical Society Press, 1984.

Auerbach, Laura K. *A Short History of Minnesota's Democratic-Farmer-Labor Party.* Minneapolis: Democratic-Farmer-Labor Party, 1966.

Baker, James H. "History of Transportation in Minnesota." *Minnesota Historical Society Collections* 9:1-34 (1901).

Bardon, Richard, and Grace Lee Nute. "A Winter in the St. Croix Valley, 1802-03." *Minnesota History* 28 (March, June, September 1947) 1-4, 142-59, 225-40.

Bell, Ida P. "A Pioneer Family of the Middle Border." *Minnesota History* 14 (September 1933) 303-66.

Benson, Thomas E. *Minnesota Resort Guide.* St. Paul: Itasca Press, 1972.

Bernstein, Irving. *Turbulent Years; A History of the American Worker: 1933-1941.* Boston: Houghton Mifflin Co., 1970.

Berthel, Mary W. *Horns of Thunder: The Life and Times of James M. Goodhue.* St. Paul: Minnesota Historical Society, 1948.

Blakeley, Russel. "History of the Discovery of the Mississippi River and the Advent of Commerce in Minnesota." *Minnesota Historical Collections* 8 (1898):375-418.

Blamer, Frank E. "The Farmer and Minnesota History." *Minnesota History* 7 (September 1926):199-217.

Blegen, Theodore C. *Building Minnesota.* New York: D.C. Heath and Company, 1938.

Blegen, Theodore C. *Grass Roots History.* Minneapolis: University of Minnesota Press, 1947. Reissued New York and London: Kennikat Press, 1969.

Blegen, Theodore C. *Minnesota: A History of the State.* Minneapolis: University of Minnesota Press, 1963. Reprinted with additional chapter, "A State That Works," by Russell W. Fridley. With additional readings.

Blegen, Theodore C., and Theodore L. Nydahl. *Minnesota History: A Guide to Reading and Study.* Minneapolis: University of Minnesota, 1960.

Boardman, Fox W., Jr. *The Thirties: America and the Great Depression.* New York: Henry Z. Walck, Inc., 1967.

Boese, Donald L. *John C. Greenway and the Opening of the Western Mesabi.* Grand Rapids, Minnesota: Joint Bovey-Coleraine Bicentennial Commission, 1975.

Borchert, John R. *A Look at Minnesota Industries.* St. Paul: Minnesota Education Association, 1954.

Borchert, John R. *Minnesota's Changing Geography.* Minneapolis: University of Minnesota Press, 1959.

Borchert, John R., and Donald P. Yaeger. *Atlas of Minnesota Resources and Settlement.* Rev. ed. St. Paul: Minnesota State Planning Agency, 1969.

Bowen, Dana Thomas. "Great Lakes Ships and Shipping." *Minnesota History* 34 (Spring 1954): 9-16.

Bridges, Leonard Hal. *Iron Millionaire: Life of Charlemagne Tower.* Philadelphia: University of Pennsylvania, 1952.

Buckman, Carol A. *Minnesota's Experimental City.* Pequot Lakes, Minnesota: Country Printing, Inc., 1973.

Buckman, Clarence B. "Lumbering and the Pine Forests." *Gopher Historian.* 13 (Spring 1959): 9-13.

Carley, Kenneth. *The Sioux Uprising of 1862.* St. Paul: Minnesota Historical Society, 1976.

Castle, Henry A. "General James Shields: Soldier, Orator, Statesman." *Minnesota Historical Collections.* 15 (1915):711-30.

Castle, Henry A. *Minnesota: Its Story and Biography.* Three volumes. Chicago and New York: The Lewis Publishing Company, 1915.

Chamberlain, John. *The Enterprising Americans: A Business History of* the United States. New York: Harper & Row, 1961.

Chamberlin, Thomas W. "The Railroads of Minnesota." *Gopher Historian.* 11 (Spring 1957):21-22.

Colwell, James L. "From Stone to Steel: American Contributions to the Revolution in Flour Milling." *Rocky Mountain Social Science Journal* 6:2 (October 1969):20-31.

Control Data Corporation. *Chronology of Key Events in Control Data's History.* Bloomington, Minnesota: Control Data Corporation, 1985.

Cross, Marion E. *From Land, Sea and Test Tube. The Story of Archer-Daniels-Midland Company.* Minneapolis: Archer-Daniels-Midland, 1954.

Cross, Marion E. *Pioneer Harvest.* Minneapolis: Lund Press, 1949.

Davis, E.W. *Pioneering with Taconite.* St. Paul: Minnesota Historical Society, 1964.

Davis, Lee Niedringhaus. *The Corporate Alchemists.* New York: William Morrow and Company, Inc. 1984.

DeKruif, Paul. *Seven Iron Men.* New York: Harcourt, Brace, 1929.

Derleth, August. *Milwaukee Road: Its First Hundred Years.* New York: Creative Age Press, 1948.

Dobbs, Farrell. *Teamster Rebellion.* New York: Monad Press, 1972.

Donovan, Frank P. *The First Through A Century: A History of the First National Bank of St. Paul.* St. Paul: Itasca Press: Webb Publishing Company, 1954.

Dougherty, Richard. *In Quest of Quality: Hormel's First Seventy-five Years.* St. Paul: North Central Publishing Company, 1966.

Downward, William L. *Dictionary of the History of the American Brewing and Distilling Industries.* Westport, Connecticut: Greenwood Press, 1980.

Drache, Hiram M. *The Day of the Bonanza: A History of Bonanza Farming in the Red River Valley of the North.* Fargo, North Dakota: North Dakota Institute for Regional Studies, 1964.

Draheim, Kirk P. *Technological Industry in the Upper Midwest.* Minneapolis: University of Minnesota Upper Midwest Economic Study, 1964.

Drenning, June. *Selections from Minnesota History: A Fiftieth Anniversary Anthology.* St. Paul: Minnesota Historical Society, 1979.

Dunn, James Taylor. *The St. Croix: Midwest Border River.* New York: Holt, Rinehart & Winston, 1965.

Eliason, Adolph O. "The Beginning of Banking in Minnesota." *Minnesota Historical Collections.* 12 (December 1908):671-690.

"EMS Systems Transmits, Records EKGs Without Loss of Fidelity." *Minnesota Scientific Journal.* (November 1961):22.

Engberg, George B. "The Knights of Labor in Minnesota." *Minnesota History.* (December 1940):372-94.

Engh, Jeri. *Hamm's: The Story of 100 Years in the Land of Sky Blue Water.* St. Paul: Theo Hamm Brewing Company, 1965.

Evans, Henry Oliver. *Iron Pioneer: Henry W. Oliver, 1840-1904.* New York: E.P. Dutton & Co., Inc., 1942.

Federal Reserve Bank, Minneapolis. *Reflections from History: First Half Century of Minneapolis Federal Reserve Bank.* Minneapolis: Minneapolis Federal Reserve Bank, 1964.

Filipetti, George, and Roland S. Vaile. *The Economic Effects of the NRA: A Regional Analysis.* Minneapolis: University of Minnesota Press, 1935.

Firestone, Harvey S. *Man on the Move: The Story of Transportation.* New York: G.P. Putnam's Sons, 1967.

First Bank Systems: The First Fifty Years. Minneapolis: First Banks, 1979.

Fitzharris, Joseph C. *Minnesota Agricultural Growth, 1880-1970.* Minneapolis: Minnesota Institute of Agriculture, 1976.

Folwell, William Watts. *A History of Minnesota.* Four volumes. St. Paul: Minnesota Historical Society, 1921-1939. Corrected editions, 1965-1969.

Frame, Robert M., III. *Millers to the World: Minnesota's Nineteenth Century Water Power Flour Mills.* St. Paul: Minnesota Historical Society, 1977.

Furness, Marion Ramsey. "Governor Ramsey and Frontier Minnesota: Impressions from His Diary and Letters." *Minnesota History* 28 (December 1948):309-28

Gadler, Steve J. *Environmental Compatibility - A Perspective.* Minnesota Pollution Control Agency. Minneapolis: University of Minnesota, 1971.

Galvin, Kevin. "The Necessities of Life Available Early on the Frontier." *Ramsey County History* 11:2; 8-14.

Gates, Charles M. *Five Fur Traders of the Northwest.* Minneapolis: University of Minnesota Press, 1933.

General Mills. *A Collected History.* Minneapolis: General Mills, Inc., 1978.

Gilfillan, Charles D. "The Early Political History of Minnesota." *Minnesota Historical Collections* 9 (1901): 167-74.

Gilman, Rhoda R. "The Fur trade in the Upper Mississippi Valley, 1630-1850." *Wisconsin Magazine of History* 58 (Autumn, 1974): 2-18.

Gilman, Rhoda R., Carolyn Gilman, and Deborah M. Stultz. *The Red River Trails: Oxcart Routes Between St. Paul and the Selkirk Settlement, 1820-1870.* St. Paul: Minnesota Historical Society, 1979.

Goldberg, Ray A. *The Soybean Industry.* Minneapolis: University of Minnesota Press, 1952.

Goldston, Robert. *The Great Depression - The United States in the Thirties.* New York: Bobbs-Merrill Co., Inc., 1968.

Gove, Gertrude. "St. Cloud Editor and Abolitionist—Jane Grey Swisshelm." *Gopher Historian* 12:25 (Winter 1957-58).

Gray, James. *Business Without Boundary: The Story of General Mills.* Minneapolis: University of Minnesota Press, 1954.

Gray, James. *Our First Century: The Story of General Trading Company, Serving Transportation's Needs Since the Days of the Oxcart.* St. Paul: General Trading Company, 1955.

Greenleaf, William, ed. *American Economic Development Since 1860.* 2nd ed., Columbia, South Carolina: University of South Carolina Press, 1968.

Groner, Alex. *The History of American Business and Industry.* New York: American Heritage Publishing Co., 1972.

Haaverson, Judy. *All Together Now, Happy Centennial.* Minneapolis: Honeywell, Inc., January 1985.

Hage, George S. *Newspapers on the Minnesota Frontier, 1849-1860.* St. Paul: Minnesota Historical Society, 1967.

Hamel, Betty Jones. *Minneapolis: Frontiers, Firsts and Futures.* Minneapolis: '76 Bicentennial Commission, 1976.

Hanft, Robert M. *Red River: Paul Bunyan's Own Lumber Company.* Chico, California: California State University Center for Business and Economic Research, 1980.

Hartsough, Mildred L. *Development of the Twin Cities as Metropolitan Market.* Minneapolis: University of Minnesota Press, 1925.

Heilbron, Bertha L. *The Thirty-Second State: A Pictorial History of Minnesota.* St. Paul: Minnesota Historical Society, 1966.

Hendrickson, Robert. *The Grand Emporiums: The Illustrated History of America's Great Department Stores.* New York: Stein and Day, 1972.

Hicks, John D. "The Origin and Early History of the Farmers' Alliance in Minnesota." *Mississippi Valley Historical Review* 8 (June-September 1921): 92-132.

Hidy, Ralph W., et al. *Timber and Men: The Weyerhaeuser Story.* New York: Macmillan, 1963.

"History of Banking in Minnesota." *Commercial West* 77:24 (June 10, 1939):19-27.

"History of the Great Northern Ore Properties." *Skillings Mining Review.* Duluth, Minnesota, 33:48 (1964):11-28.

History of Winona County. Chicago, Illinois: H.H. Hill and Company, 1883.

Holbrook, Stewart H. *James J. Hill, A Great Life in Brief.* New York: Knopf, 1955.

Holcombe, Return I. *Minnesota in Three Centuries: 1655-1908.* New York: Semicentennial Publishing Society of Minnesota, 1908.

Holmquist, June D. "Minnesota's Waterways." *Gopher Historian.* 10:1-2 (Spring 1956).

"How Glaciers Shaped the Land in East Central Minnesota." *Gopher Historian.* 13:3-5 (Spring 1959).

Huck, Virginia. *Brand of the Tartan: The 3M Story.* New York: Appleton Century Croft, 1955.

Huck, Virginia. *Franklin and Harriet: The Crosby Family.* Minneapolis: Crosby Co., 1980.

Jarchow, Merrill E. *The Earth Brought Forth: A History of Minnesota Agriculture.* St. Paul: Minnesota Historical Society, 1949.

Johnson, H. Nat. *Minnesota Panorama, Saga of the North Star Empire.* Minneapolis: T.S. Denison, 1957.

Jones, Evan. *The Minnesota: Forgotten River.* (Rivers of America Series) New York: Farrar & Rinehart, 1937.

Jorstad, Erling. "Personal Politics in the Origin of Minnesota's Democratic Party." *Minnesota History.* 35 (September 1959): 259-71.

Kane, Lucile M. "Isaac Staples, Pioneer Lumberman." *Gopher Historian.* 7 (January 1953): 7-9.

Kane, Lucile M. *The Waterfall That Built A City: The Falls of St. Anthony.* St. Paul: Minnesota Historical Society, 1966.

Karlen, Arno, ed. *Superior: Portrait of a Living Lake.* New York, Evanston and London: Harper, 1970.

Karlstad State Bank. *Golden Anniversary 1925-1975.* Karlstad: 1975.

Kelley, John L. "Present Situation of the U.S. Iron Ore Industry." *Skillings Mining Review* December 7, 1985.

King, Franklin Alexander. *The Missabe Road.* San Marino, California: Golden West Books, 1972.

Kohlmeyer, Frederick W. *Timber Roots: The Laird Norton Story, 1855-1905.* Winona, Minnesota: Winona County Historical Society, 1972.

Kunz, Virgina B. *Muskets to Missiles: A Military History of Minnesota.* St. Paul: Minnesota State Centennial Commission, 1958.

Larsen, Arthur J., ed. *Crusader and Feminist: Letters of Jane Grey Swisshelm.* St. Paul: Minnesota Historical Society, 1934.

Larsen, Arthur J. "Early Transportation." *Minnesota History* 14 (June 1933):149-155.

Larson, Agnes M. *History of the White Pine Industry in Minnesota.* Minneapolis: University of Minnesota Press, 1949.

Larson, Don W. *Land of the Giants: A History of Minnesota Business.* Minneapolis: Dorn Books, 1979.

Lebedoff, David. *The 21st Ballot: A Political Party Struggle in Minnesota.* Minneapolis: University of Minnesota Press, 1969.

Leschak, Pam Cope. "Joe Samargia - Iron Range organizer." *Corporate Report* December 1979: 54-57, 92-95.

"The Life of the Voyageur." *Gopher Historian* 11 (Winter, 1956-57): 10-13.

"Living in Minnesota Territory." *Roots* 3:1 (Fall 1974).

Loehr, Rodney C. "Franklin Steele, Frontier Businessman." *Minnesota History* 27 (December 1946): 309-318.

"Louis Hennepin, The Franciscan." *Minnesota Historical Collections* 1 (1902):247-56.

Lukaszewski, Jim. "Business Takes the Initiative in 1980." *Minnesota Business* June 1980.

Lydecker, Ryck. *Duluth: Sketches of the Past.* Edited by Lawrence J. Sommer. Duluth: American Revolution Bicentennial Commission - Northprint Company, 1976.

Lyman, Clara C. "The World and Minnesota in 1849." *Minnesota History* 30 (September 1949):185-201.

Lyman, George D. *John Marsh, Pioneer.* New York: C. Scribner's Sons, 1930.

Manfred, Fredrick. *The WPA Guide to Minnesota: Compiled and Written by the Federal Writers' Project of the Works Progress Administration.* Reprinted. St. Paul: Minnesota Historical Society Press, 1985.

Marquand, Robert E. *Minnesota Agriculture - Prices.* Minnesota Department of Agriculture. St. Paul, Minnesota: 1959.

Matz, Samuel A. *Cereal Technology.* Westport, Connecticut: AVI Publishing Co., Inc., 1970.

Mayer, George H. *Political Career of Floyd B. Olson.* Minneapolis: University of Minnesota Press, 1951.

Mayo, Charles W. *Mayo: The Story of My Family and My Career.* New York: Doubleday and Company, Inc., 1968.

Mayo Clinic, Rochester. *Physicians of the Mayo Clinic and the Mayo Foundation.* Minneapolis: University of Minnesota Press, 1937.

Medtronic, Inc. *Toward Man's Full*

Life. Minneapolis: Medtronic, Inc., 1986.

Meyer, Roy W. "The Story of Forest Mills, A Midwest Milling Community." *Minnesota History* 35 (March 1946):11-12.

Mier, Peg. *Bring Warm Clothes: Letters and Photos from Minnesota's Past.* Minneapolis: Minneapolis Star and Tribune, 1984.

Miller, Curtis. *A Summary of Minnesota Labor's First One Hundred Years.* Minneapolis: University of Minnesota Industrial Relations Center, 1960.

Mills, Stephen E. *A Pictorial History of Northwest Airlines.* First published as *More than Meets the Sky.* Seattle: Superior Publishing Co., 1972, New York: Bonanza Books, 1980.

"Miniature Hearing Device Finds New Markets." *Minnesota Scientific Journal* (November 1961).

Minneapolis Moline Power Implement Company. *Special Regulations for Women Production Workers at the Hopkins Plant of the Minneapolis Moline Power Implement Company.* Minneapolis, 1940.

Minneapolis Star and Tribune Research Department. *Retail Revolution - 1955-1965.* Minneapolis: Minneapolis Star and Tribune, 1966.

"Minnesota Association of Commerce and Industry." *Minnesota Business Journal* (May 1979):18-20.

Minnesota Business Partnership, Inc. *The Minnesota Economy, How Does It Compare?* Minneapolis: 1980.

Minnesota Chambers of Commerce. *Anatomy of a Business Climate.* St. Paul, Minnesota: 1961.

Minnesota Department of Agriculture. *Inside Agriculture.* Minnesota: Department of Agriculture, 1961.

Minnesota Department of Economic Development. *Medicine in Minnesota: Focus on Life Sciences.* St. Paul: Minnesota Department of Economic Development, 1973.

Minnesota Department of Economic Development. *Minnesota Success Stories.* St. Paul, 1980.

Minnesota Department of Economic Development. *A Review of the Economic Impact of the Iron Mining Industry on the Minnesota Economy.* Duluth, Minnesota: 1970.

Minnesota Department of Natural Re-

sources. *Forestry in Minnesota.* Division of Lands and Forestry.St. Paul, 1971.

Minnesota Department of Natural Resources. *Minnesota Resource Potentials in Outdoor Recreation.* St. Paul: Bureau of Planning, 1971.

Minnesota Economic Data, Counties and Regions. "Urbanization." University of Minnesota, No. 15, November 1969.

Minnesota Economic Date, Counties and Regions. "Wholesale and Retail Trade." University of Minnesota, No. 6, August 1967.

Minnesota Energy Policy Task Force. *Final Report and Recommendations.* Environmental Quality Council, St. Paul: 1973.

"Minnesota Firms Go International." *Minnesota Business* (November 1979) 16-19.

Minnesota Mining & Manufacturing Company. *Our Story So Far: Notes from the First Seventy-five Years, 1903-1978.* Privately published, 1978.

Minnesota Resources Commission. *Guide Book to Minnesota Industry: A Directory of Minnesota Manufacturers.* St. Paul, Minnesota: Minnesota Resources Commission, 1946.

"Minnesota: Restoring the Entrepreneurial Explosion." *Minnesota Business* (November 1980).

Minnesota State Department of Business Development. *Minnesota Welcomes New Industry.* St. Paul: 1956.

Minnesota State Planning Agency. *Iron Ore and Concentrates - Minnesota Waterborne Transportation.* Minneapolis: Minnesota State Planning Agency, 1969.

Minnesota State Planning Board. *Report of the Committee on Land Tenure and Farm Debt Structure in Minnesota.* St. Paul: Minnesota State Planning Board, 1937.

Minnesota Territorial Pioneers. *Pioneer Chronicles.* Minneapolis: Territorial Pioneers, 1976.

Minnesota Timber Producers Association. *Logging Today is Different: An Historical Review of the Minnesota Timber Producers Association.* Duluth, 1969.

Minnesota Travel and Recreation Guide. Rockford, Illinois: Rockford Map Publishers, Inc., 1984.

Morgan, Dan. *Merchants of Grain.* New York: Viking Press, 1979.

Morison, Bradley L. *Sunlight on Your Doorstep: The Minneapolis Tribune's First One Hundred Years, 1867-1967.* Minneapolis: Ross & Haines, 1966.

Morris, Lucy Leavenworth Wilder. *Old Rail Fence Corners: Frontier Tales Told by Minnesota Pioneers.* St. Paul: Minnesota Historical Society, 1976.

Neill, Edward D. *History of Minnesota.* Philadelphia: J.B. Lippincott & Co., 1858.

Neill, Edward D. "Occurrences in and around Fort Snelling, from 1819 to 1840s." *Minnesota Historical Collections* 2 (1889):102-42.

Nelson, Lowry. *A Century of Population Growth in Minnesota.* Minneapolis: University of Minnesota Press, 1954.

Nelson, Lowry. *The Minnesota Community: Country and Town in Transition.* Minneapolis: University of Minnesota Press, 1960.

Northern States Power Company. *Forever Yours.* Minneapolis: Northern State Powers, 1971.

Northern States Power Company. *Minnesota's Case for the Electronics Industry.* Minneapolis: 1959.

Northwestern National Bank of Minneapolis. *Minnesota's Electronics and Related Science Industries.* Minneapolis, Minnesota: 1968.

Northwestern National Bank of Minneapolis. *One Hundred Years of Service - 1872-1972.* Minneapolis: 1972.

Nute, Grace Lee. "By Minnesota Waters." *Minnesota Heritage* ed. Lawrence M. Brings. Minneapolis: T.S. Denison, 1960.

O'Brien, Kathleen Ann, and Sheila C. Robertson. *A Social History of Women: Linda James Bennett.* Minnesota: Women Historians of the Midwest, 1981.

Ojakangas, Richard W. and Charles L. Matsch. *Minnesota Geology.* Drawings, charts and graphics by Dan Beedy. Minneapolis: University of Minnesota Press, 1982.

Olson, Russell L. *Electric Railways of Minnesota.* Hopkins: Minnesota Transportation Museum, 1976.

Parkinson, C. Northcote. *Big Business.* Boston: Little, Brown and Company, 1974.

Peterson, Harold F. "Early Minnesota Railroads and the Quest for Settlers." *Minnesota History* 13 (March 1932):25-44.

Pfleider, Eugene P. *Minnesota's Iron Ore Future.* Duluth, Minnesota: Northeastern Minnesota Development Association, 1966.

Photiadis, John D. *Population of Minnesota: 1950-1960.* Minnesota: Agricultural Experiment Station, University of Minnesota, 1963.

Pine, Carol. *Northern States People: The Past 70 Years.* Minneapolis: North Central Publishing, 1979.

Pine, Carol. *Ticker Tape Tales: Piper, Jaffray and Hopwood 1895-1985.* Minneapolis: Piper, Jaffray and Hopwood, Inc., 1986.

Poatgieter, Herminia A. and James Taylor Dunn, eds. *Gopher Reader II: Minnesota's Story in Words and Pictures - Selections from the Gopher Historian.* St. Paul: Minnesota Historical Society, 1975.

"The Political Career of Ignatius Donnelly." *Mississippi Valley Historical Review* 8 (June-September 1921):92-132.

Posey, C.J. "The Influence of Geographic Features in the Development of Minnesota." *Minnesota History* 2 (August 1918).

Powell, William J. *Pillsbury's Best. A Company History From 1869.* Minneapolis: Pillsbury Company, 1985.

Price, Hugh Bruce. *Farmers Cooperation in Minnesota, 1917-1922.* St. Paul: University Farm, 1923.

Prosser, Richard S. *Rails to the North Star.* Minneapolis: Dillon Press, 1966.

Prucha, Francis Paul. "Minnesota 100 Years Ago, as Seen by Laurence Oliphant." *Minnesota History* 34 (Summer 1954):45-53.

Renz, Louis T. *History of the Northern Pacific Railroad.* Fairfield, Washington: Galleon Press, 1980.

Richards, Eva L.A. "Pioneers in Iron Land." *Minnesota History* 32 (September 1951):147-154.

Rippey, James C. *Goodbye, Central: Hello, World: A Centennial History of Northwestern Bell.* Omaha: Northwestern Bell, 1975.

Robinson, Edward Van Dyke. "Early Economic Conditions and the Development of Agriculture in Minnesota." *Minnesota History* 1915.

Roe, Herman. "The Frontier Press of Minnesota." *Minnesota History* 14 (December 1933):393-410.

Ryan, Ann. "Duluth and Superior: Doing the Impossible." *Corporate Report.* (April 1977) 38-41, 70-75.

Saby, Rasmus S. "Railroad Regulations in Minnesota, 1849-1875 " *Minnesota Historical Collections* 15 (1915):70-85, 120-151.

Sandvik, Glenn N. *Duluth: An Illustrated History.* Woodland Hills, California: Windsor Publications, 1983.

Sarjeant, Charles F., ed. *The First Forty: The Story of WCCO Radio (1924-1964).* Minneapolis: T.S. Denison for WCCO Radio, 1964.

Schlesinger, Arthur M. *The Coming of the New Deal.* Boston: Houghton Mifflin Company, 1958.

Schroeder, Leslie L. "Minnesota in the World of Aviation - Fifty Years of Flight." *Minnesota History.*

Schwartz, George M. "The History Behind Our Iron Ranges." Gopher Historian 6 (April 1952):1-13.

Schwartz, George M., and Thiel, George A. *Minnesota's Rocks and Waters: A Geological Story.* Rev. ed., Minneapolis: University of Minnesota Press, 1963.

Scott, Earl P. *The Growth of Minority Business in the Twin Cities Metropolitan Area, 1969-1975.* Minneapolis: Center for Urban and Regional Affairs (CURA), University of Minnesota, 1976.

Severson, Harold. *The Night They Turned On the Lights: The Story of the Electric power Revolution in the North Star State.* Privately published, 1962.

Severson, Harold. *Rochester: Mecca for Millions.* Rochester, Minnesota: Marquette Bank and Trust Co., 1979.

Shippee, Lester B. "Social and Economic Effects of the Civil War with Special Reference to Minnesota." *Minnesota History Bulletin* 2 (May 1918):404-409.

Shortridge, Wilson P. "The Transition of a Typical Frontier." *Gopher Historian* 12 (Fall 1957): 1-27.

Sister Elizabeth Kenny Foundation. *The Story of the Sister Elizabeth Kenny Foundation in the Fight Against Polio.* Minneapolis: Sister Elizabeth Kenny Foundation, 1950.

Skillings, David N. "U.S. Iron Ore Industry Continuing to operate at 50 Million Ton Production Level in 1985." *Skillings Mining Review* (July 27, 1985).

Smolen, Joseph S. *Organized Labor in Minnesota: A Brief History.* Minneapolis: University of Minnesota, Industrial Relations Center, 1964.

Smythe, Ted C. "The Birth of Twin Cities' Commercial Radio." *Minnesota History* 41 (Fall 1969):327-334.

Spalding, William W. "Early Days in Duluth." *Michigan Pioneer and Historical Society Historical Collections* 29 (1901):677-697.

Stevens, John H. *Personal Recollections of Minnesota and Its People, and Early History of Minneapolis.* Minneapolis: Privately published, 1890.

Stevens, Wayne E. "The Fur Trade in Minnesota during the British Regime." *Minnesota History Bulletin* 5 (February 1923):3-13.

Stewart, William J. "Settler, Politician and Speculator in the Sale of the Sioux Reserve." *Minnesota History* 39 (Fall 1964):85-92.

Sturm, Arthur C. "What Labor Wants in Minnesota." *Corporate Report.* (July 1975): 28-31.

Swanholm, Marx. *Alexander Ramsey and the Politics of Survival.* St. Paul: Minnesota Historical Society, 1977.

Swanholm, Marx. *Lumbering in the Last of the White Pine States.* Minnesota Historic Sites Pamphlet Series 17. St. Paul: Minnesota Historical Society, 1978.

Swanson, William. "The Spirit of '76." *Corporate Report.* (September 1975): 20-24.

Swenson, Harold. *Rochester: Mecca for Millions.* Rochester, Minnesota: Marquette Bank and Trust Company, 1979.

Ten Thousand Lakes Association of Minnesota. "Making Money for the State." *Western Magazine* 17:1 (1921).

Uphoff, Mary Jo and Walter. *Group Health - An American Success Story in Prepaid Health Care.* Minneapolis: Dillon Press, 1980.

Upman, Warren. "Groseilliers and Radisson, the First White Men in Minnesota." *Minnesota Historical Collections* 10:2 (1905):449-594.

Van Dusen, Larry. *Duluth-Superior: World's Largest Inland Port.* Au Train, Michigan: Avery Color Studios, 1977.

Wahlberg, Hazel. *The North Land.* Roseau, Minnesota: Roseau Historical Society, 1975.

Walker, David A. *Iron Frontier: The Discovery and Early Development of Minnesota's Three Ranges.* St. Paul: Minnesota Historical Society, 1979.

Walker, Platt B. *Sketches of the Life of Hon. T.B. Walker: A Compilation of Biographical Sketches by Many Authors.* Minneapolis: Lumberman Publishing Company, 1907.

Wohl, Stanley. *The Medical Industrial Complex.* New York: Harmony Books, 1984.

WPA Papers. *Works Project Administration: Writers Project.* Minnesota Papers, 1849-1942. Housed at the Minnesota Historical Society, St. Paul.

Youngdale, James M. "The Frontier Economic Boom and Intellectual Bust." *American Studies in Scandinavia* 8 (1976):1-16.

Ziegler, (William H.) Co. *Developing with Minnesota, 1914-1954.* Minneapolis, 1954.

ACKNOWLEDGMENTS

This book was written over a period of two years—on weekends and late into many nights. It was an intoxicating process of learning. But it was also a time when my friends and family saw very little of me.

My husband, Philip Gelbach, made those months bearable—and made me laugh at myself when I became too serious about the fact that I was building a business during the week and writing a book in my spare time. The narrative in this book is mine. But the emotional strength behind it is mostly his.

I also thank my business partner, Richard Lee, who carried the ball several times on Monday mornings when I'd had a little too much writing over the weekend. His confidence—week after week, month after month—gave me energy.

There are many other important players without whom I couldn't have finished on time: my parents, Bill and Betsy Downing, who always love a good read—and who paid important attention to every chapter; Pam Schroeder, of Windsor Publications, who provided editorial direction and support; Kristine Ellis and Bonnie Klosterman, who labored through every word as my supporting editors, checking and questioning thoughts as well as syntax; David Narum, Sally Stec, and Tim Sawyer, who spent long hours with the staffs of the Minnesota Historical Society and the James J. Hill reference libraries, researching, checking facts and bibliographic sources—much more work than any of them bargained for; Mary Kay Wagner and Jay Dobbs, whose word processing skills made sure that the copy was in the best possible shape; and Virginia Westbrook, photo researcher, who beautifully enhanced my words with excellent photography.

And very great appreciation to Virginia Kunz, executive director of the Ramsey County Historical Society and an author of a number of histories herself, whose incisive comments and questions helped me through the critical fact-checking phases.

Additionally, my thanks to Win Borden, of the Minnesota Chamber of Commerce and Industry, for recommending me to Windsor Publications. He introduced me to an important opportunity. I'm glad I was smart enough to tackle it.

INDEX